Extending Themselves

GRAHAM TIPPLE

Extending Themselves

*User-initiated transformations of government-built housing
in developing countries*

LIVERPOOL UNIVERSITY PRESS

First published 2000 by
LIVERPOOL UNIVERSITY PRESS
Liverpool L69 7ZU

British Library Cataloguing-in-Publication Data
A British Library CIP record is available

ISBN 0-85323-913-4 (hardback)
ISBN 0-85323-504-X (paperback)

Typeset in 10/13.5pt Meridien by
XL Publishing Services, Lurley, Tiverton
Printed in Great Britain by Alden Press, Oxford

Contents

Acknowledgements

In a large research project stretching over several years and involving several countries, there are many contributors without whom there would be no results. In each of the countries studied, a team carried out the survey, coded and entered the survey data, and provided secondary information. These were led by Shahidul Ameen in Bangladesh, Magda Metwally and Hala Kardash in Egypt, Stephen E. Owusu in Ghana and Columbus Pritchard in Zimbabwe. Their diligence and dedication to housing were fundamentally important to this study and were evident in the care with which they carried out their work. The British Council assisted us in the Ghana fieldwork by fitting some of our visits into their academic links programme. Alok Dasgupta and Azizah Salim have been faithful students of user-initiated extensions and have been generous in sharing their insights into the phenomenon in India and Malaysia. My visit to Israel was sponsored by the Academic Study Group; Naomi Carmon and Izak Kadosh gave of their valuable time and insights to help me understand the local situation.

In CARDO, Peter Kellett, Adenrele Awotona, Miles Danby and Tony Hyland have enabled the research to continue through their institutional support. Nick Wilkinson gave birth to the idea that these extensions could be important for housing and contributed greatly to the initial thinking behind the study. Aileen Coulthard, Maggie Warford and Steph Lane have been invaluable in administrative support. The Head of the Department of Architecture, John Wiltshire, has been generous with encouragement and resources. Mark Napier and Gillian Masters carried out the data analysis with great care and ability. Their meticulous and systematic approach, and willingness to follow up leads arising throughout the analysis, were essential in the fulfilment of the project objectives.

At the University of Newcastle upon Tyne, Duncan Beaton and George Taylor customized ArcInfo to carry out the GIS analysis required to relate house plans to each other and to the socioeconomic data of occupants. Ken Willis and Guy Garrod gave invaluable advice on econometric aspects of the analysis. Data entry and processing on the house plans were done by Miriam Harper, Eleanor Tipple, Peter Bird, Chris Morgan, Matt Jones, Andrew Clarence, Martin Wolf, David Tipple and David Littleton. Sarah Worrall drew the plans for publication, David and Nicholas Tipple, Maggie Warford and Steph Lane compiled the index.

The Engineering Division of the Department for International Development sponsored the research through Research Project R4865B. William Housego-Woolgar encouraged us in the beginning, Philip Perris and Michael Parkes assisted throughout, and Michael Mutter reviewed the draft report and gave very useful comments which were followed up in the structuring of this book.

Robin Bloxsidge of Liverpool University Press has been supportive and flexible in his approach to publishing the study. An anonymous reviewer gave valuable, though sometimes disconcertingly prescient, comments on the first draft.

Finally, my wife Sue has been continually supportive over my many absences abroad and with the absent-mindedness about important things that accompanies a research obsession.

1. Introduction

In January, 1984, CARDO staff were in Egypt with our Masters course students when, on a visit to 15th May City, Helwan, we passed an apartment housing area which had begun to sprout extensions on all five floors. On our free afternoon, Nick Wilkinson and I went back to Helwan, with one of our students, Shahidul Ameen, and sought out this seemingly bizarre phenomenon. Sure enough, balconies had been filled in rather more than usual for Egypt, goat and turkey cages were slung on the outside of the flats, and an occasional upper floor dweller had cantilevered out an extension. However, exploring deeper into the area revealed more spectacular feats of extension with the beginnings of the five-storey stacks with which we are now so familiar. We were at once outraged and fascinated; the gall of it was outrageous, the engineering was unconventional and daring, but the achievement was admirable.

We were so taken with what we had seen that we returned one year later, under a British Council Academic Link, and conducted a small survey with colleagues from the University of Helwan, Zamalek. Our fascination was firmly rooted by this study and the findings were published over the next few years in order to give the phenomenon a wide airing and attract some interest (Tipple *et al.*, 1985, 1986; Wilkinson and Tipple, 1987, Tipple, 1991). This was followed by a literature review (Tipple, 1991a, sponsored by the Overseas Development Administration [now Department of International Development]) and finally the study on which this book is based.

The purpose of the book

This book is the result of several years of empirical study beginning from a vaguely favourable stance towards transformations. The empirical results did nothing to counter this stance and much to amplify it. Thus, we began the writing process with a very positive attitude. The purpose of the book, therefore, is to argue that transformations are a valid activity in housing supply and should be supported as part of a country's housing policy. In order to achieve this cogently, we must do the following:

1. describe and compare the characteristics of transformation in the four case study areas, Bangladesh, Egypt, Ghana, and Zimbabwe;
2. identify advantages and disadvantages of transformation as a housing supply mechanism, and establish a balance between them;
3. establish empirical evidence to counter the negative arguments so readily used by development controllers locally, particularly that transformers are 'building slums';

4. attempt to establish causality, i.e. why some households transform and others do not in neighbouring sites;
5. suggest policies which could be applied to maximise the benefits and minimise the costs to owners, users and neighbours.

As the first major study of transformations that has had an international perspective and included both socioeconomic and physical data, the tasks of description and comparison are particularly important. They are an attempt to establish a basis on which other researchers can follow with local studies to extend our knowledge of the phenomenon around the world. Two such studies have already been started (in Malaysia and India). These will be introduced briefly in a later chapter.

We make no claim that the study is exhaustive, nor that its findings are the last word on the subject. In several cases, we can only infer correlations or trends, and make best guesses from our limited data. It is, of course, up to others to take the subject forward as new work casts increasing light on this complex, fascinating and controversial process of housing supply.

Comparative research

Gilbert (1991) offers a useful overview on the nature of comparative research. He points out that it compares two or more cases while employing a similar methodology in each. Our comparative work is what Ragin (1989: 59) calls 'empirically intensive' in that it 'examines many causal and outcome variables in different configurations in a limited number of cases.'

The virtues of comparative research are headed by the avoidance of parochialism. It would be easy, as we did several years ago with reference to Egypt (Wilkinson and Tipple, 1987), to draw conclusions from a single small study. While we avoided the temptation to generalise from this particular to all of Egypt, or worse, all developing countries, it is difficult to avoid such a tendency even if it is not spelled out in black and white. As Gilbert (1991: 82) points out, 'comparative research … regularly reminds the researcher that all cities are not the same.' Seemingly similar sets of circumstances may have very different outcomes in different cities. On the other hand, very different circumstances may generate similar responses. Within this study, we concentrate at times on the general processes and at other times on the city-specific issues arising from transformations. By using a comparative method, we are forced to account for similarities and differences among our case studies.

Gilbert (1991: 83) warns against wearing 'blinkers into the field' and 'only finding what [we] are looking for.' We tried to avoid this by not bringing well-formed hypotheses and theories to which we were committed but rather taking the grounded research view and observing what is happening before defending a theory. To a charge of being in favour of transformation before we start, we have to plead guilty but argue two points in mitigation: that our preliminary study directed us to the potential of the process, and that there is such a weight of official instinctive opposition to transformation that it needs some allies to even out the score before we start. On the last one, being what we choose to call iconoclastic, or what others could call 'bloody-minded', might have had at least some influence on our taking up the cause of the transformers more readily than that of the bureaucrats.[1]

Ethical issues arise in cross-national research, to which we have been alive. Gilbert (1991) points out that the most significant of these is the mechanism by which local participants become merely cheap labour for the researcher based in the west, benefiting only marginally in professional development. In this context, we established the principle that each collaborator would get a copy of his/her own and each other case's data and the ability to contact each other to discuss issues and write joint papers on topics of interest to each. Although the international comparative work had to be based at Newcastle, dissemination of each country study would be collaborative and joint works published internationally.

In choosing the locations of our case study, we were guided by several imperatives. First, we needed to choose countries in which transformation is occurring in government-built low-cost housing with reasonable frequency. We had seen or read reports on transformations in many parts of the world, some of which were reviewed or illustrated in our preliminary work (Tipple, 1991a, 1992). Second, we needed to have local counterparts whom we knew would carry out good work without constant supervision and who were willing to come to the transformations issue with an open mind. We had contacts in many countries and were confident that we could work effectively on transformations with our contacts in about seven. Third, we required countries which represented at least some of the diversity present in the developing world. Fourth, the countries selected had to be ones in which the ODA (now Department for International Development, henceforth DFID) would be comfortable to sponsor research.

Our choice crystallised on Ghana to represent low-income Sub-Saharan Africa and Zimbabwe to represent medium-income Sub-Saharan Africa and to stand as a proxy for South Africa where we knew many areas possessed transformed houses but in which we could not be involved at the time. The Middle East was represented by Egypt, and South Asia by Bangladesh. We are aware that no Latin American case is used and regard this as a weakness, particularly given the large scale of government-built housing in such countries as Brazil, Chile, Mexico and Venezuela.

Within the sample, different house types are represented. The multi-storey walk-up flats of Egypt present very different logistical issues from bungalows on the generous plots in Zimbabwe. Ghana's terraced single-roomed dwellings had similarities to the Bangladesh single-roomed quarters.

The structure of the book

The structure of the book is dictated by the need to tell the story of transformations in a way that fulfils its purpose. It would have been valid to arrange it with the case studies first, with a comparative section after to bring the strands of the argument together. Gilbert's (1993) comparative study of housing in Latin America takes that form. Indeed our final report to the sponsor (DFID) was structured in that way and allowed the reader to assimilate all the richness of the data before the general arguments were entered into.

However, we have now adopted a structure that 'relegates' the bulk of the detailed data to relatively long appendices so that the overall picture and the comparative analysis can take centre stage.[2] The first part of the book presents the main findings and arguments in a comparative perspective calling up data from the four case studies. It is issue based rather than following the order dictated by presenting detailed data in a systematic manner. All transformers are grouped together to compare them with non-transformers. Only sufficient detail is included of the country studies to service the argument. Univariate analysis is used mostly but we also include a summary of the multivariate analysis adopted to attempt to establish which variables are most influential on the decision to transform and its cost. We include our conclusions and policy recommendations at the end of this section so that it tells the whole story as succinctly as possible. If any part of the book is intended to be read as a whole from beginning to end, this is it.

The case studies form appendices, as does the multivariate analysis. These appendices are intended to be dipped into by most readers as and when they need clarification or expansion of data to enrich their understanding of the argument, in the way that a reader might use footnotes. Additionally, they can provide readers with particular interest in the countries represented with the detailed analysis they seek.

They have a similar structure and range of tables. However, where extra knowledge is available in a particular field, one case study may concentrate in more depth than others before returning to the roughly parallel order. The lists of contents and tables allow easy location of the data in the case studies.

The case studies divide transformers into sub-samples depending on the age of their extensions (see below) and, sometimes, by house characteristics. Detailed plans and photographs are also included at this stage rather than in the main argument. Conclusions and recommendations specific to each case study are also included here.

As with any ordering of a complex set of data, this structure will suit some readers better than others. For those who find it less than helpful, I tender my apologies and ask for forbearance.

The presentation of the data

The tables presented in this book mostly use the median and inter-quartile range (IQR) to represent centrality and spread. While it is, perhaps, more usual to use mean and standard deviation, we have adopted the other method because socioeconomic data are usually skewed. In a mean, values in the long tail of a skewed distribution (of, say, income in which a few households may have unusually large incomes) distort its value as a measure of centrality. In the income case, the mean would be quite high even though most of the sample are well below it. The median, on the other hand, is less affected by the values in the long tail as it represents the value of the middle individual in a distribution. Thus, half the sample are below (or equal to) the median value and half are above (or equal to) it. The inter-quartile range (IQR) represent the 25th percentile (the individual value which is one quarter of the way up the distribution) and the 75th percentile (three-quarters of the way up). Thus, the IQR includes the middle 50 per cent of the values in that variable.

Space syntax diagrams

In some of the analysis we have used gamma diagrams from Hillier and Hanson (1984). These diagrams represent rooms or spaces by circles and the access routes between them by lines. Two dichotomous types of syntactical arrangements can be identified using the gamma diagrams: symmetry and asymmetry, and distributedness and non-distributedness. Symmetry refers to the degree of integration or segregation between spaces in a house whereas distributedness refers to the degree of control spaces exert on the system as a whole. Put simply, if there are two rooms opening onto an open space and they are interconnected, they are symmetrical and distributed. If they are not interconnected, but a person has to pass outside to re-enter, they are still symmetrical but they are now non-distributed. Distributedness can be easily recognised by the presence of rings in the gamma diagram – where there is more than one route from one space to another. If there are two rooms arranged so that one opens only off the other, they are asymmetrical as one controls the permeability of the other. The inner space becomes relatively segregated from the rest of the system.

A gamma diagram represents a plan in a standard form which removes the influence of rooms' shapes and sizes. Although this is not the only way of representing them, all gamma diagrams in this book are shown starting outside the entrance to the house (the circle with a cross in) with spaces directly accessible from the entrance in a horizontal line above it. The next layer of spaces is also horizontally aligned, and so on, giving a measure of depth from the starting point. This justified gamma diagram can be used for mathematical interpretation of the plans but we have not done so in this book. We use the diagrams to show the relative depth of the house as a whole, and particular features of it, e.g. the original rooms, open spaces and subsequent households. We are also looking for a change from relatively non-distributed and asymmetrical plans to relatively distributed and symmetrical plans. Further clarification can be gained by reference to Hillier and Hanson's book (1984).

Sampling

In this study, the sample unit is the original dwelling which may now be transformed into a multi-household house.[3] Because of this, it is normally referred to as a house (or, in Egypt, a flat) in this study. It is the unit which is covered by a single main tenancy agreement or deed of sale from the government or its agencies. It is the unit which is controlled by the party or parties in whom lies the decision to transform or not. In cases of single-storey housing, or in which there are several storeys but the overall tenancies or ownerships are not divided horizontally, the house will be defined in two ways:

1. Where there is a plot, this defines the house.
2. Where there is no plot because single dwellings open off public space, the sampling unit is the original dwelling and all that is controlled by the party or parties in whom the decision to transform or not lies.

In cases where there are multi-storey blocks divided into flats then, as above, the sampling unit is the original flat.

Sub-samples

In the main analysis, we have divided the sample into non-transformers and transformers. Within the analysis for each country, however, transformers are further divided into recent and established.

Non-transformers

These are people who have not transformed although there is transformation being done in their area and/or to housing similar to theirs. It also includes a group which we expected to be small: people who have moved into already transformed houses but who have not done any extension work themselves. The non-transformers are chosen as a control group and to help us to examine the reasons why some transform and others do not.

Recent transformers

These are people who have transformed within three years of the date of the survey even though they may not have finished. The importance of this group lies in the assessment of transformation in the context of almost current household circumstances. They show the relationship between housing conditions and income and the nature of transformations at the time they occurred. They allow us to examine our sample in a way similar to the housing adjustment literature in the UK, Europe, America and Australia discussed below. In addition, they may give clues to any changes that are occurring in the nature or process of transformation.

Established transformers

The bulk of the transformers are those who made their transformations more than three years before the survey. They are likely to have forgotten the imperatives which led to the expansions, and their household circumstances may have changed significantly. However, they provide information about the extent and establishment of transformation activity, the quality and quantity of housing goods provided, the physical effects of extensions, etc.

We planned to sample about 100 non-transformers and at least 100 each of the recent and established transformers (but 300 of the latter two combined) to a total of about 400. In the event our sample was as in table 1.

Table 1. The sample

	Bangladesh	Egypt	Ghana	Zimbabwe
Established transformers	245	169	132	97
Recent transformers	129	84	178	91
Shacks-only transformers*	-	-	-	102
All transformers	374	253	310	290
Non-transformers	12	76	88	45
Total	386	329	398	335

* See below.

Shacks-only transformers in Zimbabwe
In the Harare sample, we included about 100 plots on which the only extensions were sectional wooden structures (known locally as shacks). They were sometimes analysed separately as they represented a very different level of investment from extensions constructed in masonry. Many of the other transformers had also used shacks for some of their new accommodation but these were not handled separately.

Government-built housing in developing countries

The context of our study is the government-built housing estate intended for low-income urban households. In developing countries, as in more industrialised nations, housing has been provided for some urban residents for several decades. Immediately after the Second World War, the government housing estate for low-income workers was a relatively new concept in anglophone Africa.[4] Housing was provided for returning veterans and the new urban labouring classes partly as a social welfare measure and partly as a means of securing a more urbanised workforce. The cyclical migration, imposed by the short-term contract working practised up to that time by such urban employers as the mines of Southern and Central Africa, did not allow indigenous workers to settle in the towns (Heisler, 1971). In the contract labour system, male workers were enticed to the urban areas, largely through the imposition of poll taxes which had to be paid in cash (a commodity available only from urban employ-ment). Then they were accommodated in barrack-like areas epitomised by the notorious hostels of Southern Africa (Japha and Huchzermeyer, 1995). In the 'stabil-isation' debate of the 1940s, the need for a more stable workforce possessed of some skills was the catalyst for allowing women and children to join their menfolk in town (Heisler, 1971). At that time, single-roomed dwellings for men only were augmented by increasing numbers of dwellings suitable for small, nuclear family households in estates reserved for certain industries or open to any employer to place valuable skilled and semi-skilled workers.

Housing was becoming a social welfare issue. Typical of the events at this time was the Eccles Commission on the financing and administration of African Locations in Northern Rhodesia (Northern Rhodesia, 1944). It spoke of improving housing condi-tions and providing for families as a means of achieving a contented, healthy and efficient workforce. Words such as 'contentment' and 'dignity' marked the reports' aims for the occupants of government-built housing.

Following Independence and the acceptance that urban life is open to anyone, government housing briefly became a means of expressing the desirability of partic-ular house-forms. Thus, single household villas of around 40 m^2 area, with three habitable rooms, self-contained services and plots of 200–300 m^2, became relatively common in Sub-Saharan Africa. Indeed, they set the spatial context for much that followed in the way of core housing or sites and services schemes. However, the policy-makers were caught on the horns of a dilemma. They had to satisfy grass-root demands for suitable houses for newly independent people[5] while balancing narrowly drawn housing budgets in times when they were firmly regarded as social welfare measures. As such, funds for housing were liable to be both a small part of total government budgets and to be trimmed to allow for over-spending in other, more overtly produc-tive, sectors. As accepted means of reducing costs, their designers tended to skimp on the finishes and the size of rooms but basic structural strength was rarely compro-mised. This was the era in which the solution to the housing problem was seen to reside in careful construction to give low maintenance through an economic life of at least 30 years. Unfortunately the standard of on-site supervision was too low to guarantee the planned construction standards and some failures have occurred. In general, however, the dwellings constructed in this way remain relatively strong many years after construction even though their appearance may be very run down indeed. Years of occupation by many more people than they were designed to accommodate and a lack of routine maintenance have taken their toll.

The experiments with high-rise, high-technology housing followed those in Europe, and took a medium-term hold in some countries despite their evident unsuitability to the lifestyles of low-income households. Companies involved in heavy-panel prefabrication of housing found that their hopes for major contracts in Europe were short-lived as the shortcomings of their housing systems became apparent. They then managed to find buyers for their factories in a few developing countries, notably those in the middle-income range such as Egypt, and many have continued production into the 1990s, for example in peripheral estates around Cairo and in the New Cities in the Desert (Stewart, 1996).[6] Studies in Egypt have shown that the heavy prefabrication of dwellings cost about 40 per cent more than load-bearing brick construction and about 25 per cent more than concrete frame construction. Furthermore, the prefabricated systems recorded no savings on materials or labour, despite expectations (Hassan, 1992).

The Egyptian estates included in our case study are not built in heavy prefabricated panels but do use a relatively high technology system, *in situ* reinforced concrete post and slab construction with brick infill. They are, however, very similar in planning and appearance to the other flats being planned in serried ranks in large estates. They represent development in the 1960s when Egypt's housing budget rose from 12 to 21 per cent of total government budget (Hassan, 1992) and thousands of similar dwellings were built.

Even in countries where low-income housing had not been a traditional concern of government or local authorities, some housing schemes have been constructed to meet particular local needs. These include the need to accommodate refugees from wars or natural disasters, and squatters who were being relocated from city-centre land. In the context of our study, housing was needed for refugees fleeing India at the time of Partition in 1947 so areas of mainly low-income housing were established in Bangladesh. Later, the struggle for independence by Bangladesh and its successful war

Figure 1. Flats built with heavy prefabricated panels in Sadat City, Egypt

of secession in 1971 created a refugee population of Bengalis who had formerly gone to work in West Pakistan. When the two countries parted company amid considerable acrimony and bloodshed, the government in Dhaka felt the need to offer at least some form of shelter for refugees returning to the newly formed state of Bangladesh. In these conditions, it is understandable if the twin, but largely irreconcilable, imperatives of cheapness and user acceptability are compromised and poor quality of construction is sanctioned from the start under the guise of a temporary solution.

The original dwellings and neighbourhoods

Mirpur, Dhaka, Bangladesh

Mirpur is located 10 miles to the north-east of the centre of Dhaka, the capital of Bangladesh. It began to grow as a satellite town after the Second World War with a major expansion during the 1960s and 1970s. The Housing and Settlements Directorate (HSD), which was formed to house refugees from the partition of India in 1947, developed Mirpur as its largest project. It covers 1357 hectares and was intended to house 150,000 people.

Initially, about half the land was developed as core houses (known locally as 'nucleus' houses), 8245 in all being built between 1959 and 1968. They were built as semi-detached units laid out in rows of 15 to 20 with access roads 9 m wide with 1.2 m service alleys to the rear carrying the utility lines. In addition, about 7900 plots were made available for residential development.

The *bastuhara* (Bastu = home, hara = less) scheme, which forms the context of our study, was proposed in 1972 to provide basic shelter for refugees from Pakistan being moved from where they had settled in squatter areas in the centre of the city. Single rooms with no services were initially planned in the form of 4304 semi-detached units in five different sections of Mirpur. Each dwelling consisted of a single room of 5.7 m by 1.9 m with a veranda 2.6 m. by 1.9 m; a total floor area of 22.2 m^2. It was built in a single leaf of brick with a corrugated iron roof, and windows were created by a chequerboard of bricks and spaces. The dwellings are joined in pairs along their long edge, which also forms the roof ridge. All the dwellings were built in rows with access lanes demarcated but no plot boundaries were drawn. They were built but not serviced; latrine blocks were constructed (in blocks between every sixth dwelling), and lavatory pans fitted but no water supply was installed, nor were the sewers laid.

At an advanced stage in the development, 662 pairs of units were converted into two-roomed dwellings (of about 44.5 m^2) for low-ranking government employees. In these dwellings, one of the verandas was converted to a kitchen, boundary walls were erected, and water supply and toilets were also provided.

The allocation procedure for the 3180 single-roomed units was handled badly and the scheme stood empty for a few years. The people for whom they were intended failed to be allocated them. Instead, middlemen (known as *mastans*) stepped in illegally to take over unoccupied units. They fitted padlocks to the doors to control access and let them to individuals against the payment of 'hush-money'; Tk2500 in 1974. Later, would-be occupants had to make initial payments rising to Tk120,000 in 1988 to vacating residents to buy possession. This sum represents a putative value whereas the earlier payments to *mastans* were arbitrarily set.

After a few years, HSD was faced with a *fait accompli*: there were too many occupants to evict so they were allowed to stay on a rental basis. Many occupants were already extending in the mid-1980s, some using bamboo matting and others brick. The extension activity has consistently involved filling the area adjacent to the dwelling, to the front, rear and side, with extra rooms and outdoor spaces for cooking and washing. The latter have often been in the narrow corridor or courtyard flanking the original dwelling.

The municipality finally constructed lanes (known locally as by-lanes) between the house blocks in the herring-bone brick paving conventional in Dhaka. The occupants have since taken the lanes' edge to be their front boundary regardless of any easements for pipes, etc. From the early days, illegal connections to the electricity mains were made, tubewells were sunk and latrines served by soakpits were fitted. Recently, when sewers have at last been laid, these have had to go under the brick-paved streets and the disturbance has ruined the surface.

The HSD is currently implementing the sale of the *bastuhara* housing to the occupants who will be charged Tk134,000 plus interest (£2230). The sale entitles the occupant to 99-year leasehold with limitations on their rights to sell for some years.

Figure 2. Panoramic view of the bastuhara *housing, Mirpur*
Although houses seem to cover the whole plot, there are still internal open spaces and a surprising number of trees.

Most of the main renter households have been in their dwellings since they were first let through *mastans* in the mid-1970s. They are not the poor of urban Bangladesh but, as the area was intended to accommodate refugees and low-grade government workers, there is no evidence that the poor were ever meant to occupy these buildings. Very few fall below the low-income threshold defined for Bangladesh and their per capita income is almost three times the absolute poverty threshold at the median. Households average 6 to 7 persons. Heads are in their mid-forties and there tend to be several young children.

Medinet Nasr, Cairo, and Workers' City, Helwan, Greater Cairo, Egypt

Since the early 1960s, the Egyptian Government has been carrying out a programme of building low-cost housing in large numbers and mainly in four- and five-storey walk-up blocks of flats. Construction of the Gamal Abdel Nasser public housing project in Medinet Nasr, Cairo, began in 1965 and allocations began in 1967. The estate has 1200 flats designed for low-income earners but some units were kept aside for emergency use, typically for newly married couples or for households suffering eviction.

The Economic Housing at Workers' City, Helwan was built in the early 1960s west of the town of Helwan and close to heavy industries. The nearly 2460 five-storey walk-up flats were built in monotonous rows.

The structures in both estates are *in situ* reinforced concrete post and slab with brick infill; the staircases provide added stiffness to the structures. Within a block, all floors are identical. The spaces between the buildings appear to be undifferentiated as to use; they are access tracks, parking, play spaces, dumping grounds, and grazing land for goats and other livestock all at the same time. The only surviving vegetation is in areas fenced off by individual households as gardens, or the occasional mature tree. While the land on both estates remains the property of the Governerate, the flats are on a hire-purchase arrangement whereby, when the 180th monthly instalment is paid, the flat passes into owner occupation. Thus, most of the sales were completed about 10 years ago. The selling prices for the flats were £E360 for one room, £E540 for two rooms, and £E1080 for three rooms. The real cost of provision is not known but it is on record that low-income housing cost £E16/m² in 1965. By 1990 it had risen to £E180/m² (Kardash, 1994).

Flats appear to have been let to workers according to their status in their company, the three-roomed flats being reserved for supervisory staff. Extensions appear to have started in earnest in 1979 (Kardash, 1990) and to have passed through at least two stages. In the beginning, ground floor occupants seem to have built load-bearing brick extensions. Their neighbours above may have taken advantage of these to add a small extension but they could not support many storeys. The concrete framed, cooperative extensions now constructed up the side of the buildings appear to have evolved out of the earlier form. The scale and pace of development in the mid-1980s can be judged from three photographs showing the same building in January 1984, January 1985 and 1993 (see Fig. 45).

Owners' household incomes (using expenditure as a proxy) are well within the broad band of what the Egyptian Government calls stable low-income earners. They have per capita incomes of twice the absolute poverty threshold. There are quite a number with much lower incomes but they are mostly retired people. The owners are workers in the industries of Cairo and Helwan, for whom the flats were intended. The transformer household heads have a median age of 53; their households are in a late stage of development with five members at the medians but only one child under 16 years old. They are mainly in nuclear family households but some now have at least one married son living in the flat for whom the extensions allow space. Non-transformers are older (median 60 years of age for the head). Even though they tend to live in originally larger flats, they have slightly smaller households. Most occupants are those who were allocated the flats new in the 1960s but the median recent transformer has 'only' been there since 1971. Almost all have no intention of leaving so there is little sign of new people coming in to take advantage of the transformations or the potential for extension.

Asawasi and Suntreso, Kumasi, Ghana

The government-built housing sector is relatively small in Ghana, representing only about 5 per cent of urban housing. The Ghana sample was chosen from two older government-built estates in Kumasi: Asawasi and Suntreso. Both areas were built in a continuous and overlapping programme between 1945 and 1956 (Tipple, 1987) as part of the post-Second World War investment in low-cost housing which was implemented across the British Empire at that time (see Tipple, 1979, for similar developments in Zambia).

Asawasi estate is situated about 1 km from the centre of Kumasi, surrounded by residential development. It was built in the late 1940s to the design and under the supervision of Maxwell Fry and Jane Drew (who later worked with Le Corbusier on Chandigarh, India). Earth blocks stabilised with a small quantity of cement were used. Small-scale mass production was set up for roof trusses and other woodwork (Gold Coast, 1948; Alcock, 1952).

Asawasi originally had 1313 dwellings of which 1041 were single rooms and 272 had two or three rooms. They vary from 25 to about 60 m² in built-up area. The single-roomed dwellings were provided with separate 2.8 × 1.7 m kitchens arranged in blocks back to back and side to side (in fours, sixes, twelves or even more). Toilets were in public latrine blocks; washing and bathing places were communal. The few semi-detached units had their own bucket latrines, bathrooms and kitchens attached to the dwellings. The dwellings cost £60 per room to build (Fry, 1946b).

Although the houses were intended for returning war veterans and established civil servants, only some of those eligible took up their options. Local Akans[7] were put off by the distance from the city centre and the proximity of Aboabo, a large northerner-migrant area. Consequently the remaining houses were allocated to northerners, some of whom had been displaced by the building of a local police station. Because of this, and its closeness to the main mosque, Asawasi is an important area for Muslim migrants from the north of Ghana and other West African countries.

Suntreso is situated to the west of Kumasi city centre, divided into North and South Estates by a wide undeveloped area to the south of the Sunyani Road. The dwellings are broadly similar in type and area to those in Asawasi. North Suntreso was started in 1949 and completed in 1952 with 360 one- and two-roomed row dwellings having detached kitchens and communal toilets and bath-houses, and 405 two-roomed semi-detached dwellings. South Suntreso followed, being completed in 1956 with 355 semi-detached, two-room and three-room dwellings and 30 detached dwellings, each with a bucket latrine and bathroom. In the late 1970s, the State Housing Corporation (SHC) built a few single- and two-storey detached dwellings along the northern boundary of South Suntreso. Most of the dwellings on these estates have been bought from SHC by the occupants.

Taking both areas together, about 35 per cent of our sample[8] (the detached and semi-detached villas) originally had their own sanitary services (toilet and water supply) while most had electricity. Now 56 per cent of our sample have their own toilet. The dwellings were originally let at a subsidised monthly rent of about 12.5 per cent of occupants' income. They were sold to the occupants from the 1960s onwards, again with subsidies to reduce their cost. Extension activity has been observed since the mid-1970s consisting mostly of single-storey additions to provide rooms strung along a corridor or grouped round a courtyard. There are only a few two-storey extensions but their scale is so impressive that they are very noticeable. They have often involved the complete obliteration of the original structure and the appearance of a double-storey compound house very similar to those that surround the study areas.

The occupants of the Ghana estates have never been the poorest households in town. The dwellings were intended for the type of workers the colonial city needed for its efficient running: junior civil servants, artisans, etc. The existing owner-occupants are likely to be mostly their descendants. They cannot be described as poor in the Ghana context; they are towards the upper end of low income. They have household incomes (using expenditure as a proxy) of about 10 times the minimum wage but per capita incomes of only twice the absolute poverty threshold of £240 per annum. Most occupants are in business but quite a large minority have wage employment. Transformers' households have a median of about seven members, while those of non-transformers have two fewer people. The households are mainly in a late phase of development with heads in late middle age but they still have some young children. The owners have been very stable in residence in their houses and have no intention whatever of selling to others. They will be followed by their heirs.

Mbare and Highfield, Harare, Zimbabwe

The city of Harare in independent Zimbabwe has inherited residential areas planned and located as, *inter alia*, means of racial control. In colonial times, the movement of Africans in and out of the urban areas was controlled, and they were regarded as temporary urbanites. Housing for Africans was rented, strictly segregated from the whites' city, and operated by a different administration, the Department of African Administration. Africans were not allowed to own land in urban areas before 1963, and after this only in designated home-ownership schemes.

 Government-built so-called 'high density' estates contribute a considerable part of the housing stock of Harare. Currently, Harare City Council administers 17 such residential areas with almost 100,000 dwellings (Rakodi and Mutizwa-Mangiza, 1989). The more recent of these have adopted sites and services approaches, with or without core houses or wet cores, usually on a 300 m² plot.

 Mbare (originally called Harare) is the oldest township in what was then Salisbury, situated to the south of the city centre. It was developed from about 1907 onwards as a township for black workers (housed as single males) with jobs in the city. Employers paid the rent for the council-built structures and later bought them for renting to their workers. During the 1960s and 1970s, core housing (two- to four-roomed semi-detached and terraced dwellings) were developed for married couples. There are about 6000 dwellings in Mbare.

 The area chosen for study in Mbare is located in the south-west of the estate, an area commonly known as 'National'. The houses there were constructed as so-called four-roomed core units, comprising two bedrooms, a living room and a kitchen. The tiny toilet/bathrooms are entered from outside. Typical dwellings in our study area are 52 m² in area set on plots measuring 27 to 29 m in depth and about 9 or 10 m wide. Each has electricity, piped water and sewerage reticulation on the plot. They are built of bricks set in sand/cement mortar and rendered in places, floors are concrete and roofs are asbestos cement sheeting on timber rafters. There are no ceilings.

 Highfield was begun in 1935 outside city limits to the south-west of Mbare by central government as a township for Africans employed in the public sector and as a response to overcrowding in Mbare. Between 1935 and 1953, two-, three- and four-roomed dwellings were built for married couples.

 In 1955, as part of the government's acceptance that some Africans would retain their urban identity after retirement, home-ownership housing was introduced. Four new areas were started in Highfield, including our study areas of 'Jerusalem' and 'Egypt', which consist of 1058 two- and four-roomed dwellings in rigid grid-iron blocks. The houses are mainly detached and vary from 47 to 56 m² in area containing four rooms and (usually) a veranda. The plots of about 12 × 21 m are shorter and wider than those in Mbare. The dwellings were allocated to Africans who could afford to own their own dwelling in the city. Thus, they unlikely to have been targeted to the poor, more to an emerging blue-collar class of Africans.

 The 'New Canaan' area was constructed at the westerly corner of Highfield in 1961 as a mix of two- and four-roomed detached, semi-detached and terraced dwellings for renting to non-government workers through their employers. The part of the study area known as 'Western Triangle' is a mixture of detached and semi-detached dwellings built in 1965. Many of the houses in this area are laid out using a wooden former for each room to produce a 6.6 × 6.6 m, 44 m² house with four identical rooms. Others are slightly smaller (42 m²) and semi-detached but have kitchen, bathroom and toilet. All the plots in the two areas of Highfield are approximately 390 m² (13 × 30 m). They are of similar construction and servicing standards to those in Mbare. There are over 10,000 dwellings in Highfield.

We have no general data about how much specific housing areas cost to construct. However, the cost of constructing a 50 m² local authority dwelling on a serviced 300 m² stand was Z$10,000 in 1980 and Z$35,000 in 1992 (Pritchard, 1993).

Extension activity has consisted of adding rooms around the original dwelling in either masonry or wood. The latter, known locally as 'shacks', are illegal but most of the former have planning approval. Many dwellings have been extended into much larger villas, entirely filling the portion of the plot within the building lines laid down by the planners. There are no upper floors in any of our Harare study areas. Transformers have added few services to those already in place. As all dwellings had toilet, water supply and electricity, there was probably little felt need to increase their provision.

The owner-occupants have household incomes (using expenditure as a proxy) at the median of three times those of labourers but less than those of managers. Per capita incomes are between 2.4 and three times those of absolute poverty. Like those in Ghana, household sizes of transformers, with a median of seven, are about two persons larger than for non-transformers. The owner households are again in a late stage of their career, with middle-aged heads but with fewer children under 16 than the Ghanaians. The current occupants have long standing in their houses. About three-quarters were in residence when the properties were bought from the city council, and most of the others inherited them. Thus, there are few new buyers. They are very permanent in both history and intention. The tenant households are younger, have fewer members and much shorter stays in the area. See Appendices 1–4 for maps of each city and the locations of the study areas. For a summary of the characteristics of study areas see table 2.

The dwellings provided in all the study estates are small, too small for the current households which occupy them. They were built for different circumstances from those now existing in the cities and they tend to be inappropriate for current lifestyles. Changes have been brought about partly by the changing locational advantages of the estates. When they were first built they were peripheral to the city; now they tend to be quite well placed for work and business opportunities as new areas are built beyond them.

The buildings are well built but rather run down, and some are at the end of their economic life. Some (Egypt, Zimbabwe) were well serviced originally but others had little in the way of services. They have had many years of neglect from the housing agencies as there have been few resources for repairs and maintenance coming from the subsidised rent and hire-purchase payments. Thus, the authorities would have had to spend substantial resources in order to renovate or replace them had they not been transformed by their occupants. However, housing budgets are severely constrained, especially in the days of structural adjustment, and there is little likelihood that such investment would be forthcoming. It is reasonable to assume, therefore, that the estates would have had only brief viable futures in their untouched state.

Table 2. Summary of characteristics of study areas

	Mirpur, Dhaka, Bangladesh	Madinet Nasr, Cairo and Workers City, Helwan, Egypt	Asawasi and Suntreso, Kumasi, Ghana	Harare and Highfield, Harare, Zimbabwe
Dwellings: Number of dwellings	3842	c.2700	2463	c16,000
Dwelling sizes	22.2 m² (a few at 44.5)	29–46 m²	25–60 m²	44–56 m²
Dwelling type	Semi-detached single rooms with verandas	One-, two- and three-roomed flats in five-storey blocks	Terraced single rooms with verandas, semi-detached two and three rooms	Detached and semi-detached two and three rooms
Services provided	None Latrine blocks built but without fittings	Piped water and WC in each flat	Public water standpipes and public latrines for single rooms Piped water and bucket latrines for each semi-detached dwelling	Piped water and WC to each dwelling
Tenure	Sub-rented privately from original renter or rented from HSD	180 months rented then owned outright	Began as rented but later bought at subsidised prices A few still rented from SHC	Began as rented but later bought at subsidised prices A few still rented from Harare City
Demarcated plots?	No	No	Not for terraced rooms. Very variable in size	Yes, 200–300 m²

Table 2 (continued)

	Mirpur, Dhaka, Bangladesh	Madinet Nasr, Cairo and Workers City, Helwan, Egypt	Asawasi and Suntreso, Kumasi, Ghana	Harare and Highfield, Harare, Zimbabwe
Occupants: Median household income	Mostly over 150% of low-income threshold	Stable low income	10 times minimum wage	3 times wages of a labourer
Median per capita income	2.8 times absolute poverty	Twice absolute poverty	Only twice absolute poverty	2.4 to 3 times absolute poverty
Employment	No information	Workers in local large-scale industry Some retired	Many self-employed, some employed in formal and informal sectors Many retired but in business	No information
Median household size and characteristics	6 to 7, non-transformers 5 Mid-forties with several young children	5, late middle age	7 to 8, non-transformers 5 Late middle age, still with children	7, non-transformers 5 Middle-aged, few children
Tenancy	Renters with a new option to buy	Owners	Owners, tenants and rent-free tenants	Owners with tenants
Permanence	Mostly since first allocation Few intend to leave	Mostly since first allocation Few intend to leave	Very long term past and future	Very long term past Few intend to sell
Intended clientele	Refugees from Pakistan and low-paid government workers	Workers in general and in the heavy industries of Helwan	Second World War veterans and low-paid government workers	African government and formal sector workers
Actual clientele	Anyone who could pay a *mastan* Most original occupants are still there	As intended Most original occupants are still there	As intended except fewer local Akans Few very low-income households Many original occupants replaced by their own children	As intended. Few very low income households 75% original buyers from City Council, most others inherited

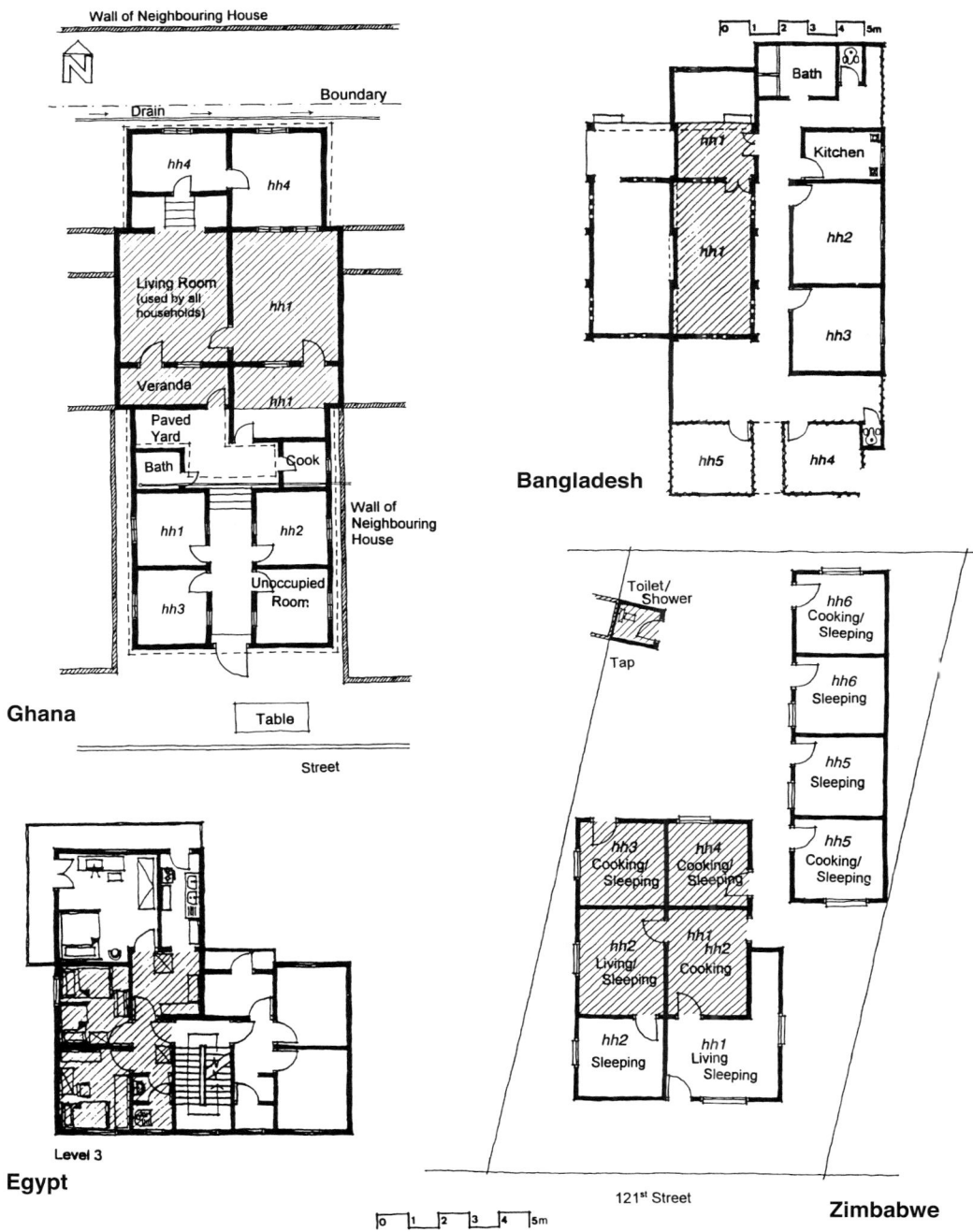

Figure 3. Plans of houses from the four case studies
All plans are to the same scale.

Notes

1   There may well be a little guilt in here as well. In 1972–5, I worked as a town planner in Zambia. I well remember turning down planning applications for extending sites and services houses with a range of independent rooms with corridor access on the grounds that they would be used as lodging houses or multi-occupied housing. Such a crassly dogmatic interpretation of the (imported) Uses Classes Order which I was expected to take to maintain the residential character of an area may have been appropriate in Slough or Harrogate but has little to commend it in a context of low-income housing supply problems in the Copperbelt.

2   On this I acknowledge the advice of Michael Mutter, Senior Architecture and Town Planning Adviser, Engineering Division, DFID.

3   Or, indeed, more than one self-contained structure, each of which could be correctly called a dwelling. See Tipple *et al.* (1994) for a discussion of the importance of differentiating house and dwelling.

4   Where two of our case studies are situated (Ghana and Zimbabwe).

5   Which usually meant satisfying the aspiration to be housed as well as the former colonial élite had been.

6   It is impossible not to wonder how successful the planting of high-technology, capital-intensive construction systems would have been in developing countries where capital is scarce and labour plentiful had not such technology transfer held great potential for the receipt of kick-backs by politicians and highly placed officials.

7   The Akans are a group of peoples who speak the Twi language, the largest being the Asantes who predominate in Kumasi.

8   Our sample has slightly more single-roomed dwellings than is representative of their numbers on the estate.

2. The housing squeeze

The scale and nature of the housing shortage

It is almost impossible to determine the shortage of housing in the developing world as not only are insufficient data available but also there is little agreement between countries on units of measurement or what constitutes adequacy. Furthermore, the relationship between households and housing is so dynamic that any data are soon out of date. In addition, it takes so long for housing data to be collated that census data from 1990 may not be available before 1996 or 1997. When dealing with people who are actually homeless, UNCHS (1996c) suggests that 100 million people in the world lack any shelter at all and sleep on pavements, in parks or shop doorways, under bridges, in transport terminals, or in night shelters provided for the homeless. Those who have very insecure or temporary accommodation, or are squatters in someone else's home, on land where eviction is threatened, in refugee camps, and in temporary shelters on public space, would number about 1000 million.

However, characteristics that expose housing shortages show that there are very many more people who cannot afford, or obtain through welfare benefits, housing which provides them with the mix of sheltered space and services which any particular society may define as adequate. Documents on housing and urbanisation created with as many resources as are available, particularly the recent Global Report on Human Settlements (UNCHS, 1996c), must rely on such characteristics to infer the scale of the problem. Specific characteristics indicative of housing shortage include crowding (in people per room and space per person), sharing of housing or multihabitation; widespread squatting (sometimes by households in a wide range of income); and the ability of landlords to raise rent advances or key money,[1] and high rents for even poor quality housing.

UNCHS (Habitat), in collaboration with the World Bank, has attempted to formalise the collection of housing indicator variables through the recently instituted Housing Indicators Programme (UNCHS, 1993; World Bank, n.d.). Forty-four indicators have been identified and have been collected as a pilot study from single cities in 52 countries. The meaning of each indicator variable is defined so that comparability may be achieved. While this programme cannot expect to provide an overall view of the state of housing in all the world at any one time, it attempts to assemble enough data to allow us to assess the progress being made over time in the battle with inadequate housing.

The number of conventional dwellings constructed annually per 1000 population is a widely collected official statistic. In Africa, Asia and Latin America, typical figures range between two and four per 1000 population. Tipple (1994b) shows that more than 10 per 1000 are needed in Sub-Saharan Africa every year for the foreseeable future. The difference is taken up with informal construction, much of which is of very poor quality, probably to the tune of 15 to 30 dwellings per 1000 population per year (UNCHS, 1996c). Thus, notwithstanding the small minority in most cities who are completely homeless, there are probably enough basic shelters but the quality of very many is inappropriate for healthy life. According to UNCHS (1996c), in low-income countries taking part in the Housing Indicators Programme, 64 per cent of dwellings in the chosen cities are not authorised by city authorities while 33 per cent of dwellings are officially recognised as not being built of permanent materials. In low–middle income countries in the programme, 36 per cent of dwellings are not authorised and 14 per cent are built of non-permanent materials. However, the same report points out that, when individual cities' returns to the study are examined against other sources, the official figures flatter to deceive. Anyone familiar with cities such as Karachi and Manila would pour scorn on the 97 and 80 per cent respectively as the claimed statistics for dwellings in permanent materials.

The rapid change in lifestyles occurring in many developing countries is creating increasing demands for improvements in housing quality. Such demands lead to obsolescence in large parts of the current stock. As we have known for many years, since it crops up in such early seminal work as Grigsby (1971), housing obsolescence is a combined function of the deterioration in the physical fabric and in changes in the acceptability of particular house types. The latter occurs with housing fashions and with the need for different space configurations, for example with the growth of technology in the home. In the 1990s, we are seeing a combining of the forces of physical decline and a crisis of acceptability for large numbers of dwellings that were built in the 1950s and 1960s, often through colonial policies and in the days before rapid city growth. Thus, we might expect a higher-than-historical rate of obsolescence in the housing stock to occur during this decade and into the next. As a consequence, any process that increases renovation and maintenance could be very valuable in increasing the viable housing stock.

In addition to the needs and demands[2] created by the inadequacy in the existing housing stock, there will be great need for new housing through the addition of many millions of new households every year as the particularly youthful populations in developing countries achieve adulthood. This is clearly a daunting task and one that is unlikely to be fulfilled without major changes in the way we approach housing supply.

The Global Strategy for Shelter to the Year 2000 (GSS) (UNCHS, 1990) calls on all countries to develop realistic housing policies to enable them to make serious inroads into the housing supply backlog before the year 2000 and establish a policy framework which will keep pace with housing need in the long term. In order to fulfil this, governments are encouraged to adopt an enabling approach, setting in place policies and fiscal arrangements that will enable the construction and maintenance of housing rather than providing it directly through government activity. To this end, GSS calls for governments to encourage all actors in the housing process to be involved in the process at the level at which they are most effective. Such 'actors' would include house-holders, communities, community-based organisations, non-governmental organisations, construction contractors, employers, and local and national govern-ments.

In addition, GSS recognises that housing is a positive contributor to local and national economic development. Where it is provided in a labour-intensive way (using local building materials, small- and medium-sized contractors, and local labour) housing provision can be an important provider of employment especially for the poorest groups in society (UNCHS/ILO, 1995).

In recognition of the continuing scarcity of housing for most people in developing countries, the GSS calls for a scaling-up of housing programmes to encourage output. Key strategic improvements will be needed in shelter delivery and one of the purposes of this book is to point out that user-initiated extensions are one of the key ways in which occupant participation can be harnessed as a housing supply mechanism.

Housing adjustment theory

There is a growing literature on the way people adjust their housing in industrialised countries where households usually have the option to move house or to stay and make changes through home improvements – the 'move or improve' choice. In recent years, home improvements have been made mainly to improve the accommodation of the single household rather than to accommodate more households or increase the stock of dwellings (Seek, 1983).

The final decision to make a housing adjustment is conceptualised as a two-stage process. The first is a decision to adjust housing consumption; the second is a choice between moving or improving, or a combination of both. The first decision springs from a mismatch between consumption and demand; the second depends on the balance of costs and benefits associated with each alternative (Seek, 1983).

Housing stress, shocks and triggers

It is obvious that, as a household increases in size through the addition of children or other dependants, or reduces when the children leave to marry and form their own households, needs and demands for space and other housing goods will change. While a newly married couple may require only a single room, by the time they have (say) two daughters and a son, and an elderly mother-in-law in residence, they will need more space and several separate rooms.

Seek (1983) conceptualises this trend as a growing mismatch over time between current levels of consumption of housing and the demands and preferences of the occupiers. The gap between consumption and demand may also spring from changing socioeconomic circumstances, tastes and preferences, changes in housing attributes and prices. There will also be other external influences such as public decisions relating to land use or transportation. As it is relatively difficult to change housing, the gap between consumption and preference grows gradually but with increasing intensity over time and is termed 'housing stress'.

Households will vary in their threshold of stress, the point at which some action is taken to relieve rather than continue to tolerate it. They may adopt various forms of coping behaviour until their threshold is reached and something is done to relieve it. Even when a previously intolerable situation is reached, financial or other circumstances might make it impossible to change housing conditions. In this case, the tolerance level must rise and the household may have to adapt to the situation by changing its housing aspirations (Michelson, 1977).

Seek (1983) suggests that there are discrete events (which he calls 'shocks' and Gosling *et al.* (1993) call 'triggers') such as the arrival of children or of elderly parents, which markedly increase housing stress. They may, however, be seemingly less dramatic, e.g., when the oldest child starts school and pressures increase for play or study space, privacy and possibly location near desirable schools (McLeod and Ellis, 1982).

Lansing and Kish (1957) classified households into eight types, seven of which follow the life of a couple (and the surviving partner) from formation, through the growing phase to mature family, and then the contracting phase to death. The eighth is for singles or couples who have no children. Seek (1983) found that, up to the mature family stage, improvements made were mainly for bigger rooms and additional rooms, while those made in the contracting phase tended to be renovations and alterations.

The choice between moving and improving

Michelson (1977) characterises stages of housing provision for a household as beginning (stage one) in inexperience and shortage of capital with a dwelling that is unlikely to cope with lifestyle changes. In stage two the household forms a concept of an ideal dwelling and carries out some improvement, extension and moving strategies as means to move towards the ideal. The third and final stage is attaining as near to the ideal as they can (Gosling *et al.*, 1993).

If adjustment is achievable through either moving or improving, i.e., in well-developed housing markets, Seek (1983) believes that most households will improve. The main impediment to moving is high cost. First, the difference between the value of the current dwelling and the price of the new one must be met. In addition, there are costs in the transactions (legal fees, duties, commissions, etc.), and in the moving of furniture and household goods. Staying put while improving through building work has disturbance and inconvenience 'costs' as well as the price of the construction, redecoration, etc. However, improving is perceived to offer the highest net benefits. The sum of transaction costs, additional price and changes needed to make the new house suit the new occupants can finance about twice as much extension as the increase in space achieved by moving (Seek, 1983).

Intangibles are often important. The inertia element is very powerful; social ties, the bother of moving, etc., cannot be quantified but are accounted for in the decision (Seek, 1983). Dynarski (1986) attempted to quantify the value of residential and neighbourhood attachment and posited that, where the loss of residential attachment outweighs the benefits of moving, a household will remain in its existing dwelling. Harmon and Potepan (1988) identified adjustment costs as more important than other demand factors including income, in determining patterns of housing consumption (Gosling *et al.*, 1993).

Households who rent and those who have to relocate through marriage, divorce, new employment elsewhere, etc., tend not to consider improving. When housing adjustment is needed, they move. Those who wish to reduce their housing consumption also tend to move as it is less easy to reduce the size of a house than to increase it, especially when subdivision is often prevented by planning norms. When movers were compared with improvers in a study in Adelaide, Australia (Kendig, 1981), some movers had made large changes in the value of their housing, such as could not easily be done by improving. In addition, about half the movers had a newer dwelling than before.

Extension can be likened to moving house while standing still, reinforcing the idea that the decision to extend is likely to be explained in the same terms as residential mobility (Gosling *et al.*, 1993). Improvers tend to make an upward adjustment to get more and better housing and most believe that the dwelling is more valuable after the improvement. In Kendig's Adelaide study, there was almost no difference in socio-economic circumstances between those who moved and those who improved to get more space.

There may be economic advantage from extension (or the extendibility) of a house but, in industrialised societies, this will normally only be acted upon when it is necessary to relieve housing stress. Whatever choice is made in response to the need for adjustment, Seek (1983) holds that the perceived benefits must be seen to cover the 'dissatisfaction' and the adjustment costs before action is taken. At the same time, the householder is likely to anticipate future 'shocks' in order to lengthen the time before another adjustment has to be made. In his survey in Melbourne, Australia, Seek (1983) found:

(a) that improvements were mainly undertaken in response to changes in households' demographic or economic circumstances; and

(b) that expenditure on improvements was constrained by households' income, wealth and financial commitments.

Seek's evidence suggested that young households bought a house and extended it from time to time over a very long period of occupation. This was counter to the argument that households adjust their housing consumption by moving and that vacated houses filter downwards to lower income households. Only 3 per cent of owner-occupier households in Australia move per year so that the mean length of stay in a house is 33.3 years.

Seek (1983) and others point out that a typical newly married couple can only afford a small house initially but they expand it over time and as finances allow, sometimes doing much of the work themselves in order to save money. The mean amount of expenditure on improvements has been found to increase with household head's income although lower income households add their own labour input to reduce the cost.

Many households will decide that adjustment by either moving or extending is simply not worth the bother and stay as they are, tolerating the housing stress. At the other extreme, some do both as 'move' and 'improve' are not mutually exclusive options. Many extensions are made as part of the moving-in process as a way of reducing immediate costs of moving and spreading the costs over a period. A household selects a relatively small, inexpensive house with the intention of extending it imme-diately or in the short term. About half the Australian samples intended to improve after they moved in (Kendig, 1981; Seek, 1983).

Littlewood and Munro (1997) found that the move-and-improve option was so common in Scotland that about one-third of movers in the previous year had under-taken works costing £500 or more since their move. This was a higher proportion than owners who had not moved (about one in four). They found that recent movers' housing choices do not represent equilibrium between their demand and the supply offered by the new home, as many commentators have held (see Harmon [1988] for a review of these). However, this does not mean that they have moved to the 'wrong' houses. They are, instead, embarking on a process of purchase and improvement which will result in a house to suit their needs in the medium term.

Although the above arguments are set in the context of well-developed housing markets, the theory they represent is useful in our consideration of less developed housing markets. Moving is much less possible in our case study areas than in the USA, Europe or Australia but the improve (extend) option is obviously chosen by our transformers. We will examine the market implications in chapter 6. For now, we will concentrate on the effects of transformation on the households' accommodation to see whether, *inter alia*, they have more room to enjoy or simply crowd more people into the extended space.

Household size and composition

As much of the housing adjustment literature revolves around the concept of housing stress as a determinant of the need to extend or move, it might be expected *a priori* that household size and composition would be major influences on the transforma-tion process. This might be simply expressed as 'large households would be more likely to transform than small ones.' Data on household size before the transformation were available only in Egypt where our two-stage model (see Appendix 5) found it was insignificant as a determinant in either the decision to extend or the value of the extension. However, we can test whether transformers' households currently have more people than non-transformers'.

Table 3. Household size and composition (main household)

Medians (and IQRs)	Bangladesh	Egypt	Ghana	Zimbabwe
No. of people in household:				
Transformers	7	5	7	7
	(5, 8)	(4, 7)	(5, 10)	(5, 8)
Non-transformers		4	5	5
		(3, 6)	(3, 8)	(3, 7)
No. of adults in household:				
Transformers	4	4	4	4
	(2, 5)	(2, 5)	(2, 5.5)	(2, 6)
Non-transformers		3.5	3	2
		(2, 5)	(2.0, 4.5)	(2, 5)
No. of children in household:				
Transformers	3	1	3	2
	(2, 4)	(0, 2)	(2, 4)	(1, 4)
Non-transformers		1	2	2
		(0, 1.3)	(0, 4)	(1, 3)
Dependency ratio (no. of children per adult)				
Transformers	0.75	0.2	0.8	0.5
	(0.3, 1.3)	(0, 0.7)	0.4, 1.0)	(0.2, 1.0)
Non-transformers		0.2	0.5	0.7
		(0, 0.5)	(0, 1)	(0.3, 1.5)
Expected household size in 3 years:				
Transformers	7	5	7	8
	(5, 9)	(3, 6)	(4.5, 10.0)	(4, 8)
Non-transformers		4	6	5
		(2.8, 6.0)	(4, 8)	(4, 7)
Number of guests per annum:				
Transformers	10	1	3	4
	(2, 20)	(0, 4)	(0, 6)	(2, 10)
Non-transformers		0	1	4
		(0, 4)	(0, 5)	(2, 10)

In table 3 there is a consistency among transformers in all the samples in their household size and composition; all tend to feature more than just a nuclear family household of one or two adults and their juvenile children. With medians of seven members (but only five in Egypt) including four adults, all show signs of transformers having large households and being in a relatively advanced stage of family life. This is reinforced by the IQRs of 5 to 8 or 10 (4 to 7 in Egypt) which demonstrate a concentration of our sample in large households with a majority of over-16-year-olds. The presence of four adults at the medians indicates a greater need for privacy than might have been expected when the original dwellings were designed for nuclear family households of parents and children.[3] In most cultures, a married couple with both a grown up son and daughter (in our data over 16 years old) would require three rooms. Thus, most of the original dwellings in their unaltered state are incapable of providing adequate space or sufficient privacy for all the occupants. Non-transformers tend to have smaller households, fewer adults and marginally fewer children than transformers. They are closer to the nuclear family household for which the dwellings were originally intended so may have had less housing stress than transformers.

There appears to be no pattern for who has the higher dependency ratios; transformers are higher in Ghana, non-transformers are higher in Zimbabwe, and they are the same in Egypt. The expected household sizes and numbers of guests per year again show no discernible pattern across countries to suggest obvious housing stress from these sources leading to extensions. Guests are numerous only in Bangladesh and are not likely to have influenced matters much anywhere.

Table 4. Household sizes for households with a planned extension

Medians (and IQRs)	Bangladesh	Egypt*	Ghana	Zimbabwe
Number of people in the household	8.5 (7, 9)	-	6 (4, 8)	6 (4, 8)
Expected household size in 3 years	8.0 (6, 9)	-	7 (5, 10)	6 (4, 8)

* No planned extensions were admitted.

As table 4 shows, households with planned extensions are currently smaller than average in Ghana but are expecting to increase in size (to the equivalent of transformers) over the next three years. Those in Zimbabwe are also smaller than average but those planning to extend in Bangladesh are larger than average (by 1.5 persons at the median). As most households in Mirpur have already extended, we can gain no clear indication of how far household size correlates with current plans for extension.

Those occupants of transformed houses who are now in a late stage of family life are likely to find that they have more room than they need in their declining years.

In industrialised countries, they would be likely to move out of their over-generous dwellings as the children leave and find somewhere smaller. We could expect this to happen to some extent in our Egyptian sample where the flats are difficult to subdivide. However, even here and certainly in the other countries, the likelihood is that the old folk will stay on but allow a son or daughter to establish him or her self as the main household (see chapter 6).

This has important ramifications for transformations. While extension activity in industrialised countries is unlikely to take account of the retirement needs of the occupants, it is more likely to do so in developing countries. In our sampled countries, the extended house may be expected to provide a combination of a rental income to augment a meagre pension, a social system for support in declining years, and a small place to provide comfort and dignity for the old folk among the next generation's activities (see chapter 3).

Increase in housing space

Increase in house size through transformation

It is obvious that one of the main factors contributing to transformation is likely to be the shortage of accommodation; the main need in housing in the countries studied appears to be for more space. The effectiveness of transformation in providing more space is, therefore, one of the main concerns of this study and the findings point to quite impressive levels of provision.

In Bangladesh, property size begins with particularly small dwellings (22 m²) as standard while in Zimbabwe they are at least twice as large (around 50 m²). In Egypt and Ghana the flats and houses built have reasonably similar median floor areas despite their extremely diverse characteristics.

The houses as currently extended have median areas of between 55 and 87 m². Some transformers have undoubtedly made prodigious increases in space (in Bangladesh, 149 per cent at the median). However, the medians for our samples generally show more modest increments (of 48 to 75 per cent in Egypt, Ghana and Zimbabwe) than previous work without a random sample would suggest (especially Tipple and Owusu, 1994). This is only a snapshot in an ongoing process, however, and there is no reason to expect the current stage to be the end of extensions.

In Zimbabwe (where the floor space index is 30 per cent for transformers), there is still plenty of potential to extend within the plots (see table 23). However, there is less room in Ghana (where the floor space index is about 60 per cent for transformers) and Egypt, and virtually none in Bangladesh. However, in Bangladesh, the recent (1995) proposal to sell the houses to the tenants is likely to signal a market in plots and could lead to the demolition of some houses and replacement with multi-storey development. There are several blocks of flats close to the *bastuhara* housing in Mirpur and it seems likely that the opportunity would be taken to maximise the income through rents by building a multi-storey apartment block. However, steps are taken

Figure 4. The first two-storey extension in Mirpur

against this in the lease document which declares that demolition of the original house would render the plot liable for *pucca* development only. This would introduce building lines and limit legal new development to a relatively narrow band and prevent blocks of flats from covering the plots. Since our survey, however, two-storey development has begun on the extensions. Multi-storey development on the whole plot has taken place in high-density single-storey estates elsewhere, e.g. in Umoja 1, Nairobi, Kenya, where housing is similarly scarce (see Fig. 5).

Table 5. Increase in floor area through transformation

Medians (and IQRs)	Bangladesh	Egypt	Ghana	Zimbabwe
Floor area of original houses	22 (22, 22)	36 (34, 44)	37 (25, 47)	50* (45, 52)
Floor area of transformed houses (m²)	55 (51, 82)	65 (60, 72)	87 (55, 127)	79 (61, 100)
Estimated increase in floor area achieved by transformers (%)**	149	57	75	48

 * For comparative reasons, these figures reflect the original house type without being influenced by whether any of the original has been demolished.
** This does not necessarily reflect row 2 median minus row 1 median as the median individuals are likely to be different.

Figure 5. Flats in Umoja 1, Nairobi, Kenya
In this core housing scheme, some owners have completely demolished the small
single-storey dwelling and replaced it with a block of flats occupying the whole plot.

As table 5 shows, the original dwellings in each of our case studies were relatively
unvaried; only in Ghana where the terraced rooms differ markedly from the semi-
detached types do we have IQRs higher than 13 m². The transformers have, however,
not only increased the sizes of houses considerably but they have also introduced a
greater range of house size into the estates studied with IQRs of 32 m² in Bangladesh,
72 m² in Ghana and 39 m² in Zimbabwe. Advantages of variety include the likelihood
of attracting and keeping a heterogeneous population, the likelihood that housing
more closely fits the requirements of its varied occupants than is possible from a small
range of designs, and the smoothing out of lumpiness in the housing stock so that
filtering can proceed with greater facility (Ferchiou, 1982 and chapter 4).

Habitable space

Habitable space within a dwelling is that which is used as living, dining and bedroom
accommodation. It includes halls in Ghana, where the name is used for living rooms
(as in 'chamber and hall'), but not elsewhere. It does not include kitchens, bathrooms,
toilets, balconies, verandas, passages, storerooms, commercial space or any open space.

There is a two-stage process of capturing extra habitable space. First, the original
space is redivided into more rooms (albeit some are very small, e.g., original verandas).
Second, new rooms are added which are generally smaller than the originals.

Table 6. Habitable space characteristics of the houses

Medians (and IQRs)	Bangladesh	Egypt	Ghana	Zimbabwe
No. of habitable rooms	1	3	2	3
in the original houses	(1, 1)	(2, 3)	(1, 3)	(3, 3)
No. of habitable rooms in	5	3	6	6
the transformed houses	(4, 6)	(3, 4)	(4, 8)	(4, 7)
Percentage change	500	50	217	67
through transformation*	(400, 700)	(25, 50)	(100, 400)	(33, 100)
Habitable area in the	14.1	26.4	24.1	30.0
original houses	(14, 14)	(26, 26)	(19, 35)	(25, 35)
Habitable area in the	34.6	41.8	53.5	53.1
transformed houses	(30, 47)	(36, 48)	(35, 85)	(41, 65)
Percentage change	144	57	124	58
through transformation*	(109, 217)	(33, 73)	(64, 206)	(24, 105)

* The percentage change does not necessarily correspond to the differences between the median and IQR values shown in adjacent rows.

Data in table 6 show the impressive scale of housing supply currently achieved by transformers in terms of habitable rooms and habitable space. Although rooms in flats in Egypt have only increased marginally (still three rooms at the median), houses in Bangladesh have increased to five rooms and those in Ghana and Zimbabwe to six at the median. These constitute increases in habitable rooms of between 50 and 500 per cent at the medians.

On the other hand, habitable space has increased by 60 per cent in Egypt and Zimbabwe, twice that in Ghana and a prodigious 144 per cent in Bangladesh. Although the rate of increase in Bangladesh is greater than elsewhere, the houses that result are the smallest of our four samples with a median of only 35 m² habitable space. While the particular circumstances of flats in Egypt render spatial expansion very expensive, the transformers have achieved impressive extensions and have a median of 42 m² habitable space. In Ghana and Zimbabwe, habitable space is now about 53 m² at the medians.

Proportion of space which is habitable

In each case study, there is a high proportion of habitable space to total built space as clearly seen in table 7. Transformers have made living space out of earlier verandas, balconies and kitchens to the extent that the lowest country median (Zimbabwe) shows 78 per cent of the area habitable. In Egypt, non-transformers who are mainly in three-roomed flats have managed higher shares of habitable space than transformers because they have rearranged the unextended flats to confine the kitchen to a very small area. The percentage improvements in habitable space show how effective transformers have been in comparison with the original provision. In Bangladesh, where the original veranda was more than one-third of the dwelling, very large percentage gains have been made as almost any non-habitable space has been expunged from the house. Elsewhere, balconies and verandas were much smaller in proportion to the original dwellings and some non-habitable spaces have been added.

Table 7. Percentage of housing space which is habitable

Medians (and IQRs)	Bangladesh	Egypt	Ghana	Zimbabwe
Non-transformers' current	63	90*	65	72
percentage habitable	(63, 63)	(73, 91)	(61, 67)	(66, 79)
Transformers' *original*	63	73	66	76
percentage habitable	(63, 63)	(73, 85)	(60, 72)	(71, 79)
Transformers' *current*	90	80	81	78
percentage habitable	(80, 96)	(73, 82)	(72, 88)	(72, 83)
Transformers' percentage	41	0	10	5
improvement over original	(26, 51)	(-2, 11)	(0, 36)	(-3, 11)
Transformers' change in				
veranda/balcony space	-8.2	+2.0	-3.5	0
(m² per house)	(-8.2, -8.2)	(-0.9, +4.3)	(0, -8.2)	(0, +3.6)

* Only in Egypt are there differences between original and current habitable space for non-transformers. The original can be seen in the cell below.

Most samples have chosen to trade off balconies or verandas for habitable space. This has not occurred in Egypt where, counter to our expectations, transformers have increased their balcony space. Though most have absorbed the original balcony into new habitable space, they have added a new balcony, 2 m² at the median larger than the original. As we have seen above, the Bangladesh sample have completely sacrificed veranda space in favour of habitable space.

The lesson from this is that, while balconies and verandas are extremely useful for allowing transformers to break out of the original building envelope through extensions, their importance as a long-term space user is very questionable. In designing dwellings, therefore, it might be wise to regard balconies and verandas as roofed but unenclosed future living space, rather than as having a long career as open areas.

> The pattern is clear. When the family looks around for some space to expand, which it always does, the easiest, cheapest, and quietest direction (no building inspectors, please) is into existing 'raw' space whose initial function is deemed dispensable – the porch, the garage... . Houses evidently need more low-definition space for later expansion, and it's easier to add in than add on. (Brand, 1994: 162–3).

More space per person: the 'smoking gun' of successful housing supply

Two of the most important aims of any housing policy in a context of shortage are the reduction of occupancy rates (people per room) and the increase of dwelling space per person. Success in either or both of these is the most likely demonstrator of whether extension activity succeeds in relieving housing stress (Seek, 1983; Gosling *et al.*, 1993)[4] or simply creates more space for more people to crowd into (allows an increase in population without improvements of most people's occupancy). If the transformation has been made to benefit the original household, we would expect main households in transformed houses to have more habitable rooms and more habitable space per household than non-transformers. As a corollary, we might expect non-transformers to have higher occupancy rates because they have not adjusted their housing to provide more space (we might say they have not yet adjusted). If, on the other hand, transformers are providing space for renting out or for commercial activity, we might expect there to be no difference in rooms and space occupied, or even for non-transformers to have lower occupancy rates. Within a house which is multi-habited, owners could be expected to enjoy better space standards than other households but not necessarily more than they would have had if they had not transformed.

In earlier work (Tipple, 1991a), we suggested that small dwellings are more likely to be extended than large ones; similarly, households who originally have only a few rooms would be more likely to extend than those with many. In addition, we suggested that transformations would tend to increase the local population, and generate higher population densities but, at the same time, they are likely to reduce occupancy rates (Tipple, 1991a: 77). In this study, we measure occupancy in terms of both habitable rooms and floor area. The latter is particularly recommended by the Housing Indicators Programme (UNCHS, 1993) as the most reliable indicator of occupancy as it reduces bias arising from variability in room sizes.

Occupancy rates of main households

It seems plain that transformers benefit from increased space for themselves. In each sample where we have non-transformers' data, transformers have more habitable space for the main households than non-transformers. They occupy 47 per cent more habitable space than non-transformers in Ghana, 20 per cent more in Zimbabwe, but only 4 per cent more in Egypt at the medians. Egypt has the largest median habitable space use at 41 m² per household and 8 m² per person. The latter is 44 per cent higher than Ghana, 65 per cent higher than Zimbabwe, and 146 per cent higher than Bangladesh.

Table 8 demonstrates that, except in the Bangladesh sample, there is little difference in the median amount of habitable space which the current main households occupy (34 to 40 m²). Egyptian main households, however, have considerably more space per person than the other samples reflecting *inter alia* their difficulty in using additional space for anything but their own household. Their options to rent out space or use it for commercial purposes are, of course, strictly limited by the design of their multi-storey flats and the difficulty of dividing their transformed flats into more than one independent dwelling. This is a constraint not experienced by our other samples and one which the Egyptians may prefer not to have, especially in the light of their comparatively low income, the difficulty of finding independent dwellings for the next generation, the different needs of the next (inheriting) generation, and the windfall gains to be made through key-money payments on newly rented rooms.

Table 8. Measures of occupancy for main household

Medians (and IQRs)	Bangladesh	Egypt	Ghana	Zimbabwe
Habitable space occupied by main household (m²):				
Transformers	23.0	41.4	39.7	34.4
	(8, 32)	(33, 47)	(28, 54)	26, 45)
Non-transformers		39.8	24.1	27.5
		(26, 40)	(19, 35)	(22, 36)
Habitable space occupied per person in main household (m²):				
Transformers	3.3	8.0	5.8	5.2
	(1, 5)	(6, 12)	(4, 9)	(4,8)
Non-transformers		7.1	4.9	4.5
		(6, 13)	(3, 8)	(4, 9)
Occupancy rate of main household (persons per room):				
Transformers	2.5	1.5	1.8	1.8
	(1.75, 3.0)	(1.0, 2.3)	(1.2, 2.7)	(1.3, 2.6)
Non-transformers		1.5	3.0	2.2
		(0.8, 2.0)	(2.0, 4.5)	(1.5, 2.9)
Habitable rooms occupied by main household:				
Transformers	3	3	4	3
	(1, 4)	(3, 4)	(3, 5)	(3, 5)
Non-transformers		3	2	2.5
		(2, 3)	(1, 2)	(2, 3)
Future occupancy rate:				
Transformers	2.5	1.3	1.8	1.8
	(1.8, 3.3)	(1.0, 2.0)	(1.1, 2.7)	(1.3, 2.6)
Non-transformers		1.3	3.0	2.0
		(0.8, 2.0)	(2.3, 5.3)	(1.4, 3.0)

The Bangladesh sample has significantly higher occupancy rates than the other three case studies but the real differences are most obvious in terms of habitable space. In Bangladesh, main households occupy only 23 m² of habitable space at the median, 10 m² less than the next lowest (Ghana), and only 3.3 m² per person. This is considerably lower than the other medians but is quite high compared with other households in Dhaka and only a little lower than the Housing Indicators Programme mean for Dhaka of 3.72 m² per person, which is probably an over-estimate (UNCHS, 1993).

Transformers in Egypt have slightly better occupancy rates (i.e., fewer persons per room) and more rooms occupied per household overall than non-transformers. However, habitable rooms occupied vary between transformers and non-transformers by more than is evident from the medians. The means show the difference made; transformers in Egypt occupy 3.7 rooms, non-transformers, 3.3. In line with our suggestion in Tipple *et al.* (1985), a major imperative in Helwan and Medinet Nasr appears to be to obtain three rooms for the household; 79 per cent of transformers in our Egyptian sample have at least three rooms and non-transformers are concentrated in the flats built with three rooms.

In Ghana, the number of habitable rooms occupied per household is very significantly better for transformers (it has doubled at the median). The increase in space is almost 16 m² per household (up from 4.9 to 5.8 m² per person). Thus, transformers have made major gains in space in a city where 73 per cent of all households occupied one room in 1986 (Malpezzi *et al.*, 1990). In Zimbabwe, transformers have 0.5 more habitable rooms per household than non-transformers at the median, even though extra renter households are relatively common. In the top quartile, the difference increases with transformers having at least two more rooms than non-transformers.

Whatever difficulties and exogenous pressures exist, all our samples have achieved more habitable space at the median for the current main household than was originally available in the whole house. Thus, as we suggested, higher population densities have been achieved with lower occupancy rates in the main household (see table 8). Even with the extensions, however, main households are still not generously housed. In Bangladesh they only have 3.3 m² per person at the median while those in Egypt have 8.0 m², in Ghana they have 5.8 m² and in Zimbabwe they have 5.2 m² per person. In the Zimbabwe sample, space has improved for the main households at the expense of a particularly large difference between main and subsequent households' spaces (see below).

From the foregoing, we see that main households fare well in gaining considerably more space and rooms, and the transformation process is a way in which households improve their own space use and that of other residents in their houses. This is one of the most cogent arguments in favour of transformations as a valid housing adjustment mechanism and against the 'building slums' accusation of local planners.

Contrary to Oxman and Carmon (1986), who found that Israeli transformers tended to add larger rooms than were originally provided, our transformers have provided smaller new rooms than the originals, except in Egypt where they are similar in both median and range (table 9). In Bangladesh and Ghana, the original one-roomed dwellings had exceptionally large rooms but the relatively small median for the new rooms must owe something to the constraints of small sites and to cultures where (for different reasons) many smaller rooms are more advantageous than a few larger ones. The Zimbabwe shacks tend to be small but this affects many transformers there who supplement permanent structures with additional shacks as well as the shacks-only transformers themselves.

Table 9. Size of habitable room, original and current (medians and IQRs)

Medians (and IQRs)	Bangladesh	Egypt	Ghana	Zimbabwe
Size of original rooms	14.1	10.1	13.9	9.5
	(14.1, 14.1)	(9.2, 12.6)	(12.2, 15.6)	(7.9, 12.5)
Size of new rooms	8.7	10.1	9.2	7.9
	(6.6, 13.4)	(7.8, 12.9)	(6.5, 12.6)	(5.9, 10.1)
Size of current rooms*	7.6	10.0	10.6	8.6
	(5.7, 9.8)	(8.2, 12.5)	(5.9, 14.2)	(6.7, 11.3)

* Original and new combined including division of original rooms.

Space and rooms occupied before and after transformation

Increase in space per person through transformation

In order to measure the improvement in space use that households enjoy through transformation, we have attempted to model the likely space use of households in the absence of their transformations through three proxy measures. The current circumstances (HcOc) for transformers equal 100:

1. *Non-transformers' space use:* This assumes that non-transformed houses would represent the occupancy rates in the area if it had not experienced extension activity.

2. *HoOo – only the current main household (standing for the original occupants – Oo) in the original house (Ho):* This assumes that the same number of people would belong to the main household whether or not the house had been extended and it is the only household in the house. Thus, it demonstrates the best housing conditions which the household would be tolerating in the absence of extensions. The number of non-transformed houses with additional households (see below) demonstrates that some would not have these relatively favourable conditions.

3. *HoOc – all the current occupants (Oc) in the original house (Ho):* This assumes that all the occupants of the current house would occupy it even if it had not been extended. It represents the worst crowding likely in the absence of transformations but is, perhaps, the least likely scenario except in Egypt, where it is virtually the same as HoOo.

Although we have a variable of occupants before transformation in Egypt, we use the same proxies as in the other samples for this comparative analysis. It is clear from table 10 that transformation adds considerably to the amount of habitable space and number of habitable rooms per person, whatever way those are measured. For example, households in Egypt, and in Ghanaian main households (HoOo), would have only two-thirds of the space currently available in the absence of transformations. Transformers have improved less over non-transformers (the difference between the value shown and 100) than over the other proxies but there are many cells in the tables where values of about, or less than, 50 show that transformation has achieved about, or more than, a doubling of space per person by that measure. Rooms per person have generally increased more than habitable space; a reflection of the increased privacy gained as a consequence of building smaller rooms. It is particularly marked in Bangladesh where habitable rooms have increased fivefold (see table 6) and in Ghana. In both places, the main households would have only 42 per cent of the rooms currently available. There are very few flats in the Egypt sample with more than one household.

Table 10. Various measures of original habitable space and rooms per person as indexes of current habitable space per person (HcOc) (transformed HcOc=100)

	Bangladesh	Egypt	Ghana	Zimbabwe
Habitable space per person:				
Non-transformer's space per person as an index of HcOc	-	90	79	93
HoOo as an index of HcOc	73	66	67	97
HoOc as an index of HcOc	40	66	43	65
Habitable rooms per person:				
Non-transformer's rooms per person as an index of HcOc	-	100	56	78
HoOo as an index of HcOc	42	75	42	91
HoOc as an index of HcOc	23	75	30	58

HoOo uses current main household only as a proxy for original household.
HoOc uses all current occupants as a proxy for original household.

This analysis demonstrates that transformers are responding at least partly to the inadequacies of the original dwellings for the main households. The comparatively large original dwellings in Zimbabwe are the exception as the main households seem to have provided themselves with little extra space through the transformations process. Elsewhere, main households would have had only two-thirds to three-quarters as much habitable space as they have now. As the main household represents those who would occupy the dwelling even if it had not been transformed, it seems that at least some of the impetus to extend has probably come from the inadequacy of the original. In this case, the population is unlikely to have increased as a result of the extensions.[5]

This is in line with the findings of the two-step econometric analysis reported in chapter 6 and detailed in Appendix 5. In each country, area or number of rooms before the extension is an important variable in determining whether transformation occurs and/or how much is spent on it.

The difference between existing occupancy and that of non-transformers is relatively small because of the latter's smaller households. We cannot, however, discern whether the difference in household size is intrinsic or has been generated because the extra space has attracted extra household members. The difference between existing occupancy and HoOc, of course, represents the effect of increases in population on the estates enabled by the transformation. We will see, later, how many more households there are in the houses after transformation than were originally intended.

The foregoing data give ample support for three of our preliminary expectations:

1. That among the urban poor, several small rooms are preferable to one or two large ones. Transformations, therefore, are likely to provide more rooms as well as more room. As space has been added, it has tended to be in smaller rooms than the original provision. In addition, many households have divided up the original space into more (smaller) rooms, showing that internal privacy is more important than the original designers reckoned.
2. That the need for greater external and internal privacy is one of the major motivators for transformation.
3. That transformations increase the local population and generate higher population densities but tend to reduce occupancy rates (Tipple, 1991a: 76–7).

Notes

1   Key money is a payment demanded for the tenancy (the key) which is extra to monthly rental payments. It is almost universal in Egypt. Rent advance is the payment of several instalments of rent ahead of time with a rent holiday until the advance is exhausted. This is common in Ghana. The former is a means to increase rents without affecting official monthly payments; the latter is a means to increase the net present value of the rent to be paid in that $200 in hand is worth more than $20 per month for the next 10 months.
2   Put very simply, demands are needs backed up by an ability to pay.
3   In the case of the Ghana single-roomed dwellings, it is likely that most were expected to be occupied by men living alone.
4   Just as a smoking gun in the hand is a sure sign of a murderer.
5   Except some may have stayed who would have moved out if the space had not been available, e.g. mature children, or some may have come to fill the extra space, e.g. poor relatives.

3. More than just a dwelling

Every house is a work in progress. It begins in the imagination of the people who built it and is gradually transformed, for better or worse, by the people who occupy it down through the years, decades, centuries. To tinker with a house is to commune with the people who lived in it before and to leave a message for those who will live in it later. Every house is a living museum of habitation and a monument to all the lives and aspirations that have flickered within it. (Owens, 1991)

Introduction

A house is more than just a dwelling. It is a source of identity and status and a demonstrator of both to the outside world. It may become identified with, and a place of assembly for, a wider family or lineage than occupies it from day to day (a family house). It may also be a location for the business which provides the basic necessities of life or for one that augments a main income. In this chapter, we can see how transformations assist in turning a simple dwelling into a structure which can fulfil some or all of these functions.

Transformation as occupant participation

In government-built housing areas, transformations could be expected as a manifestation of the alienation which occupants are bound to feel, according to Habraken (1975), in 'mass housing'. He argues that mass housing cannot satisfy the needs of the occupants because, by its very nature, it must be built in the absence of consultation with future occupants. Moreover, it is impossible to predetermine occupants' requirements as these will only become apparent through their activity in the dwellings. While mass housing assumes that the dwelling is a consumer item, Habraken argues that no one can live satisfactorily within a fixed environment in which they have no input:

> Dwelling is indissolubly connected with building, with forming the protective environment. These two notions cannot be separated, but together comprise the notion of man housing himself; dwelling *is* building. (Habraken, 1975: 18)

Thus, the acts of alteration and extension to mass housing environments would appear to be as inevitable as that night follows day:

It has to do… with the sudden urge to change as well as the stubborn desire to conserve and keep. It is related to the need to create one's own environment, but also to share that of others or to follow a fashion. The need to give one's personal stamp is as important as the inclination to be unobtrusive. In short, it all has to do with the need for a personal environment where one can do as one likes, indeed it concerns one of the strongest urges of mankind: the desire for possession… To possess something we have to take possession. We have to make it part of ourselves… put our stamp on it. Something becomes our possession because we make a sign on it… because it shows traces of our existence. (Habraken, 1975: 12)

The argument is that one cannot really identify with an area unless one has made some contribution in the way of construction or alteration; that a sense of belonging can only really be achieved through leaving physical traces:

> To build is to exercise power and to change the environment… Only when users themselves exercise power, by directly influencing and controlling a part of the physical environment, can we expect healthy, vital, steadily improving environments. (Habraken, 1980a: 1)

Much of the early work on transformations concentrated on these notions of how they allowed residents to have some input to their housing conditions in a context in which initial provision was an entirely 'top-down' imposition. Steinberg (1984), Benjamin (1985) and Beinart (1971) all stress the importance of transformations as participation by the occupants in not only increasing their living space but in reducing alienation and increasing the feeling of belonging and having a stake in the housing they occupy.

Brand (1994) suggests a more positive context, beginning not with alienation but a less destructive but nonetheless real feeling of not belonging. He argues that the process of alteration of one's environment is inevitable as a consequence of inhabitation, a highly dynamic process referred to by biologists as 'ecopoiesis' (home-making), or the process of a system making a home for itself. 'The building and the dwellers must shape and reshape themselves to each other until there is a tolerable fit' (Brand, 1994: 164).

Writers such as Turner (1976) and Rapoport (1969) have also emphasised the creative dialogue between people and the environment which is played out in the construction of their dwelling. The concept of building a home is seen as a socially vital part of integration into urban life and the assignment or assumption of status (Kellett, 1995). Holston (1991) sees the expression of different levels of relative affluence in the design and construction of the dwelling as means of creating differences among the poor. He sees construction of better housing as a representation of a passage from disrespect and denigration to competence and knowledge through 'the production and consumption of what modern society considers important' (Holston, 1991: 462).

Brand (1994) demonstrates that buildings which survive usually experience changes through their lifetimes as occupants change. He argues that the time dimension deserves more attention in design and demonstrates how flexibility can be designed in. He shows, for example, through the work of Moudon (1986), how the 'San Francisco Victorian' house gains greatly in flexibility from having the hall and side passageway almost 2 m wide rather than just wide enough for a passage. Its added ability to contain cupboards, bathrooms, etc., give it a function as a support core rather than just an access way. The rooms themselves are small, squarish and unspecialised in function. Whilst there was no intention that the design should allow flexibility through time, it was probably intended to appeal to a variety of tenants and this amounts to more or less the same thing. Moudon (1986) draws a conclusion in his work that we should return to the room as module in designing resilient housing. The problem with the dwelling as the design unit is that it encourages over-specialisation of rooms which make it difficult for later occupants to change their function. On the other hand, autonomous rooms can be constantly readapted without stress to the building (Brand, 1994).

In this vein, buildings can be seen as multi-generational contexts for housing and transformers are expressing not only housing needs but also the desire for identity, a sense of belonging, and a search for status among neighbours and in the world at large. It is almost a case of 'I build therefore I am.'

The importance of ownership

In our previous work, ownership was recognised as a factor likely to contribute towards transformation. We did not go as far as Carmon and Oxman (1984b) in arguing that it is a necessity but we suggested that ownership was likely to be a catalyst, rather than a prerequisite, for transformation (Tipple, 1991a). It might also be argued that transformation is a means of extending property ownership, of increasing the amount of housing owned and, thus, its effectiveness in whatever varied functions a house performs. Thus, the ownership of more rooms allows more space for one's own household to develop their personalities and activities in the home, more patronage of relatives, and more opportunities for rental or other income-generating activities. A larger unit of real estate increases investment wealth so increasing status and the ability to raise capital in an economy where housing is marketable (in our cases, Bangladesh, Egypt and Zimbabwe). Thus, transformers could be said to be moving up the ladder of society in their neighbourhood by their housing adjustment.

Table 11 shows that, apart from in Bangladesh, ownership is predominant among our samples and most are the owners who actually paid for the house. Also, transformers are more likely to own than non-transformers. It is interesting that renters are capable of transforming if conditions are favourable. Their willingness to transform in Bangladesh goes against earlier work in Israel (Carmon and Oxman, 1984a) and in industrialised countries (see chapter 2) suggesting that renters have only the moving option in housing adjustment.

Table 11. Tenure characteristics of transformers and non-transformers (percentages)

	Bangladesh	Egypt	Ghana	Zimbabwe
Transformers:				
Owner	0	94	90	57
Renter	100	0	2	8
Family owned	0	2	2	9
Owner's representative or other	0	4	6	26
Non-transformers:				
Owner	-	87	58	43
Renter	-	0	19	11
Family owned	-	0	10	11
Owner's representative or other	-	13	13	35

Two market quirks are worth attention. In Bangladesh, the buying of possession has bestowed opportunities to rent government-built houses on those to whom they were not allocated and who are probably well outside the low-income group. This represents a method of passing the occupation of the housing either up or down the income scale, an opportunity for 'raiding' by middle-income groups (see chapter 4). In Ghana, there are significant minorities who inherit (25 per cent) and who live in the house because of a family relationship with the owner (20 per cent). None of these 45 per cent needs resources sufficient to acquire the house 'in the market' and they represent a potential for passing ownership rights down the income scale. Inheritance enriches people with a dwelling (or a share in one) and may signal further expenditure on improvements and extensions to cope with the new household circumstances. In our samples, inherited ownership is currently common only in Ghana but it is bound to increase as mortality takes its toll of the original owners.

Table 12 shows that our Egypt and Ghana samples overwhelmingly have no other house, though virtually all Ghanaians have part of a rural house to which they have rights of occupation. In Bangladesh and Zimbabwe, however, considerable minorities have a rural house and many are likely to have land. In Bangladesh, some transformers pay for the new construction through selling land or property in the rural area. It might be expected, therefore, that their percentage in this variable will fall over time. A house in another town might tend to ease the pressure on the sampled house as a status symbol and a place to fulfil obligations of accommodation to kin. Thus, it is unsurprising that fewer transformers than non-transformers have a house in another town in both Egypt and Ghana.

Table 12. Ownership of another house (percentages)

	Bangladesh	Egypt	Ghana	Zimbabwe
No other house:				
Transformers	69	89	88	53
Non-transformers	-	88	83	48
House in home rural area:				
Transformers	29	5	4	35
Non-transformers	-	4	0	48
House in another town (not home area):				
Transformers	0	0	2	1
Non-transformers	-	6	9	0
House in the city:				
Transformers	1	5	6	2
Non-transformers	-	1	8	0
Owns more than one other house:				
Transformers	0	0	1	9
Non-transformers	-	0	0	4

Home ownership and extension in mature years

We could expect two characteristics to be dominant among heads of households in government-built housing in the survey:

1. that they are relatively old as the houses are quite old and little turnover in tenancy takes place in such estates;
2. that they would be established workers when they received the house and so are very well established now.

However, the Mbare estate in Zimbabwe is so old that many of the original heads of households have died and have been replaced by their offspring.

It comes as no surprise, therefore, that the heads of the main households demonstrate the expected characteristics. There is remarkable consistency among transformers in age at moving in: all medians are around 30, with first quartiles in the early twenties and third quartiles in the mid-thirties. Non-transformers moved in particularly early in Zimbabwe. Many probably lived there as children and then bought the houses from the authorities when they had taken over from parents as the *de facto* household heads (only 10 per cent of households inherited their house after it had been bought). Household heads now tend to be in late working life or retired, having stayed in the house most of their working lives. Non-transformers tend to be even older than transformers (by five to seven years at the medians for Egypt, Ghana and

Zimbabwe) and just as long in the house (in Egypt and Ghana though not in Zimbabwe).[1]

Table 13. Age and establishment of heads of main households

Medians (and IQRs)	Bangladesh	Egypt	Ghana	Zimbabwe
Age at moving into house (years):				
Transformers	30	30	29	29
	(25, 38)	(24, 36)	(21, 37)	(23,35)
Non-transformers		30	30	20
		(22, 31)	(13, 39)	(9, 28)
Age of head (years):				
Transformers	45	55	59	54
	(40, 51)	(45, 56)	(48, 66)	(42, 61)
Non-transformers		60	52	48
		(50, 65)	(40, 65)	(34, 60)
Age at first transformation (years):				
Transformers	38	49	43	41
	(31, 44)	(41, 57)	(33, 53)	(32, 54)
Non-transformers	-	-	-	-
Length of stay in house (years):				
Transformers	15	27	30	25
	(11, 19)	(20, 31)	(20, 40)	(17, 32)
Non-transformers		30	30	20
		(22, 31)	(13, 39)	(9, 28)
Length of time in current employment (years):				
Transformers	15	27	9	5
	(7, 22)	(10, 33)	(2, 18)	(0, 14)
Non-transformers		30	5	6
		(10, 34)	(0, 17)	(0, 12)

In most of the samples, transformation began when the household heads were in their late thirties and early forties, eight to 14 years at the medians after they had moved in. This is a time when the households are probably much larger than when they had moved in and really feeling the stress of increased demands for space. The exception is the Egypt sample, who tend to have waited until their 15 years rent was paid and they became owners. This put them in their forties.

We initially suggested that long residence would increase the likelihood of transformation (Tipple, 1991a). This appears to be supported here but only indirectly. It is inevitable that the longer a household is in the house, the more likely it is to have transformed. On the other hand, there is no evidence that transformers have been in the house longer than non-transformers. Neither is there evidence here that non-transformers are potential transformers who have yet to extend through lack of time. Lengths of stay in the house for all groups are prodigious and two points can be considered:

1. The longevity at one dwelling reflects that adjustment by relocation is very difficult in many developing country housing markets and thus emphasises the consequent importance of transformation as a housing adjustment mechanism. Thus, the long time in the house probably reflects the general difficulty facing would-be housing adjusters rather than being a characteristic associated only with transformers.
2. The benefits to be derived from relatively costly extensions (the use-value of the work done) can be increased by long residence. Very settled households need not be too concerned about the difference between extension cost and added value as they will have plenty of time to enjoy using the extensions (Gosling *et al.*, 1993).

The latter would appear to be the opposite of what would be expected of a household whose head is ageing and soon to retire. We might feel that (s)he would have little time to enjoy the housing goods provided. However, it shows how the perceived use value is increased by the expectation that the transformed house will be enjoyed by the next generation to whom the transformer is acting as a benefactor.

Needs of the next generation

A house can be expected to provide a flow of housing services for many years after the original household head has died. Many household heads regard their house as the only real asset which they can pass on to their heirs. Furthermore, many societies place burdensome responsibilities on one generation to give the next an especially good start in life. This is often expressed in terms of a house to live in. In countries with ready markets in housing, the posthumous benefits matter little to the occupants apart from their value as an inheritance capable of being sold to enrich their children. In many developing countries, however, the likely needs of the next generation, and how best the house can serve them, appear to be very important in the decision to transform. Why else would relatively old people be increasing the size of their houses, often with financial help from their grown-up children? Indeed, the needs of the next generation are probably more important to Ghanaian transformers than those of the current one. Such considerations are combined, in Ghana at least, with a tradition not to sell the house of a deceased owner and divide the money up between the heirs but, instead, to keep the house and live in it. Thus, many similarly sized, independently accessible rooms can more usefully be inherited by several heirs than a suite of rooms of differing sizes opening off a living room. This is in line with Moudon's (1986) argument that the room is a useful basic unit for planning. In this way, inheritance and the inheritors' needs for accommodation become important for the house owner's decision-making process.

It follows, then, that house size and design after transformation are likely to reflect factors other than current household size. All heirs may require at least a room in the house and maybe even more if their children are to be accounted for. Even if an adult heir has left the house, his/her need for a room to inherit in the family house (Amole *et al.*, 1993) may well be accounted for in the decision on the number of rooms in the transformed house.[2]

When asked their intention for disposing of the house, only in Zimbabwe is there even a small minority of transformers who intend to sell their houses eventually (table 14). The overwhelming majority either refused to entertain the idea of moving or asserted their intention of leaving the house to their heirs. Thus, transformation is probably both a function of, and a response to, the static nature of housing in the cities of the developing world. It is unlikely, therefore, that transformed areas will suffer from displacement of population by middle-income or richer households coming to buy them out (raiding or gentrification)[3] and, thus, the occupants will benefit from any upward filtering inherent in the transformation process (see chapter 4). However, if prices rose significantly in relatively active markets like that in Zimbabwe (and, in future no doubt, Bangladesh), owners who currently see no possibility of moving might receive offers too good to refuse.

Table 14. Intention on leaving the house (percentages)

	Bangladesh	Egypt	Ghana	Zimbabwe
Sell it	2	1	1	14
Pass it on to family	2	13	61	54
Will not leave	95	85	32	27
Other	1	1	5	6

Accommodating extra households

When the estates under study were first built, they were intended to house nuclear family households or single men. Furthermore, those in Ghana and Zimbabwe were intended to be simply a rented shelter for them for such time as they stayed in the city or in the employment through which they gained their rights to be housed at that time. The concept of single nuclear family households occupying independent dwellings, though basic to the design of the estates, is uncommon in the countries studied and many others. Tipple *et al.* (1994) demonstrate that, in some West African cultures, there is no concept of a dwelling, defined as the place of abode of a single household. The latter is a group of people who live and eat together. We found this to be true in the languages used for the surveys (Bangla in Dhaka; Arabic in Cairo; Twi, Ewe, and Ga[4] in Kumasi; and Shona and N'debele in Harare).

Similarly, there appears to be no word for household as defined in the survey. All cultures represented had a preference for living in extended family households of some sort. They may be horizontally extended to include brothers, sisters, nephews and nieces of the head or spouse, or vertically extended to include three generations. Over the years, these forms of living have successfully been established in the estates studied, or are preferred if the dwelling permitted them (e.g. by the Egyptian flat dwellers), leading to demand for more rooms, extra privacy, and other conditions that allow the operation of complex households.

There is remarkable consistency in the number of people per house in the Bangladesh, Ghana and Zimbabwe samples, considering the differences in the original provision (table 15). The medians of around 10 and third quartiles of 14 to 15 fall between the expectation for single household dwellings and multihabited rooming accommodation. Except in Egypt where there has been little or no increase in population parallel with the transformations, there are about 50 per cent more people in transformers' houses than in non-transformers' and probably at least twice the originally planned population (non-transformers in table 3 may represent these quite well).

Table 15. People currently accommodated

Medians and (IQRs)	Bangladesh	Egypt	Ghana	Zimbabwe
Persons per house:				
Transformed	11	5	10	10
	(8, 15)	(4, 7)	(7, 14)	(8, 14)
Non-transformed	-	4.5	6	7
		(3, 6)	(3, 8)	(5, 9)
Households per house:				
Transformed	3	1	2	3
	(1, 4)	(1, 1)	(1, 3)	(1, 4)
Non-transformed	-	1	1	1
		(1, 1)	(1, 1)	(1, 2)
Percentage of houses with tenant households:				
Transformed	71	2	27	70
Non-transformed	-	1	13	38
Percentage of houses with rent free (family) tenants:				
Transformed	n.i	7	33	13
Non-transformed	-	4	2	5

The difference between types of renting can be seen here quite clearly. In Bangladesh and Zimbabwe, renting is a business venture for at least some profit. Seventy per cent of transformed houses there have tenants and a total of three households per house at the medians. In Zimbabwe, even 38 per cent of non-transformed houses have a tenant in residence as well as the main household. In Ghana, however, renting rooms to tenants is not normally a business venture. As Korboe (1993a) points out, rooms tend to be rented out when family members do not need them or as a means of raising sufficient money to keep the house in repair. Thus, not surprisingly, even though privately rented rooms are the largest source of housing in urban Ghana, only 27 per cent of transformed houses have renters while 33 per cent of them have rent-free (family) tenants.[5] The latter demonstrate housing's role as a social safety net for the poorer members of families (see Amole *et al.*, 1993 and Korboe, 1992). There are only two households per house at the median for Ghana's transformers.

Characteristics of subsequent households[6]

Who are these subsequent households? How do they differ from the main households?

As we would expect, tenant households in transformed houses have younger heads with far fewer years in the house and in employment than the owners but they are roughly as well educated (table 16).

Table 16. Characteristics of subsequent (tenant) households in transformed houses

Medians (and IQRs)	Bangladesh	Egypt*	Ghana	Zimbabwe
Age of head (years)	30	-	37	29
	(25, 35)	-	28, 42)	(26, 33)
Length of stay in house (years)	1	-	9	2
	(1, 2)	-	(3, 18)	(1,4)
Years in employment	5	-	6	4
	(2, 8)	-	(3, 10)	(2, 6)
Years in education	8	-	10	11
	(5, 10)	-	(10, 14)	(9, 11)
Household size	3	-	3	3
	(2, 4)	-	(2, 5)	(2, 4)
Dependency ratio	0.33	-	0.5	0.5
	(0, 0.67)	-	(0, 1)	(0, 1)
Percentage owning no other house	56	-	97	52

* There are too few subsequent households in our Egypt sample to make a valid data set.

There is also considerable consistency in household sizes with medians of three (and 75th percentiles of four or five) in each case study. Thus they are much smaller than main households (half as many people or less) and have lower dependency ratios. Marginally fewer tenants own another house than main households. We will see in chapter 4 that they generally have lower household incomes than owners but higher per capita incomes.

Household shares of the houses

Main households have occupied the lion's share of the habitable space in their houses, from a low 56 per cent in Bangladesh to 100 per cent in Egypt at the medians (table 17). In the very tight sites of Bangladesh, a minority have reduced their space used in order to accommodate sub-tenants but more space is available for most households in the sample even though they are only tenants. Most main households occupy the original house while accommodating any extra households in the extensions. However, in Bangladesh and Zimbabwe quite a large minority have given up some space in the original house and occupy some of the extended space instead.

Table 17. Distribution of space among households in the house*

(Medians and IQRs)	Bangladesh	Egypt	Ghana	Zimbabwe
Percentage of habitable space in the current house occupied by the main household	56 (23, 100)	100 (100, 100)	100 (64, 100)	69 (52, 100)
Habitable space occupied by the first subsequent household (where there is one) (m²)	7.4 (6.2, 10.9)	22.0** (13.4, 31.1)	14.2 (9.5, 19.9)	7.8 (5.6, 9.6)
Percentage of habitable space in the house occupied by the first subsequent household	23 (15, 35)	37** (27, 48)	18 (12, 28)	17 (12, 22)

*This includes both transformers and non-transformers.
** From a very small sample.

Subsequent households, however, fare much worse than main households. Those in Ghana, where the rooming house culture is more favourable to subsequent households than in our other samples, do best in areal terms with 14 m². Those in the Bangladesh and Zimbabwe samples have very small habitable areas indeed. Their 7–8 m² at the median is equivalent to one small room about 2.4 m × 3 m. Subsequent households each occupy only about one-fifth of the house except in Egypt where the few that exist have more than one-third of the habitable space.

Subsequent households have only one-third as much space as main households in Bangladesh, 36 per cent in Ghana, and 23 per cent in Zimbabwe (table 18). However, their occupancy rates do not differ as markedly from those of main households. In

Ghana and Zimbabwe, they have only marginally higher occupancy rates while those in Bangladesh are 50 per cent higher. Thus, smaller households reduce the crowding effect of having much smaller spaces than the main households.

Table 18. Measures of occupancy for subsequent household

Medians (and IQRs)	Bangladesh	Egypt	Ghana	Zimbabwe
Occupancy rate of subsequent household (persons per room):				
Transformers	3	2.5	2	2
	(2, 4)	(-, -)	(1, 3)	(1, 3)
Non-transformers	-	-	2.5	2
			(1, 4)	(1, 4)
Habitable rooms occupied by subsequent household:				
Transformers	1	2	1	1
	(1, 2)	(1, 3)	(1, 2)	(1, 1)
Non-transformers	-	-	-	-
Habitable space occupied by subsequent household (m²):				
Transformers	7.4	22.0	14.2	7.8
	(6.2, 10.9)	(13.4, 31.1)	(9.5, 19.9)	(5.6, 9.6)
Non-transformers	-	-	-	-

Home-based enterprises (HBEs)

For many low-income households, the dwelling is also one of the few resources they have for generating income. This may be through relatively passive activities, chiefly renting rooms, or it may take the more active form of a home-based enterprise (HBE). In both of these endeavours, the modification of existing space and the addition of extra space through transformation can be essential prerequisites.

The ability to rent rooms out for profit is an important source of income for home-owners even though it may mean that they have to crowd or endure relative strangers sharing some of their domestic space. In addition, it is a vital means of supply for low-income households who want a room to rent. Though commercial renting is seen to be a very poor business indeed (see Gilbert and Varley, 1990), low-income households seem to find it both convenient and profitable. Indeed, in some circumstances, it is regarded as very anti-social not to allow others to rent space in your house for money or gratis because of family or other connections.[7] This is in stark contrast with the attitudes of many government officials towards landlords[8] who rent otherwise empty rooms to low-income households.

The symbiotic relationship between owners and tenants has been seen to be the chief motivator for much of the low-income housing construction and consolidation which has taken place in recent years (Woodfield, 1989). Indeed, the renting of rooms appears to be the most common income-generating use to which dwellings are put and one which is favoured because of its low demand for working time.

A wide range of home-based enterprises (HBEs) can be found in low-income neighbourhoods including baking, sewing, repairing, giving injections, cutting hair, keeping livestock and general trading (Strassmann, 1986; Nientied *et al.*, 1987). Piece-work for formal industrial concerns is also common in Southeast Asia, but reasonably uncommon in Africa. However, it has attracted more attention than other forms of home-based small-scale enterprises because of the propensity of workers to be exploited. The types of product manufactured in the home in India, for example, include *beedis* (or *bidis* – very slim hand-rolled cigarettes), garments, textiles, footwear, food products, and handicrafts (Bhatt, 1989), incense sticks and polished diamonds (Mehta and Mehta, 1990).

Small shops in dwellings are an almost universal phenomenon. Food items are sold from houses in and around low-income housing areas. Such premises may also function as a meeting place, with recreation options such as TV, tables for billiards, cards and other games (Treiger and Faerstein, 1987).

In Raj and Mitra's (1990) sample in Delhi, a large number of households have not allocated separate space in the house for the HBEs (renting, regular retailing and specialist services are exceptions). Indeed 50 per cent of HBE operators acknowledge that the possibility of mixing the two kinds of uses is the main advantage of HBEs.

In low-income areas, the complex web of economic linkages present in and between the HBEs allows all but the destitute to eke out a living and have access to some shelter. As with rental rooms, there is believed to be a symbiotic relationship between housing and HBEs. Owners may be enabled to consolidate their dwellings through the income and many households would not have their dwelling without the HBE. Likewise, many enterprises would not exist without the use of the dwelling. Thus, housing plays an important part in the existence and operation of the informal economy in many countries (UNCHS/ILO, 1995).

In Strassmann's (1986) work, 68 per cent of respondents said that they needed the HBE in order to afford the dwelling. Thus, he assumes that housing conditions would have been worse without HBEs:

> Conversely, 70 per cent of [Strassmann's] HBE operators said that their enterprise would not exist if the dwelling space were not available. Over 80 per cent of repair workers and male-head-dominated 'sturdy' manufacturing operators said the business income was necessary for the dwelling. Less than half the dwellings with women weaving or dispensing medical services were dependent on such income. Yet these female-operated businesses, including laundries, retail trade, and personal services, were the ones most dependent on the dwelling as a site. About three-quarters could not operate elsewhere, while about half of the 'sturdy' activities were considered moveable. Although the income of the male-headed HBEs was more, their dwellings had lower value than those with HBEs

operated by women, partly because total household income was less. (Strassmann, 1986: 497)

Lipton (1980: 190–1) stresses the advantages that HBEs derive from being able to treat resources fungibly, i.e. a resource can be converted swiftly, conveniently and without loss from one use to another. The HBE allows fungibility to extend beyond the bounds of the enterprise and to impinge on the domestic sphere as well. Thus, time spent in domestic activities can be converted to time spent in the HBE as the ebb and flow of domestic work permits; food intended for sale can be consumed for the family's evening meal; space which is used for, say, sleeping during the night, can be utilised for making paintbrushes during the day and, if a person is ill and needs to lie down, can be converted back to sleeping space even in the daytime; money can be spent on improvements in living conditions or in working conditions (or both at the same time). All these changes are made virtually without cost and inconvenience.

The aspect of extended fungibility which most interests us in this study is that of space. It appears that the distinction between reproduction (domestic activities) and production (economic activities) is not clearly drawn in developing country households (Hays-Mitchell, 1993). However, planning policies and land-use regulations have been based on the separation of these two functions. In these, the formal sector, acting through the state, is seen as:

> …defending itself against externalities – whether they are unseemly sights and smells and (usually exaggerated) health hazards, or family mode of production enterprises' [HBEs] competitive challenges – …through inappropriate rules on building, housing and trading. (Lipton, 1980: 223–4)

Policy-makers and commentators have often been highly critical of home-based enterprises from several standpoints.

1. In countries where the government is a large-scale housing provider, there is a moralistic bias against private economic gain arising from social housing support (Strassmann, 1987).
2. Single-use zoning has been a tenet of town planning for decades. Thus, residential areas should not be sullied with commercial or industrial uses. In Delhi, income generation within planned neighbourhoods is illegal and so requires some form of political patronage to continue (Benjamin, 1993).
3. The isolation and lack of visibility of home-workers allows exploitation of the HBE proprietor by factories and middlemen, and of the workers by the proprietors. This is especially evident in outworking systems whereby an industrial establishment employs workers to carry out processes in their homes, ostensibly as self-employed entrepreneurs but, in reality, as dependent workers or disguised wage-earners.
4. Control over HBEs is virtually impossible because, by their very nature, they blend into the residential environment as much as possible.

In the housing markets in our study areas, dominated as they are by shortage, we would expect that transformations would tend to add living space and only secondarily rooms for employment and other activities. On the other hand, in societies where the need for gainful employment is increasing, through the maturing of a young population, we would expect that transformers would like the opportunity presented by extended space to carry out some home-based enterprises. As we were not engaged in a specific study of home-based enterprises, we have not assiduously sought them out. As they may be consciously or unconsciously hidden by their very nature (Peattie, 1981), we cannot claim to have found all such activities in our sampled houses. We have only charted the structures and spaces specifically given over to commercial or other non-residential uses. Thus, our data are likely to be on the low side in demonstrating the extent of the forward linkages (Tipple, 1993; UNCHS/ILO, 1995) available from transformations.

Commercial uses are quite common in each case study area except Egypt where the staircase-access, multi-storey environment make them less easily set up except on the ground floor (table 19). Kardash (1990) reports 61 shops in the Helwan estate, almost all of which are at the ends of blocks close to the streets. Where they occur in Bangladesh, commercial uses tend to occupy a larger share of the house than elsewhere (more than one-fifth at the median).

Table 19. Frequency of commercial uses

Medians (and IQRs)	Bangladesh	Egypt	Ghana	Zimbabwe
Percentage of houses with commercial space	11	1	25	11
Percentage of house used for commercial activities where these occur	22 (11, 38)	18 (5, 28)	11 (7, 20)	7 (5, 12)

Although they are most common in Ghana (in one in four houses), they only occupy 11 per cent of the space in those houses at the median and only 20 per cent at the third quartile. Thus, though the areas may present quite a commercial aspect to the main roads, and even allowing for our incomplete cataloguing of commercial and other uses, the areas are still overwhelmingly residential in their land-use characteristics.

Employment is relatively uncommon in the flats in Egypt (where only five of our 256 sampled flats had any employment in them) and on the plots in Zimbabwe (with 23 houses out of 398) (table 20). In Bangladesh, however, there are very many jobs but relatively little obvious use of space for commercial and manufacturing activities. Only 18 house plans had shops or factories in dedicated space but 43 householders reported commercial space on the plot. It may be that the 256 people work in only

Table 20. Number of people employed on the plot (percentages)

	Bangladesh	Egypt	Ghana	Zimbabwe
0	85.7	98.0	72.4	94.2
1	2.9	1.6	7.7	4.3
2	1.0	0	5.7	1.3
3	1.8	0.4	4.0	0.3
4	2.1	-	4.0	-
5 or more	6.5	-	10.1	-
Total workers in sampled houses	298	7	379	30
Workers per house with employment on the plot (means)	6.9	1.4	4.2	1.9
Workers per house (whole sample)	0.85	0.02	0.95	0.09

Figure 6. Home-based enterprises in Mirpur

Figure 7. Home-based enterprises in transformed houses
Opposite, from top: a carpentry workshop in Mirpur; a formal sector (licensed) chemist in Kumasi; a 'tuck shop' (small general store) in Harare.
Above, from top: various trades on one plot in Kumasi; a general store in Mirpur.

43 houses (at about six people per house). Indeed, commercial uses reported on the plans include 40 shops (some plots had five in a row along a street frontage at the side of the house) and three factories, two of them manufacturing shoes.

In the Ghana sample, 65 houses had commercial, manufacturing, or other uses on them. This would, again, mean about six persons employed per house with commercial uses. The commercial activity varies from hairdressing (usually plaiting) done on a veranda through to large bread-baking concerns. There may be a simple wooden kiosk or a two-storey hotel and night-club. People keep livestock on a part of the yard, they brew *pito* and *akpeteshi*,[9] they have shops and lottery kiosks. One semi-detached house on a large plot now has all the following: a carpentry workshop, a building materials shop, a photographic studio, a vulcaniser (tyre repairer) and tyre sales outlet, a battery repairer, a motor spares shop, a lottery kiosk and a dressmaker. There are also a fully equipped church, at one end of the spectrum, and a tiny school in an extension to a detached kitchen less than 2 m wide at the other.[10]

The Zimbabwe sample has 17 sources of employment on the plots of which nine are retail outlets (mainly 'tuck-shops' selling food, soft drinks and a few household items). There are five workshops (carpentry, welding and general handicrafts), a bar and a traditional healer's consulting room. One house has an office in the rear. Thirty people find employment in these workplaces, a mean of less than two per site.

Table 20 shows that for every hundred houses in the estates, approximately 85 jobs will occur in Bangladesh and 95 in Ghana. Thus, we can calculate that the 4304 *bastuhara* houses of Dhaka probably provide job opportunities for 3660 workers. In Kumasi, government estates probably have almost 4000 jobs in their 4200 houses. There are fewer job opportunities per hundred houses in Egypt and Zimbabwe. Given the known link between working in the home and survival strategies among the poor (Tipple, 1993; UNCHS/ILO, 1995), it is likely that the house is acting in a very supportive manner to the households whose workers find economic activity within them. In addition, the retailing, commercial and industrial services which occur in the houses add to the comfort and well-being of neighbours (unless, of course, they generate negative externalities such as noise, fumes, harmful effluents, increased heavy traffic, etc.) as they cut down journey times for routine shopping, nursery schooling, visits to health practitioners, etc. and, therefore, reduce their transport costs.

Notes

1   Bangladesh is the exception here where non-transformers are actually living in transformed houses. They are the same age as transformers and all are younger than in other case studies.

2   The construction of several rooms to convert a single household dwelling into a suitable family house after the owner's death has a short-term benefit for the ageing owner and his/her spouse. As Amole *et al.* (1993) report, being a head of house or an elder in the house gives the old folks a useful role in life long after they have ceased to be physically active.

3   The evident raiding which has taken place in Bangladesh seems to have occurred before transformation through the badly managed allocations.

4   We also used Hausa for some of the interviews in Kumasi and it is the only exception to this in having a word (*sassa*) for that part of a house occupied by a household (Tipple *et al.*, 1994).

5   There is much overlap between houses which contain rent paying and non-rent paying tenants, thus the total number of houses containing either is not the sum of the two.

6   We have socioeconomic data for one tenant household and one rent-free (family) household in each house in which they exist.

7   A rather extreme case of this came to my notice while visiting a friend who is a highly placed government officer in Accra with an official bungalow. He told how an old school friend who had been evicted came and begged to be allowed to live on his front veranda. This was acceded to and the whole household moved in. The same process brought a second acquaintance together with all the household paraphernalia to the side veranda. It was only with difficulty that he was able to draw the line at the covered passage to the outside kitchen's being used by a third household in need.

8   Landlords are often characterised, officially or merely covertly, as officious, rapacious and profit motivated. Many recent studies (brought together in UNCHS, 1989) have shown that landlords are often very supportive of their tenants and many do not charge as much rent as they could.

9   Local beer and gin.

10   What it loses in size, the school makes up in pretension. The owner calls it an International School!

4. The financial element: transformation as an investment

Income and wealth

It is necessary to examine measures of income at this stage as the issue of housing investment hinges on the financial resources of the households. In our consideration of incomes in this comparative study, we have followed Summers and Heston (1988) in the use of Purchasing Power Parity (PPP), which adjusts local costs through multiplying the official exchange rate by a factor related to the cost of living in that country to a hard currency, in our case pounds sterling.

Experience has shown that income and expenditure questions elicit very different data. Previous work in Ghana has consistently found that expenditure is stated to be an average of 2.4 times stated income (Malpezzi *et al.*, 1990; Tipple, 1984). Obviously this cannot be so as, except in the very short term, no one can spend anything which is not income in some form but wages, gifts, bribes, produce in kind, business profits, etc., can all form parts of an aggregate income considerably higher than the bottom-line wage income stated to a gullible interviewer.

While it might be more correct to refer to expenditure in the analysis, we refer to income instead. This is because our expenditure data are standing for a measure of long-term income and most housing studies talk in terms of income relative to house cost, affordability, etc. We thus feel it would be valid for a reader to compare our data directly with income data from their own context, as long as such data contain all forms of income for all household members.

Regular savings, where a household lives below its income and puts money away for the future, are probably rare among low-income households. It is more likely that so-called savings are only deferred periodic spending on furniture, clothing, school fees, festivals, etc. The study collected data on both income and expenditure so the decision on the most useful could be made country by country. In the event, expenditure was universally used. We also have a wealth indicator as a back-up measure.

Data on the percentage of income spent on food are also presented, and are likely to be inversely proportional to income. Thus, they make a reasonable measure of wealth and ability to spend on housing to augment expenditure and the wealth indicator (Tipple *et al.*, 1997).

Most house owners regard their house as an investment, as a possession expressing their wealth. This might be in terms of status: 'they must be successful/wealthy/astute if they can live in a house like that'. This is referred to by Price (1974) as 'the big-man syndrome'. On the other hand it might be in monetary terms as an equity investment and/or a hedge against inflation. This is especially important in countries where there are few alternatives for yield-bearing monetary investment. We could expect that any sitting tenants who had the opportunity to buy their dwelling at a discount would do so if they possibly could. However, when extra expense is required to transform, we might expect those who opt to do it to be better off than non-transformers.

The ability to afford to extend would appear to be the most basic issue for a would-be transformer. Income, status and financial commitments have proved important determinants of housing improvements in most housing adjustment studies in industrialised countries (e.g. Kirwan and Martin, 1972; Seek, 1983) but income has not always been found to be significant (Ziegert, 1988).

Although many households make improvements for other than purely economic investment reasons, some large-scale extensions may be implemented out of a desire to make money. However, the housing adjustment literature introduced earlier leads us to expect that income is not a prime determinant of whether extensions are constructed but does affect their cost once the decision has been taken.

Table 21 shows the income data in comparable PPP£ for the four case studies. The people in our samples are not numbered among the very poor within their country. Clearly, they are neither destitute nor rich by any standards, having household incomes of £2000 to £4000 per annum. The Egyptian sample probably has the most stable working population as they are mainly wage-earners in heavy industry who probably enjoy a high level of job security with a regular monthly wage. They were allocated their flats because they worked in the factories of Helwan and Cairo but many are now retired, which will drive down the income levels.

In contrast with our preliminary expectations, the Egyptian sample has the lowest annual household income and highest proportion of income spent on food, but they are more optimistic about their future earnings than anyone else. Their median household income of £2440 is almost as low as the 25th percentile in the Ghana and Zimbabwe samples and its 75th percentile is as low as the 25th percentile in the Bangladesh sample. However, per capita incomes are much closer to the other samples at £530 per annum.

The Ghana and Zimbabwe samples are much more mixed in their economic activity. Although we have no data on employment, we asked from where income was derived. About 81 and 32 per cent of households in Ghana and Zimbabwe respectively derived income from business activities and 38 and 82 per cent had wage income. Their median household incomes are £3430 and £3770 respectively. However, per capita incomes vary much more with the Ghana sample being the lowest of the four and considerably lower than those of their Zimbabwean peers.

In our research design, we assumed that Bangladesh would represent a very low-

Table 21. Incomes and wealth in PPP pounds*

Medians (and IQRs)	Bangladesh	Egypt	Ghana	Zimbabwe
Annual household income:				
Transformers	4210	2440	3430	3770
	(3400, 5500)	(1800, 3400)	(2400, 4700)	(2400, 5500)
Non-transformers	-	2280	3160	3150
		(1500, 3200)	(2400, 4000)	(2500, 4100)
Annual per capita income:				
Transformers	650	530	480	630
	(490, 860)	(320, 760)	(360, 710)	(380, 970)
Non-transformers	-	460	620	720
		(340, 880)	(420, 1020)	(430, 910)
Food expenditure as a percentage of household income:				
Transformers	59	68	61	39
	(51, 68)	(56, 77)	(51, 70)	(29, 50)
Non-transformers	-	73	60	40
		(63, 80)	(51, 71)	(33, 49)
Percentage with Relative Wealth Index (RWI) of zero:**				
Transformers	23	0	10	11
Non-transformers	-	1	17	4
Percentage expecting to be better off next year:				
Transformers	1	37	10	18
Non-transformers	-	32	3	16

*PPP functions inflate the currency values by the following: Bangladesh = 4.1524; Egypt = 3.259; Ghana = 2.6051; Zimbabwe = 2.2831 (UNDP, 1993: Table 1). Thus, for example, instead of C1000 per £ sterling in 1993, there would only be C384 per PPP£.
**Relative Wealth Indexes (RWIs), used within countries (see Appendices 1–4) are not used for between-countries comparisons as their source values differ. Only RWI = 0 is comparable.

income country but we find that our transformers do not have the lowest income among our samples. The Bangladesh sample enjoys the highest income in both household and per capita terms but has higher percentages with none of the consumer goods in our Relative Wealth Index. The allocation of houses officially to refugees from Pakistan, and unofficially to whoever paid the *mastans* (see chapter 3 and Appendix 1), has ensured that the occupants of Mirpur are not among the poorest in Dhaka. Refugees are poor at the time because of their flight, but probably are closer to an income cross-section of the whole population than a group identified through low income. The median household income of transformers in Bangladesh is 70 per cent higher than for those in Egypt but per capita incomes are only 22 per cent higher.

Of the households in our Bangladesh sample, 80 per cent have wage income and 24 per cent have business income.

It is clear that, at the medians, transformers do indeed have higher household incomes than non-transformers and this seems to be the only consistent pattern among the various measures in table 21. In Zimbabwe, for example, transformers have the higher household incomes (and lower percentage expenditure on food which is a good indicator of wealth), but they have lower per capita incomes. In Egypt, on the other hand, per capita incomes of transformers are higher than non-transformers' and percentage expenditures on food are lower. In Ghana, per capita incomes are higher for non-transformers and there is no difference in expenditures on food. The effect of income on the choice of transforming, and on its cost once the choice is made, is examined in Appendix 5.

Are transformers' households low income?

Taking the £240 per year per capita[1] absolute poverty threshold adopted by Ravallion *et al.* (1991), we can see (table 22) that our median transformers vary from twice the threshold in Ghana to 2.7 times in Bangladesh. At the first quartile they exceed the absolute poverty threshold by 35 per cent in Egypt and up to 105 per cent in Bangladesh. Very few households in the samples have incomes below the absolute poverty threshold; only in Egypt does it exceed 10 per cent of transformers.

Table 22. Per capita incomes in relation to the absolute poverty threshold of PPP£240 per annum

Medians (and IQRs)	Bangladesh	Egypt	Ghana	Zimbabwe
Index (absolute poverty threshold = 100):				
Transformers	271	222	200	261
	(205, 359)	(135, 318)	(150, 296)	(157, 403)
Non-transformers		193	259	302
		(140, 366)	(175, 425)	(181, 380)
Percentage with incomes below the absolute poverty threshold:				
Transformers	2	13	4	7
Non-transformers		6	2	9

In Ghana and Zimbabwe, transformers have slightly higher household incomes but lower per capita incomes than non-transformers. Median annual household incomes for transformers range from £2400 in Egypt to £4200 in Bangladesh. Median annual per capita incomes range from £480 in Ghana to £650 in Bangladesh. Except in Egypt, transformers have higher RWIs than non-transformers.

As we would expect, most of the transformers have wage income (in Bangladesh and Zimbabwe) or business income (in Ghana) but a few rely on rents (17 per cent of income at the median in Bangladesh) or gifts (remittances) for much of their income. Only in Bangladesh and Zimbabwe are rents significant income sources. We have no breakdown of income for our Egypt sample but most are likely to be wage earners in the nearby heavy industries.

Income of subsequent households

Incomes of subsequent households are a little over half as much as the main households (table 23). They are remarkably similar across the three cases for which we have tenant households at about £2000 per annum. Thus they have incomes between 60 and 75 per cent of those of the main households. However, because of smaller households, median per capita incomes are higher than those of the transformer main households at about three times the absolute poverty threshold of the smaller households.

Table 23. Income of subsequent households in PPP pounds

	Bangladesh	Egypt	Ghana	Zimbabwe
Household income	2200	-	2000	2200
	(1600, 2900)	-	(1400, 3000)	(1600, 3300)
Per capita income	754	-	669	750
	(570, 1050)	-	(520, 860)	(480, 1320)

Spending on transformations

In Kendig's (1981) study among house owners in Adelaide, Australia, expenditure on extension had a mean of 13 per cent of head's annual income. However, as we can see in table 24 total spending on transformations in our sample is consistently about one year's income at the median. The expenditure varies from £2500 (Egypt) to £4800 in Ghana with transformations in Bangladesh and Zimbabwe costing similar totals at around £3750. The variability within samples is perhaps as interesting as the median and the variability between samples. Where large plots are available to at least some of the sample, we see very large variability (IQRs of £17,500 in Ghana and £13,500 in Zimbabwe). On the other hand, in neighbourhoods with small plots or where the extensions must conform to neighbours' requirements, as in Egypt, variability is much reduced. In Egypt, there is only £2200 (less than the median) between the first and third quartiles.

Although spending on transformations is between 90 and 120 per cent of a year's income at the medians, the upper quartile in Ghana and Zimbabwe respectively spent more than 5.7 and 4.2 times annual income. If the transformers in our samples are at all representative of owners in similar estates in other countries, this may indicate that there is a latent willingness to spend about one year's income at the median on house extensions and much larger amounts at the third quartile. This is a huge resource which could be utilised if careful policy formulation could enable its implementation (see chapter 8).

Table 24. Spending on transformations in PPP£s

Medians (and IQRs)	Bangladesh	Egypt	Ghana	Zimbabwe
Spending on transformations	3880	2500	4790	3660
	(2190, 6800)	(1800, 4000)	(1200, 18,800)	(440, 13,900)
Transformation cost /	0.9	1.2	1.2	0.9
household income	(0.6, 1.5)	(0.6, 1.9)	(0.4, 5.7)	(0.2, 4.2)
Total cost of transformations	940	1100	750	750
per room	(540, 1870)	(760, 1650)	(290, 3240)	(250, 2000)
				1580*
				(760, 3040)

* Total costs for Zimbabwe *without* shacks-only transformers are given in italics.

Costs per room are high in Egypt because of the multi-storeyed nature of the construction and the relatively few (large) rooms which are added. In Ghana, they are very cheap at £750 at the median as most transformers add as many small rooms as possible. However, the third quartile in Ghana is very high, at over £3000, as some are very high quality. The Zimbabwe picture is one of relatively cheap rooms if all are included but the costs double if we only consider those transformers who are building at least some of the rooms in permanent materials. They then become the most expensive of the case studies with a median of over £1500 and third quartile of £3000.

Transformation costs per room are remarkably diverse not only among the medians but also within countries as shown by the IQRs. This shows that there are now major differences in the standard of construction and finishes among the transformed houses.

House value

Expenditure on housing usually must be justified on simple cost-benefit terms,[2] and show a positive rate of return (Kirwan and Martin, 1972; Mayer, 1981; Boehm and Ihlanfelt, 1986). Although many households make improvements for other than purely economic investment reasons, some large-scale extensions may be implemented out of a desire to make money. The most basic financial issue, however, is that the households must be able to afford the improvements.

In earlier work, we suggested that households are capable of undertaking and financing incremental alterations and additions to their dwelling units (Tipple, 1991a).

The following demonstrates that this is true. We also suggested that transformations involve relatively low-income households in capital investment which would be unlikely through the formal system (Tipple, 1991a: 77). This is probably true not least because the formal financial systems are undeveloped for low-income households.

In asking questions on both house value and cost, we expected to compensate for the inaccuracies contingent on collecting only one. In most countries, it is likely that owners would include locational variables and some notion of land value within their estimates. They may, however, over-estimate value in a bid to maximise their apparent wealth. In countries where there is little or no market in low-cost housing, as in Ghana, costs of building may be very familiar but value might be completely unknown and estimates would probably be wildly inaccurate. In addition, they are likely to be inaccurate with respect to land as our study areas are no longer peripheral to the cities and what land market exists is likely to be locationally distant from our estates.

We suspect that our data on value are reasonably accurate in Egypt and Zimbabwe, but not in Ghana. The Bangladesh sample is unique in that, though they are renters, they are being confronted with a right to purchase, for a price of Tk134,000, and they are aware of the market of sorts as others buy possession of the houses for a roughly similar price. As the Bangladesh sample of non-transformers is not occupying non-transformed houses, the value of the least valuable transformed house is used as a proxy for the value of the uniform non-transformed house. All values are expressed in PPP£.

Table 25 shows that transformers have increased the value of their houses above those of the non-transformed dwellings[3] at the median by between £600 in Egypt and £3400 in Zimbabwe (9 to 33 per cent). In Bangladesh, the difference in value between the non-transformed house and the median transformed house is 300 per cent; values have risen from £3500 to £10,400 at the median. This probably betrays the difference between the perceptions of value of the original houses among our samples more than it demonstrates how much improvement there has actually been in the houses, although the latter is undoubtedly significant. Alone in the sample, the Bangladesh occupants had a very low opinion indeed of the value of the original dwelling. On a walk around the site with Shahidul Ameen during the period when the HSD announced their intention to sell to occupants, several household heads argued with us that there should be no charge for the original structure, just for the land. They regarded the old structures as worthless.[4] This is not the case elsewhere; even in Ghana among occupants of terraced single rooms, non-transformers regarded their houses as more valuable per unit area than transformers.

While the original houses (excluding Bangladesh) have values of between £6400 and £10,300 at the medians, the transformed houses range from £7100 to £13,700. The houses have undoubtedly increased in value but there is also the important effect that they have become much more varied (the IQRs express this). For example, in Bangladesh, from a uniform stock worth about £3500 each, transformers have produced a varied stock with an IQR of £6900.

Table 25. House value in PPP pounds sterling

Medians (and IQRs)	Bangladesh	Egypt**	Ghana	Zimbabwe
Value of house/flat:				
Transformers	10,400	7060	11,700	13,700
	(6900, 13,841)	(5400, 9300)	6500, 20,500	(10,300, 20,500)
Non-transformers	3460*	6430	6510	10300
		(5500, 6500)	(3900, 13,000)	(9100, 12,600)
Percentage increase				
through transformation	300*	10	80	33
Value of house/flat per habitable room:				
Transformers	2310	2130	1950	2660
	(1700, 3100)	(1600, 2700)	(1300, 3000)	(1900, 3600)
Non-transformers	3460*	1610	3910	3040
		(1600, 2500)	(2600, 6500)	(2600, 3800)
Value of house/flat per square metre:				
Transformers	163	134	158	228
	(110, 210)	(110, 150)	(97, 240)	(170, 290)
Non-transformers	155*	146	164	228
		(146, 146)	(120, 290)	(210, 290)

* The least valuable transformed house was chosen as a proxy for a non-transformed house: Tk50,000 = £3460.
** Non-transformers in Egypt were not asked the value or the cost of rebuilding the property. Consequently the figures above have been generated by using the average value per square metre and rebuilding cost per square metre from the transformers' information. Also only the cost of transformation was asked rather than the cost of rebuilding the entire flat. To estimate this we used the cost per square metre and assumed this would apply to the flat as a whole. In later discussions, these relatively poor quality data are not used.
PPP functions: Bangladesh = 4.1524; Egypt = 3.259; Ghana = 2.6051; Zimbabwe = 2.2831 (UNDP, 1993: table 1).

Except in Ghana, the range of values per habitable room is much smaller than the range in values of the whole houses: only 36 per cent difference between the highest and lowest medians (compared with 93 per cent for the house as a whole) with medians in the range of £2100 to £2660. In Bangladesh, Ghana and Zimbabwe, values per room reduce with transformation. However, they rise in Egypt by 32 per cent at the median. On the other hand, value per square metre shows a different distribution and one in which the unpredictability of room size is removed. The pattern is slightly to reduce value by transformation in Egypt, Ghana and Zimbabwe, but to increase it in Bangladesh. Thus, housing is becoming cheaper per unit area in Egypt, Ghana and Zimbabwe, and more expensive in Bangladesh.

House cost

This variable is derived from households' estimates of the cost of rebuilding the house should it be destroyed (or some other scenario where this was unacceptable for cultural reasons).

Cost of housing is likely to be accurate as a measure of value in Ghana except that land is unlikely to have been accounted for. These data (table 26) show the very high cost of housing resulting from transformation in Ghana with a median of over £15,600 – the highest median cost or value in all our samples. Furthermore, the third quartile of £26,000 exceeds any other third quartile value or cost by £5500. Bangladesh and Egypt have achieved quite modest costs in comparison with Ghana and Zimbabwe, around £8000 at the medians and around £12,000 at the 75th percentile.

Table 26. House cost in PPP pounds sterling

Medians (and IQRs)	Bangladesh	Egypt**	Ghana	Zimbabwe
Cost of house/flat:				
Transformers	8300	8000	15600	13700
	(6900, 12,500)	(550, 11,700)	(7800, 26,100)	(9100, 20,500)
Non-transformers	2770*	6720	7820	9130
		(5700, 6700)	(5200, 13,000)	(5700, 11,400)
Percentage increase				
through transformation	200	20	100	50
Cost of house/flat per habitable room:				
Transformers	1940	2510	2610	2280
	(1400, 2800)	(1600, 4000)	(1600, 4200)	(1400, 3300)
Non-transformers	2770*	1690	5210	3040
		(1700, 2700)	(3900, 6500)	(2300, 3800)

* The minimum rebuilding cost was chosen from the group of transformed houses as a proxy for a non-transformed house: Tk40,000 = £2770.
** Non-transformers in Egypt were not asked the value or the cost of rebuilding the property. Consequently the figures above have been generated by using the average value per square metre and rebuilding cost per square metre from the transformers' information. Also only the cost of transformation was asked rather than the cost of rebuilding the entire flat. To estimate this we used the cost per square metre and assumed this would apply to the flat as a whole. In later discussions, these relatively poor quality data are not used.
PPP functions: Bangladesh = 4.1524; Egypt = 3.259; Ghana = 2.6051; Zimbabwe = 2.2831 (UNDP, 1993: table 1).

Proportionate increases in cost through transformation are very marked in Ghana, in fact they constitute a doubling at the median and at the third quartile. This is greater than in Zimbabwe where a 50 per cent increase is achieved at the median and 80 per cent at the third quartile. However, the Bangladesh sample has achieved a tripling of investment in the housing, adding double the estimated original building cost at 1993 prices. In contrast, there is a reduction in cost per room with transformation, to the tune of 50 per cent in Ghana and Bangladesh through the reduction in room size which accompanies the extension process.

Although increases in value (cost for Ghana) for the whole house are quite substantial, the portion of the house occupied by the main household has only increased in value by a small amount (table 27). This shows that much of the increase has been devoted to accommodating subsequent households as tenants or, occasionally, rent-free (family) tenants in much smaller (less valuable) portions of the house. Such portions have median values around £2000 (with a relatively narrow range between extreme quartiles from £1100 to £3700 – both in Ghana).

Table 27. Value for the portion of the house occupied by the main and subsequent households

Medians (and IQRs)	Bangladesh	Egypt*	Ghana**	Zimbabwe
Value of portion of house occupied by the main household:†				
Transformers	6230	6520	10,300	9140
	(3800, 9000)	(5400, 8300)	(5200, 16,800)	(5800, 13,700)
Non-transformers	6900	6400	7600	9700
	(43, 11,900)	(5300, 6500)	(5200, 11,700)	(8000, 11,400)
Value of portion of house occupied by subsequent households:†				
Transformers	2000	-	2800	2000
	(1400, 3500)	-	(1400, 4900)	(1300, 3100)
Non-transformers	2300	-	-	2590
	(-, -)	-	-	(2100, 3000)

* Non-transformers were not asked the value or the cost of rebuilding the property. Consequently the figures above have been generated by using the average value and rebuilding cost per square metre of the extensions.
** Costs from table 26 are used as a more accurate estimate of real value than perceived values from table 25.
† Calculated from: Value per m² × area occupied.
PPP functions: Bangladesh = 4.1524; Egypt = 3.259; Ghana = 2.6051; Zimbabwe = 2.2831 (UNDP, 1993: table 1).

As we have seen, subsequent households have lower household incomes than main households but their per capita incomes are higher. Their smaller households occupy fewer rooms but at similar occupancy rates to main households. The housing they occupy in our transformed areas tends to be much lower down the market than that of the main household.

In considering whether transformation is good value for money, we can assess how its cost compares with the increase in value and rebuilding cost as estimated by the occupants (table 28). However, as we have seen earlier, transaction costs in moving house can be very high, not only in the legal costs of sale and purchase but also in the refurnishing of a new house. We have no data on their scale so they cannot be discounted against improvement costs to achieve a fair assessment of the comparative costs or benefits of moving rather than improving. The effect of this shortcoming is to inflate the cost of transformation against the increase in value or rebuilding cost. Thus, transformations are probably better value than we are showing in table 28.

Table 28. Increases in value and cost in comparison with spending on transformations in PPP£s

Medians (and IQRs)	Bangladesh†	Egypt	Ghana	Zimbabwe
Increase in perceived value*	5190 (1700, 8700)	2270 (430, 4300)	3400 (-2000, 8600)	2910 (-510, 9800)
Increase in rebuilding cost*	2080 (690, 6600)	2520 (9, 6600)	3630 (3000, 13,900)	4360 (-210, 11,200)
Spending on transformations	3880 (2190, 6800)	2500 (1800, 4000)	4790 (1200, 18,800)	3660 (440, 13,900)

† Using lowest value/cost of a transformed house.
* Using mean values/costs of non-transformed examples of same house type for comparison.

In Bangladesh, Egypt and Zimbabwe, the spending on transformations is reasonably commensurate with increases in perceived value and/or rebuilding cost. In each case, the median cost of transformation falls between the other two estimates though these are not always in the same order. In Ghana, however, increases in neither perceived value nor rebuilding cost cover the cost of transformations completed. In this case, the extensions could be said to be a relatively poor investment purely from the market value point of view.

The cost of transformation gives us a measure by which we can assess the aggregate investment in housing made by our samples. For it we use the mean costs of transformations which are higher than the medians, inflated by some expensive projects. We have removed four especially expensive extensions in Ghana (including a church) which bias the mean upwards by PPP£50,000.

The mean sums spent are considerably higher than the medians in Ghana and Zimbabwe. Taking the data in table 29, we can calculate aggregate spending by multiplying these means by the number of houses in the estates as follows: The residents of 4304 *bastuhara* houses will have added housing worth PPP£22 million; those in the 3660 flats in Helwan and Medinet Nasr, Egypt, will have built PPP£12 million worth of housing. In Ghana, if we aggregate the mean spending up to the 5000 or so government-built houses in Kumasi, we could estimate a massive investment of PPP£200 million. The 13,113 township houses in Mbare and Highfield, Zimbabwe, represent an investment potential of PPP£170 million. On the other hand, the 100,000 township houses throughout Harare would represent a possible investment on exten-sions of PPP£1.3 billion.

Table 29. Mean spending on transformations (PPP£)

	Bangladesh	Egypt	Ghana*	Zimbabwe
Mean spending on transformations	5193	3307	39,729	12,708

* Excludes four extremely expensive transformations.

Relationship between house value/cost and income

Table 30 shows that transformation has increased house value/cost to income ratios universally. In Zimbabwe (value) and Ghana (cost), ratios in excess of four have been achieved by transformers at the medians with almost eight at the third quartiles. In Ghana, these represent a large increase over non-transformers (about two annual incomes at the median and nearly four at the third quartile), probably indicating that non-transformers are radically below their demand curve.

In Zimbabwe, the difference of only 18 per cent in value (0.7 times household income) is likely to include quite a strong downward pull exerted by the larger than representative sample of shacks-only transformers. Thus the quite impressive value-to-income ratio of 4.63 is rather conservative. Indeed, if the shacks-only transformers are excluded, median house value increases to 5.4 times household income (IQRs = 3.6 and 8.8). This is a very impressive level of investment in housing at the median and a remarkable one at the third quartile.

There seems to be little similarity across the countries except that transformers' houses are regarded as more valuable in relation to the household's income than non-transformers'. However, the margins are quite variable. The smallest margin is in the Egyptian sample where many of the non-transformers' flats were already larger and allocated to workers higher in the income range. It is, perhaps, surprising that some of this differential still appears to be maintained after almost 30 years. Transformers in Egypt have achieved lower value-to-income ratios than in Ghana and Zimbabwe. This is probably heavily influenced by the restricted site and the difficulty in acting apart from a five-storey cooperative effort. As a result, the transformers in the Egypt sample are probably still under their demand curve.

Taking value for Egypt and Zimbabwe and cost for Ghana, house-cost-to-income ratios vary from almost 3 to 4.7[5] for transformers and they have added between 0.7 and 2.1 annual incomes to the house cost at the median.[6] Thus, the capability of house-holds to undertake and finance incremental alterations and extensions to their dwellings has been strongly demonstrated by the data.

Value and cost per room variables show a different relationship with income.

Table 30. House value and cost in relation to annual income

Medians (and IQRs)	Bangladesh	Egypt**	Ghana	Zimbabwe
Value of house/household income:*				
Transformers	2.3	2.9	3.7	4.6
	(1.6, 3.5)	(2.2, 4.0)	(2.0, 6.0)	(3.0, 7.9)
Non-transformers	-	2.6	2.1	3.9
		(1.8, 3.5)	(1.3, 3.5)	(2.8, 6.2)
Rebuilding cost of house/household income:*				
Transformers	2.0	3.3	4.7	4.0
	(1.4, 2.8)	(1.9, 6.2)	(2.5, 8.0)	(2.5, 6.7)
Non-transformers	-	2.8	2.6	3.1
		(1.85, 3.65)	(1.70, 4.14)	(2.15, 4.95)
Value per room/household income:*				
Transformers	0.5	0.4	0.4	0.6
	(0.4, 0.8)	(0.3, 0.6)	(0.2, 0.5)	(0.4, 1.0)
Non-transformers	-	0.5	1.5	0.8
		(0.3, 0.6)	(0.9, 2.0)	(0.6, 1.3)
Rebuilding cost per room/household income:*				
Transformers	0.5	0.5	0.4	0.5
	(0.3, 0.7)	(0.3, 0.9)	(0.3, 0.7)	(0.3, 0.8)
Non-transformers	-	0.5	1.7	0.7
		(0.3, 0.6)	(1.1, 2,4)	(0.5, 1.0)

* Expenditure as a proxy.
** Non-transformers were not asked the value or the cost of rebuilding the property. Consequently the figures above have been generated by using the average value and rebuilding cost per square metre from the transformers' information.

Without exception in Egypt, Ghana and Zimbabwe, transformers' rooms are less valuable/costly than non-transformers' with a major collapse occurring in Ghana where cost reduces from 1.7 household incomes for non-transformers to 0.4 for trans-formers. This is partly a matter of quality, with a likely perception that not only are informal sector-built rooms much cheaper to build but that they are also somehow of lower value (cf. Martin's comments about self-built housing in Lusaka quoted in Bamberger *et al.*, 1982). It is probably also much affected by the smaller size of new rooms and propensity to subdivide the original house to gain extra rooms with little added value or cost. There may also be an additional factor in the equation: that there is a perceived value for non-transformers in being able to occupy even a small house unencumbered by tenants sharing the open space near the house and the services connected with it.

What is happening in the market

Housing development is generally regarded as responding to broad market signals. It can be hypothesised that extenders will respond to the same signals and form part of the adjustment mechanism by which housing market equilibrium can be restored after a shift in demand. Within this context, it could be expected that extenders would take the value of the most desirable houses in the neighbourhood as representing some ceiling to their own investment. In this case, the price of a small house with extensions is unlikely to exceed the price of a large house. On the other hand, there seems to be no reason why the price of a small house with large extensions should not keep pace with the price of a large house with smaller extensions.

Similarly, rising housing prices in a market may provide an incentive to extend when an owner can see that the price of a large house exceeds the price of his/her smaller house plus extensions (Gosling et al., 1993). 'Prisoners' dilemma' issues also arise here.[7] There may be advantages in 'free riding' on neighbours' increasing value through extensions, and these may exceed the net return from one's own improvement expenditure. Therefore, a household may decide that the added value is achieved without the necessity of extending. On the other hand, there is a risk in being the first to improve as others may not follow suit and increase the general level of values in the area. This would tend to reduce the value of one's pioneering extension.

At one level the householder is acting as a housing developer, capturing value by constructing housing (or by having the ability to construct at some future date), but it is arguable whether households can be classified as developers in the normal sense. Their motive may be that of extracting financial return from the development, like the developer, though this seems unimportant for many in our samples. But housing is also a consumption good so the extension also has value in being enjoyed by the occupant-developer and this may be their real motive.

The effect of transformations on housing demand can be demonstrated by the consumption model shown in figure 8. The original demand for housing is shown as a shallow parabolic curve D as the quantity of housing demanded increases as the price declines. Supply in the estates (and, for housing available to the households in our study estates, in the city as a whole) is inelastic (fixed) at S. The price of housing quantity Q0 is P0. Over time, demand increases so that we can model its current position as a higher curve D1. If the quantity of housing to satisfy the new demand D1 were to be consumed in a static housing supply, it would cost more per unit (P1) to satisfy. However, transformers have the option to extend and have shifted the supply curve to a more elastic S(T) at which demand for quantity Q(T) can be satisfied at price P(T) – the price of the original house plus the price of transformation. The saving provided by transformation is, thus, P1 minus P(T).

In most of our cases, house value per room reduces with transformation, thus quantity of housing increases more rapidly than price as transformations take place. Thus supply is relatively elastic compared with demand, indicating that it is occurring where there is a relatively steep slope on the demand curve (i.e. that demand increases

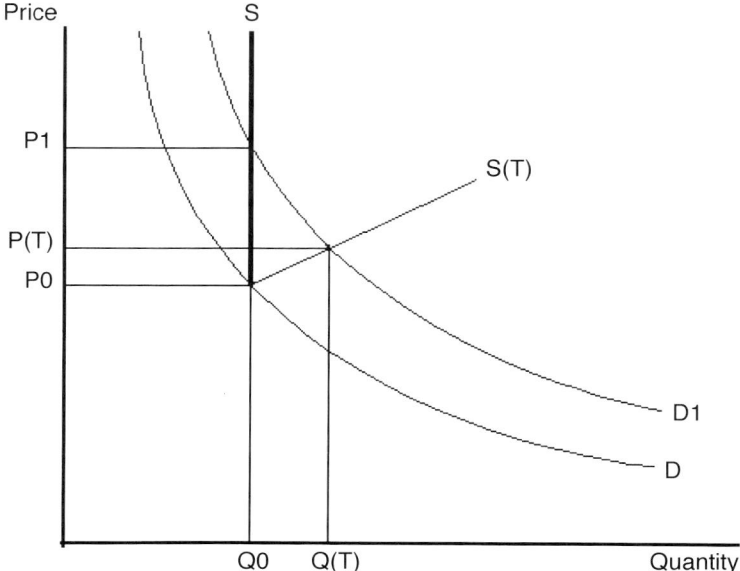

Figure 8. Supply and demand in the context of transformation

relatively slowly with reductions in price) and a relatively shallow gradient on the supply curve (i.e. increases in price produce relatively large quantities of housing goods). Furthermore, the steep demand curve and shallow supply curve suggests that P(T) would be closer to P0 (the original price) and further away from P1 (the demand price if no transformations had occurred) than if the value increased per room with transformation (if the demand curve was shallower and the supply curve steeper) as large unsatisfied demand continued to drive up the price.

Increases in house-cost-to-income ratios

In the literature, house-price-to-income ratios are seen as a useful indicator of how efficiently the housing supply system is operating with respect to demand. If there are uncertainties, administrative complexities, bottlenecks in the building materials and finance markets, etc., price of housing is likely to be high in comparison with the demand from any income group. Therefore, that income group's house-price-to-income ratio is likely to be higher than it would be in a smoothly operating supply system and an active market. Thus, a high house-price-to-income ratio is seen to be a bad thing, to the reduction of which policy must be addressed. In industrialised countries, the median urban house-price-to-income ratio is about four, while for developing countries it is 5.5 (World Bank, 1993). In the Housing Indicators Programme (World Bank, n.d.), the values for our study countries are stated at 6.3 for Bangladesh (Dhaka), 6.7 for Egypt (Cairo), 2.5 for Ghana (Accra), and 2.8 for Zimbabwe (Harare).

At the micro level, the price-over-income ratio (PI) is used as one of the measures of affordability by mortgage lenders (Landeau, 1991). Assuming a fairly low deposit (10 to 20 per cent), a PI of five would be regarded as highly risky. It would, however, be regarded as satisfactory if the owners already owned a large proportion of the equity in the house so that loan payments were a relatively low proportion of income. In general, however, at both the macro and micro levels, caution is expressed over high house-cost-to-income ratios.

Our study has not collected data on house price specifically but has modelled it through the collection of data on house value and cost. For most purposes these should be a very reasonable approximation and we will use cost here to compare our sample with the country data above. In Bangladesh and Egypt, our sample median cost-to-income ratios (2.0 and 3.3 respectively) are well below the medians for the city. Even the 75th percentile in Egypt (6.2) does not reach the country median of 6.7. These low levels may well be a function of their restricted space for extensions rather than of any economic decision to limit expenditure to the current levels. However, in the Sub-Saharan African case studies, our samples' cost-to-income ratios exceed the country medians. In Zimbabwe, our sample median of 4.0 is well above the country median of 2.8 while in Ghana, our sample has a median of 4.7, almost twice the country median (table 27).

We would argue that the transformations context gives a new slant to house-cost-to-income ratios and one contrary to the normal assumption that a high cost-to-income ratio shows a constrained market and is to be avoided. The high ratios in Ghana and Zimbabwe show that transformers are willing and able to increase their spending on housing. Thus, when we are concerned to maximise the slice of the investment cake coming to housing, the high values represent a voluntary increase in housing investment and should be welcomed. Transformers at the medians in Zimbabwe and Ghana are showing their willingness to increase their house-cost-to-income ratio by 50 or 80 per cent respectively above non-transformers. Furthermore, those at the 75th percentiles are now occupying houses costing 6.7 and 8.0 times their household incomes.

At the micro level, however, the issue of financing an increase in house-cost-to-income ratio from, say, three to six times could raise serious problems for a potential borrower in the formal sector. Imagine, if you will, the reaction of a banker to the unfolding of such a plan! But this level of spending and increased spending is undoubtedly happening in transformations on a regular basis and is financed in cash or from informal borrowing.

The concept of filtering: 'there goes the neighbourhood!'
One sign of obsolescence would be the alteration (and sometimes extension) of the original buildings in order to accommodate multiple households. Typical in this process is the conversion of large middle-class residences on the fringes of British city centres into flats as the prices of energy and domestic servants render large dwellings unsui-

able for modern affluent lifestyles. As the new occupants move into the smaller, cheaper housing units, the once proud neighbourhood deteriorates.

In developing countries, officials tend to be jealous of the quality of urban environments, especially those which have been planned. Imposing standards developed in Europe on new construction over which they have control, they see the later conversion activity, especially where accretions appear like carbuncles on the faces of old friends[8] or involve conversion to multi-occupation, as 'creating slums'.[9] The process is perceived as a means of causing housing to filter down and bringing the neighbourhood with it. This has positive and negative aspects. The negative are the 'there goes the neighbourhood' syndrome. The positive concentrate around the filtering of housing down to lower income households than could previously afford to live there.

Filtering theory was developed in the 1940s mainly in the USA as an explanation of how the poor were housed in the absence of welfare housing. Ratcliff (1949: 321–2) describes filtering as 'the changing of occupancy as the housing that is occupied by one income group becomes available to the next lower income group as a result of a decline in market price, i.e., sales price or rent value.' Initially, filtering was conceptualised as a straightforward process in which the turnover in occupants of a dwelling brought ever lower income households into it in a one-way cascade. This led to at least some claims that housing interventions should be directed to high-cost housing rather than low cost so that the cascade would be as long as possible and affect many households.

It is usually assumed that the filtering down of dwellings and filtering up (percolating) of households occur simultaneously as opposite sides of the same coin, but Grigsby (1971) argues that it need not necessarily be so. The price may reduce sufficiently for the new occupants to be paying no more than for their previous dwelling. However, Fisher and Winnick (1961) prefer to separate the downward price movement (which they regard as the filtering process) and the changes in occupancy which are the effect of this process. As the price decline of a dwelling may or may not be accompanied by a change of occupants, Fisher and Winnick (1961) regard filtering as 'a change over time in the position of a given dwelling unit or group of dwelling units within the distribution of housing prices and rents in the community as a whole.' This introduces the complicating factor of what is happening in the rest of the housing stock. If other dwellings move upwards in their value relationship with a particular dwelling, the latter will filter down even though its own value and its occupants may remain constant. Thus, if new dwellings are built higher up the price scale, a dwelling whose absolute value remains constant will actually filter down because the mean price of dwellings increases.

This inclusion of the relative position of dwellings in the market divorces filtering from arguments of whether it works in policy terms, as a means of making housing available to the lower income groups without building welfare housing. Lowry (1960) reverted to the examination of whether filtering could be relied upon to provide adequate housing for the poor in his definition that, if prices and rents of a particular group of dwellings and apartment units do not advance as much as prices generally, they have filtered down. On the other hand, if they advance more than prices generally, they have filtered up (Grigsby, 1971). In this definition, a dwelling does not filter down simply because someone has built a more expensive one elsewhere. Also, filtering can occur without change of occupants as it simply relies on a change of price. Thus, and importantly for our work, a dwelling can filter up or down (or fail to do so) while occupied by the same household. Such filtering does not provide poorer households with housing.

As Ferchiou (1982) and Malpezzi (1990) point out, filtering plays a less important role in developing countries, partly because of the small existing supply compared with the very brisk demand as urban areas grow very rapidly, and partly because supply is lumpy, housing in the middle of the price range being relatively uncommon. If older housing is progressively improved, however, and does not filter down, poorer households who cannot afford new dwellings will experience increasing shortages of suitable accommodation.

Recently, filtering studies have been largely replaced by vacancy chain studies which explore the turnover of households within a market in response to newly built dwellings. In the large study in Southern England by Forrest, Murie and others (Forrest et al., 1993; Forrest and Murie, 1994), the vacancy chains were found not to be cascades down the income or former-dwelling-price scales, as filtering theory implies, but much more complex. Many households traded down or across, large dwellings were bought by childless couples, and income did not correlate with dwelling price. As Forrest et al. (1993: 116) argue, 'the pattern of change is a matter for empirical study rather than conforming to any theoretical model.'

In this work, we are generally dealing with a non-mobile population. As we saw in table 13, lengths of stay in the houses are impressive with Bangladesh by far the most mobile population with 'only' 15 years stay at the median. At the other end of the scale, the Ghana sample have a median of 30 years in the houses. Thus vacancy chains and the aspect of filtering which involves turnover are not relevant to us, except when households move into newly created rooms. However, the concept of filtering, in so far as it deals with housing goods increasing or decreasing in value and the effect that has on the stable resident households, offers us some useful indicators of neighbourhood and housing quality changes.

In filtering theory, dwellings are added when first constructed and subtracted when demolished, taken out of residential use, or subdivided into two or more dwellings. Grigsby (1971: 110) cautions that these conversions should be regarded as 'independent sources of housing supply that sometimes result from, but are not equivalent to, filtering.' However, the creation of accommodation for extra households through subdivision and/or through renting out added rooms is important in this study and not necessarily equivalent to the conversion of one old dwelling into several flats.

In conceptualising building extension as an improvement activity, Seek (1983), Kendig (1981), and Gosling et al. (1993) argue that the filtering down is stopped as the properties are extended and so the poorer households have no opportunity to occupy them. If this became general, the suspension of filtering down could create welfare problems where little public rented housing is available to poor households as in Bangladesh and Ghana.

Householders who transform may be upgrading the neighbourhood by increasing the value of both their own dwellings and the aggregate housing goods in the neighbourhood. Both are present if upgrading (upward filtering) is indeed occurring. Extending a £50,000 dwelling into one at £60,000 filters the occupant household up the market and can be said to be upgrading. However, adding value by converting, say, one £50,000 dwelling into two £30,000 flats (total value increases by £10,000) cannot be said to be upgrading the neighbourhood as it results in the housing filtering down to (or the creation of new dwellings in) cheaper markets.

It can be argued that, as a dwelling is converted and extended, it tends to become less cohesive. Though there may be five bedrooms after extension, the living room and kitchen may well be suited to the occupants of only a three-bedroomed dwelling. Additions may require rooms to serve as both living spaces and passageways, and the dwelling becomes less convenient. Increased depth from extending outwards from the façade may reduce daylighting and ventilation, especially in inner spaces. It would follow that the spending on extensions and alterations would not be fully reflected by an increase in value. Thus, while increasing in value overall, the dwelling could become less valuable per square metre and, to that extent, would filter down. The balance of this filtering process in transformations is explored as part of this study.

Filtering through transformation

We have been given some clues by the data on cost and value to determine whether and in what direction filtering, in the broadest sense of the word, is taking place. We are limited to some extent by the low awareness of value in the context of a free-market sale (except in Zimbabwe). However, as they stand, our findings on house value and cost have several implications for filtering:

- Transformation has improved the housing by a significant amount so it can be said in general to be filtering up. As expected, transformation appears to be preventing the houses from filtering down.
- Because other households occupy some of the new housing provided, main households have not benefited in value of the space they occupy by the same degree as the housing has increased in value/cost. But we have seen that they have more space per person than they could be expected to have had in the absence of transformation, and more cheaply per room (table 25). Thus, main households are generally filtering up slightly.
- Through transformation, some accommodation has been provided at a considerably lower value than the original dwellings and than the accommodation occupied by the main households. These parts of the houses (usually single rooms)

could be said to be filtering down in that they are available in lower cost units which constitute fewer housing goods (space and services). Alternatively, they may be providing new housing goods at the bottom end of the market. Thus, our initial suggestion that the supply of housing at the bottom end of the market is being augmented appears to be true even though the neighbourhood in general is moving slightly up the market.

- The value of non-transformed houses seems to have held up well, usually more than rebuilding cost[10] and more than transformed houses for value per square metre and per room. Therefore, there are no traces of negative externalities, reflected in reductions in value, arising from the transformations in the neighbourhood.

As we have seen, subsequent households have lower household incomes than main households but their per capita incomes are higher. Their smaller households occupy fewer rooms but at similar occupancy rates to main households. The housing they occupy in our transformed areas tends to be lower down the market than that of the main household and confirms the impression that the filtering down of the housing stock that is prevented by the transformation process is counterbalanced to some degree by the lower cost new accommodation provided by transformers for tenants.

Notes

1   A dollar a day.
2   Even if this is the most rudimentary 'back of an envelope' calculation including only the most obvious costs and benefits.
3   This distinction is important in Egypt where the larger original flats tend not to have been extended.
4   It should be said in fairness that we agreed and have argued the case with Mr Mushfiqur Rahman of the Housing and Settlements Directorate. That good-natured gentleman expressed no opinion either way but listened attentively to the argument. The current plan for the sale values the original *semi-pucca* structure at Tk70,567 (PPP£4880) and the land plus structure at Tk133,927 (PPP£9270).
5   Or 5.4 if shacks-only transformers are excluded in Zimbabwe.
6   Because this is an estimate of rebuilding cost for the whole house, the difference made by the transformation will not necessarily be similar to the spending on transformation of roughly one year's income at the medians.
7   'Prisoners' dilemma is a situation in which it pays several economic agents individually to behave in a particular way even though it would pay them as a group to behave in some other way' (Willis, 1991: 166).
8   To misquote slightly His Royal Highness The Prince of Wales.
9   This passage has been written in India during a week in which each official with whom I have informally mentioned transformations has used this phrase at least once.
10 Ghana is the exception but then its value and rebuilding cost relationship is different from the others owing to the lack of a market.

5. Sustainability issues

Sustainable development[1]

Following the UNCED 'Earth Summit' in Rio de Janeiro, the concept of sustainable development has been in the forefront of international thinking about human settlements. As set out in Agenda 21 (UNCED, 1992), sustainable development implies a new concept of economic growth – one that provides fairness and opportunity for all the world's people, not just the privileged few, without further destroying the world's natural resources and without compromising the carrying capacity of the globe; development which is economically, socially and environmentally sustainable.

Agenda 21 recognises that urbanisation offers unique opportunities for the supply of sustainable environmental infrastructure, and that the overall human settlement objective is to improve the social, economic and environmental quality of the living and working environment. In the fleshing out of Agenda 21 which has been exercising UN and other international agencies since 1992, there has been some focusing on the effects of its proposals on urban development (e.g. UNCHS/ILO, 1995) and some of the issues raised that are pertinent to our study are outlined below.

The achievement of sustainable development in the urban context is widened from just a governmental concern. People should be involved in the planning of improvements which affect their everyday lives, translating their concerns into positive action, with responsibilities to ensure such improvements are maintained and operated in an efficient manner. International agencies and governments have signed up to empowerment of ordinary people through their communities. Sustainable development demands decision-making to take place at as low a level as is commensurate with success (known as subsidiarity), from the household level at one end to inter-government level at the other.

In chapter 7 of Agenda 21 there is a clear call for a realignment of responsibility from the traditional services-oriented concerns of local authorities to enablement and promotional activities. They are urged to redirect their role away from controlling and towards enabling. Furthermore, both the planning process and local government need to be 'sustainable'. Local authorities should be encouraged to improve their tax collection powers, especially with respect to land and property taxes. Services provided by local authorities should be charged for, to at least cover costs.[2] Currently, planning is almost exclusively concerned with limitations and regulations; it is unnecessarily complicated; unrelated to the needs and programmes of public agencies and the private sector; and beyond the reach of those it was meant to serve. In order to redress these drawbacks, planning should be decentralised, participatory, responsive, accountable, realistic and imaginative. The process of transformation impacts on these concerns in ways which are, perhaps, unexpected but, nevertheless, real and worthy of encouragement.

In this chapter we consider the contribution transformation makes to conserving housing which is probably close to the end of its economic life if left unrestored. We demonstrate the level of upgrading which has taken place so far in the study areas through examining the physical conditions and servicing levels which have been produced. The plan forms that result from transformation are examined and shown in many cases to be contributing to the continuity of families through allowing the next generation to occupy them conveniently. We also consider the tendency for transformations to supply accommodation which we would otherwise need to find on the periphery of cities. At the same time, the tendency to crowd too much accommodation onto the available plot space is considered.

The need to conserve resources and to upgrade existing estates

The rhetoric of sustainable development impacts on the existing housing stock as a context in which existing structures are an important resource for the future. Within sustainable development, the conservation of existing resources is fundamental to planning strategies. Prolonging the usable life of a house delays the need to build a new one, sometimes for generations.

In the old days of wholesale redevelopment of poor quality housing, the material and social fabric of whole areas could be swept away with only a passing glance and an occasional protest from a few radicals. As the policy-makers discovered that the fiscal austerity of the 1980s would not allow the clean-slate approach to housing improvements, the upgrading of existing areas became economically attractive and politically fashionable. This was accompanied by a recognition that the ordinary resident has a role to play in planning and implementing such improvements. Not only is this desirable so that the occupants will 'own' the improvements and, therefore, look after them, but also they will be able to translate their concerns into action and produce an environment in which they have a sense of well-being and belonging.

In this approach, existing housing is seen to have a value which exceeds its salvage price and the benefits of continuing to use the construction materials. It is the fragile context in which groups of people live their lives and conduct their relationships. It is easy to romanticise life in the mean streets of low-income housing areas, investing the poor with metaphysical wealth which enriches them above the suburbanised middle classes. The reality is often that poor quality housing allows only poor lifestyles and the continual danger of disease and injury. However, all but the meanest housing can be improved *in situ*, making use of the current materials and adding only those which are required to improve the structures to more acceptable levels of amenity.

Such intervention may damage parts of the social and economic fabric of the neighbourhood, for example when some occupants must be displaced to allow the remainder to have more space, but there is a good chance that at least some will be sustained.

Transformers are involved in physical neighbourhood upgrading, albeit in a piecemeal and centripetal manner. They are conserving the existing structures, or parts of them and, therefore, conserving the materials and energy inputs which they comprise. In addition, transformers are reinforcing the existing structures with extra materials and energy to add value, lifespan and amenity.

House physical conditions

To an observer, the original dwellings in the estates appear to be fairly run down and reaching the stage when major renovations would be needed, even though they may not be physically unsafe or have obvious defects such as leaks and cracks. In Egypt, for example, our survey data show very low levels of physical problems. However, the general appearance is of blocks of flats in need of renovation. There are signs of physical damage, especially to balcony rails and exterior pipework. The plumbing leaks so that there are areas of efflorescence spalling on the outer wall of most flats.

There are overt problems of walls cracking (nearly half the houses in Bangladesh and Ghana) and leaking roofs (half the houses in Bangladesh and one in three in Ghana and Zimbabwe). Most houses in the Ghana sample have rotten windows.

In most cases, the extensions are in slightly better physical condition than the original buildings using the objective measures of traces of damage. Indeed, the Ghanaian sample has considerably better conditions in the new rooms except with respect to windows. In Zimbabwe, the presence of so many wooden shacks leads the wall condition scores to be worse in the extensions. However, anyone touring the areas would agree that, in general, masonry extensions appear to be in better condition than the original houses and to have higher standards of finish and more expensive fittings than the original buildings. There are also decorative touches: in Bangladesh, walls tend to be plastered and the door in the boundary wall may be emphasised by a carved and painted panel; in Egypt, paint and decorative surface treatment of the outer rendering give variety and opportunities for self-expression. In Ghana, it is not uncommon to have finishes that are normally associated with high-cost areas: stucco rendering, decorative fascia boards and boundary walls, and terrazzo floors. In Zimbabwe, expensive doors and gates suggest higher status occupants, and modern styling of bungalow fronts gives a middle-income atmosphere to several transformed houses.

As table 31 shows, transformers are not innovative in their use of building materials; they appear to use whatever is available and popular. Thus, although some of the Ghanaian sample were built in stabilised soil blocks, none of the extensions use this non-conventional material. Cement blocks are preferred, probably because they are what the contractor is used to and they are easily obtainable. In Zimbabwe, however, some changes are being rung as both bricks for walling and corrugated asbestos–cement sheet roofing (despite health risks) are popular in transformations instead of cement blocks and corrugated iron sheeting as used in so much of the original construction.

Table 31. Materials used in extension construction
(and the difference from the original use of materials)

Percentages	Bangladesh	Egypt	Ghana	Zimbabwe
Walls:				
Cement blocks	0 (-1)	-	96 (+58)	15 (-59)
Bricks	82 (-17)	2 (+2)	0	48 (+22)
Earth/Laterite	-	-	0 (-58)	-
Timber	-	-	-	37 (+37)
Reinforced concrete frame and brick infill	-	98 (-2)	-	-
Bamboo matting	6 (+6)	-	-	-
Bricks & bamboo matting	12 (+12)	-	-	-
Other	-	-	4 (=)	-
Roof:				
Corrugated metal sheets	98 (-1)	-	91 (+91)	4 (-62)
Reinforced concrete slab	-	99 (-1)	4 (+4)	-
Corrugated asbestos sheets	-	-	0 (-100)	91 (+58)
Bamboo matting	2 (+2)	-	-	-
Other	-	-	5 (+5)	5 (+5)
Windows:				
Glazed	20 (+8)	95 (-5)	29 (+26)	74 (-10)
Not glazed	80 (-8)	5 (+5)	63 (-34)	26 (+10)
Combination of above	-	-	8 (+8)	-

Apart from the Zimbabwean shacks-only transformers and some Bangladesh households who have erected bamboo structures as part of their extensions, construction is in permanent materials of generally similar strength and life span to the original estate and similar to the standard in common use locally. Some economies are made, however. A good example is the use of bricks laid on their side to produce a minimum thickness wall in the tight circumstances of the Bangladesh sample. Both the Bangladesh and Ghana samples have quite high frequencies of unglazed windows, using local alternatives to expensive glazing, such as wooden shutters.

As indicated above, therefore, little of the physical conditions information suggests that the neighbourhood is being spoiled by transformations. On the contrary, much of it suggests the physical upgrading of the neighbourhood which the Israeli and South African writers claim (Andrew and Japha, 1978; Carmon and Oxman, 1984b; 1984a).

Service levels
As expected from Benjamin (1985) and Dasgupta (1990), transformation has improved the servicing enjoyed by residents in number and in some cases in services per household. Though toilets and water supply were universal in the Egypt and Zimbabwe samples originally, the Bangladesh and Ghana samples did not have one per dwelling (table 32). In fact, in the Bangladesh case, the utility lines were only recently laid and then not to the (now demolished) latrine blocks. Both Bangladesh and Ghana have shown a considerable increase in services through transformation. In Zimbabwe, however, while all dwellings had a toilet and water supply at first, the increase in rooms and households in the houses has not been accompanied by an increase in services. Thus, while every house has a toilet and water supply, there are more households per toilet and tap than planned.

Table 32. Servicing characteristics of the houses

Percentages	Bangladesh	Egypt	Ghana	Zimbabwe
Houses provided with a toilet:				
originally	0	100	31	100
currently	87	100	54	100
Houses provided with a water source:				
originally	0	100	35	100
currently	100	100	97	100

Increases in service provision have differing ramifications in the study areas. In Egypt and Zimbabwe, where mains reticulation to the dwelling existed from the original construction, there will simply be demand for greater flows with the effect of a reduction in water pressure and increased blocking in the sewers. In Bangladesh and Ghana, however, the reticulation was not provided for each dwelling at first; in Ghana most were served by communal aqua-privy toilets and taps only. Now, in Bangladesh, tubewells are almost standard in the houses and pour-flush toilets drain to soakaway pits. In Ghana, we have no data on reticulation but there must have been an increase in connections running from individual houses to the mains, some of which are probably illegal. Thus, problems are likely to exceed those simply of increased demand for flow: they will also include disruption of flow through inconsistent engineering practices, and through pipe breakages where they are exposed by erosion.

On the other hand, the households moving into transformed areas are more likely to have water supply and toilets than those finding accommodation in informal subdivisions or squatter areas which are the alternative for low-income renters. Thus, our data support our earlier suggestion that levels of utilities provision would be improved by transformation activity, particularly with regard to avoiding the use of public latrines and water standpipes (Tipple, 1991a).

Plan forms

The dwellings as constructed were suitable for a limited range of household sizes and single-household occupation. As we have seen, the occupants have moved on in their needs, not only requiring accommodation for more household members than were originally envisaged, but also for extended family members, renters, commercial activities and a host of other less obvious space users. In addition, the dynamics of household growth, attrition and dissolution, suggest that flexibility is a desirable characteristic of their housing. The changes which we describe in this section are valuable for their own sake but, in addition, they tend to create flexibility in the structure that contributes to the long-term suitability of the housing and to its sustainability as domestic infrastructure.

Writers on extensions activity in industrialised countries have found that house improvements can be influenced by the physical characteristics of the property (Kirwan and Martin, 1972; Seek, 1983), sometimes because they influenced the value of improvements but also because of the physical constraints that they imposed, especially on extensions. The most significant of these for us is that many terraced houses do not permit significant extension opportunities (Gosling *et al.*, 1993). This is particularly relevant to our Ghana sample as many are in very narrow terraced houses. Gosling *et al.* (1993) also suggest that (in the UK), as development continues in a town, the density of previous styles of housing will begin to look intrinsically low, resulting in pressure to intensify use of this land by means of extensions. We could expect this to be increased in its effect in rapidly developing cities such as those in our study because the estates, which were peripheral when they were developed, are now quite central to the built-up areas. While low density may have been appropriate in the past, higher densities are more normal now; while paternalistic authorities value open space for public use,[3] local norms tend to favour maximising private and covered space.

The original built forms in the estates studied in Bangladesh, Ghana and Zimbabwe have certain common elements, notably that dwellings take the form of small, rectangular blocks set in relatively large open spaces. Thus, the open space surrounds the dwelling and the rooms look outwards into the public or semi-public space, what some space syntax writers would call nuclear form (Mills, 1989). Transformation has tended to reduce the outward-looking characteristics of the houses. Many are now inward looking and others, though still outward looking, are surrounded by private space cut off from public gaze and unrestricted access. The larger buildings now often surround smaller open spaces, closer to a linear space syntax (Mills, 1989).

Bangladesh

In the original plan in Bangladesh, the pairs of dwellings stood in rows with their verandas facing each other at the rear. Entrance to the interior of the dwellings was gained through the veranda. Each block, of a dozen or up to 40, was flanked by access roads and rear alleys. Pedestrian circulation within the area was unfettered by bound-

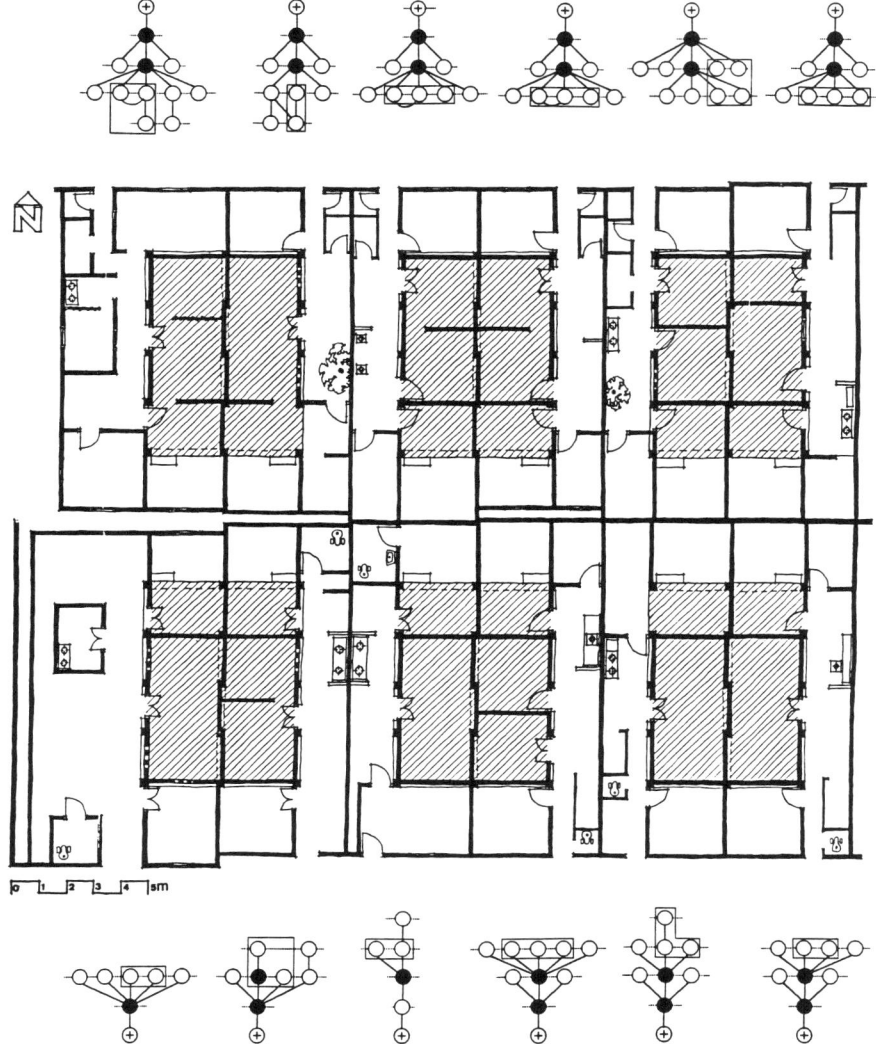

Figure 9. A group of twelve houses in Section 7, Mirpur following transformation
The pattern of development is similar but does create some variety, especially in the plan
syntax and at the ends of the rows. It is evident how the space available is being fully
utilised with only the narrow courtyards remaining open to the sky. Kitchen spaces are
mostly in the courtyard and open. The original rear verandas have universally been
extended into a large room. The original room veranda tends to be accessible directly from
the courtyard. As the plan syntax diagrams show, almost all rooms open directly off open
spaces or corridors.

aries so, in theory, anyone could walk across any part of the site. Currently, however, access around the site is much more restricted as there is a tendency to create a 'plot' and then turn it into a secluded walled area to which access is gained by a single narrow door leading into an open corridor. This corridor of varying width serves as a courtyard for outdoor cooking and other domestic activities and also for access as it tends to run from front to rear with doors into the original building and any new rooms, which usually open directly off it. Some washing and cooking areas may be inside rooms. As we shall see in table 33, the open corridor/courtyard tends to take up about one-third of the 'plot' area. Many of the entrance doors have smaller doors within them, allowing access and through draughts without exposing more than a glimpse of the threshold to passers-by.

Within the house plots, circulation is now more formalised within the narrow corridor/courtyard. Many households have installed doors on the side of the original single room (which is often subdivided). Thus, entry to the original private room through a transitional space provided by the veranda has been replaced by access to each room directly through the semi-private courtyard. The road space has been compressed to leave only the 4 m wide brick carriageway itself (and sometimes the roadside stormwater drain) between the front walls of the houses.

At intervals, toilet blocks were built but not fitted out. The dwellings that are adjacent to these have wider spaces at the sides, especially as many of the superstructures intended for the toilets have been removed. These are approximately 4 m in width and can accommodate an extra row of rooms. Alternatively, a much wider courtyard can be flanked front and back by substantial rooms. This flexibility is also available on some end blocks where spare space has often been left by the original development and is now fully utilised, often with sideways-facing shops or workshops.

In terms of Hillier and Hanson's (1984) gamma analysis, the original plan was asymmetric and non-distributed, with two cells in a straight, vertical relationship with each other and with the outside world. The current internal space syntax is still non-distributed (i.e. there is invariably only one route from one space to another) except where the original room has been given a side entrance and the original opening to the veranda is still intact. Otherwise, the very restricted sites lead mainly to two genotypes (figure 9): a relatively shallow, symmetrical one of three levels, with rooms strung out in horizontal clusters springing from the main courtyard; or a deeper one (four levels) with clusters at several levels where the corridor is divided up into distinct parts. The original rooms are now usually as deeply placed as any rooms in the house. The placing of layers of spaces between private rooms and the outside world is a process which we would expect in a society that values privacy. In our sample, the vestibule at the gate, narrow because of the toilet's sharing the less than 2 m width, has been treated as one space and the courtyard opening out beyond the toilet as another. Thus, two spaces now interpose between the doors of the most shallowly placed private rooms and the outside world. Where the sites are wider, the plans continue to be mainly non-distributed and tend to have room clusters springing from circulation spaces at several levels. Very few rooms are only accessible through other rooms. As we have little information on which rooms are used by subsequent households in our Bangladesh sample, we can say nothing about whether they occupy deep or shallow spaces in the genotype. However, toilets appear to occupy either very deep spaces or those literally on the threshold.

Ghana

In Ghana, it might be expected that households would start their extension at the entrance veranda and continue out from there without a break. While it is not uncommon for householders to alter and extend their verandas with a lean-to structure, most are necessarily small as the current roof slope does not allow long extension unless the new one is made much shallower. In fact, few householders continue the extension without a break. Most have a courtyard outside the veranda and then a free-standing addition beyond. Where single-roomed units interlock, with alternately facing verandas, it is common for a householder to wrap an extension around the rear of the next-door dwelling, by negotiation, usually leaving a narrow space for air and light to reach the neighbour's rear window. In some cases, however, this space has been reduced to only the width of the eaves or missed out altogether. This wrapping round allows the extensions to be about 8 m wide (instead of about 4 m where it has not been done) and capable of containing one row of 4 m wide rooms or two rows of 2 m wide rooms flanking a narrow corridor. Very few terraced dwellings appear to be extended in both front and rear although this practice of wrapping round the neighbouring dwelling's rear gives the impression that most are extended both ways.

Occupants of terraces that are close to the next row have less scope for outward extension than those where there are larger open spaces. In the latter case, three or more rooms can be stretched along a corridor at right angles to the terrace. Owners with corner terraced houses have the opportunity to use the land flanking the terrace where it is a simple matter to reproduce the wall and roof lines of the existing building to contain rooms several metres wide. In addition, the land to the front and rear of the terrace, along the whole new width, is also available and easily accessible from the original rooms by careful planning.

Thus, end terraces are similar to the semi-detached dwellings in scope for extension except that they do not have firm boundaries within which to work. Some terraces have surveyor's beacons set into the ground to represent the SHC's notion of their limit of extension. While these appear to be honoured in some blocks, in others anything seems to be done as long as the neighbours acquiesce.

The houses which have either demarcated plots or space that can be captured as plots have been extended in a wide variety of designs and proportions from the simple extension of a front veranda to the conversion of a small house into a 28 roomed two-storey compound. Where space permits, there is a tendency to create inward-looking houses with many of the features of the traditional compound house. External spaces

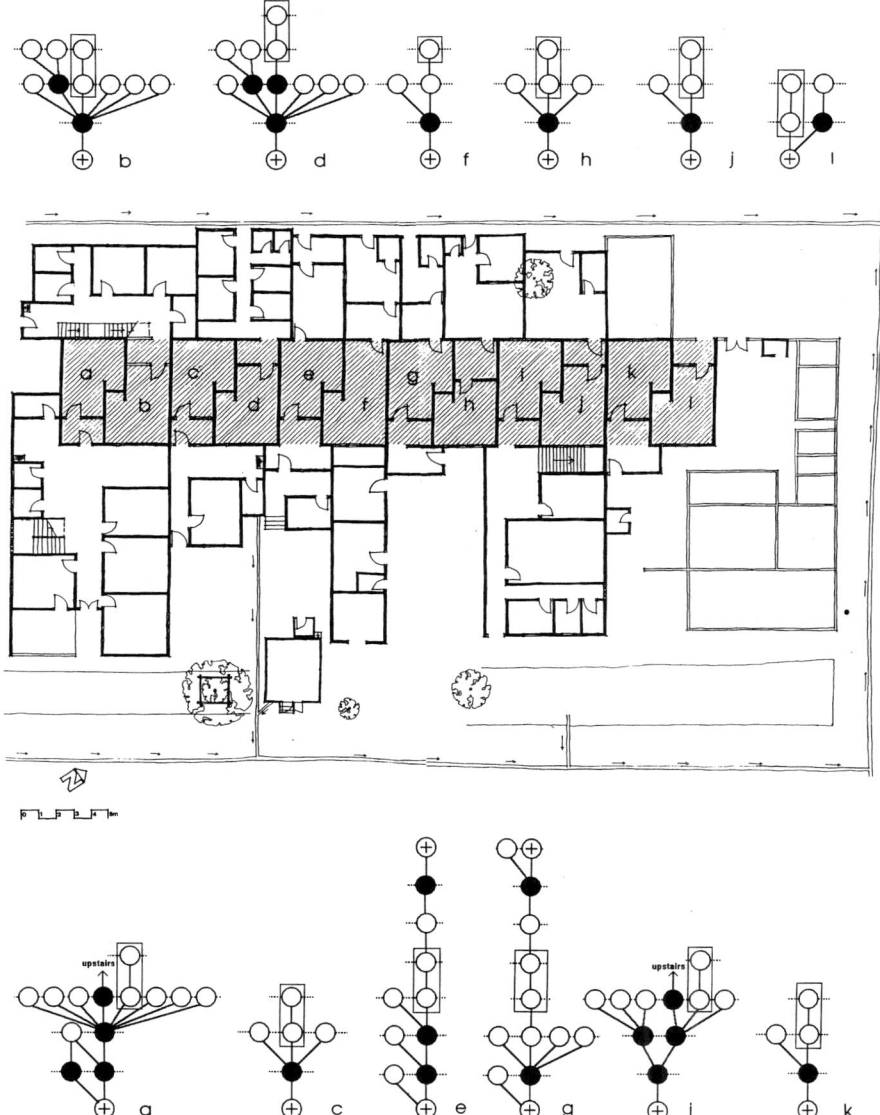

Figure 10. A twelve dwelling terrace in Asawasi built in about 1950 has now been extended into a complex block

The wrapping of rooms round the rear of the neighbour's original dwelling allows greater flexibility of form than would otherwise be possible. The rooms on the south side of 'b', 'd' and 'j' belong to 'a', 'c' and 'i', while the north side extensions there belong to 'b', 'd' and 'j'. 'E', 'g' and 'k' appear to have extended in both directions, with 'g' wrapping round 'f' rather than 'h'. The plan syntax diagrams generally show the non-distributed plan form with clusters opening off open spaces. The original rooms are normally as deep as any spaces.

Figure 11. Photograph of the left-hand end of the Asawasi block
The two-storey extension to 'a' dominates the picture.

Figure 12. Photograph of the right-hand end of the Asawasi block
The houses visible are the two storey extension to 'i', the small 'porch' on 'k', and the
foundations for the large extension to 'j'.

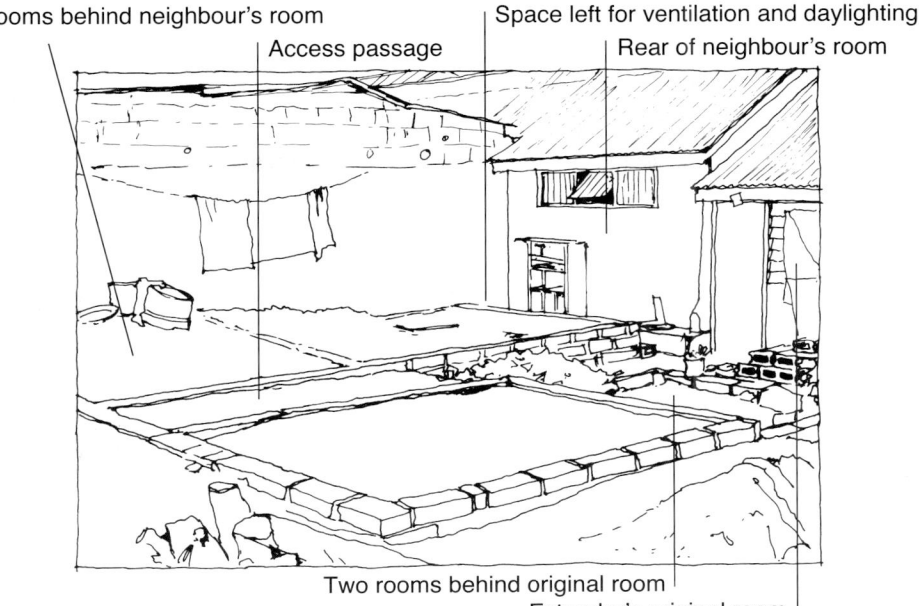

Rooms behind neighbour's room

Access passage

Space left for ventilation and daylighting

Rear of neighbour's room

Two rooms behind original room

Extender's original room

Figure 13. A typical extension in Kumasi being built round the back of the neighbouring house

within, and often slightly beyond, site boundaries are enclosed in such a way as to render them private and, therefore, usable for household functions (cooking, washing, relaxing and drying of clothes). In some cases, this is simply achieved by erecting a boundary wall or fence with an entrance off the street. In most cases, however, the house is extended through adding single rooms or rows of rooms built along or close to plot boundaries, facing towards the original dwelling. Where space permits, there is often a roughly rectangular open space off which rooms open. About 45 per cent of the sampled houses have assumed the compound form, with a courtyard as an internal space and the focus of circulation, despite many being very constricted before extension. Where the space available for extensions is narrow, a corridor or an irregular narrow space may allow access to the new rooms. About 24 per cent of the sampled houses in Ghana have this narrow corridor. Very few extended houses in Ghana are simply larger rectangles in the style of a western villa.

As is implied by the increasing use of the compound form, most of the new rooms open off a corridor or open space rather than off another room, giving flexibility of use. Such a room can be occupied by a household member or rented out to an individual or household who live independently and use the outdoor space for cooking and other activities as they would in a traditional compound house. It also slightly reduces the problems of ventilation in the hot humid climate. If the extensions had generally kept to the plan form implied in the villas originally provided, rooms would open off or be accessible through an internal living room. That this is not the case infers that the flexibility offered by the compound form is being actively sought by transformers.

On the very narrow sites, the original dwelling is now the deepest part of the house. Hillier and Hanson's (1984) internal syntax diagrams for single-room terraced dwellings (figure 10) show non-distributed asymmetric arrangements, of only three or (rarely) four levels with almost all the new rooms clustered from one space (a corridor or courtyard). It is rare for rooms to open off other rooms; the verticality in the diagrams arises from the series of courtyards and corridors which tend to lead to the rooms and from the original dwelling where the veranda gives access to the room. The original dwelling is, again, very deep within the current house but subsequent households can be found at any level.

In the two-roomed terraced units of Suntreso, non-distributed and asymmetrical layouts with many levels and access to different outside public space at each end are common. Where space is less of a constraint, for semi-detached dwellings on plots, plans become more distributed as several open spaces in and around the buildings allow alternative routes between nodes. The original buildings were at least three levels deep but the toilet and bathroom were only on the first level, being accessible directly from the public area. After transformation, five and six levels are common in these more complex plans, because of the series of open spaces, but the very flat syntax of clusters of (often more than five) rooms opening off single open spaces is a common feature. The toilet and bathroom is now usually much deeper than in the original plan, often only accessible through a rear enclosed courtyard. Subsequent households tend to occupy rooms at deep levels, usually levels three or four.

Zimbabwe

In Zimbabwe, there are two distinct forms of transformations. As the houses have ample space in front, behind and to at least one side, owners can extend the house itself or they can add free-standing structures. The former tends to conform to planning and building regulations, particularly with respect to avoiding contravening the set-backs and building lines. About 36 per cent of the sample have extended the house, about 30 per cent have built only free-standing buildings,[4] and 34 per cent have built both extensions and free-standing buildings.

In terms of Hillier and Hanson's (1984) internal space syntax, the semi-detached houses with a few shacks attached lead to non-distributed and quite deeply branched plans with the new rooms at the third or fourth levels. The more extended villas lead to two different spatial arrangements. Where a corridor has been installed at the rear to give access to a range of rooms, there is usually a distributed plan up to levels three or four, sometimes with three routes from front to rear, and then a highly branched arrangement at level four. The extended villas without courtyards are distributed (usually because of the two routes around the villa to the rear yard) but to a lesser extent, and are capable of branching at any level as rooms may open off side yards, front rooms or each other. In all forms, subsequent households tend to occupy very deep rooms while the main household has rooms at all levels.

In her study of our Zimbabwe sample, Turnbull (1998) found that transformed houses were deeper and more asymmetric in plan than the originals. They show signs of becoming more segregated. Indeed, some rooms have been converted from spaces which controlled others or provided through-access to terminal spaces, those with access but no egress. This is especially the case with kitchens that were originally spaces with egress from the rear space to the living room. With transformation, many kitchens are now terminal spaces. Her work showed that our expectation that the house would become more like a traditional compound (with shallow, integrated plans) was, in fact, occurring.

Egypt

In Egypt, the estate design is totally different from the other three, being in five-storey blocks standing like dominoes in monotonous ranks with spaces between them a little wider than the structures. The building façades are generally flat or with very small protrusions for balconies. The internal plan of the transformed flats depends largely on the original flat type and the rooms which present themselves to the extendible façade (usually the one with the balcony). It is quite clear that the balcony provides the means through which the plan breaks through the original built envelope so its position can affect efficiency in the plan. The kitchen is also commonly used for access into the new rooms so that, with almost all the transformed flats, a very small area is left with fittings to act as the kitchen. This seems inappropriate in what are now large flats with a median of seven residents whose demands on food preparation must be quite substantial.

In Helwan, the two-roomed flats are usually extended over half or two-thirds of the façade, leaving a space for ventilating the toilet which is adjacent to that façade. These extensions usually contain only one room. Some flats in Helwan take up only half the depth of the building and so are arranged back-to-back. In these, two rooms are present at the façades and so the extension can have two rooms side by side each opening off an original room. These extensions tend to be quite shallow, about 2 m being common, but covering the entire façade. This also occurs in some of the Medinet Nasr flats. In the remainder, however, the kitchen and toilet are so arranged that ventilation is required for at least half the façade. Rather than only extending on this part, however, some transformers leave a 1 m wide ventilation shaft and light well across half the façade. As a result, access to the two new rooms must be achieved through the former living room and then through one of the new rooms to the other. This adds greater depth to the circulation pattern so that a room may be reached only by passing through two others in contrast with the original flats in which all living rooms were accessible directly from the hallway.

The few three-roomed flats that have been extended are wide enough for two rooms to be added side by side to the façade while leaving the kitchen and toilet façades untouched. Extensions are usually of two rooms and there is often a new balcony. In almost all transformations, the original balcony is subsumed into other rooms or simply acts as circulation space. Where balconies are provided in transformations, they are usually a whole room wide and, therefore, larger than the original ones. End flats have major advantages, first in the ability to ventilate inner rooms through new windows punched through the end wall, and second in having the potential to extend beyond the end wall of the blocks.

In terms of Hillier and Hanson's (1984) plan syntax, most of the plans are non-distributed. Most extensions involve adding a deep room (at level three or four) and extending spaces which already existed at that level (e.g., balconies) into living rooms and using balconies and kitchens as their striking points. The new living rooms in the extensions are thus much deeper than the originals which are invariably at level two. Where larger balconies have been fitted, they often have access from more than one room so adding a degree of distribution at the deepest level.

Summary

Some transformations are simply the extension of existing rooms to create a larger version of the original dwelling. The Egyptian flats and some villas in Ghana and Zimbabwe have been transformed into larger and slightly more complex dwellings without fundamental changes in layout. They are still, basically, single dwellings but have an extra room or two.

However, most houses in Bangladesh and Ghana, and many in Zimbabwe, have

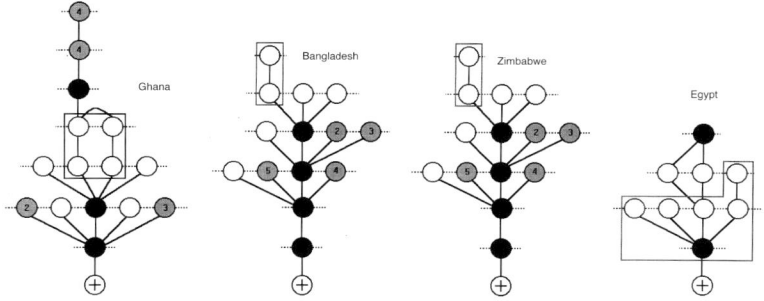

Figure 14. Plan syntax diagrams of the four transformed houses in figure 3
Circles represent spaces, lines represent access routes. The circles are coloured, black for
circulation spaces, grey for those occupied by other households (with a household number
added). The spaces existing from the original dwelling are outlined in a rectangle or irregular
polygon. All syntax diagrams start at the space outside the plot (the circle with a cross).
Ghana, Bangladesh and Zimbabwe show the new spaces opening out directly from
circulation spaces at various depths, and the original rooms now occupying deeper space
than most of the new development. In Egypt, the new spaces are deeper than the original.

been more radically altered. Not only have they more rooms but also they are noticeably more complex. Gone are the simple rectangles[5] set at relatively consistent
distances and surrounded by contiguous open spaces. Instead, rooms are distributed
around open space or corridors; several that used to open off the living room are now
accessed from outside. The houses are now adapted to multi-household occupation
and, even, multi-heir inheritance.

Internal plans demonstrate more sensitivity to local cultures than when they were
first built. For example, toilets tend to be further from the public gaze. Segregation of
the sexes is easier when there are more rooms and these have been the major products
of the transformation process in each country.

Open areas now have a radically different relationship with built spaces. The open
space is no longer contiguous in Bangladesh and Ghana. Much of the open space
which was public or at least open to public view, is now private; some is only accessible through covered space. Many of the buildings now extend right to their front
boundary so that the street is bordered by walls rather than grass or other vegetation.
Many rooms are now inward looking, facing the open space within the plot, and most
have immediate access to the open air or a corridor rather being reached through
another room.

The growing urban footprint: issues of urban sprawl

There is obvious scope for debate about the desirability of high-density development,
as a land-saving strategy, or low density development for the pleasant 'Garden City'
environment and future flexibility. On the one hand, extending existing housing
increases urban densities. On the other, it reduces the demand for peripheral development and the spread of the 'urban footprint'.

Where building control is lax and unplanned housing or extensions are common, spaces between houses may be too small and winding to permit efficient access for fire appliances and other emergency services. As a result, life becomes unnecessarily endangered and the likelihood of large amounts of property being lost is magnified. Over-dense development also has adverse implications for the provision of housing services such as water, drainage and electricity. Where spaces between buildings are narrow and irregular, machinery may not reach places where it is required for repair work. In addition, there is an increased likelihood that service lines will be built over and damaged by extra loadings or excavation. Crowded development reduces the area of permeable ground which can absorb rain and other surface water. Increased volume and speed of run-off can cause significant erosion between buildings, spoiling streets and open spaces and threatening the integrity of the buildings themselves. In addition, the cumulative effect downstream can increase the incidence of floods.

Very high intensity of land use, unless accompanied by sophisticated engineering, leads inevitably to accelerated degradation of the land surface and pollution of the substratum and atmosphere. Soil contamination, for example, affects children in particular as parasites can readily infect them through ingested dirt or enter through the feet. Crowding also means that any hazardous spill-offs originating from one dwelling easily affect the quality of life in adjacent dwellings or even neighbouring areas. Such nuisances may take the form of unsafe sanitation practices, poor drainage and indiscriminate refuse disposal. The economic consequences of the spread of any communicable diseases can be crippling for the poor, requiring high expenditures on imported antibiotics (which, in any case, are not always easy to find) and causing loss of productivity and income.

Very low density is, of course, also unsatisfactory: underpopulation of the land is expensive both to local governments and to individual households in the sense that *per capita* servicing and amenity provision costs can become unduly high. Provision of under-used utilities that drain the coffers of financially weak municipalities cannot be sustained in the long term.

One common cause of low-density development in developing countries is the enforcement of wasteful plot-ratio stipulations. In some cities (in Ghana, for example), no more than one-half of a plot may be built upon, even when standard plot sizes are in the region of 1000 m². Together with over-generous road rights of way and excessive building set-back reservations, low plot ratios encourage urban sprawl, with significant financial and economic implications. In some countries, especially where land markets are dominated by inept public land allocation agencies, low densities may be encouraged by sub-economic land pricing, and generous land-tax structures. By lowering the price of land artificially, such practices give rise to over-generous land-consumption habits.

If left unchecked, extravagant subdivision standards will raise the costs and lessen the availability of further land for urban uses. Eventually, sprawl will stifle the provision of priority public infrastructure – water, drainage, electricity and roads. In turn, longer commuting distances imply increases in energy utilisation; higher green-house-gas emissions and associated air pollution; more severe ozone depletion and possible thermal inversions; and lead and particulates from motor vehicle exhausts. Additionally, low-density development requires further stocks of rural land to be acquired and turned over for urban uses. Such conversions necessarily degrade periph-eral agricultural land and forest vegetation, extending the urban area's ecological footprint. Clearly, there is an urgent need for more judicious exploitation of urban land resources.

With transformation activity, especially in estates such as those in Ghana and Zimbabwe, we have the phenomenon of a garden-city suburb being subverted and turned into something more akin to high-density development. In so far as it makes more intensive use of land, it is a positive contribution. If, however, it causes the ills associated with very high densities, its effect would be negative.

The rising price of peripheral land

It can be argued that transformations become an important housing supply strategy at a time when alternative housing adjustments cease to be straightforward. Gilbert (1993) and others have argued that invasions of land by squatters in Latin America, and their African equivalent of squatting on land peripheral to the city, have ceased to be a viable alternative for the poor masses because land is now commercialised. For example, Strassmann (1994) reports that peripheral plots of land in Manila, Philippines, now cost as much as the annual household income of the occupants and half the price of houses built on them. As this land commercialisation developed, the massive squatter urbanisations of the 1960s and 1970s slowed down or stopped in the 1980s. Instead of a group cooperatively dividing the land up amongst themselves without money changing hands, it is now more likely that someone will assume control of the land and become a broker, 'selling' a spurious ownership or charging a fee for annual 'leases'. Thus, commercial interests divide up the land into plots and sell it. These informal (or illegal) subdivisions have taken the place of mass squatting in very many cities. Traditionally-held land requires increasing amounts of tribute to be paid to the holding community until, instead of being a token for the gaining of accep-tance, it is now a market 'price' even though the title gained is no stronger than that of temporary surface user (see, for example, Tipple and Willis, 1992).

It seems self-evident that building a squatter house on a relatively unobtrusive site on the periphery was a less risky activity than adding several rooms to a house in a well-regulated formal suburb. While the squatting option was available, the decision to move might be more likely to take first place, even in the face of increased transport costs involved in peripheral locations. However, the commercialisation of land makes transformation more attractive. As peripheral settlement now costs money, benefi-ciaries of subsidies, i.e., those who have bought for lower-than-market prices, will be alive to the comparative value of their housing. Thus, rent-seeking behaviour will cause them to stay put. We might, therefore, expect to see considerable increases in the incidence of transformation in the medium to long term now that (and for as long as) mass squatting is much reduced in frequency and scale.

Increases in intensity of development

One of the major concerns of local planners has been the idea that extensions create too much built area. This is voiced in conversations locally as a common apprehension about 'over-development' or (horrible expression!) 'over-densification'. In order to check how true this is, we have generated data on floor-space indexes. Except in Egypt, these are virtually identical to plot ratios as very few houses have had additional storeys (only a few in Ghana, making a difference of 0.02 between the median plot ratio and floor-space index there).

In table 33, floor-space indexes are calculated where the house has a plot by using the covered floor space as a proportion of the plot area. Where there is no plot but simply undefined open space, a plot is imputed from the mean size of spaces captured as plots by transformers in the same type of house.

Table 33. Plot areas, plot ratios and floor-space indexes

Medians (and IQRs)	Bangladesh	Egypt	Ghana	Zimbabwe
Plot area:				
Transformers	57.5	65.3	143.8	251.2
	(51, 85)	(60, 73)	(85, 313)	(228, 293)
Non-transformers	-	51.3	39.7	274.1
		(42, 51)	(33, 55)	(223, 306)
Original floor-space index:*				
Transformers	0.39	0.63	0.26	0.17
	(0.27, 0.44)	(0.6, 0.7)	(0.2, 0.4)	(0.1, 0.2)
Non-transformers†	-	0.68**	0.24**	0.2
		(0.6, 0.7)	(0.2, 0.3)	(0.1, 0.3)
Current floor-space index in estates studied:§				
Transformers	0.68	1	0.59	0.29
	(0.51, 0.93)	(1, 1)	(0.4, 0.7)	(0.2, 0.4)
Percentage change in transformers'	77	53	110	62
floor-space index	(56, 140)	(39, 68)	(61, 203)	(26, 129)

* Original built area divided by current plot area.
† Assumes mean plot for transformers in the same type of house.
** Since the majority of non-transformed houses do not have official plots, we have used the average plot size from each transformed house type to give some idea of the plot size a non-transformer might expect.
§ Current built area (all floors of the house) divided by plot area, and see text for Egypt.

We can see from table 33 that the Ghana and Zimbabwe areas, where the British colonial practice of building small cottages on plots is prevalent, had very low original floor-space indexes – even in Ghana where there were many terraced rooms. In Zimbabwe, the increase with transformation is 62 per cent to 0.29 (and only 0.4 at the third quartile) which cannot be said to represent crowding or over-development of plots. In Ghana, transformation has produced a floor-space index of just over double the original, to a median of 0.59 (with third quartile of 0.7) which shows high levels of development and could be argued by some to be over-development. Furthermore, the impression gained on the ground, walking round the areas, is of higher density than the floor-space index would indicate. In some parts, particularly once the houses are surrounded by high walls, the spaces left in public use are narrow and intensively used. This is particularly so where houses in the upper half of the floor-space index distribution occur in groups. However, the presence of many open spaces within the houses as courtyards means that an outside observer gains an exaggerated impression of plot coverage.

There is clearly a problem of surface water drainage in the estates. Their original drainage system is well past its best but the problem has been exacerbated by the increased intensity of building. When heavy rain falls, as it does in Kumasi on many days in a year, pathways soon become drains as the lack of soft ground and vegetation increase the intensity of run-off. This problem is relatively straightforward to eradicate but requires investment from the under-financed Metropolitan Assembly. It represents a clear example of why transformers should also be property-tax payers.

In Bangladesh, the story is similar. The original provision (index = 0.39 at the median) has been increased by 77 per cent by transformation until it appears to be very densely built up indeed. Walking around the areas, or viewing them from a distance, gives the impression of about 100 per cent coverage. However, as in Ghana, there are open spaces within the houses, albeit individually quite small (and particularly quite narrow), which reduce the index to 0.68 at the median and only allow it to rise towards saturation by the third quartile (0.93).[6]

The Egyptian case study has been dealt with differently. There, our sample is random on both orientation and floor level so we cannot generalise our data to the block and its immediate environs. These circumstances require that we deal with each flat as a horizontal slice of the block at that point and allow for no plot definition. Thus, we can only look at the increase, which results from transformation, in coverage of a putative plot and horizontal slices through its projection upwards. Thus, we had to accept the transformed flat (including any internal light wells) as constituting the plot. Almost all households have covered the entire envelope with covered space; only a few have left a ventilation shaft or light well. Thus, we achieve floor-space indexes of one for transformers in Egypt but this does not mean that there is no space for further extensions as it would if there were plots. Non-transformers' plots are assumed to be the mean area used by transformers for extensions to that type of flat. As they vary little around the median of 0.68, we can assume that transformers have increased the intensity of use of the area by 53 per cent. Earlier (Tipple *et al.*, 1985) we estimated the original net ground coverage of the flats in Helwan to be 16 per cent and transformers to have increased this to 21 per cent. Our current data and Kardash's plan in figure 15 allow us to estimate the original ground coverage, including open spaces in the estates, to be around 25 per cent. Extensions have increased this to about 40 per cent. However, in areas tightly drawn around the rows of flats, original ground coverage was about 33 per cent and is now 55 per cent. If all five floors are assumed to be equal, we obtain an overall floor-space index in Workers' City Helwan of 2.0 compared with the original 1.2.

As might be expected, overall there is more variety in plot areas (with a factor of about five between medians) than between house built areas (only a factor of about two between medians). Where large plots are the norm, the coverage which occupants achieve is lower than where small plots are customary. There must be a balance between the amount of housing that a particular household is liable to provide (for themselves and others) and the amount of space in which they can operate. This would result in an optimum floor-space index. In any country, this point of equilibrium could be regarded as indicating an optimum plot size (or range of sizes) for areas in which transformations are likely and which would result in the most efficient plans for residential areas.

Summary

The pattern which we can discern from this chapter is that transformers are practitioners of sustainable development. They are improving the condition of generally run-down buildings in neighbourhoods that are unlikely to have been suitable for modern urban life if they had remained pristine. The estates were built as special environments owing more in appearance and dwelling types to foreign philosophies of urban living (from the Garden City to the Modern Movement) or the need to provide many shelters for little money than to the forces which shape the rest of the city. The transformers' activity has built something much closer to an ordinary low-income neighbourhood in the city; their area has become more like any other low-income area rather than a non-conforming special area. Its house forms, space syntax, densities and other characteristics are moving towards those of its surroundings while at the same time becoming more flexible in the functions that can be performed within it.

At the same time, increases in density are making more intensive use of existing built-up areas and current services. Thus, transformers are making a contribution to reducing urban sprawl. Increases in density within the estates are still mostly within reasonable bounds.

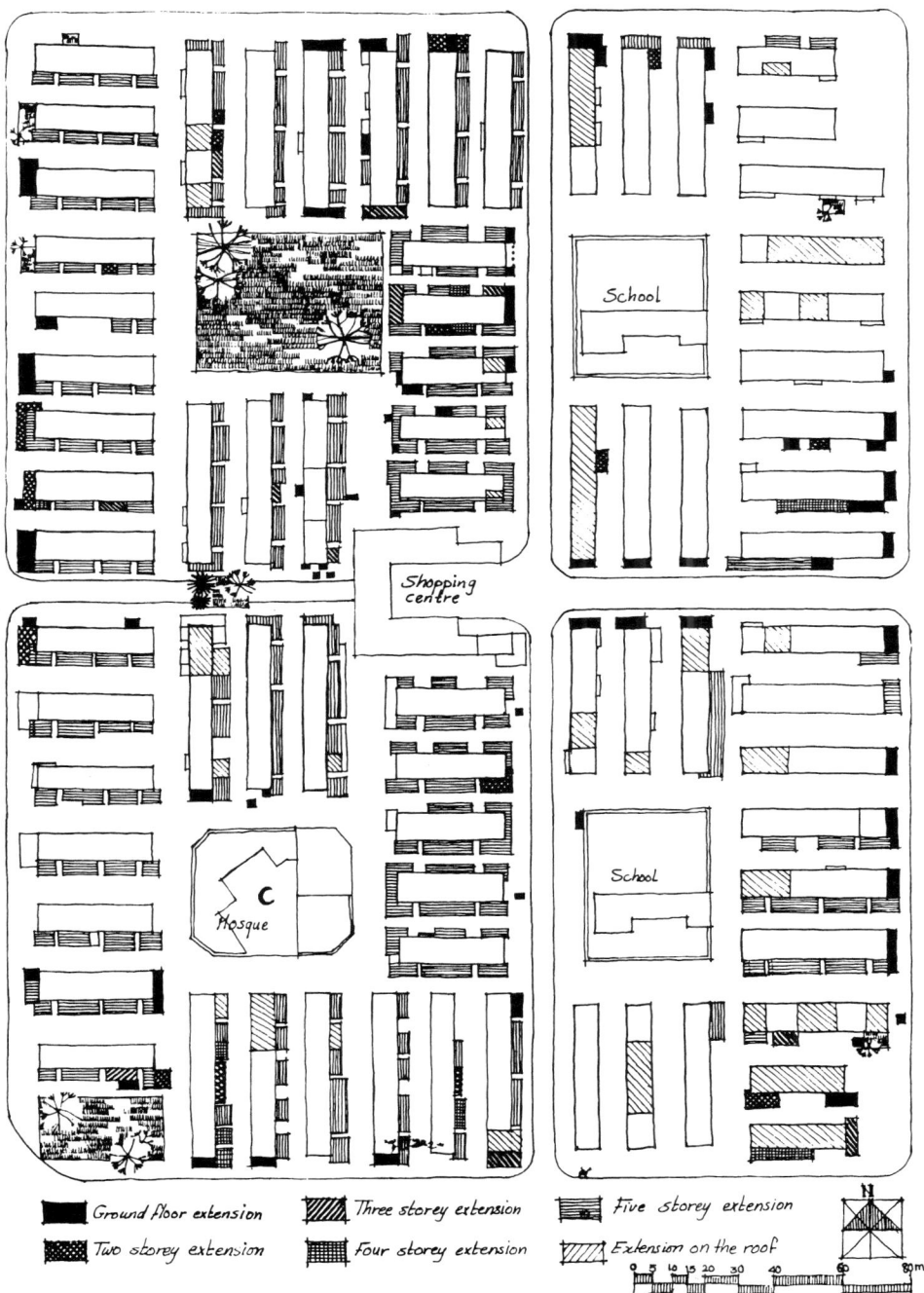

Figure 15. Kardash's plan of the northern two-thirds of the Helwan estate
The extreme south-west corner block is pictured in Fig. 45.

Notes

1   This is drawn from material published in *Habitat International* (1996) 20 (3): 367–76.
2   Suggestions for future taxation of extensions, as a *quid pro quo* of permission, are made in chapter 8.
3   One wonders how far authorities would value public open spaces if they were not traditionally coloured green on the map. If, instead, they were coloured light brown or a dirty grey as they are in reality in so many cities when goats, children, garbage dumpers, vehicle parkers and hawkers have interacted with the space in their usual manner, they might be replaced by private open space which can be justifiably coloured green as it is usually well looked after and watered.
4   This is, of course, heavily influenced by the purposeful sampling of about 100 shack transformers (28 per cent of the sample) which are, we think, considerably over-represented.
5   Whether the rectangles represent one dwelling or a number.
6   There are also a surprising number of trees within the courtyards, see figure 2.

6. The transformation process

Informal settlements clinging to existing buildings

Transformation of government-built housing can be likened to attaching informal development to the most formally developed areas found in many cities. In the past, we have become used to informal housing supply taking place in particular areas, typically on unused land within the urban built-up area (railway reservations, land assigned to future government use, steep slopes, land liable to flooding, etc.) or on its periphery. These settlements often present acute discomfiture to land-use planners because they create obstacles to smooth implementation of planned development, e.g. the Klong Toey settlement and port facilities in Bangkok (Durande-Lasserve and Pajoni, 1993), or put their residents in potentially serious danger, e.g. from mud slides during heavy rain. As they occur mainly on public land, the removal of development puts the authorities in the awkward position of being the oppressors of the poor when they would prefer to be seen as the protectors of the poor and oppressed.

Transformations, on the other hand, occur close to existing dwellings and often on the private land attached to them. The informal 'settlement' takes place within the interstices of the current formal settlement on land that is already serviced, integrated within the city fabric, equipped with social and other infrastructure, and suitable for residential occupation. While interstitial development has many of the inconvenient features of the conventional informal settlement, it does not tend to obstruct major future developments as many informal settlements do. Instead the development which may be prejudiced is more local and likely to affect only the close neighbours. It may be fairly serious in its local ramifications, e.g. blocking access for fire appliances or building over service lines, but it is unlikely to affect meso- or macro-scale projects in the city.[1]

The construction process

Extensions to existing houses are ideally suited to self-help through family labour if there is a propensity to build this way in the local culture. The work is close by so any spare hour can be used to add to the building. Thus, the potential exists to convert surplus time into capital value very efficiently (Turner, 1976) and we have previously referred to the phenomenon under study as 'self-help transformation' (Tipple, 1991a). However, as in many sites and services schemes (Laquian, 1983), few householders are involved in active construction themselves; there is little 'sweat equity'. In most cases, separate tradesmen, engaged, controlled and paid by the householder appear to be the norm, as we can see from table 34.

Table 34. The implementers of the extension process (percentages)

	Bangladesh	Egypt	Ghana	Zimbabwe
Self-help, household members	30	0	3	15
Single contractor	0	97	29	12
Separate tradesmen	70	3	66	65
Self-help plus tradesmen	0	0	2	7
Other	0	0	0	2

Self-help in the form of actually building the structure is relatively uncommon except for shacks-only transformers in Zimbabwe who can purchase the room in sections ready to be nailed together at the corners. Contractors who bring together several trades are also uncommon in the transformation process; the single tradesmen dominate the scene. One of the main reasons for this is the form of payment customary in each case. If a contractor is engaged, payment tends to involve a few large sums as the work proceeds quickly and all processes are completed in a short time. If single tradesmen are engaged, however, the owner can have delays between them so that money can be gathered and payments strung out to suit the owner's resources.

Egypt is the exception in having a heavy reliance on single contractors who bring all trades and labourers with them. This may be an inevitable (and in this case prudent) consequence of the multi-storey nature of the stacks. In both estates studied, the contractors who were interviewed were well known in the community. They employ skilled workers on a permanent basis (paying medical insurance, social security and bonuses) and unskilled workers on temporary terms (paid by the day, hour or job) for each kind of work. No women are employed. Skilled workers constitute at least half of the work-force; they are used for concrete mixing and casting, block laying, finishings, etc. Some contractors insist on a written contract with the client, others do not. All provide materials and all the labour; some provide mains services, others depend on the householder to negotiate for their supply. Where permissions are applied for (e.g. in Medinet Nasr), they are the responsibility of the owner.

The engineering design of these five-storey structures is done by the contractors based on experience rather than any formal training. As is common in hot climates where rapid drying of the concrete reduces its strength, the framework tends to be over-designed with columns of greater thickness than necessary. There are, however, likely to be some problems with exposed reinforcement bars owing to poor concrete pouring.

In Bangladesh, the informal sector construction process presents a typical mixture of artisan and owner collaboration and cooperation in the small-scale construction

Figure 16. Construction under way in Helwan
This extension spans two neighbouring stacks of flats.

processes involved in transformation. It occurs in roughly the following way. An occupier who decides to extend a house seeks out a *rajmistri* (master mason) through recommendation from a friend or neighbour and an introduction. The *rajmistri* usually works with an assistant (*jogali*) who is less skilled and who may become a *rajmistri* in due time. He may also have one or two labourers with whom he commonly works or he may hire them by the day by going to particular places in the city where they gather for hire early in the morning.

No plans of the proposed extension will be drawn but agreement will be reached about the nature and extent of the work, the approximate price and the amount of materials required. If changes are required during the work, negotiation will be entered into. The householder may appoint someone close to him/her as a project manager or may act him/herself. This person will go with the *rajmistri* to select and purchase materials (using the householder's money) and arrange their transport to site. This is usually done by pullcart or rickshaw (ordinary rickshaw for a few bags of cement, a flat-bed rickshaw 'van' for bricks). The *rajmistri* will have no means of transport for materials nor will he own any mechanical tools such as a cement mixer.

Much construction of single storeys uses walling only one brick thick (5 inches or 125 mm) and this is common in our study area. First-class bricks are used for structural walls, second-class may be used for boundary walls and internal partitions. In order to add stability, the mortar will be mixed 1:4 cement to sand rather than the more usual 1:6. Ideally, the labourers will water the newly finished wall section occasionally to cure the mortar but, if it rains, work is covered in polythene or jute sacks. If there is to be a septic tank, the *rajmistri* builds it, but a soak-pit would be dug by the labourers.

A carpenter (*kathmistri*) will be engaged by the householder for fixing the windows, doors, wood strips for the electrical wiring to follow, roofing timbers and corrugated iron sheets. Electric wiring and fitments would be fitted by someone from the shop where they are bought as there is little complicated circuitry involved.

Labourers are paid daily by the householder while the *rajmistri*, his *jogali*, the *kathmistri* and other skilled workers are usually paid partly in the middle of the job (by negotiation) and partly at the end. If rain stops the work, the householder does not have to pay the workers but usually gives them transport money if they have had a wasted journey to the site.

Figure 17. Construction under way in Kumasi
The roof corner is left unsupported while the walls are built in this extension to a kitchen in Asawasi.

The process in Ghana has been described in Owusu and Tipple (1995) and is very similar to the Bangladesh case. Usually, the owner engages a 'mason' to construct the foundations, floor and walls and he becomes the leader of a group of artisans and may influence their selection. Such *ad hoc* groups of tradesmen are quite capable of tackling very large jobs but their efforts in our sample have a median of four rooms.

There is a long tradition in urban Ghana of collecting materials over many years against the day when building can start. Piles of cement blocks are a familiar site in all cities and aluminium roof sheets are stored under or behind beds. When the mason is engaged as the main artisan, there is usually no written contract but the arrangements are discussed in front of witnesses. The client is usually responsible for providing all materials and must pay for portions of the work at frequent intervals because the artisans are unlikely to have capital with which to pay the labourers. The artisans' contract fees are negotiated partly with respect to the expense of the job but also partly

Figure 18. 'Shack' components for sale in Harare

on the basis of whether they perceive the client to be rich or not. A rich client will be expected to pay much more for the same work than a poorer client.

In Zimbabwe, self-help is utilised for less costly extensions (especially shacks) and, combined with tradesmen, in the largest. This suggests that, for the very large jobs, owners are reluctant to leave all the tasks to paid help and feel the need to economise by having household members help.[2] Such extensions are likely to be so large and complex that the opportunity for tasks to be accomplished over the weekend or between stages is greater than simple room additions. Single tradesmen and contractors both tackle large extensions and both have a large range of job costs.

Thus, we can see that labour-intensive methods of construction are almost universal in the transformations observed in our study. All tend to use little in the way of heavy equipment. Even in the multi-storeyed construction in Egypt, such tasks as hauling materials to the fifth floor will be done by ropes and pulleys or wheelbarrow ramps rather than cranes. Similarly, transport of materials to the site is commonly done by the small-scale transport contractors; taxis and 'mammy-wagons' are the order of the day in Ghana, flat-bed rickshaw vans in Bangladesh.

It should also be remembered that many building materials are made locally (often on the plot itself as in Ghana) by the most labour-intensive means. A most remarkable case is found in Bangladesh where there is so little stone that aggregates are made by crushing burnt bricks. This process involves a pile of bricks, a bamboo mat, a hammer, and a resulting pile of aggregates of various grades. The agent of destruction for the bricks is commonly a woman, sometimes assisted by her children.[3] A SKAT report looked into the manufacture of artificial aggregates by making the equivalent of tiny irregular bricks but came to the conclusion that they were not likely to be cheaper than crushed brick (SKAT, 1991).

Permissions

Only in Ghana do a majority claim to have asked for planning permission though everywhere those who asked are likely to have been granted it (table 35). The Zimbabwe figures are, of course, skewed by the larger than representative sample of shacks-only transformers who are largely outside the planning system. Those transformations that simply extend the original building within the limits set by the building lines usually have full planning and building regulations approval and are registered as such in council records.[4] The Bangladesh sample is completely outside planning control as it is classified as a *semi-pucca* area where regulations do not apply. When the proposed sale is complete, however, each plot will be reclassified as *pucca* and full planning approval would be required for any new development.

Table 35. Permissions (percentages)

	Bangladesh	Egypt	Ghana	Zimbabwe
Permission asked	n/a	8	58	44
(Of those who asked) permission granted	n/a	60	97	93

Though the authorities may flex their bureaucratic muscles on transformers who do not bother to ask for permission and threaten action in a minority of cases, usually no great change emerges and transformers who have not applied for or received permission carry on regardless.

As we can see in table 36, only in Zimbabwe have more than 14 per cent been threatened with action by planning authorities. The most common consequence of a threat from the authorities has been inaction; the sabre has been rattled but no *coup de grace* has been delivered. Where action has resulted, only in Zimbabwe did a significant proportion (one half) result in stopping the work or demolition. This unsuccessful wielding of control by planning authorities and building regulators appears to support our initial suggestion that laws and regulations to prevent transformation activity are only effective while a dwelling is rented from the owner of the property, and then only if the owner is vigilant and opposed to such activity (Tipple, 1991a). In Bangladesh, where the properties are still rented, the owner (HSD) appears to hold a completely benign view of transformations.

Table 36. Householders who have received threats from authorities and action taken against them (percentages)

	Bangladesh	Egypt	Ghana	Zimbabwe
Threat	11	14	13	40
	$n = 383$	$n = 257$	$n = 305$	$n = 294$
Actions taken				
(percentages of those threatened):	$n = 43$	$n = 34$	$n = 40$	$n = 117$
No action	1	90	88	15
Forced a change in what was built	98	7	8	24
Stopped work going ahead	1	0	2	58
Demolished the work done	0	1	0	3
Demanded a penalty in monetary terms	0	1	2	-

Phases of transformation

Up to the time of the surveys, the majority of transformers had only carried out one phase; only in Bangladesh had more than 30 per cent added a second or subsequent phase (table 37). However, it is likely that the numbers of second and subsequent phases will increase as time passes as transformers appear to be largely embarked on a process of incremental improvement; they add a room or two when they can. There are exceptions to this, the most notable being found in the Egypt sample where most have had only one phase and may not add any others. However, evidence from photographs taken over a decade demonstrate that at least some Egyptian flats are extended time and again. This phasing represents the most effective way for low-income households to invest: to build as much as can be afforded for cash at any one time. The pattern of phasing in houses is shown in some of the plans in Appendices 1–4.

Table 37. Number of phases in the extension process (frequencies and percentages)*

	Bangladesh	Egypt	Ghana	Zimbabwe
Phase 1	370	249	237	293
	(100)	(100)	(100)	(100)
Phase 2	244	16	68	64
	(66)	(6)	(29)	(22)
Phase 3	85	1	14	12
	(23)	(0.4)	(6)	(4)
Phase 4	18	-	4	-
	(5)		(2)	
Phase 5	6	-	-	-
	(2)			

* Percentages are in parentheses.

Scale

As shown in table 38, there is considerable variety in the area of extensions. Those in Bangladesh are much smaller than the other countries', each being equivalent to only

Table 38. Scale of transformation phases in square metres

Medians (and IQRs)	Bangladesh	Egypt	Ghana	Zimbabwe
Original floor area	22.3	36.2	36.6	50.0*
	(22.3, 22.3)	(33.6, 44.1)	(24.5, 47.3)	(45.0, 52.0)
Phase 1	9.7	21.9	30.6	25.7
	(5.8, 16.7)	(17.4, 27.2)	(18.3, 67.8)	(12.8, 44.8)
Phase 2	9.7	24.8	28.7	20.9
	(6.7, 19.7)	(18.4, 35.8)	(14.1, 58.9)	14.2, 27.2)
Phase 3	12.2	4.1**	24.6	23.1
	(6.4, 23.2)	(-, -)	(14.7, 46.4)	(11.1, 35.5)
Phase 4	10.2	-	10.5	
	(7.5, 18.2)	-	(7.1, 19.5)	
Phase 5	5.6**	-	-	-
	(-, -)	-		

* For comparative reasons, these figures reflect the original house type without being influenced by whether any of the original has been demolished.
** $n = 2$.

a single small room. The first phase in Ghana is unusually large, not only at the median of 30.6 m² but especially at the third quartile of almost 70 m² (the equivalent of seven small rooms). Otherwise, early phases in Egypt, Ghana and Zimbabwe tend to be 20–28 m² at the medians.[5] The most recent phase in each country except Zimbabwe is substantially smaller than all the rest.

In relation to the original dwellings, extensions tend to be quite substantial. They average about half the size of the original in each phase (except very late ones which tend to be much smaller). This may be as much a function of the small size of original houses in comparison with average rooms as of the ambitions of the owners. The Ghana transformers achieve the largest extensions in proportion to the original. They and their Zimbabwean counterparts are still achieving a median extension half as large as the original house all the way through to the third phase. Though Bangladesh transformers build small, their efforts supplement the original dwelling by almost half its original size consistently through each of the first four phases.

Timing

The data in table 39 are only of established transformers and, therefore, not influenced by the inevitable bunching caused by the inclusion of the recent transformers who have been working in the last three years. Transformation activity began decades ago in Ghana and Zimbabwe (1953 and 1958 respectively in our samples). The Ghana sample led the field through the 1960s and 1970s but Egypt and Bangladesh have seen very strong trends to transform since the early 1980s. Our earliest example in Bangladesh is 1974 and in Egypt is 1980.

Table 39. Dates of phases in the extension process (for established transformers only)

Medians (and IQRs)	Bangladesh	Egypt	Ghana	Zimbabwe
Phase 1	1987	1986	1978	1983
	(1984, 1989)	(1983, 1987)	(1970, 1983)	(1975, 1987)
Phase 2	1989	1988	1985	1989
	(1986, 1990)	(1985, 1989)	(1978, 1989)	(1982, 1990)
Phase 3	1990	1989*	1981	1990
	(1989, 1991)	(-, -)	(1977, 1986)	(1991, 1992)
Phase 4	1991	-	1984*	-
	(1988, 1992)		(-, -)	
Phase 5	1989	-	-	-
	(1988, 1992)			

* $n = 2$.

One of the issues arising from these data is the continuity of work available for contractors and artisans in the construction sector. Within a short-term pattern of boom and hiatus, there seems to be a general rise in work which may achieve some degree of continuity in the longer term.

Cost

Considering the rather uninspiring original structures and the modest circumstances which the occupants could be expected to enjoy, it is impressive that such a large amount of construction has been achieved. Not only is the total amount spent considerable but so is the cost of each phase. We can see from table 40 that phase one is the most costly and amounts to PPP£2–3000. There is remarkable consistency in costs across the countries, at least for the first two phases. The range of medians for phase 1, from Bangladesh to Ghana, is only £950 (about 40 per cent of the Bangladesh median).

Table 40. Cost of phases in the extension process, PPP pounds

Medians (and IQRs)	Bangladesh	Egypt	Ghana	Zimbabwe
Phase 1	2310	2480	3260	2620
	(1200, 4200)	(1700, 4000)	(1000, 18000)	(400, 12300)
	($n = 370$)	($n = 249$)	($n = 237$)	($n = 293$)
Phase 2	1550	1359	1785	995
	(900, 2900)	(300, 3200)	(570, 5200)	(400, 4400)
	($n = 244$)	($n = 16$)	($n = 68$)	($n = 64$)
Phase 3	1094	482	2358	430
	(500, 2000)	(-,-)	(400, 16400)	(300, 3800)
	($n = 85$)	($n = 1$)	($n = 14$)	($n = 12$)
Phase 4	851	-	922	-
	(500, 1900)		(400, 1500)	
	($n = 18$)		($n = 4$)	
Phase 5	851	-	-	-
	(500, 1400)			
	($n = 6$)			
Total cost of transformations	3880	2500	4790	3660
	(2200, 6800)	(1800, 4000)	(1200, 18800)	(400, 13900)

All costs are adjusted to 1993 values.

There is also remarkable consistency in the pattern of costs per room through successive phases (table 41). In general, the cost per room is highest in phase one (at £820–1800 per room) and then reduces steadily in the later phases. There is no evidence that rooms in later phases are smaller than those in earlier ones (except, oddly enough, in Zimbabwe where open space is most available). Thus, the reduced cost per room is likely to be because those transformers who embark on several phases are more likely to use cheap materials and finishes. Those who build one large extension, on the other hand, are those with high aspirations in terms of room sizes and finishes.

Table 41. Per room cost of phases in the extension process, PPP pounds

Medians (and IQRs)	Bangladesh	Egypt	Ghana	Zimbabwe
Phase 1 rooms	1120	1140	820	670
	(480, 2130)	(750, 1690)	(270, 3260)	(260, 2150)
				1800
				(670, 3240)
Phase 2 rooms	800	830	880	360
	(370, 1440)	(210, 1650)	(260, 2290)	(170, 1020)
				500
				(230, 1270)
Phase 3 rooms	520	140	520	300
	(260, 970)	(-, -)	(130, 4560)	(95, 700)
				360
				(150, 800)
Phase 4 rooms	390	-	590	-
	(91, 850)		(260, 670)	
Total cost of transformations per room	940	1100	750	750
	(540, 1870)	(760, 1650)	(290, 3240)	(250, 2000)
				*1580**
				(760, 3040)

* Total costs for Zimbabwe *without* shacks-only transformers are given in italics.

Finance

We can see from table 42 that there is almost no current involvement of credit from the formal banking system in transformation; almost all finance the building from

Table 42. Main source of finance for transformations (percentages)

	Bangladesh	Egypt	Ghana	Zimbabwe
Own funds	89	22	57	72
Bank credit	2	0	2	7
Own funds + bank credit	0	0	0	1
Borrow from friends/relatives	1	74	29	20
Credit from contractor or materials supplier	0	4	0	0
Borrow from savings scheme	8	0	0	0
Others	0	0	11	0

their own savings or borrow informally from family or friends. The absence of viable mortgage sources for the low-income majority is graphically expressed in these data.

The housing adjustment process through transformation

The housing adjustment literature is clear that the increases in demand for space caused by increases in household size ('shocks') are a major generator of decisions to increase housing consumption. In parallel, the changing needs for space and privacy ('triggers') of a constant household where children are getting older are also influential in creating housing stresses which lead to adjustment (Michelson, 1977; McLeod and Ellis, 1982; Seek, 1983).

In our study countries, moving house is not common; only Zimbabwe has an active housing market in which moving is a common option. In the others, and for many in Zimbabwe who choose not to move, owners must improve (extend) in order to increase their housing consumption. Figure 19 models the housing needs of the household of a couple and their three children in a small dwelling allocated to the couple at the start of their married life.

The original dwelling provides a fixed quantity of housing (Q1) which is slightly in excess of the couple's need for accommodation. When they have their children, their need increases in a lumpy upward gradient as children are added (the verticals) and their growth generates more need (the upward sloping gradients). Soon after the first child is born, the household's need for space increases beyond the quantity delivered by the original dwelling and they begin to feel housing stress. Let us assume that, after the birth of child number two, the couple extend their dwelling to provide sufficient space for their needs and some to spare (Q2). A few years and a third child later, say, 12 to 15 years into their household history, a second extension is made to relieve the stress from the increasing needs for space of the adults and growing children, and once more to provide a little extra (Q3). However, only a few years later, a longer lasting but relatively mild case of stress sets in as the children pass through the teenage phase. This is relieved when the first child marries and/or leaves home and the other children follow in relatively quick succession, much as they had come. The need for space then reduces below supply (Q3), flattens out as the parents are left alone and finally collapses in two stages as first one and then the other dies.

In figure 19, the housing stress is represented by shading; the lighter shade shows the relatively small and short-lived amounts which are relieved by the two stages of transformation activity. If the original government provision had been occupied for the whole of the household's career, there would have been substantially more acute and long-lasting housing stress shown by adding the darker shade to the lighter shading above Q1.

If the second extension had not been possible, the medium shading between lines Q2 and Q3 would be added to the small amount of stress shown by the light shading

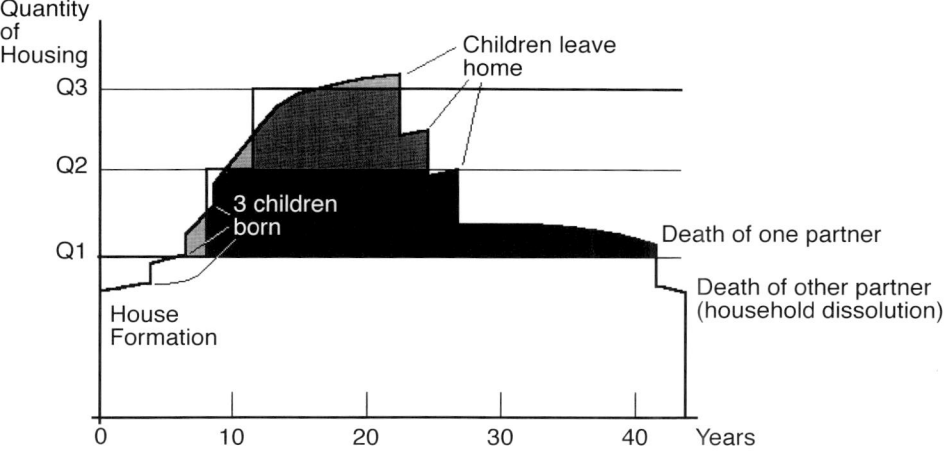

Figure 19. A model of housing consumption over time for a transformer household

between Q2 and Q3. It would remain until the second child leaves.

Once the house is transformed to size Q3, the spare housing space in the later stages of the couple's life together is clearly evident. This provides clear potential for one of the children (especially the younger or later married ones) to stay at home either sharing with the parents or forming a second household by dividing up the house into two dwellings, still within Q3. If this does not occur, the couple have the option to rent out the space instead, providing at least some income as physical strength declines. The elderly couple would have the choice to maintain as much space as they felt appropriate, probably consuming somewhere between Q1 and Q2 to be comfortable, or reverting close to Q1 if the housing stress was compensated for by rental income or by the peace of mind of having the next generation of family close at hand.

Why do occupiers extend?

We tackled data collection on the decision to extend in two ways. First, a straightforward question was asked on what factors were most important, giving a limited range of options (plus 'others [specify]') to choose from (table 43). Second, multivariate analysis was attempted on the range of variables available from the survey to test which had the most influence on the fact of whether the household had transformed recently or not.

Answers found by questioning
If our case study countries were to follow the western pattern, we would expect that 'more people joining the household' and 'children getting older' would be the most important reasons cited in response to our question on factors in the decision to extend.

The choice 'to house the family' would also pick up the obligations to accommodate members of the extended family, albeit not in their own household.

Table 43. Important factors in the decision to extend (percentage as first choice)

	Bangladesh	Egypt	Ghana	Zimbabwe
Housing stress reasons:				
More people joining the household	17	58	38	13
Children getting older	48	2	34	25
To house the family	1	6	9	7
Total housing stress reasons	66	66	81	45
Economic reasons:				
To rent out rooms	32	14	7	42
To have a business	1	1	7	4
To increase the value	1	5	1	4
Total economic reasons	34	20	15	50
Other reasons:				
To have better services	1	2	4	0
For storage	0	0	0	4
Forced to join with neighbours	0	12	0	0
Total other reasons	1	14	4	4

The housing stress reasons are, indeed, predominant for respondents in each country. Only in Zimbabwe did the three reasons relating to this score less than 50 per cent. At the other end of the scale, they constitute 81 per cent in Ghana which would indicate little interest in building for renting and business/investment purposes. In the light of this, it is, perhaps, surprising that so many tenant households are in residence in the extensions. However, the recent literature on renting in Ghana suggests two reasons that many rooms are rented. First, as an (albeit fairly long-term) interim measure until family members want to use them[6] and, second, as a means of generating enough money to keep the rest of the building in good repair (see Korboe, 1993a). The latter is especially important in buildings that have been inherited by family members who hold them in common (Amole *et al.*, 1993).

From our preliminary study (Tipple, 1991a), we guessed that rental income had probably been important in motivating extensions in Bangladesh and Zimbabwe, and in a change of use of the detached kitchen to rented accommodation in Ghana. However, only in Zimbabwe do householders hold these economic reasons to be close to housing stress reasons in importance; 42 per cent there quoted renting as the main motive.

Only in Ghana is what could be called loyalty to the area a major force in the decision to extend rather than to move. Here, 54 per cent either did not consider a move or preferred to stay in the area. Elsewhere, where there are markets of sorts, a majority (60 per cent or more in each case) seem to have at least considered a move and decided against it. In Bangladesh and Egypt (and even in Zimbabwe), therefore, if mobility were easier, transformations may be less important as an adjustment strategy. The lack of area loyalty is very marked in Egypt where only 4 per cent preferred to stay in the area; people are potentially mobile but they cannot fulfil their requirements by moving in the current market. If the hurdles facing potential movers were withdrawn (and the rent control-generated 'key-money' must be the most important of these), then many more households would be likely to eschew extending and move to a different flat.

Answers found through multivariate analysis
A two-step econometric analysis of the decision to transform was carried out on data on transformers and non-transformers. In the first step, we examine the factors which influence the decision to make an extension in the period 1991–3 (the three years before our survey). The second step examines which variables influence how much is spent on the extension. The process and results are described in detail in Appendix 5.

Table 44. Cross-country comparison of variables which appear to affect the decision to transform

Bangladesh	Egypt	Ghana	Zimbabwe
Not included in this stage of the model	Estate	Method of acquisition	Area before extension (-)
	Years in education	House type	Estate
	Rooms before extension	Rooms before extension (-)	Plot area
	Area before extension (-)	Household size	
	Income difference	Income difference	
	Method of acquisition		

Variables related to house characteristics are shaded.

It is chiefly noticeable that house characteristics are important in each of the three countries which could be included at this stage.[7] Area and/or rooms before extension are influential[8] in all three samples. House type, with the related characteristics of space round the house (expressed as estate, plot area, or whether or not there is a plot), is influential in each. The importance of house variables in this analysis suggests that physical planning policies which affect plot size and estate layout could have a major influence over the decision to transform and that, whenever small dwellings are planned, they are likely to be extended.

The variables expressing household characteristics tend to be less influential than house characteristics and less, perhaps, than would have been expected. However, where they do occur, they are the ones we would expect: measures of household expenditure (income difference is positively correlated with extending) and household size. Only in Ghana has the latter any significant influence on the decision to extend.

House characteristics are influential in deciding the cost (scale) of transformations (table 45). Rooms or area before extension are significant and positively correlated in each country except Bangladesh where space is so cramped that the variable 'more rooms' is heavily linked to there being less space available. Rising floors in Egypt, and the freedom to build shacks in Zimbabwe, reduce spending.

Table 45. Cross-country comparison of variables which appear to affect the cost of transformation 1990–1993

Bangladesh	Egypt	Ghana	Zimbabwe
Rooms before extension (-)	Rooms before extension	Area before extension	Female head of household
Total household expenditure	Years in education (-)	House type	Shack (-)
Method of acquisition	Male head of household	Method of acquisition	Length of stay in house (-)
	Floor (-)		Rooms before extension
	House type		

Variables related to house characteristics are shaded.

Household variables such as total household expenditure, education, sex of head (in varying directions) and length of stay in the house are influential in some samples and more than in the decision to extend. In addition, housing tenure (method of acquisition) is influential in two case studies.

The importance of house characteristics in both of these analyses demonstrates that inadequate housing provision is a major generator of extensions. Even where the external spaces make extensions difficult, they still occur if the residents need them.

Problems encountered

The problems which would-be transformers encounter in the construction process should point up areas in which intervention might improve the delivery of housing in this manner. The factors which inhibit transformations are, superficially, fairly obvious and some have been indicated in the last section. In the formal questionnaire, we asked about five of the six inputs to housing supply identified in the literature (e.g. Malpezzi, 1990),[9] and which are usually amenable to government policy interventions. We also included 'avoiding the local authority' to explore the scale of disadvantage arising from being unauthorised (table 46).

Table 46. The most difficult problems encountered in the extension process (percentages)

The most difficult problem	Bangladesh	Egypt	Ghana	Zimbabwe
Finance	73	59	87	46
Building materials	0	0	3	17
Labour	0	7	7	2
Services	4	2	0	0
Permissions	0	-	-	11
Avoiding local authority	0	-	-	23
More than one main problem	0	7	-	-
Others	23	25	2	-

Transformers claim that finance is the number one problem facing them, although its importance varies from country to country, and in Zimbabwe only receives 46 per cent of the vote. No other problem even approaches it in importance. But then, as the cynical might say, 'they would say that, wouldn't they.' We could point out that finance cannot have been too severe a problem or such large amounts of money would not have been spent so readily by the transformers. However, the combination of the predominance given to finance here, and the low rate of borrowing (even in the informal sector) found among transformers (table 42) demonstrates that official policy is not assisting the financing of these extensions.

It is obvious that transformers can obtain building materials, construction labour and service connections (if they want them) relatively easily. Most have no problem with permissions: either they are granted or they are irrelevant. The only major source of problems among those listed, other than finance, is the avoidance of the local authority by the Zimbabwean shacks-only transformers (one-quarter of the Zimbabwe sample).

Summary

We have seen that the majority of transformers engage small contractors or artisans to construct their extensions, thus it tends to be a labour-intensive, locally based process. More than expected have had planning permission and, even where they have not, very little action has been taken against them, except in Zimbabwe. While most transformers have only extended once so far, some have built many phases in an incremental process, potentially increasing the accommodation in an estate over many years. The first phases tend to cost around £2–3000 while later ones tend to be smaller and cheaper. But, overall, rooms tend to cost about £1000 each. They are built using savings and family resources, even though this saving and building process may take years. Only in Egypt was credit readily available, but from the contractor not the banks! The transformations allow step-by-step improvement of housing space to relieve stress. They are likely to occur wherever people need more space whether or not the layout of the estate allows for it or hampers it.

Notes

1   As part of this research project, draft codes of practice have been developed to help intending transformers to avoid such unhelpful practices.
2   Alternatively, it may be similar to the propensity for better-off households to be involved in DIY maintenance in UK housing (Littlewood and Munro, 1996: 1093). The reasons cited there include the relative poverty of older owners who may be unable to do heavy work and the barrier represented by the cost of the necessary tools or equipment.
3   Advocates of labour intensive construction and building materials industries (including me) must be aware of the unresolved tension between the need to work for however paltry a living and the sheer inhumanity of some jobs. The women brick crushers of Bangladesh must rank among the borderline cases where oppression and the joy of having a job intersect.
4   Indeed, we used these records to make a first identification of our sample.
5   There is some evidence that the earliest extensions were quite small (see the first photograph in figure 45) and have been demolished to make way for a larger extension. Thus, we may assume that our data represent the first phase which is still extant – even though it may be phase 1, mark 2.
6   The rent legislation in Ghana allows tenants to be evicted to make way for family members.
7   As there are almost no non-transformers there, we cannot model this for Bangladesh.
8   Though in varying directions; see Egypt case study for an explanation.
9   Land acquisition is not an issue for transformers so is left out.

7. The case for transformations

Widespread practice of transformation

Just as the sheer ubiquity and scale of squatting in the 1960s led writers and officials to argue that something had to be done to allow, regularise and improve such development, we can argue that one part of the case for transformation is its widespread popularity among residents. It is so popular that it may be reasonable to ask whether transformation is a universal phenomenon wherever it is allowed either actively or passively. Our experience is that it certainly seems to be very widespread throughout the developing world. In addition to our study countries, I have seen it in Nigeria, South Africa, Zambia, Kenya, Ethiopia, Guinea, Venezuela, Bahrain, India, Malaysia, Indonesia and the Philippines. Published studies included in the annotated bibliography to our literature review of transformations (Tipple, 1991a) and completed more recently show its occurrence in Algeria (Bouchair, 1984; Kraria, 1989; Angal, 1991), Chile (Arditi *et al.*, 1990; Kellett and Toro, 1990; Sepulveda and Carrasco, 1990), Colombia (Peinado, 1980), Hong Kong (Wojtowicz, 1984), India (Benjamin, 1985; Greger and Steinberg, 1988; Sarkar, 1988; Dasgupta, 1990), Israel (Carmon and Oxman, 1981, 1984a, 1984b, 1986; Carmon and Gavrieli, 1987; Oxman and Carmon 1989), Libya (El Fortea, 1989), Peru (Fromm, 1985), and South Africa (Beinart, 1971, Andrew and Japha, 1978). Other studies have described it in our study countries – Ameen (1988) in Bangladesh; Aref (1989); Behloul (1991, 1996); Habraken (1980b), Kardash (1990); Kardash and Wilkinson (1991); Sakr (1983), Salama (1997); Steinberg (1984), Tipple *et al.* (1985, 1986), Wilkinson and Tipple (1987, 1991) in Egypt; and Blankson (1988), Building and Road Research Institute (1970), and Danby (1989) in Ghana.

Some recent unpublished work by Joyce Malombe at HABRI, Nairobi, shows it occurring in some owner-occupier estates in Nairobi though it is markedly absent from rented estates. There is also a body of work arising from our study which has used similar questionnaires and sampling techniques to maintain some comparability. A study in Malaysia, by Azizah Salim, and one in New Delhi, by Alok Dasgupta, are briefly reviewed here to draw out some preliminary findings or observations. We also review some Israeli experience of positive policy towards transformations.

Transformations in Malaysia
In doctoral work carried out in CARDO after the main four-country study, Azizah Salim has surveyed three settlements outside but close to Kuala Lumpur in 1994

(Salim, 1998). Her study areas consist of three estates:

- Kampung Sungai Ara, an estate of 131 two-storey terraced dwellings built in prefabricated concrete panels in 1985–7;
- Kampung Batu 30 Ulu Yam, an estate of 197 single-storey terraced dwellings constructed with reinforced concrete frames with brick infill, in three phases in 1969, the late 1970s, and 1991;
- Kampung Sri Serendah, an estate of 412 detached dwellings, constructed in the traditional manner on wooden stilts almost 2 m high, with timber construction for the main rooms and a ground-level cement-block kitchen at the rear. In contrast with the other estates, these have spacious plots.

The recipients of government-built low-cost housing in Malaysia are meant to have a gross income no higher than RM9000 (PPP£5900) per annum. The median household income of the transformers in the sample is PPP£9000, making them twice as well off as our highest income sample (in Bangladesh) and 53 per cent richer than the target maximum. Their households are similar in size to our samples (six for transformers and five for non-transformers – the latter having one fewer adult), so per capita incomes are reasonably buoyant (PPP£1600), almost three times as high as our samples. Non-transformers in Malaysia have marginally lower household incomes and higher per capita incomes than transformers.

All the Malaysian transformers are living as single households in the dwellings. While all have a median of about 50 m² from the original dwelling, transformers add about 30 m², about the same amount as is added in Zimbabwe. The largest extensions tend to be in Sri Serendah (33 m² at the median) where the plots are spacious. However, even in very constricted plots in the terraced estates, 15 m² are added at the median. Transformers have about 14 m² habitable space per person at the median, while non-transformers have only 10 m². These are more than twice the space available to our sample in Zimbabwe, and considerably greater even than our most generously accommodated sample in Egypt.

The number of rooms enjoyed by the households in Malaysia is also much larger than our samples. Transformers tend to have six rooms and maintain the one person per room occupancy rate enjoyed by non-transformers. Thus, extensions are keeping up with additions to the household but the sample cannot be generally held to be suffering overcrowding.

In some estates they are using the plots very intensively. In the Sungai Ara estate (two-storey terraced dwellings), the floor-space index is now 80 per cent, and in Batu 30 Ulu Yam (single-storey terraced dwellings), the floor-space index is 58 per cent. However, in Sri Serendah, there is plenty of spare room on the plots and the overall current floor-space index for transformers in the Malaysia sample is only 50 per cent.

The value of the dwellings as built is considerably greater than their subsidised price. All the dwellings were sold for RM25,000 (PPP£16,500) which is a standard price set for low-income housing provided by the government. However, the Malaysian sample valued their non-transformed dwellings at RM40,000 (PPP£26,300) and their transformed dwellings at RM60,000 (PPP£39,500). The cost of rebuilding was quoted at half these values, based on experience of having new rooms built. This demonstrates that, through not having to buy extra land and the buoyant state of the market (should they wish to sell), extension activity yields a very high return on money invested. The additional investment in housing goods achieved through the current transformations in the three estates is 58 per cent of the purchase price of the dwellings.

Householders are about 40 when they begin to transform and only carry out one or two phases, at least to date. The extensions concentrate on providing more habitable space and particularly on extending the small kitchens in Sungai Ara and Batu 30 Ulu Yam into larger rooms which can fulfil the traditional requirements of a local kitchen, i.e., cooking, eating, socialising (for women), sleeping (for infants), etc. In addition, a car port is usually a priority to protect cars and/or motor cycles from the intense sunlight and provide a covered play area for the small children.

Unlike all our samples, the Malaysian transformers extend the dwellings almost as soon as they move in. They appear to be capturing the benefit available from increasing the value and utility of their subsidised dwellings as soon as possible and converting inadequate and poorly designed dwellings into ones which better suit the local lifestyle.[1] Thus, transformations may be symptomatic of a middle-income group 'raiding' housing provided for a low-income group and immediately uplifting its standard and value to suit their requirements. They are limited in this by the very tight plots in Sungai Ara and Batu 30 Ulu Yam, but in Sri Serendah the more spacious layout allows them full rein to create really large dwellings.

Salim has found that, on the spacious plots in Sri Serendah, spending on transformations increases steadily with income. In the more constricted estates of Sungai Ara and Batu 30 Ulu Yam, spending does not rise as far or as steadily against income. This is fairly conclusive evidence that lack of space inhibits investment in housing in Malaysia; where space is available, householders can build the ambitious and expensive extensions to which they aspire (Salim, 1998).

The Malaysian case reflects some aspects of Littlewood and Munro's (1997) move-and-improve strategy. They worked in the context of Scotland and included all improvements whether or not they resulted in more space. They argue that households do not irrationally move into a house which does not fit their requirements. The households are:

> … aware of the equilibrium housing they will need in the longer term, but do not intend to reach this at the time of moving. Instead, they can choose an option embodying a relatively lower amount of housing services but intend to increase the amount through time in investing in improvements. (Littlewood and Munro, 1997)

Recent movers (in the last year) in Scotland appear less content with their current house than longer term residents. This is not because they have moved into the 'wrong'

Figure 20. A typical kitchen extension in Salim's sample in Malaysia

house but that they are in this process of progressing to a longer term equilibrium (satisfaction) point, only part of which was the move. They may have moved into their preferred neighbourhood and will then modify the house to suit their needs.

The Malaysian experience differs from Littlewood and Munro's findings in featuring new property. In the Scottish study (Littlewood and Munro, 1997), movers into older property are more likely to improve than movers into new housing. This is understandable in a context in which all improvements and renovations are included and might be expected to be different from Malaysia where the criterion for improvement was extensions to built area.

Transformations in India

A second doctoral research project is under way at CARDO to examine the characteristics of transformations in New Delhi. Following on from his earlier work (Dasgupta, 1987, 1990), Alok Dasgupta is surveying households in three housing projects in South Delhi but results are not yet available. Two of the projects are refugee housing from the 1950s built as two-storey blocks of flats ranged round courtyards in a 'doughnut' configuration. The third is a newer four-storeyed project with dwellings intended for several low-income and very low-income groups but occupied mainly by middle-income households.

In the very constricted doughnut blocks, flats have been extended outwards and into the courtyards until they are four to six rooms deep. Upward extensions have been added so that the blocks now have four or five storeys. The original buildings are all but hidden in a mass of development but they are obviously in fairly poor condition and would have required major refurbishment had the extensions not led to piecemeal and rather anarchic physical renewal.

In the newer blocks, the residents are not confident about their status as extenders and have taken steps to camouflage their handiwork. The new rooms are finished with the same stucco work, painted to match the original. Details of balcony balustrades, windows, and other features, are slavishly copied in the new work. The result is that it takes an expert on what the original buildings looked like to tell whether they have been extended and where. These precautions are probably wise as forced demolitions of extensions have taken place in Delhi.

There are obvious problems in the very narrow sites in that the original rooms become internalised with neither ventilation nor daylighting. Inevitably, the new rooms become the most commonly used for daily activities but the internal ones may be used for sleeping, doing homework and many other functions. In the very hot dry climate of Delhi many residents find that an electric fan and a 60 watt bulb are all that are required to provide comfort and sufficient lighting. As the rooms are not the only living area, they can be abandoned temporarily at times of real discomfort.

No empirical evidence is available from the Delhi study at the time of going to press but figure 21 gives us an impression of the energy and innovation of transformations there.

Enabling transformations: the Israeli experience[2]

Israel is the only country I know to have actively encouraged transformations. Project Renewal in Israel is a multi-sectoral programme focusing on low-quality neighbourhoods, most of which consist of government-built flats erected in the 1950s and 1960s for migrants flocking to Israel after its independence, many from the less developed countries of North Africa and Asia. Its aims are to reduce social disparities, to improve the image of project neighbourhoods and to prevent further neighbourhood deterioration (Carmon and Hill, 1988). The project started in earnest in 1979 and gradually expanded to include 90 neighbourhoods housing 600,000 people (15 per cent of Israeli citizens) (Carmon, 1992). Though the backing of overseas Jewry[3] focused the project exclusively on Jewish neighbourhoods, Arab areas within Israel were included later.

Project Renewal consisted of employment, education and welfare programmes as well the renewal of physical infrastructure and housing renovations; indeed the former programmes took about half the budget which amounted to US$600 per household per annum up to 1985 (Carmon and Hill, 1988). The neighbourhoods chosen were regarded as the ones with the most serious problems of ageing populations, poor education achievement, unemployment and poor housing conditions. Within the neighbourhoods, everyone was equally eligible for assistance, thus the targeting was by residential area rather than by any household criteria. The dwellings are mainly

Figure 21. Extensions to two storey 'doughnut' blocks in Dasgupta's sample in Kalkaji, New Delhi
The original block has almost completely disappeared under layers of extensions outwards and upwards.

flats in two-, three- and four-storey blocks but there are some of eight. Almost half had 55 m² floor area or less while new apartments were being built in the late 1970s averaging 120 m² (Carmon and Hill, 1988). Thus the occupants could justifiably feel deprived, especially as large households were common. At first, the intention was to carry out 'enveloping'[4] to improve the appearance and durability of the buildings. However, a scheme for encouraging the extensions which were already making an appearance was adopted and it is on this that we will focus.

At the beginning of the project, about half the apartments had already been purchased by sitting tenants. In line with Israel's welfare approach, the prices were highly discounted (to 40–60 per cent of value) and the loans for buying the flats were very generous (up to 90 per cent of the cost of the flat) payable over 30 years at a very low rate of interest.[5] The flat was transferred in this way from the public holding and management companies such as Amidar and Amigoor to the occupant. However, the land remained in public ownership with a 49 or 99 year lease to the occupier. The project had an element to persuade more households to buy, which entailed reducing the real cost to 10–20 per cent of market value (in 1982) and providing even more generous loans. Its success was limited, however, as there is probably a ceiling to those wishing to be owners, especially as renters had very secure tenancies and paid very low rents (or none if on welfare). In 1987, the Project Renewal neighbourhoods' flats were 60 per cent owner-occupied compared with 70 per cent in Israel as a whole (Carmon, 1992).

The subsidised loans required households to pay US$25–50 per month at a time when their household incomes were about US$500. The process resulted in a mixture of owners and tenants in each block and considerable numbers of owners in even the poorest estates.

As the renovation programme began to show results, several households added quite large extensions to their flats without public support. Some project managers and academics – particularly the team from Technion, Haifa (see Carmon and Oxman, 1981) – recognised the potential of this process for renovating the estates and lobbied the Ministry of Housing to allow and encourage it. The project, therefore, took on new elements: small loans for interior functional changes or replacement of damaged sewage and water pipes, and larger loans for extensions. The loans for extensions changed irregularly to keep pace with the rampant inflation at the time; for example, their dollar value varied from US$4000 to almost US$13,000 (US$140 to US$360 per m²) between 1980 and 1984 (Lerman *et al.*, 1985). The average size of loan between 1979 and 1983 was US$6000 and the households added an average of US$5000 (Carmon, 1992).

Both the improvement loans were intended for self-help programmes in that the occupier instigated, planned, supervised and sometimes carried out the work. The threshold of dwelling size at which occupants were ineligible for a subsidised loan was raised in this programme to 114 m² (larger for households of eight or more) (Carmon, 1992). However, only 40 to 80 per cent of the cost of the enlargement could be financed from a public loan: the rest had to be raised privately, usually from employers, savings or less favourable loans.

There were no qualifications for the loans other than ownership of a flat in the Project Renewal neighbourhoods. Small households could build large enlargements if they wished, as could elderly occupants. In the two-storey buildings where the enlargements started, households were doubling their space on average to about 90 m² (Carmon and Gavrieli, 1987). In 1983, a start was made on three- and four-storey walk-up flats but these require much more complex social organisation and technical competence. The mean size of extensions also tends to be smaller in the taller blocks (60 per cent) than those with two storeys (Lerman *et al.*, 1985). In the early 1980s, the mean area of original flats in the study by Lerman *et al.* (1985) of three neighbourhoods was 55 m² and the mean extended area was 102 m². At the same time, mean area per occupant had risen from 16.9 m² to 25.5 m².[6]

The Project Renewal's local officers proved invaluable in regulating the process and sometimes being the instigator, persuader of the fainter-hearted, and general cheer-leader.[7] They also arranged for Project Renewal to finance the extensions of tenants whose flats were sandwiched between owners involved in an enlargement scheme. In the 1982–7 period, 17,000 enlargements were carried out through the project (in 15 per cent of the flats) (Carmon, 1992), and the figure must be much higher now.

Lerman *et al.* (1985) explain that it is difficult to define the cost of extensions per square metre as it may be impossible to separate the costs of improvements such as new kitchens from the extension itself. They estimate two costs per square metre: US$350 as an overall average and US$250 as one just including the extension itself. In the case of the former cost, the owner would have to find about 20 per cent of the money for a 25 m² extension in 1983 and about 50 per cent in 1984. If US$350 were the true cost, however, (s)he would have to find about 30 per cent in 1983 and about 60 per cent in 1984.

There is a fine line between persuading the faint-hearted to join in something which they feel is to their benefit, even if they cannot imagine actually succeeding, and bullying reluctant people to join a scheme which may be in others' best interests rather than their own. An example of the latter has taken place in an estate in Jerusalem where the Project Renewal staff decided to extend blocks as a whole to a very high standard of exterior appearance. From a student project in Technion, it appears that the occupants had no option but to join in and several households were visited and told that they were the last objectors. On completion of the exterior work, many occupants cannot afford to use the new space properly as they cannot finish it off with floor surfaces, etc. There is much dissatisfaction even though the block looks magnif-icent. This is not just because many occupants have the problem of paying back their loan. It is also because they have used up their once-for-all chance of a government housing loan.

Given that there is danger in it, the use of a project manager to persuade, cajole, enable and encourage, coupled with the availability of loans, appears to offer real

Figure 22. A transformed block in Neve David, Haifa, Israel (rear elevation)
The government's enveloping scheme (top right) is augmented by user-initiated extensions
designed, financed and built through Project Renewal. Isak Kadosh, the Project Co-ordinator
for Neve David, can be seen near the building.

benefits in terms of efficiency and appearance, to remove much of the sting in the 'building slums' argument (figure 22 shows a block extended in this controlled way).

The extensions in Neve David are remarkable for their quality and general conformity in design. As many of them have been done as part of a 'renovate and improve' package, they have incorporated the detailing and finishing in general use in the building. Thus, where walls are painted (say) white with pink string courses, so the extensions follow suit. Great care has been taken to minimise the visual intrusion of extensions; joints between original and extension are carefully detailed, fenestration and other design details are maintained in the extensions. The plans of flats in extension stacks conform with each other vertically, and neighbouring stacks are similar in massing and detailing. In fact, in many cases, if an observer did not know the original buildings well, (s)he might be unable to tell whether they had been extended. In addition, landscaping has been added between blocks to increase their identity and the occupants' ability to feel new pride in their once low-status address.

Where occupants have chosen not to take part in an extension, the framework which passes outside their flats has been carefully finished and fitted with a parapet wall to resemble a completed balcony rather than being left as an obvious gap in the Egyptian fashion. Where individuals have chosen to extend alone and outside a renovate-plus-extend project instigated by the project manager, they have been advised on designs, detailing and finishes.

Israeli transformations as leaven in the lump
In assessing the success of the enlargement programme in Project Renewal, Carmon (1992) examines its impact on the potential for further housing improvement. She feels that the main change in improvement potential involves the taller buildings; when successful extensions appeared on these buildings, the main Israeli housing type became liable for transformation. These flats are usually well spaced out with plenty of land ripe for extensions and it is clear that all income groups have begun to exploit the potential for expanding these blocks in all directions. It is now quite common for residents of middle- and upper-income blocks to cooperate and employ professionals to design a complete transformation and enlargement of their flats. Values can rise by double the cost of the extension (though most would claim to have done the transformation to benefit from the use value). In addition, the changes improve the social status of the building and higher status people are likely to move in when flats change hands.

Despite the long time taken in the negotiations amongst residents and for obtaining licences, the occupants persevere in a high level of collaboration. They hire professionals for design and a single contractor to do all the extensions as one job. There are several striking examples where only the column and slab structure remains of the original and the new exterior (several metres further out) features postmodernist architectural detailing (Technion, Haifa: architecture student seminar presentations).

In order to accommodate the extension activity, and in contrast with the internationally common 'building slums' attitude of local authority officials, Project Renewal enlargements have inspired local authorities in Israel to modify their building and planning regulations to enable transformations. In Givat Olga in Hadera, the site of much of Carmon's earliest work (Carmon and Oxman, 1981), local regulations were reinterpreted to allow more built space on each plot. In Jerusalem, Akko and Hetzliya, the committee procedures were streamlined for enlargements in Project Renewal neighbourhoods through using special committees, increasing meeting frequencies, or dealing with the applications together (Carmon, 1992).

There is also a positive impact from the goodwill shown by local authorities in the potential for extensions and the willingness of householders to carry them out. If householders feel secure and approved of in what they do, they will maximise their efforts in comparison with those in our study who may have been harassed and may detect disapproval from the authorities. Also, government investment in infrastructure seems to increase the impetus to extend. Examination of aerial photographs by Mayer and Enis (1981) has demonstrated that most extensions occur within five years of the paving of the road.

A second analysis of project effectiveness has been attempted by Lerman (1988) who found that the value for money obtained by extenders varies depending on location. He demonstrates relatively inconclusive findings. Because the housing supply in Israel is very lumpy, and there are large numbers of flats of 55 m² or less (at least a quarter of the stock) and very few of, say, 90 m², the conversion of a smaller flat to a larger would gain a premium over the cost of the addition.[8] Thus, transformers in estates whose locational value is high, i.e. those close to the large city centres, are likely to find their extensions better value for money than those in less advantaged areas. However, he concedes that, in some of the estates, values are so low that the cost of the extension will be higher than the added value. Furthermore, because it is difficult to separate improvement costs from extension costs, the calculation of value for money is more complex than it would at first appear. There is some anecdotal evidence of two new trends:

- that extenders have found that they can sell off their enlarged flat and move into a better neighbourhood, so beginning to undermine the policy of trying to keep young, upwardly mobile households in the areas;
- that young couples buy unaltered flats with the intention to extend. This coincides with Seek's (1983), Kendig's (1981) and Littlewood and Munro's (1997) findings of a move-and-improve strategy and may make up for the loss of the ambitious households above.

Enablement and the balance of advantage

The key concept of the Global Strategy for Shelter is that of enabling, of governments' stepping back from housing production and measures to control the price of outputs and, instead, working to enable the current and potential suppliers of housing to do what they do best. Transformers are undoubtedly housing suppliers and governments should contemplate whether they could or should enable transformations. We have seen how the Israeli government enabled transformations and are sure that it is possible in other places and circumstances.

The first stage in enabling is to discover what drives and what hinders the current process. Thus, we have analysed the reasons why households in our samples become transformers and the problems they claim to have had on the way. We then consider what policy interventions might be suitable to enable transformations with respect to physical planning policy and regulations, finance, and promotion of the construction industry.

We have shown how transformations undoubtedly increase the supply of housing. In the current housing shortages which beset so many developing countries, we could say that this is reason enough to encourage them. We would argue that, if anyone is supplying housing, it is beholden on us to assist them. However, for others involved in the housing process, the argument that they are 'building slums' hangs like a Sword of Damocles over any suggestion of allowing a free-for-all, such as a transformed neighbourhood appears to represent. Thus the questions remain, 'Should transformations be encouraged?' 'Have we more to gain from this than from attempting to prevent them?' 'Should we relax controls to allow such development in any government-built estate?' 'Should we help these maverick developers to take advantage of their location to build more housing than was planned or should we nip such activity in the bud and preserve the estates as built?' Table 47 attempts briefly to summarise the advantages and disadvantages of encouraging or enabling transformations. It is compiled from the data in this study but acknowledges that not all neighbourhoods are represented by our sample. Thus, though we have shown that physical conditions seem to be improving in our areas, there is no guarantee that this will be the case elsewhere. Therefore, we admit that there is unpredictability where control is relaxed and this is a valid argument for those opposing transformations.

It would be foolish to argue that table 47 shows an unequivocal case in favour of transformation activity. This is the paradox with which we must wrestle if we are to garner the positive potentials while avoiding the negative effects of *laissez-faire* policies.

On the one hand, transformation supplies housing through people who would not be expected to supply it (relatively low-income consumers of government-built housing) on already built up and (usually) serviced land. The new housing is generally of at least as high a standard as the existing housing in the neighbourhood. Very high plot coverage is only evident where plots are small. Transformation allows households to adjust their housing at their own pace and in their cost limits, and allows residents to express themselves through their built environment. It provides housing much more cheaply than new-build projects. Standards of finish are generally higher than existing structures.

On the other hand, housing provided by transformers is usually uncontrolled, may be unplanned, and is unpredictable in its consequences for the physical and

Table 47. The balance of advantages of transformations

Transformations as neighbourhood improvement	'There goes the neighbourhood!': transformations as 'creating slums'
Transformation supplies housing through people who would not be expected to supply it (not particularly well-off consumers of government-built housing) on already built-up and (usually) serviced land.	Housing provided by transformers is usually uncontrolled, may be unplanned, and is unpredictable in its consequences for the physical and demographic conditions in the neighbourhood.
Transformation renews low-quality housing at no cost to the government. The new housing is generally of at least as high a standard as the existing housing in the neighbourhood. Very high plot coverage is only evident where plots are small.	There are some localised problems of very high floor-space index and plot coverage creating environmental problems.
There are lower occupancy rates for the main households. Occupancy rates for subsequent households are not much higher than main households. The new population is more varied and so gives a wider age and income spread for the demand for neighbourhood facilities (shops, etc.) and public services (schools, etc.).	Transformation encourages increases in population leading to higher demand for utilities and public services. Service lines are likely to be compromised by the narrower and less regular spaces between buildings and encroachment onto road reserves and access lanes.
Transformations increase fixed capital stock. Transformations allow households to adjust their housing at their own pace and in their cost limits. This allows residents to express themselves through their built environment. Standards of finish are generally higher than that of existing structures. They can create new supply at the bottom of the market for renting or rent-free occupation much more cheaply than new-build projects.	Transformations look chaotic rather than disciplined, they do not follow current government-favoured designs, they change the look of the neighbourhood from that which was planned. Some of the new rooms are small and built to minimal standards of space and utility. They generate some rooms which do not conform to building regulations minima for dimensions, lighting, ventilation, etc.
Transformation allows economic activity in the houses (home-based enterprises) including renting rooms (passive), retailing and production (active). No evidence of devaluation of surrounding and non-transformed properties was found.	Non-conforming uses may create negative externalities (nuisance, traffic, danger) which can reduce the enjoyment of the residential area and lower market values.

demographic conditions in the neighbourhood. There are some problems of inade-
quately ventilated, small rooms, very high floor-space index and plot coverage creating
environmental problems. Transformations look chaotic rather than disciplined, they
do not follow current government-favoured designs, they 'spoil' the look of the neighbourhood.

On the positive side, there are lower occupancy rates for the main households. Even
occupancy rates for subsequent households are not much higher than main households. The new population is more varied and so gives better age and income balance
for the demand for neighbourhood facilities (shops, etc.) and public services (schools,
etc.). Transformation allows economic activity in the houses (home-based enterprises)
including renting rooms, retailing and production. No evidence of devaluation of
surrounding and non-transformed properties was found.

On the negative side, transformation encourages increases in population leading to
higher demand for utilities and public services. Service lines are likely to be compro-
mised by the narrower and less regular spaces between buildings and encroachment
onto road reserves and access lanes. Non-conforming (commercial and industrial) uses
can create negative externalities (nuisance, traffic, danger) which may reduce the
enjoyment of the residential area and lower market values. We have no evidence of
this in our samples but it could happen elsewhere.

The most important feature of transformations, however, is that they provide large
amounts of new housing goods and in ways which are unlikely to occur on new sites
or through wholesale renewal of the obsolete estates. We would contend that we have
established that transformations are not of low enough quality to be regarded as unacceptable housing by and for the people who provided it or their tenants and family
members. This is the crux of the issue.

On balance, we can find little support for the 'building slums' or 'there goes the
neighbourhood' arguments and more support for the assertion that transformation is
acting as an agent for upgrading. It is our belief from the evidence of this comparative study that the balance of advantage lies with allowing transformations rather with
preventing them and that the advantages would increase by enabling transformations
rather than merely tolerating them.

Transformations in the context of sustainable development, the Global Strategy for Shelter and the Global Plan of Action

It is obvious that transformations can contribute to the urban environment in several
ways that are congruent with the aims of sustainable development, the Global Strategy
for Shelter and the decisions of the Habitat II Conference, particularly the Global Plan
of Action (UNCHS, 1996b).

In transformations, housing consumers become producers of housing

The Global Shelter Strategy advises governments to involve all actors available in the production of housing and to move decision-making down to the lowest appropriate level (subsidiarity). In addition, the Global Plan of Action calls for encouraging individuals, families and communities to 'play a proactive role in identifying local needs and priorities and formulating new policies, plans and projects' (UNCHS, 1996b: para. 182). These issues are both addressed in transformations, but in unexpected quarters. The actors expected to be involved include different levels of government, non-governmental organisations, employers, the construction industry, community groups and individuals in need of housing.

In transformations, however, the decision-making on housing production is taking place at household level, a much lower level than conventional subsidiarity assumes. The involvement of households in housing supply through transformations is, of course, directly in line with the Global Plan of Action.

In the past, housing policies have not been sufficiently supply oriented to provide shelter for all. Control has been more important than promotion of supply; orderly development according to arbitrary norms has been more desirable than efficient construction of more housing.

In transformations, individuals who are not officially counted among those in need of housing, and who are expected to be merely passive consumers of housing, are involved in the process of supplying housing. They are constructing housing on already developed plots. This is entirely unexpected in policy and is usually ignored in the way that squatters tended to be ignored in the early 1970s. However, we argue that it is neither efficient nor advisable in policy terms to ignore the contribution of extensions to the housing stock, nor is it reasonable to dismiss the efforts of transformers as invalid and to be discouraged. We have found that they have added between 60 and 150 per cent more accommodation onto their houses to date and are likely to add more in the future. An enabling approach to housing cannot afford to eschew the contribution of transformers and has much to gain from improving the conditions under which they make their extensions.

Transformations make efficient use of existing finite resources, particularly serviced land, infrastructure and construction materials

The Habitat Agenda arising from the Istanbul Conference commits countries to:

> ... promoting the redevelopment and reuse of already serviced but poorly utilised commercial and residential land in urban centres in order to revitalise them and reduce development pressures on productive agricultural lands on the periphery. (UNCHS, 1996a: para 43)

In addition, it contains a commitment to:

> [the] promoting of upgrading of existing housing stock through rehabilitation

and maintenance and the adequate supply of basic services, facilities and amenities. (UNCHS, 1996a: para 40)

Particularly in areas developed by the colonial governments (or in the style inherited from them), government-built housing areas are often the least densely developed residential neighbourhoods within the established urban area. Their peripheral location more than 20 years ago is now relatively central and, therefore, valuable. Through transformations, we have seen that the density of development on these prime sites is being upgraded to be more appropriate to their central locations. The land is more efficiently used. As a corollary, as there can be more people living on such centrally located land than before, fewer would require to use new urban land which would have to be carved out of economically and ecologically valuable agricultural land or forests. This is very important in Egypt where only 4 per cent of the surface is fertile and most cities are located on that land. In Kumasi, urban growth continually encroaches into highly productive agricultural land, especially cocoa farms and market gardening areas. In addition, as villages lose their farming land, the local people lose their only means of survival and must commute to the city for employment instead. In addition, the reduction in demand for peripheral land should reduce the number of poor households who have to occupy land which is subject to flooding, landslides, mudslips or the many other disasters which strike those most vulnerable areas. This is especially important in Dhaka where so much peripheral land is below annual flood level.

The intensification of use of currently serviced land also has major effects on infrastructure provision. Where serviced land is more intensively used, the existing investment in infrastructure can be economically utilised. In addition, the extension of utility lines into yet more remote areas is delayed as peripheral development slows down. This has important transport spin-offs, also. Housing more people close to the city centre reduces the commuter load. Not only does this reduce total mileages for public and private transport, it is also likely to reduce the scale of the peak flows and the difference between peak and off-peak flows. In Harare, the 'high density' residential areas are generally close to the belt of industry which stretches to the west of the city centre and to the arterial roads with good transport links to the central business district. The main alternative areas for low-income accommodation are in peripheral squatter settlements and Chitungwiza, miles to the south of the city. For every room added to the housing stock in Mbare and Highfield, there could be one commuter fewer on the long distance routes. Of course, intensification of service use only makes more efficient use of investment up to its capacity; beyond that problems begin to arise. This is one reason why proscriptive norms may be necessary at the upper margin of intensity of use.

There is a need for infrastructure surveys in areas where transfomations are taking place or might be expected. We need to know how much load the current infrastructure can cope with so that adequate response can be made to increasing demand (Tipple, 1991b). This may require periodic improvements in infrastructure at public expense.

Current housing is providing a flow of goods (shelter facilities) without the use of additional materials. If the old housing is demolished, the materials will cease to provide those housing goods and new ones must be utilised. In so far as transformations allow currently existing houses to remain standing, they make a contribution to sustainable development in making the best use of existing resources. It is clear from our analysis that much of the original housing stock under study is nearing the end of its economic life in the absence of transformation. As, through transformation, this economic life is extended, new building materials resources will not be consumed in replacing the originals.[9]

Transformations improve the social, economic and environmental quality of the living and working environment

There is a growing recognition that quality of life is an important issue in urban policy. The Global Plan of Action refers to 'liveability' as 'those spatial, social and environmental characteristics and qualities that uniquely contribute to people's sense of personal and collective well-being and to their sense of satisfaction in being residents of that particular settlement' (UNCHS, 1996b: para. 135). It also recognises that 'civic engagement' (in the sense of an active engagement in society) is of importance in achieving sustainable human settlements (UNCHS, 1996b: para. 181). Both 'liveability' and 'civic engagement' are regarded as things to be promoted by urban policy.

It has long been accepted that the involvement of residents in the process of neighbourhood development engenders a sense of belonging and care for the environment, elements of which are 'liveability' and 'civic engagement'. Transformations have the potential to involve local people in environmental improvements at an intensity which is difficult to conceptualise through any other means except total self-help. Transformers are engaged at the interface at which the environment can be either improved or damaged. Their activities affect 'liveability' and are likely to improve the level of 'civic engagement'.

We have argued that residents of housing gain status, identity and self-worth from the activity of altering their living environment and the products of their endeavours. Though we collected no data on this, it is likely that our transformers have benefited in these ways from stamping their personalities on the neighbourhood. Collectively, this is likely to have a positive effect on their sense of belonging and pride in the neighbourhood, and on strengthening sound ties with neighbours. We have no data on the effects that neighbourhood negotiations prior to extensions may have on social sustainability. Nor do we have information on any conflict as a result of extensions where negotiations have been avoided or were unsuccessful. Each of our study areas (with the possible exception of the Egyptian flats) scored reasonably well on loyalty measures and appeared to be sought after by outsiders wanting to move in. This suggests that few conflicts arise which are serious enough to reduce the general enjoyment of the area.

Neighbourhoods appear to be more socially heterogeneous after transformation than before. In Egypt, for example, almost all the owners in the sampled neighbour-hoods are now middle-aged with grown-up children. Through the extension activity, the second generation can remain in the neighbourhood, introducing the young marrieds back into the social scene. In Bangladesh, Ghana and Zimbabwe, rented rooms (and rent-free family tenancies) allow younger, smaller and lower income households to move into the area while larger dwellings produced through transfor-mations encourage prospering long-term residents to stay. In addition, the opportunity to rent out additional rooms is important for many households' ability to pay for and maintain their houses or as a means of livelihood for the old. Between 27 and 71 per cent of our samples in Bangladesh, Ghana and Zimbabwe rented out at least one room.

Reductions in occupancy rates appear to follow transformation. Transformers are less crowded than non-transformers in each country. With three to four habitable rooms now available to main households at the medians, children of opposite sexes can sleep apart and the parents can sleep away from the children. Those with school homework to do are more likely to find a quiet corner than members of households with only one or two rooms. Thus transformers will reap the social benefits of reduced crowding.

Additional space can be used for economic activities if desired. These are dealt with below. The elderly can gain rental income from rooms rented out and/or can have a worthwhile role in their declining years as matriarch or patriarch over the extended family living in the rooms they provided. Such social inclusion of the elderly is in line with the Global Plan of Action.

Housing is productive; transformations increase that productivity

The productive 'worth' of housing *per se* has been difficult to prove even though it seems self-evident that better housing conditions will promote a healthier, happier, more productive population. However, we can assert that housing is productive in the sense that it provides a flow of goods and services over a very long period. In so far as transformations extend the period over which housing continues to deliver these benefits, it is increasing this productivity. Our data show that the improvement in conditions and services is considerable and available to all who live in the houses.

It is well known that the production of housing provides excellent opportunities for employment, local income multipliers, and strong forward and backward linkages in the economy (UNCHS/ILO, 1995). The Global Plan of Action requires that countries promote 'the use of labour-intensive construction and maintenance technologies that generate employment in the construction sector... at the same time promoting the development of skills in the construction sector' (UNCHS, 1996b: para. 70). We have demonstrated that transformers use local artisans and small-scale building contrac-tors in their extension operations. These, in turn, tend to use labour-intensive construction methods, locally produced materials (which usually have a high labour content) and local labour in carrying out the building operation. Thus, local backward linkages into the economy and local income multipliers are likely to be large from transformation activity (Tipple *et al.*, 1994; UNCHS/ILO, 1995).

In addition, forward linkages into the economy are also likely to be quite signifi-cant in transformed housing. It is widely accepted that working in the home is an effective poverty alleviation measure where even poorly paid out-working can make a real difference. Furthermore, it is a means of providing some employment security for children (Gilbert, 1988). This could reduce their need to move out of the area when they are grown up and allow their childhood local social system to serve them into adulthood.

For those who wish to use their dwelling as a workplace, transformation may be an essential prerequisite, providing the extra space so that economic activity can occur. We found that between 11 and 25 per cent of houses in our Bangladesh, Ghana, and Zimbabwe samples had a commercial use within the house. In addition, the ability to rent out rooms can provide a flow of income to the owner which would be absent without the extra rooms in the extension. In the light of these characteristics, trans-formations can be seen to be an efficient means of increasing economic activity. This activity is important for those who have insufficient resources to operate a business in a formal industrial or commercial site. In addition, women are disproportionately involved in home-based enterprises so are likely to be especially assisted by transfor-mations. This aspect of transformations is in line with the Global Plan of Action commitment for 'developing housing that can serve as a functional workplace for women and men' (UNCHS, 1996a: para. 42).

Transformations make efficient use of existing social resources

Sustainable development stands on three pillars: environmental, economic and social sustainability. The last of these is, perhaps, the most intangible and the most difficult to address with policy. While positive steps can be taken by reducing social exclusion, one important element of social sustainability is the maintenance of existing social networks, often manifest as local social systems or that elusive concept: community.

We have already addressed the existential benefits of involvement in modifying the environment. The maintenance of existing housing areas and, better, their continual improvement over time through local initiatives, is likely to maintain long-term social relationships which make city life viable. We have found that most of our transformers are long established in their neighbourhoods. They are, thus, likely to have rich networks of social, cultural and economic relationships which might be vulnerable if the area had to be redeveloped. As social cohesion is very difficult to build, we must be cautious about any developments that fracture it and favourably inclined towards ones that preserve or enhance it. Transformations allow residents stability of residence in one place despite the housing stresses and shocks which would otherwise cause them to move with the attendant breakdown of social relationships made in the area. Thus, transformations are likely to encourage social cohesion and to allow it to survive the end of the notional economic life of the dwellings.

Transformations require realism in regulations and standards

The Global Strategy for Shelter goes so far as to state that:

> The whole basis of a workable shelter strategy is that Governments should review existing legislation and regulations and their impact on shelter production and improvement, and remove those which clearly appear to be pointless and largely unenforceable. (UNCHS, 1990: para. 33)

This review is seen as 'a matter of highest priority' (para. 67). This issue is taken up again in the Global Plan of Action which calls on governments to 'avoid inappropriate interventions that stifle supply and distort demand for housing and services.' Governments are called upon to 'periodically review and adjust legal, financial and regulatory frameworks, including... building codes and standards' (UNCHS, 1996b: para. 72). Appropriate planning standards are held to be those which 'match the actual needs of the local communities' (para. 90). Furthermore, the presence of unenforced standards and the partial nature of development control are rejected in favour of 'more transparent government regulatory and inspection systems' (para. 90).

We have seen that many transformers have permission but we suspect that much has changed between the permitted plan and the edifice constructed. Certainly, the study draws attention to the gap between that in which low-income households are prepared to invest their hard-earned money and that which the authorities regard as acceptable. Realism in regulations would include rethinking the reasons for limiting plots to single-household occupation. In addition, the reasons behind restricting uses in residential areas to exclude most economic enterprises should be re-examined.

We may be able to establish what realism in regulations may mean by studying the designs, structural qualities and space provision of the extensions constructed in government-built estates. We have insufficient data from our study as there was no examination of how the occupants or neighbours feel about room sizes, ventilation and daylighting circulation spaces, materials and standards of construction, services provided, and all the other components of the physical environment provided by the informal transformation activity. However, such a study could provide important insights to assist in developing revised building codes based on local realities rather than imported norms.

Transformations can promote a balanced approach between shelter upgrading and new shelter construction

In recognition of the fairly small proportion of the housing stock that is newly built per year, making best use of the existing stock is an important part of the housing process. The Global Strategy for Shelter recognises that, with the limited resources in most developing countries and the difficulty of assembling land for low-income housing schemes, improvement of existing shelter units should have a high priority as a means of increasing the housing stock. This is not only to preserve the assets of the country but also to protect households from losing their main, and sometimes only, capital asset. In addition, cost-effective use of land is fundamental to urban development. We have seen that the process of transformation not only helps to conserve the existing housing stock but also increases its value. In addition, it increases the value of property per hectare ensuring more cost-effective land use than was originally existing. It also gives the neighbourhoods a broader role in supplying a variety of housing goods (see below).

Transformations involve the efforts of citizens in planning and implementing improvements

Faced with the enormous task of not only providing new urban areas but also of maintaining and improving currently developed areas, city authorities need all the help they can get. The now orthodox way of soliciting citizen participation in neighbourhood improvement takes place from the outside first, through improving the utilities and environment (often with citizen participation in some form) in a hope that the householders will improve their houses. Transformations demonstrate the reality of citizen participation in urban renewal but done from the dwelling outwards. Although the public domain is largely unimproved by the *ad hoc* character of transformations, there is potential for local authorities to complement the improvements made by the residents through a programme of upgrading the utilities. This public–individual partnership for urban renewal (which is discussed in more detail in chapter 8) could thus transform the entire neighbourhood. In this context, transformation can be seen as a means of empowerment through which the residents can maintain the fabric of the neighbourhood. In other words, transformations can create sustainability in the neighbourhood.

As mentioned earlier, we suspect that the intention in the subsidiarity argument is that decision-making on the scale of housing provision in a neighbourhood should only pass down to local authorities. In transformation, however, it passes so far down the scale as to result in *ad hoc* development control by individual households and groups of neighbours. The principle is in line with sustainable development but its practice may need some intervention if negative externalities of blocked light and ventilation, excessive narrowing of public rights of way, and obstruction of surface drainage and sub-surface services are to be minimised. To this end, the DFID-sponsored project has generated some, as yet unpublished, draft codes of practice (Higdon, 1995) for discussion with relevant authorities in the four countries.

Transformers add value to an area and increase the potential property tax base

The necessity of building sustainability into local authority structures has re-emphasised the need to raise sufficient revenue to maintain and enhance services and staffing. One of the most popular and least troublesome means of raising revenues is through property taxes. As transformations increase the value of property in an area, they present the potential for raising property taxes. Thus, as houses are extended, municipal revenues can rise. This may be particularly important when matched with the increase in demand for servicing which may follow from the population growth on site. Governments are being encouraged by the Global Plan of Action to improve and monitor performance on revenue collection through property taxation (UNCHS, 1996b: para. 189). We discuss the importance of revenue collection as a *quid pro quo* for transformation in chapter 8.

Transformation promotes rental housing

The Global Strategy for Shelter and the Global Plan of Action recognise the increasing importance of rental housing for accommodating the poor in urban areas. Increasingly in the literature (Rakodi, 1995), renting is being recognised as advantageous for significant sections of the urban population. The majority of the supply of rental housing is in the private sector, and much of that is in the form of a room or rooms in owner-occupied houses. The Global Plan of Action challenges countries to 'promote the supply of affordable rental houses' (UNCHS, 1996b: para. 68).

We have seen that transformers add rental rooms to their houses and accommodate lower income, smaller households. In Bangladesh and Zimbabwe, 70 per cent have at least one renter household and the median per house is two. Despite their own, seemingly constrained, space consumption, owners find it worthwhile to rent out space. It is likely, therefore, that the addition of rental rooms to low-income housing will continue to be a survival strategy for the owners and a source of affordable accommodation for would-be tenants. Many of the new rooms open off semi-private space, allowing independent access and egress for households therein. They are thus particularly well suited to letting out room by room – the form most essential to poor householders who cannot afford self-contained dwellings (Tipple, 1994b).

Transformations change the emphasis of physical planning and residential area design

In the past, despite the long-term view which gives town and regional planning its character, physical planning has tended to be quite short sighted. Plans for residential development have been treated in the same way as a blueprint for a bridge. The end product has been assumed to be that which features on the plan in hand unless dwellings were specifically designed to be extended (i.e. core housing). Plot sizes, street layouts, plot ratios and other such components of the physical planner's arsenal have tended to be aimed towards a finished item envisaged by the designer of the area. Thus, if an area is intended for the construction of three-roomed dwellings in terraces, design has concentrated on the most efficient way to place the dwellings in relation to each other and on the plots. It has been oblivious to any changes which might be made in the future. Similarly, the number of rooms in an area has been assumed to be static.

This work has shown that, even where the plots are so narrow or constricted as to allow hardly any expansion, extensions have indeed happened. Twenty to 40 years after 'completion', the estates retain only vestiges of their original characteristics. Thus, transformations suggest that the emphasis of physical planning and residential area design should be on a longer term development process, one which accommodates the likely growth of the dwellings. It should provide for increasing populations, increasing ratios of built to open area, and proliferation of land uses. Thus, flexibility is as important as or more important than an elegant solution to an initial design problem. We discuss it in detail in chapter 8.

Variety out of uniformity

One of the most interesting features arising out of this study is that transformers are producing variety out of uniformity. The variety is expressed in the following features.

Variety of house size

The houses provided in the estates studied tend to be of a few standard designs. In some, these designs varied considerably in size: in Ghana, for example, the IQR of original dwellings is about 23 m². In others, there was little variation: in Egypt, IQR is only 10 m², while in Bangladesh all were identical. Transformers have superimposed a variety of house size upon this more or less uniform canvas. This variety, which is a hallmark of self-help transformers, allows many housing solutions to be present in one place. Very cheap single rooms and spacious apartments to rent can stand amongst multi-roomed compounds accommodating polygamous extended-family households in owner-occupation.

In Bangladesh (where all the sampled houses started the same), there is an IQR of almost 32 m² which is 45 per cent larger than the original uniform dwelling area. In Egypt, the flats have been extended so that, even where the five-storey stack construction imposes a level of conformity, there is 12 m² difference between the first and third quartiles. In Ghana, the variation between quartiles is a massive 72 m² , double the original median dwelling size, and in Zimbabwe, the IQR of 39 m² is similar to the original dwelling size.

Variety of accommodation for the main household

Main households have a greater variety of space than the original dwellings provided. For example, in Bangladesh, where there was no variability in the original dwellings, the IQR of habitable area used by the main household in the current houses is 23 m² (from 8 to 31 m²). Main households have the option of occupying more space (and most do), and space in either the original or new structures (which may be of different quality). They can occupy less space by allowing tenant or rent-free (family) households to occupy part of their original space or by moving into a new smaller portion of the transformed house. They can choose to have their own bathroom, toilet and kitchen, or share with others, and to have outdoor space or enclose a smaller or greater part of it.

Variety of house value and housing cost

While the original dwellings tend to be of very similar value and cost (especially if measured per square metre), the new housing is very varied in value and cost. For example, in Bangladesh, house values have an IQR of PPP£6900, twice the value of the original dwellings. In Egypt, a sample in which the value per square metre was very uniform, there is now a perceived difference from the first to the third quartile of PPP£50 per square metre. The value of that part of the house occupied by the main household tends to vary greatly (e.g. in Ghana IQR is from PPP£5200 to £16,800) and also to differ from that occupied by subsequent households (by factors of three or four).

The variety of accommodation provided now in the estates has a varied filtering effect; some households filter up (mostly the main households in the houses), some filter down through occupying less housing or building cheap extensions, both of which reduce the value of their portion of the house. Others benefit from new housing provided at the bottom of the market.

Variety of use

As we have seen, the original residential estates now have a variety of uses within them. Of course, people carry out business activities from the home even if no alterations or extensions are possible. For example, they may sell beer and soft drinks from the kitchen or sew clothes for neighbours in the living room (Muller, 1995). Through transformation, however, opportunities arise for doctors' surgeries, shops, manufacturing activities, and many other space-consuming non-residential activities. There are examples in our surveys of mosques, churches, nursery schools, maternity clinics and night clubs.

All these provide not only employment and income-generating opportunities in otherwise economically barren areas but also serve the local people for their social, cultural and religious needs and provide opportunities to obtain goods and services without leaving the neighbourhood. Although specially designated plots are provided for such activities, and are undoubtedly used as such, converted and extended dwellings provide cheaper opportunities for these activities and may deal with a lower income clientele than use the formal shopping areas and social facilities.

S. V. Sethuraman of the International Labour Organization posits that small-scale enterprises have a greater chance of survival if the income density in the neighbourhood is reasonably high (personal communication, 1993). This means that the income of each household is less important to shopkeepers than the income per hectare. Thus, a poor neighbourhood can support a range of shops and other commercial activities if population densities are quite high. Transformations have the effect of increasing population densities and so may enable the survival of a wider range of shops, etc. than would have survived in the areas without transformations. They thus allow for and encourage a wide range of uses in the neighbourhood.

Variety of tenure

The recent trend towards a much more complex tenural split than just owning or renting (as described in Gilbert, 1993, for example) is clearly reflected in the opportunities for variety in tenure arising in transformations. Out of a uniform hire-purchase or renting-from-government tenure regime, transformations create opportunities for tenancies and sub-tenancies in the private sector, rent-free (family) tenancies, sharing and other tenural forms.

In two of the three case studies where most original dwellings are now owned by the occupants (Ghana and Zimbabwe), there are now numerous private-sector tenancies. In Ghana, rent-free (family) tenancies that allow poor members of lineages to live in the city cheaply (Amole *et al.*, 1993: 18) are quite common in our study areas. In Egypt, little renting of rooms occurs but there are examples of sharing where married children and their spouses may have a private room in the extension plus use of the sitting room and kitchen. In Bangladesh, despite reluctance to admit to them, there are many sub-tenants in addition to the numerous households sharing with the main household. Transformations also allow a variety of tenure within a particular income group. Instead of there being no choice for the poorest households in Harare but to join squatter settlements miles from the city, single rooms in extensions are available for them to rent. Similarly, better-off households in the Ghana and Zimbabwe samples have the choice to be owner-occupiers without tenants or to become petty landlords.

Variety of occupants

When they are completed, houses in government-built estates tend to be allocated to homogeneous groups of people (young middle-ranking factory and government workers with children) who, having won the lottery of obtaining a highly rationed and subsidised good, are loath to leave. Thus, there is a tendency for all the households to be in a similar phase of life, growing older together. This may lead to a boom in demand for schooling followed by a dearth of children, and later a concentration of retired people for whom the dwellings are unsuited.

We have seen how transformers tend to create space for new households in different stages of their lives to move in as tenants or rent-free (family) tenants. New rooms can be created for the next generation. The availability of single rooms allows relatively poor households to find accommodation in the area. The extension and renovation of the original small dwellings encourages original allottees who prosper to stay and to express their new higher income and gain status without moving away.

Notes

1   In this, they are carrying out the move-and-improve process described by Littlewood (Littlewood and Munro, 1997, p. 1775) in the context of Scotland. They are obtaining a property that is relatively unsuited to their needs (the 'wrong' house) and converting it to one that is closer to their ideal.

2   This section was compiled with the invaluable help of Naomi Carmon of Technion, Haifa.

and Izak Kadosh of the Project Renewal Office in Neve David, Haifa.

3   Jews in the Diaspora shared the expenses of the project with six ministries. Jews in partic-
     ular places sponsored chosen settlements; for example, those in Britain contributed
     towards a neighbourhood in Ashkelon. This source of funding was later replaced by full
     government backing. Throughout, however, the housing elements were financed solely
     by the Ministry of Housing.

4   This involved enveloping the exterior in new finishes; tarring the flat roofs, repairing and
     painting the stucco finishes on the wall, some replacement plumbing, renovating window
     shutters, fitting entrance doors, and some landscaping.

5   These loans are available to all Israeli households below average income wishing to buy
     a moderately sized dwelling. Thus, owners in the project had benefited from both
     discounted prices and soft loans.

6   This is probably an underestimate as there are about one-third of the sample in the '35
     m² plus' category in Lerman and colleagues' table (p.47 in the Hebrew version) which we
     have represented by 37.5 m².

7   A morning spent in Neve David, Haifa, with the charismatic Izak Kadosh, showed me the
     value of a strong project manager. It is obviously a skilled task to keep the peace among
     12 to 24 households in planning a large extension project for a multi-storey block and to
     ensure that even the most wary is enthused by the unfolding reality of the extension
     process and its promised results. The generally high esteem in which the residents seem
     to hold him is testimony of the gratitude they seem to feel for the chivvying to which he
     undoubtedly subjected extenders to get them involved.

8   He enumerates that a flat of 90 m² would be twice as expensive as one of 60. In addition,
     those of 90 m² would tend to be newer (as the standard of living increases) and more
     valuable.

9   Even where parts of an original building are demolished to make way for the extension,
     the materials are often reused even if only as hardcore in the new foundation slab. In
     Zimbabwe, when buildings constructed with prefabricated reinforced-concrete panels are
     extended, the displaced panels are often reused as security fencing. Windows, doors,
     timber and roof sheets are often salvaged and reused.

8. Policies for enabling transformations

Introduction

As we have seen from the analysis (and from our case studies in the appendices) transformers add considerable amounts of housing goods to the current stock. This varies from about 50 per cent extra in Zimbabwe to 150 per cent in Bangladesh. They do so in areas which are already developed so no new land is required (the urban footprint does not expand except indirectly). Furthermore, they do not appear to receive any assistance from the housing budget but succeed in increasing the share of investment accruing to housing and, by so doing, increase Gross Fixed Capital Formation. Thus, as we argue, transformation is a form of neighbourhood upgrading.

On housing supply grounds alone, governments have much to gain from encouraging transformations. On the other hand, there are potential, incipient or established problems of crowding of structures for which some development control would be advisable. These include lack of ventilation, daylighting and open space around or within the dwelling, access, surface water drainage, etc. These are, of course, exacerbated in some areas by the very small and/or narrow plots which are provided in many government-built housing areas. Our Bangladesh and Ghana samples show the problems which arise here. The accusation that transformers are building slums is a difficult one to counter as long as breaches of planning and building regulations are common. It is particularly difficult where they have been done without reference to the planning authorities. The multi-storey stacks in Egypt have been built in defiance of planning officials and the extensions in Bangladesh are in areas where planning controls do not apply. Even where planners admit that the planning and building regulations in force are inappropriate for the economic and social circumstances in a country, they still find a *laissez-faire* alternative unpalatable and it would be naive of us to assume that it could be accepted.

We suggest, however, that governments could benefit greatly from an essentially permissive attitude towards transformers. At one end of the spectrum, there would be light control. This would prevent the worst excesses which can be characterised (in a spirit of hyperbole) as a dominant neighbour sweeping all local objections before him (or her) to erect a giant edifice of rented rooms for personal profit. At the other end of the spectrum, they could practise enablement through loans and officers responsible for promotion of extension activity (as in Israel).

On the other hand, governments have much to lose through heavy-handed, unhelpful policies which freeze out the potential extensions through introducing bureaucratic delays and interference. It must be remembered that regulations need not be fully upheld for their presence to inhibit development. There are costs to circumventing regulations; the timid will be put off and may not add the housing they would in the absence of regulations. For the less timid, bribes add up against the price of construction but the regulations avoided in that way have had no positive effect on the environment. There is a need for a balance between control which inhibits and control which enables.

Turner (1972, 1976) has long argued that prescriptive standards (those that prescribe action in specific ways) inhibit the ingenuity of potential house-builders. He proposed that standards should be proscriptive, proscribing activities which are unacceptable and allowing a wide range of actions within the field of acceptability. The difference between the two can be likened to stages of parenting children. When the children are young, parents need to set out (prescribe) quite detailed 'dos and don'ts' to keep them from danger and point them in the way they should go. When the children mature into young adults, parental influence must decline to a measure of guidance within a fairly broad field of acceptable behaviour. Within this they have greater freedom of action but it must have firm boundaries (proscriptions) across which they cannot go without incurring opprobrium and active sanctions. With the onset of transformations, it could be argued that a neighbourhood comes of age. It follows that control must be proscriptive towards the totally unacceptable but liberal within the bounds of acceptability. Our experience of transformations leads us to argue in favour of an attitude to development control which accepts that residents should have a high degree of control over what happens within their neighbourhoods. These proscriptions, sensitively developed and agreed by community leaders, should limit development only when absolutely necessary.

Carmon's strategy for encouraging housing renovation: the public–individual partnership

Flexibility
>   Responsive housing is the name of the game. (Carmon, 1992: 67)

From her experience with Israel's Project Renewal, Naomi Carmon (1992) has developed a strategy for encouraging renovation, based on the concept of housing as a service not a product. She argues that, just as continuous interaction is a vital element of a good service, so there must be continuous interaction between housing authorities and occupants. This requires some changing of attitudes and behaviour among the actors in the process. She suggests that public officials should adopt a permissive approach to suggestions for changes in the size and form of buildings through time. This has implications for existing estates, in allowing extensions to alter the form and massing of the housing stock. It also implies that designers of new dwellings should integrate the fourth dimension, time, into their designs, especially to consider the future and build flexibility into residential areas. The latter is particularly relevant in Egypt and Zimbabwe where government agencies are still attempting to build dwellings for the low-income groups, and to a lesser extent in Ghana where the now-privatised State Housing Company builds estates.

Public–individual partnerships

Private ownership is a key for this strategy as relatively low-income households are prepared to spend considerable portions of their means to achieve it and then are more prepared to renovate their dwellings than other tenure groups.[1] The second issue central to the strategy is public–individual partnership. This is fundamentally different from the public–private partnerships in which large private firms are coupled with public authorities to establish economic enterprises to provide employment or other services to the poor, and for which they usually take a profit. In the public–individual partnership, Carmon argues that the needy individual (house-buyer, would-be extender, etc.) directly receives some goods or services from the public sector and adds something from their own resources as a multiplier. However, it requires a bottom-up approach, involving the individuals in the decision-making process. In this way, the real needs of low-income households are met rather than imposing upon them some norms from middle-class policy-makers (as in the beautiful though unpopular transformations in Jerusalem discussed above and the widespread official condemnation of 'building slums').

Area targeting

A third important component is targeting of benefits to particular areas. Personal need intuitively appears to be the most efficient criterion for distributing benefits as this avoids inefficiencies arising from giving welfare payments to those not in need of them. In most welfare distribution, area targeting is seen to be inefficient as not all residents of a particularly needy area will, themselves, be in need. However, experience in Israel has shown that area targeting of benefits is important for enabling transformation activity as housing renovation and extension gains much from the clustering of activities in one neighbourhood. As one household renovates and extends, neighbours stand to benefit from the positive externalities as the area increases in value and status. The example of one is also infectious and soon everyone wants to be extending. As extensions are grouped together in one neighbourhood, their effect is likely to be much larger than if they were scattered wherever poorer households live. The inclusion of the few better-off households in the area in the benefit distribution may be inefficient in direct welfare terms but it will encourage them to stay rather than moving. Their staying on in the area avoids homogeneously poor neighbourhoods which tend to be stigmatised by the rest of the population. Finally, targeting support at only moderately deteriorated neighbourhoods tends to give a better chance of success than targeting at the worst neighbourhoods from where all the moderately well-off have already fled. In this way, improvement through extension is seen as a measure to prevent the worst deterioration in housing and to promote housing supply, rather than as a means for tackling the housing problems of the poorest areas in a city (Carmon, 1992).

Projects for transformations; a proactive approach for local authorities

The productive environment of Project Renewal's enlargement policy appears to hold some lessons for those willing to adopt a proactive role in enabling transformations. It could increase the efficiency of supply currently demonstrated in our case study estates, especially with regard to financing, the field of construction and increased conformity of design.The public–individual partnerships proposed by Carmon (1992) and operating in Project Renewal may be just what is required to maintain the investment momentum while achieving a measure of control.

A local authority could identify an area which is 'ripe' for transformation, or one in which it has already begun. A project manager should be appointed and, through him/her, enthusiastic transformers can be encouraged to cooperate with neighbours, to adopt designs, detailing and finishes which are in keeping with the general design of the existing fabric, etc. The project manager would also be the catalyst through which transformations can be accepted by the bureaucrats who would otherwise oppose them as 'building slums'.

Residents who are unsure about their ability to afford and carry out extensions can be reassured, cajoled and assisted to realise their potential and that of their dwelling. For many of these, extensions may come too late, when most of their family have moved on. However, they may make them anyway for the benefit for the next generation. There is a very high demonstration effect in Israeli transformations and we can recognise it in our case studies although we have no data to demonstrate it empirically.

In Project Renewal in Israel, many processes have been streamlined by user-friendly paperwork. By adopting this approach in other countries, our would-be transformers can be assisted to obtain permission, advised on structural and design problems, and guided through the procedures for raising a loan. If desired, the project manager would act as a supervisor of contractors, checking the work and disbursing the money as the building proceeded. Where agreements must be made amongst residents or with outside agents, the project manager would act as a broker. He/she would secure the participation of as many of any group as possible and represent the group to the authorities with respect to planning and building regulations approvals and finance.

From the Project Renewal experience, the major improvement in design seems to accrue from a proactive approach with local organisation and loans finance. Within this, it should be easier to achieve designs that are compatible with the existing structures and high-quality construction. Both of these should lead to extensions which fit into the local context without appearing intrusive. Thus, we recommend a proactive approach to encouraging and enabling transformations.

Public–individual partnerships and area targeting are both methods of benefits distribution which are non-income specific. They are intended, primarily, as housing-supply strategies not as welfare or income redistribution as so many housing strategies have been, overtly or covertly. Thus, spending on the housing budget has been directed primarily to increasing housing first.

Whether occupants have been 'deserving' on grounds of income or other measures has been only a secondary consideration. We have seen that transformers are not the poorest in society and so readers whose first concern is poverty reduction are likely to be unhappy with some of what follows. They might object to public resources being spent on those who are not the poorest. They might feel that policies that favour owner-occupiers to increase their capital holdings are inappropriate. However, our study has shown that transformers are very efficient suppliers of housing both for their own use and for other, younger, smaller and poorer households. On these grounds, we would defend helping transformers to transform and providing new housing areas that take account of their likely future activities, even if both cost public money.

Physical planning policy and regulations
Plot size and shape
Physical planning practice for low-income housing layouts in the recent past has encouraged smaller plots rather than larger and narrower rather than wider:

> Research suggests that square plots or rectangular ones where the frontage is on the longest side lead to considerably increased circulation and utility network costs. ..the most economic result for any given area is with rectangular plots of which the frontage is the shortest side. (Davidson and Payne, 1983: 41–2)

An efficient plot shape, in the Egyptian context, is expressed by Davidson and Payne (1983) as a rectangle in which the frontage is at least 6 m and the depth of the plot is at least twice but no more than five times the frontage. In addition, the frontage should be wide enough for an entrance hall and a room. These recommendations are based on a minimum plot to accommodate a single household and the minimisation of both public and private costs. They also acknowledge that there should be space, preferably on the ground floor, for extra rooms.

In discussing a range of shapes and sizes, Davidson and Payne (1983) suggest that the 6 m frontages provide economical but tight layouts, 7.5 m widths are economical and reasonable, 9 m gives flexibility and 12 m could be regarded as very flexible. They also make the point that, when a plot has been laid out, it is extremely difficult to increase its size, regardless of household needs. Thus, adequate plot sizes should take priority over utilities or superstructure. Davidson and Payne are advocating a more resident-friendly approach than has, perhaps, been usual. Experience in layout design in a Town Planning Department of a local authority in Africa demonstrated to me that servicing concerns tend to carry the day and the pressure on plot size and shape is towards small and narrow.[2] It is usually argued that larger plots will lead to lower densities and higher service costs and this is demonstrably true if the assumptions of stability are made.

Apart from their acceptance that extra households may be housed by the occupants, Davidson and Payne's advice reflects what has been regarded as good practice for decades. It is, indeed, sound advice where a single household per plot will be the dominant form of settlement, and a narrow range of alternative house designs or sizes are expected. However, our experience of transformers indicates that other assumptions may be required of physical planners. These are that:

- The development envisaged at the outset may bear no resemblance to that which will exist 20 years later except in its plot boundaries.[3]
- Single households per plot may be unusual; instead several households per plot may be predominant after a few years.
- Consumers of housing are likely to become producers of housing.

As a result of this work, we would argue that plots should be large rather than small and wide rather than narrow. When suggesting this, we are arguing that the plan as drawn up for official implementation is not a blueprint for a static system. Instead, it represents only one stage in a dynamic system of development as residents extend and alter their living environment through the life of the houses – a period that is likely to exceed 60 years. The larger and wider plots will provide broader private open spaces to allow efficient additions to the accommodation through user-initiated transformations. Though larger and wider plots lead to fewer plots per hectare and more expensive services per plot in a controlled environment, such controls are rarely achieved in cities in developing countries. The ongoing process of transformation is, however, likely to make up any initial difference over the first few years. Soon, therefore, user-initiated transformation may provide as great efficiency in terms of people per hectare and services per person or per household. The short-term increase in servicing and land cost will be offset against the longer term increase in people accommodated at no further cost to the exchequer. There will probably also be an increase in value as residents invest privately held capital in fixed goods of a varied nature.

The plea for wider plots in an environment where extension is likely may sound too obvious to require articulation but it is salutary to remember the planning of Dandora in Nairobi, Kenya. Here, plots of 100, 120 and 140 m² were planned with a width of only 6.3 m, purposefully too narrow to range rooms along both sides of a central corridor. Only in the few corner plots of 7.35 m width was this possible without one side's rooms being very narrow. Although only 50 per cent plot coverage was expected (Chana, 1984), later development has tended to feature an extra row of very narrow rooms filling in the intended yard spaces. Thus the plot coverage has increased very considerably and in a manner which flies in the face of the plans and reduces the quality of accommodation because of the narrow rooms. In parts of Dandora, two-

and three-storey buildings are common, even though original foundations are unlikely to be designed for extra storeys.

Design and siting of the dwelling on the plot
Cost cutting in housing provision has inevitably led to small dwellings. Recommended minimum room sizes have become design norms as centimetres are pared off the building envelope to reduce costs to an 'affordable' level. However, this leads to less adaptability of internal spaces in direct contrast with the need for flexibility inherent in transformations. It is contrary to Moudon's (1986) praise of the flexibility inherent in the square rooms and wide hallways of the San Francisco Victorian houses (chapter 3). Thus, transformations direct us towards designing in flexibility of use and future subdivision and coalescence of spaces within dwellings.

It is relatively common for government-built housing to be a series of similar detached bungalows set centrally on the plots with narrow spaces on either side and set-backs to front and rear. The Zimbabwe case study areas, reflecting Southern African township layouts, are the ideal type of this (Mills, 1989). A fat rectangle captures the maximum closed space within the minimum wall lengths, so the open spaces around it are relatively narrow and fragmented. Daylighting and ventilation are achieved from the outer walls; the direction of the pitched roof is determined for aesthetic reasons. In other circumstances, terraced dwellings are built across the centre of a row of narrow plots, leaving only small spaces at the front and rear. In all these circumstances, the quantity of accommodation likely on site in the long term may not be much greater than that originally planned.

In areas where there are no delineated plots, a first step in the transformations enablement process would be to demarcate some. It may also be very useful to mark the limits of acceptable extensions on buildings which stand in public space. This has been used as a joint promotional and control measure in Israel's Project Renewal with some success[4] but with less success in Ghana where control was the aim but insufficient staff resources were available to implement it (see Appendix 3).

In designing new residential areas with transformers in mind, it would be most efficient to align the original building close to at least one plot boundary or even at a corner. In this way, the remaining open space is relatively wide and unfragmented.[5] In addition, transformations suggest that the fat rectangular building may be efficiently replaced by a long narrow rectangle, a single-banked series of rooms, with clues and cues for extension. These clues and cues would include verandas and balconies, walls against which lean-to construction is possible, high eaves to allow the roof line to continue downwards over another room, simple gable ends so that the roof is easy to extend, and stub walls protruding from the frontage. In addition, internal plans should allow easy access to all the new rooms without having to use other rooms as corridors.

The effectiveness of verandas as cues for extension has been shown in Bangladesh, Ghana and Zimbabwe. In addition small rooms suitable as future corridors to new rooms, such as the kitchens in Egypt, may act as clues. When these are present they need sufficient outdoor space, appropriately located, for an extension to take advantage of them.

Review of building regulation and planning norms

On a visit to a city, which is regarded as in the forefront of housing provision in one of our study countries, I was taken on a field trip round the city with several housing managers from other cities in the country. The housing managers were continually bemoaning the shortage of housing and asking, graciously, whether their foreign visitor had any solutions to offer to increase housing supply. Of course, I had plenty of ideas but insufficient knowledge of the country to give them credibility so declined to offer advice. In a site and service scheme, splendid dwellings had been built down one side of the wide plots provided and I asked my companions if the owner would be allowed to build another dwelling in the ample space left over. 'No', came the reply, 'it would be against the regulations. Single plots are meant for single households and single dwellings.' It seemed that there was no compromise possible as the regulations were clear and their fulfilment more important than increased supply.

We can, however, learn lessons from transformers just as we learned from squatters through the work of a long line of researchers from Turner (1972, 1976) and his colleagues in the late 1960s and 1970s to Kellett (1995) and others in the 1990s. Just as squatters showed us what people are willing to accept and are prepared to provide in housing in peripheral and marginal land, so transformers may show us what people are prepared to accept and provide within the conventional city. They point us away from the 'policing' method of development control and towards the 'enabling' method (UNCHS, 1996c).

The housing estates which we have studied are not peripheral to the urban milieu. Government-built housing areas tend to be, if anything, the most formal areas in the city occupied by civil servants and formal sector industrial workers. Except for Mirpur, our sample areas are built fully to the government's own adopted standards and are well serviced (at least with mains pipework if not house-level fittings).

The estates under study, and those around the world which we would claim they represent, were built on the western 'suburban' assumption that the nuclear family household occupying the dwelling would be the norm for residents over the life of the housing. As we have seen, this is no longer the case on the ground. Even in Egypt where additional households are yet to feature strongly in the transformed flats, the extended family household is evident. In addition, the housing needs of mature and married offspring are being addressed by at least some transformers. Elsewhere, commitments to assist members of the wider family, and the ability to afford more housing if some rooms are rented out (at least temporarily), are displacing the suburban expectation of a single household per plot. In this context, the appearance of informal accretions, more often officially permitted than we had expected, is a significant sign of what people will accept and do for more accommodation.

Throughout this, there is a tension between the wish of bureaucrats to control the transformations, often for the best of reasons, such as keeping services operational and preventing unhealthy or hazardous living conditions,[6] and the logic of allowing transformers relatively unfettered opportunities to supply much needed housing goods for themselves and for others. While local planning authorities insist on a 5 m set-back at the front of the plot (Zimbabwe, 1976), householders appear to prefer the ability to site a kiosk close to the roadway. Where road widths cannot officially be less than two-thirds the height of the flanking buildings (Egypt), residents' extensions are reducing spaces between blocks of flats to the shady 3 to 5 m wide canyons typical of Old Cairo. Some households show that they are willing to accept a room entirely devoid of windows or ventilation[7] while such a thing is officially completely unacceptable.

Such regulations as currently exist are designed to promote the 'amenity' of the area.[8] Front set-backs promote traffic safety (they allow car drivers to see and be seen at junctions) and safeguard the intended appearance of the estate (by disallowing forward extensions). Side and rear building lines permit access to service pipes, reduce intrusion from building up to the neighbour's fence, hinder the spread of fire, and allow all-round access in case of emergency. Our experience of transformations activity is that these regulations are ignored by many occupants and only paid lip-service to by development control officers. Why, for example, should someone be allowed to erect a 2 m high chain-link fence covered in creepers (and, therefore, a solid barrier to sight) along their front boundary but are unable to build rooms in the front garden? Similarly, why should two neighbours who agree to build rooms adjoining their side boundaries be prevented from doing so by a bureaucrat who does not live in the neighbourhood?[9]

We are persuaded that the building regulations and planning laws should be modified to allow and enable extensions rather than to continue to outlaw them and, thus, leave them completely uncontrolled (Turner, 1972). Currently, planning authorities appear to be taking a generally benign view of breaches of planning regulations. Even Zimbabwe's shack builders rarely suffer demolition of the structures that contravene building lines and regulations on materials.[10] However, the presence of regulations, even if they are not imposed, can cause problems. They can increase the time taken to develop and the building cost (either in inflationary delays or in bribes and backhanders). More importantly, as Turner (1972) pointed out way back in the 1970s, buildings which do not qualify for full legal recognition are not eligible for loans from the formal-sector financial agencies. Furthermore, where this illegality increases risk of sanctions (including demolition in extreme cases), it is likely to reduce the quality of extensions because investment which is risky is likely to be less generous than that which is safe.

Our experience of transformations suggests that it is better to admit that current and likely future levels of centralised planning control are inadequate to make much difference to the micro-environment within neighbourhoods. If we are to enable transformers and other individual actors in the housing supply system, such shibboleths as one dwelling per plot, building lines, road reserve widths, etc. may need to be abandoned in favour of realistic proscriptive statements concerning a narrower range of developments that are to be completely unacceptable.

An alternative is required which does not allow the exploitation possible with complete *laissez-faire* but which removes the illegality from all extensions to the original housing. There is much sense in introducing areas in which planning is the province of local community groups and neighbourhood leaders. These might be expected to include whole neighbourhoods apart, perhaps, from main road frontages and major areas of non-residential use. Within these areas, certain minimal proscriptions could be determined through discussions between the local authority and neighbourhood leaders. These would include not building over roads or main drains, avoiding high-tension electricity lines, blocking a neighbour's light or air, etc. The members of the community, through their chosen leaders, should then be responsible for controlling the scale and nature of development by transformers. In Ghana, for example, there are chiefs in each estate to whom residents owe allegiance and who settle disputes. They would be ideal as chairmen (they are all male) of development committees over-seeing extensions in their neighbourhoods. Alternatively, in such areas, the main criterion for allowing development within plots should be the agreement of (say 75 per cent of) the neighbours. If most of the neighbours on all sides agree, there seems to be little reason for higher authorities to interfere.

Proposals for the switch from local authority control to community control of trans-formation activity would appear to be timely and appropriate with regard to the Global Strategy for Shelter and the Global Plan of Action from Habitat II (see chapters 5 and 7). Current discussions about the effectiveness or otherwise of privatising service provision have pointed out the suitability of community control over the supply of infrastructure and the day-to-day delivery of water, waste disposal, and other formerly centrally controlled functions (UNCHS/ILO, 1995).

Three measures could be put in place by local authorities as enabling legislation whether or not they are willing to adopt a community-based approach to planning:

- relaxation of set-backs and building lines to allow development close to side and rear boundaries and to allow commercial streets to develop where appropriate;
- acceptance of rental rooms or complete new dwellings adjoining owner-occupied dwellings as a valid housing supply mechanism;
- introduction of classes of permitted development within which planning permis-sion is not needed. In Britain, for example, an extension up to 70 m^3 (or 15 per cent of the original volume whichever is the greater) can be added to the rear of a dwelling for residential use by the household without requiring planning permission.

In places where permission has not been granted for large numbers of transforma-tions, there is much to be said for legalising the currently illegal extensions. The Global Plan of Action calls for integrating and regularising self-built housing as a means of supporting the efforts of people to produce shelter (UNCHS, 1996b: para. 740). We would argue that the unauthorised extensions merit this treatment as much as complete dwellings in informal settlements.

Service lines

Service lines may be affected in several ways by transformations and these should be taken into consideration either in proscriptive control measures in existing areas or in planning new areas with transformation in mind. The main issues for service lines are:

- They may be built over in the transformation process with consequent problems of damage and of making repairs and maintenance difficult. This is more likely to affect lines close to buildings rather than the major distribution lines.
- They may be disturbed or damaged as the ground is broken for the building operations as extensions are constructed close by.
- They may be 'trapped' between buildings in spaces too confined for repairs and maintenance to take place. Two examples of this are evident from our study; the pipework servicing kitchens and toilets in the Egyptian flats can easily become trapped between proximate extensions; and the rear storm-water drain between some plots in Mirpur, Bangladesh, is now bordered so closely with rooms that a sweeper cannot squeeze down the space to unblock the channel.
- The increasing population in some areas is likely to create higher demand for water supply and the removal of storm water, grey water and sewage. In addition, the fitting of extra (or completely new provision of) toilets, taps, air-conditioners, etc. may place loads of a scale and type for which the infrastructure was not designed.
- The increasing use of space for commercial or manufacturing activities is likely to increase demand for services. Such uses are likely to create loading demands for electrical power, water and drainage which are substantially different from those of residences and which may have the effect of levelling out otherwise narrowly peaked domestic demand cycles. More likely, however, is that strains will be placed on the infrastructure to cope with, for example, high-powered machinery, noxious wastes and heavier vehicles.

The reaction of the servicing authorities should be tempered in the light of the contribution that transformers have been making to the housing supply within the currently serviced city limits. In some cases, no action will be necessary as the services may not be operating to their capacity in relatively low-density developments such as in Zimbabwe. In others, the *ad hoc* development of services by individuals should eventually be replaced by a planned network capable of coping with overall demands of the area so that blockages and breakdowns can be minimised.

The infrastructure in the government-built estates would need renewing if the houses had been allowed to remain untransformed and would, thus, soon reach the end of its economic life. There is, therefore, a latent cost building up against the day when redevelopment is needed and the old infrastructure must be ripped out. Thus, if infrastructure investment is required as a consequence of the increased demand from transformers and their tenants, two issues should be taken into account:

1. the likelihood that major infrastructure renovation or installation would be required soon anyway;
2. the fact that extra infrastructure elsewhere on green-field sites is not required for these households.

These issues cancel out at least part of the cost of relatively major improvement in service lines to cope with increasing and different demands. As a *quid pro quo*, it is reasonable to expect transformers to avoid service alignments, to make connections in the correct way, and to pay for supply and maintenance of the service to the relevant agency. Thus, there should be investment in infrastructure in areas in which transformations are occurring or where they seem likely. They should ensure that the existing infrastructure is in good enough condition to cope with additional loads or upgrade it so that expected loads are easily managed. This should be regarded as part of the enabling housing function of local authorities.

Within the tenets of sustainable development, the due payment of service charges on a scale to ensure the continual delivery of the service is essential. The action of transformers, especially those improving the service provision in their house, indicates that they are economically committed to the neighbourhood, that they want a service, and that they can afford quite substantial levels of investment. It would seem reasonable, therefore, that residents should pay the economic cost of the service.

Where a service is compromised by an extension, for example, when pipes or drains are crossed or broken, the owner of the house should be expected to reinstate a similar level of provision so that flows are maintained. It is important that, as soft landscaping is replaced by hard construction, storm-water drainage channels are included in each transformation; then the local authority or community group should design a modified system to remove water from the site without its becoming an agent for erosion. This is already an issue in parts of our Ghana estates.

In new areas, pipe runs should be designed to avoid problems from likely extension activity. Thus, mains in the roadway with spurs directly to each house provide a more flexible environment than pipework which runs close to the front or rear of several houses or which cuts diagonally across a plot. Pipe sizes should reflect the likely demands of an increased population rather than just coping with the originally planned population. Public or shared taps and toilets are likely to be unpopular in most cultures and to be superseded by *ad hoc* private provision within a few years.[11] Mains reticulation should be designed to cope with this change. If it involves increased costs, the viability should be tested against the likely future population benefiting from it rather than the population expected in the first instance.

Finance

While transformers undoubtedly show their ability to manage without formal-sector finance, it is likely that they are considerably delayed while gathering together cash or informal loans. We have seen that, in Bangladesh, Ghana and Zimbabwe, construction of the extension is financed from savings and current income. Long lead times and extended periods of construction generate inefficiencies. Contractors are laid off while money is collected for the next stage, with all the inconvenience and expense of interruptions in the building work. Investment may be tied up in incomplete rooms which can deteriorate when left exposed to the elements for months or years on end.

Credit finance could take the waiting out of housing adjustment and relieve the housing stress earlier in the household's life-cycle. Furthermore, the current standard of construction may be poorer than the household could afford if credit finance were available to people on average incomes at market rates. Loan finance would probably allow transformers to afford more expensive extensions than they can achieve using cash and informal borrowing only. Housing finance is, therefore, one lubricant which could substantially improve the efficiency and quality of transformation activity.

Availability of finance for extensions

We have seen that about one year's household income is invested in transformations at the medians. Such large amounts of money are difficult to collect for spending over a few months, or a year or two. It is likely that the capital cost of transformations would be greater if credit financing were available. This is so because any household which can raise a whole year's income over a short period could probably afford substantial annual loan repayments. These would finance a larger capital sum over a longer period for a more costly transformation.

Formal housing finance systems have been generally unsuccessful in reaching the poor or even the moderately well off. Most formal mortgage schemes have been limited to a few salaried workers in the top 20 per cent or so of the population. Ghana is a case in point here where even the Home Finance Company, instituted especially to serve the low-income group, has so many conditions attached to loans that only the salaried élite can qualify. Furthermore, the loans can only be applied to the single household villas built by members of the Ghana Real Estate Developers Association (GREDA).

The characteristics of finance suitable for transformations are similar to those required for loans for low-income housing in general: relatively small loans (£1000 to £3000) need to be available from local offices, over shorter terms than are normal with mortgages (say 5–15 years), and with repayments at frequent intervals (daily, twice weekly, or weekly, as well as monthly). Formal-sector financial institutions value large loans rather than small ones, because the administration costs are relatively constant whatever size the loan may be. Thus, small-scale mutual credit institutions, and such initiatives as the Grameen Bank in Bangladesh, are more likely than the large banks and building societies to provide small loans. They can also cope with frequent small payments through large numbers of branch offices.

The collateral issue that dogs loans for new housing is less difficult with transformations because the original house is usually already owned by the occupants and can stand as security for the loan. However, it is vital that land registration is efficient so that clear titles are available. Otherwise, the existing house will not be sufficiently secure to act as collateral on an extension loan.

The Global Strategy for Shelter specifically calls for 'small loans to owner occupiers willing to build cheap rental housing through additions to their dwellings' (UNCHS, 1990: para. 85). We have seen that transformers are prepared to do this but they may require incentives from the public purse to ensure that a high standard of accommodation is provided within the affordability range of low-income tenants.

In calculating acceptable lending levels, loans agencies should be encouraged to take expected rental income from the extension into account and to allow higher than customary debt-to-income ratios. We have argued elsewhere (Tipple, 1993; UNCHS/ILO, 1995) that small business loans should be available for home extension where the rooms are to be used for a home-based enterprise. Kellett (1995) chronicles how the loans for floor surfacing, toilets and washing facilities, etc., for small private nursery schools in Colombia have allowed women to upgrade their houses as well as earn an income.

The Egyptian study has shown how a contractor is willing to have multiple clients who each pick up part of the bill for the contract against his initial financing of the job. In other countries, there may be potential to finance joint extensions and joint service installations (septic tanks, water connections, tubewells, etc.) as one loan paid for mutually, with each debtor acting as a control against default by free-riders.

Finance for contractors and artisans

As we have argued elsewhere (Tipple, 1994a), small-scale builders need finance for their operations. This is also recognised in the Global Plan of Action which states that governments at the appropriate levels should 'support private-sector initiatives in providing bridging loans to builders at reasonable interest rates' (UNCHS, 1996b: para. 90).

Governments spend large amounts of money on job creation in urban areas, usually through grants, loans or subsidies channelled towards the large- and medium-scale enterprises, and in industry or commerce. But these are rarely channelled towards enterprises active in house construction. If there are occasions when small-scale enterprises are currently assisted, they are almost always in the formal sector. However, most firms involved in transformations are very small and in the informal sector.

Informal-sector producers could be much more efficient if they could obtain credit on the same terms as formal-sector enterprises but they often have no formally recognised collateral to offer. Currently, they are obliged to seek finance directly from the clients through payments in advance or in very short-term arrears, or to use informal sources of finance. At worst, they resort to borrowing from money-lenders on highly unfavourable terms.

Many building contractors in developing countries operate with virtually no capital. We have seen how they often rely on the client to assemble the materials and to pay the wages of hired workers as work progresses. But this has attendant problems of cash flow and discontinuity of work which can result. Efficient development can be assisted by giving small-scale construction firms access to amounts of capital sufficient to launch and carry forward a project until payments are due. At the smallest level, this would require sufficient money to equip and pay workers, buy and transport all materials for a single contractual phase, e.g. foundations and slab, walls, roofing, etc., for a single room. This would remove the uncertainty and delay of relying on the client for working capital (Tipple, 1994a).

Both front-end capital for firms and end-user capital for occupants are required in increasing the efficiency of transformations. These complementary functions would not be served by a few, preferentially structured (i.e. subsidised), loans. Instead, it would require that the financial market should deal with borrowers with less conventional forms of collateral (such as jewellery, vehicles, community guarantees, or informal sector housing), over relatively short periods and for relatively small amounts. This may require some form of loan guarantee from the government but the cost of the risks involved should be viewed against the benefit to be had from bringing forward housing investments, increasing the efficiency of small-scale construction firms, and speeding up development (Tipple, 1994a).

Land and property taxes: a *quid pro quo* for enabling transformation

Property taxation has a pivotal role in municipal finance (Devas, 1992) and in ensuring the sustainability of local authorities and their services. However, the introduction of realistic land valuation practices is frequently politically difficult. In Ghana, for example, where official rates and valuations have been kept artificially low (Korboe, 1993b), a genuine tax-paying culture has still to be developed and a history of unaccountable governance has left the population most unwilling to pay up on property taxes and other broad charges.

Much revenue is also being lost because urban authorities are failing to recover the costs of installing and maintaining municipal infrastructure. Unrealistically low tariffs and other user charges simply leave city administrations broke and unable to discharge their civic and capacity-building responsibilities effectively. In addition, they are often less than assiduous in levying and collecting property taxes. However, sustainability considerations are forcing municipalities to realise that they must collect realistic taxes from property if they are to survive to offer services into the next century (UNCHS, 1995). While it is reasonable to argue that low-income households should be taxed at minimal levels, on welfare grounds, many of the owners or main occupants of houses in our case-study neighbourhoods are in the upper echelons of low income. The fact that they have managed to gather the resources together to make the extensions serves to demonstrate that they may be quite capable of paying additional tax.

In areas where transformations have occurred, renovating the mains infrastructure to cope with increased demand can provide a trigger for introducing full repayment of the cost of water, sanitation, waste disposal and electricity.[12] In addition, their legal recognition may offer the leverage required to introduce realistic levels of property taxation. We would propose, therefore, that property taxation takes account of increases in value of extended houses, extracting greater value from the larger houses. Once this is done, local authority attitudes are much more likely to be positive towards extenders.

Summary and conclusion

Our proposals can be summarised as taking a positive view of transformers as providers of valuable housing. In times of great need in the housing sector, it makes good sense to follow the evocation of the Global Strategy for Shelter in involving all actors in the housing process in 'scaling up' the housing supply system (UNCHS, 1990). Just as squatters were, perhaps, not the most welcome actors in the process in the 1960s and 1970s, but were eventually accepted as making a valid contribution, so transformers, today, should be accepted. Their means may be unconventional, and their location unplanned, but their contribution is undeniable and a very positive story has emerged from our international empirical work.

The story that has emerged is remarkably similar in the four very different places chosen for the work. The small dwellings provided as part of the social welfare approach to housing have become places where their residents can build a long-term solution to their housing needs and a base for their heirs. They do so with no help from the authorities, apart from the subsidised sale of the poorly maintained structures or the blind eyes of institutional landlords. Consumers of housing have turned into producers and have changed their relatively monotonous estates into places of variety, self-expression and even whimsy. Furthermore, the 'building slums' criticism of transformers is very difficult to support in any but highly subjective terms. The scale of investment achieved in the estates varies from impressive to staggering, even where the physical constraints against extensions (small and narrow plots, multi-storey original structures) are quite severe. They have done it, often despite unhelpful original layouts, because government-built housing tends to be too small and inflexible for family life in the modern city, especially in the context of obligations to relatives in the present and in the future.

The ubiquity of transformation indicates that our findings could be useful in many countries at various stages in development. The successful promotion of renovations and extensions in Israel has given some clues as to the way forward. Transformers show us that the initial plan for a residential area is only the beginning in a poten-tially fruitful process of extensions and renovations over several decades. Any expectation that residents will permanently concur with the original designers on the suitability of the environment to their needs should be banished as fantasy. The validity of residents' desires for change should be accepted as a normal part of estate life. Thus, flexibility and compromise are important watchwords for designers and development controllers respectively.

If the policy-makers can adopt a positive view, and implement some enabling policies, in financing, building control and regulation, and physical planning of new estates outlined earlier, it is likely that transformations will increase in frequency and quality to the benefit of all concerned. We will, thus, be able to utilise the full potential of these relatively low-income households who are unexpectedly active in the housing sector.

This book forms only the beginning of a process of understanding and planning for extensions in low-income housing in Africa, Asia and Latin America. I hope that other researchers will examine user-initiated transformation activity in their countries, in both public and private housing. Others' empirical studies will allow for adjustment, alteration and even refutation of the preliminary ideas formed here, and lead us closer to understanding the housing needs, demands and behaviours of ordinary people across the world.

Notes

1   This is not to say that there is no place for rental housing in the future. Indeed we have argued elsewhere in this book that it is becoming more important as time passes. It is just that transformations as a housing supply mechanism are likely to be less successful in a rented neighbourhood because residents will either fear to make additions at all or they will spend little knowing that they may be turned out of their dwellings at any time.

2   I agreed with this at the time and argued for it in Planning Committee meetings.

3   If no plot boundaries are provided, the changes are likely to be even more radical. In parts of our Ghana case study, it is impossible to trace the original plan on the ground.

4   In Neve David estate in Haifa, there is a plan on the Project Renewal office wall with each of the existing blocks of flats surrounded with a red rectangle large enough to give significant scope for extensions while maintaining open spaces between the blocks.

5   This pattern would have been reasonably represented in Mirpur if the plots had not been so narrow.

6   But also often from rather subjective reasons such as preserving the appearance of an area regardless of the needs of its occupants. One sometimes wonders if city administrations have a sort of bureaucratic anorexia in which they have ideas about beauty that drive them into behaviour which is damaging the health of the city.

7   This is even so in Israel where many residents expect very high standards in their housing.

8   But what amenity means is usually not defined in law. It seems to be one of the concepts whereby everyone knows what they mean by it but could not agree where the margins are. For example, a development control planner may reject an application to build a brick house in a stone area but 95 per cent of the population may not regard it as seriously damaging their amenity. Furthermore, they may be far more concerned with whether the occupants play loud music.

9   Apart from the fire hazard, which can be minimised by fire-proof party walls, the argument about leaving room for emergency vehicles and personnel to pass into the rear of the plots is about the only cogent one in this context. However, there is no regulation of other boundaries (walls, etc. across the plot) or trees which may as effectively limit movement from the front to the rear of houses in case of fire.

10   As we saw above, 40 per cent of transformers in Zimbabwe (the worst case) received threats of action from the local authority but half of them had no action actually taken against them.

11   The sharing of a service by several households on one plot is much more likely to be
      continued than sharing by inhabitants of several plots. Indeed, sharing the use of services
      in the multihabited house is likely for an increasing proportion of the urban population
      (see Tipple, 1994b).
12   Except where it is stolen through illegal connection, electricity is usually charged for at
      full-cost-recovery tariffs. That it is very common in relatively low-income homes demon-
      strates that services do not have to be subsidised to be popularly used.

Appendix 1. Transformations in Bangladesh

Introduction to the Bastuhara Housing, Mirpur, Dhaka

Dhaka is the capital city of the People's Republic of Bangladesh, the largest city in one of the most densely populated countries on earth. It is situated about 150 km above the mouth of the River Ganges. It stands on the northern bank of the Buriganga River about 12 km above its confluence with the Dhaleswari. Although the Ganges delta is low-lying, Dhaka is sited slightly above the general level on the southern edge of an alluvial terrace. Its commanding position and the presence of ground which does not flood in average years led Islam Khan, the Mughal Subahdar, to transfer his capital there from Rajmahal in 1610. Large areas of the present site of the city flood annually and are left clear of official development though many areas do have squatter populations. Only the military area in the spine of the city is never flooded.

Although the urban population is only 15 per cent of the national population, urban areas have severe problems. Old Dhaka, which lies near the north bank of the river, contains some of the most densely populated residential areas anywhere in the world. The population density of the city overall is 3990/km^2 (Bangladesh, 1993). A survey in 1993–4 showed an estimated 2 million people living in 'slums' and squatter settlements in Dhaka and about 3 million could be classified as living below the poverty line. The likely future growth of Dhaka was estimated to be from 6 million currently to 12 million in 2010 (Bangladesh et al., 1995).

The average monthly income for urban households in Bangladesh was Tk4832 in 1991–2 (£80), considerably higher than the national average of Tk3341 (£56).[1] Some 48.7 per cent of the urban population (6.8 million people) live below the poverty line, defined as the income needed to consume 2122 KCal per person per day and 26.2 per cent live in hard-core poverty, below 1805 KCal per person per day. Although they do not seem to be expressed in money terms in official documents, corresponding per capita monthly incomes appear to be about Tk8800 (£145) and Tk6200 (£100). The lowest 20 per cent of the urban population have only 8 per cent of the urban income while the top 10 per cent have 30 per cent (Bangladesh, 1995).

There are 1.04 million households in Dhaka, 39 per cent of which own their dwelling, 53 per cent rent and the remainder live rent-free. Just under 50 per cent of households are reported to have tap water and most of the rest have a tubewell supply. Only 4 per cent rely on shallow wells or surface water sources; 55 per cent of households have a 'sanitary' (usually pour-flush) toilet but the rest rely on pit latrines or the open ground. Almost 70 per cent have electricity.

Less than half the households in the city are reported to occupy dwellings built in brick or cement-based materials; 34 per cent have bamboo, straw or jute stick walls;16 per cent have corrugated iron sheet walls; and 6 per cent have mud walls. However, 60 per cent of households are protected by corrugated iron roofs and most of the rest have concrete-slab roofs. Only 12 per cent rely on straw, bamboo, jute or polythene sheets to keep off the sun and rain.

The city has spread north for many miles and Mirpur is located 10 miles from the city centre at the north-east periphery. It began to grow as a satellite town of Dhaka after the Second World War with a major expansion during the 1960s (when the 1961–74 intercensal growth rate was 265 per cent for the 14 years) and the 1970s (103.9 per cent 1974–81) with influxes of residents to the new residential development (Bangladesh, 1993). The Housing and Settlements Directorate (HSD), which was formed to house refugees from the partition of India in 1947, developed Mirpur as its largest project. It covers 1357 ha and was intended to house 150,000 people.

Initially, about half the land was developed as core houses, 8245 in all built between 1959 and 1968. They were built as semi-detached units laid out in rows of 15 to 20 with access roads 9 m wide with 1.2 m service alleys to the rear carrying the utility lines. In addition, about 7900 plots were made available for residential development.

Despite the plan to accommodate only 150,000, the 1991 population of Mirpur *Thana* (district) comprised 120,000 households with a mean of 5.2 members, giving a population of 640,000. The intercensal population growth rate 1981 to 1991 was 6.8 per cent per annum. The density of population is 11,000/km^2 (giving a gross area of only 91 m^2 per person). Water supply is better than in Dhaka as a whole with 72 per cent of households having taps to the dwelling and 21 per cent using tubewells; 68 per cent have a sanitary latrine (pour-flush or WC), 27 per cent have non-sanitary latrines and 5 per cent have none at all; 76 per cent have electricity (Bangladesh, 1993).

The *Bastuhara* (Bastu = home, hara = less) scheme, which forms the context of our study, was proposed in 1972 as probably the first mass housing scheme for the low-income group undertaken by the Ministry of Relief and Rehabilitation and later executed through the HSD. The scheme was intended to provide basic shelter for displaced persons: only a room but no services were initially planned. In 1975, about 175,000 people were evicted from a squatter settlement from an old railway line in the city centre which was converted into a major road. There was, therefore, a great need for low-cost accommodation for rehousing these and other displaced persons (Ameen, 1995).

A total of 4304 semi-detached units were originally planned in five different sections of Mirpur. Each consisted of a single room of 18 feet 8 inches long by 6 feet 2 inches wide (5660 by 1880 mm) with a veranda 6 feet 2 inches long by 8 feet 9 inches wide (1880 by 2640 mm); a total floor area of 22.2 m^2, built in a single leaf of brick with a corrugated iron roof. Windows were created by a chequerboard of bricks and spaces.

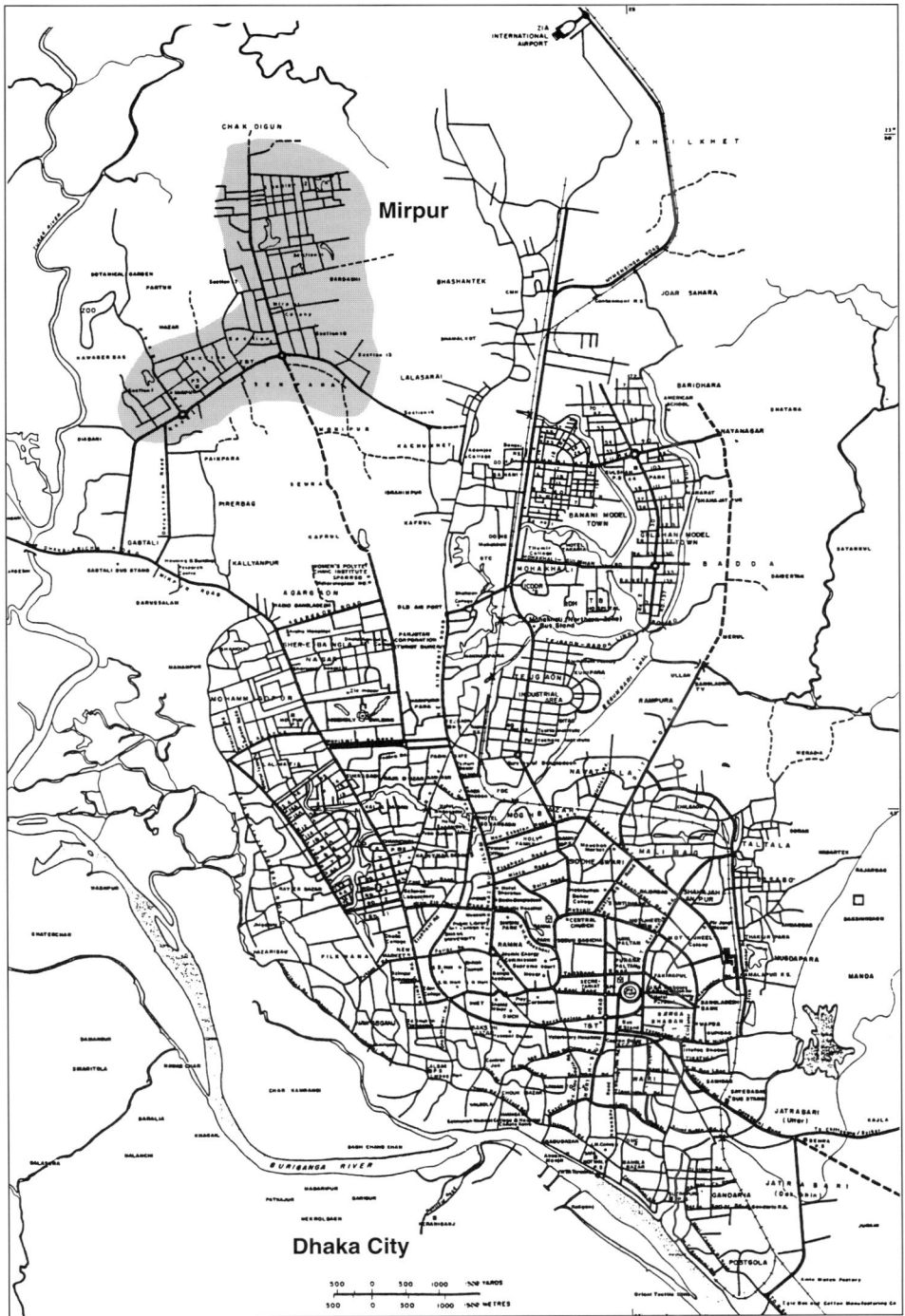

Figure 23. Map of Dhaka showing the location of the Mirpur study areas

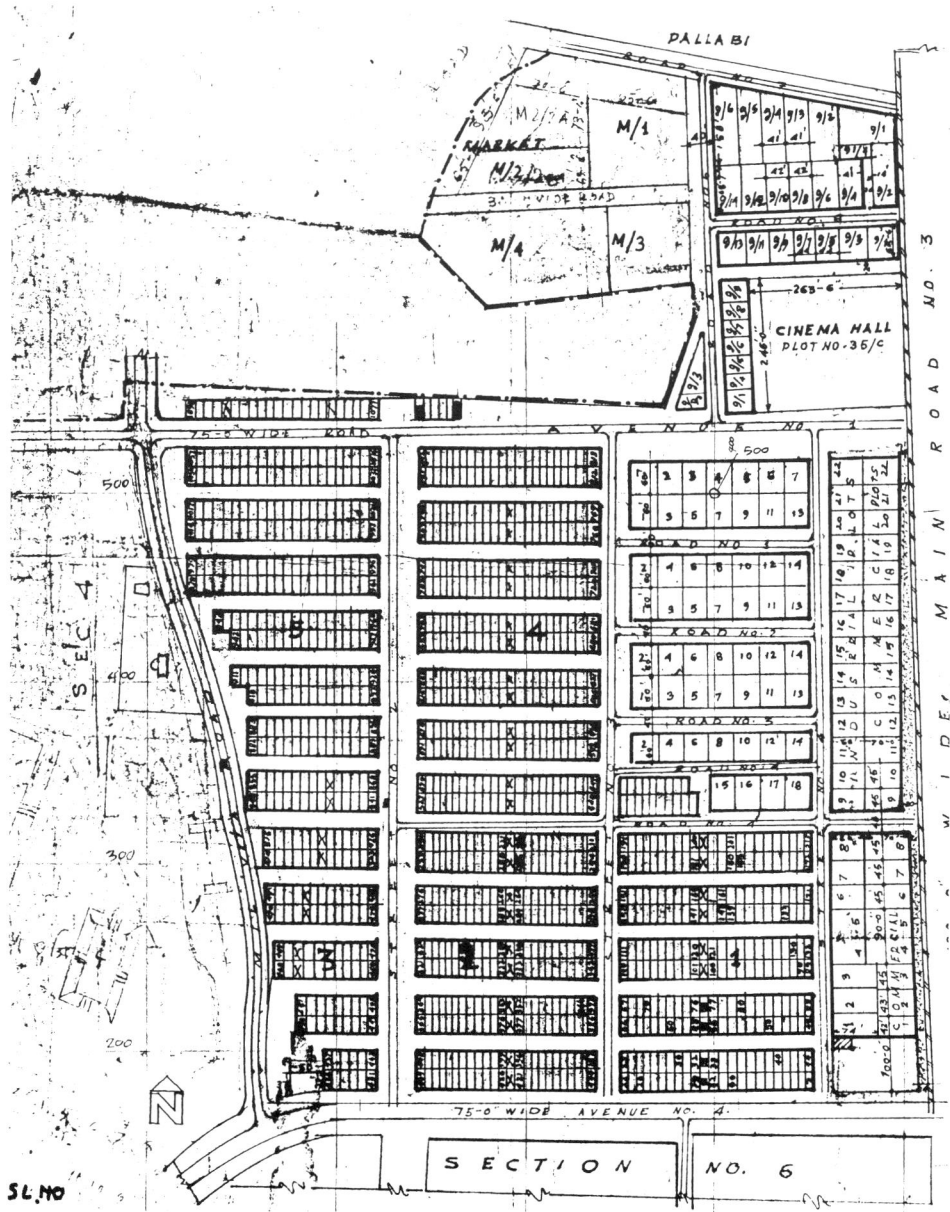

Figure 24. Plan of part of Mirpur showing a typical layout of the bastuhara *housing*
Figure 2 looks north east across the site from five blocks south of the north west corner.

The dwellings are joined in pairs along their long edge, which also forms the roof ridge. All the dwellings were built in rows with access ways demarcated but no plot boundaries were drawn. They were built but not serviced; latrine blocks were constructed (in blocks between every sixth dwelling), and lavatory pans fitted but no water supply was installed, nor were the sewers laid. The scheme stood empty for a few years.

At an advanced stage in the development, 1124 units were converted into 662 two-roomed dwellings (of about 44.5 m²) for government employees in class III and IV occupations. In these dwellings, one of the verandas was converted to a kitchen, boundary walls were erected, and water supply and toilets were also provided.

The allocation procedure for the 3180 single-roomed units was handled badly. The people for whom they were intended failed to be allocated them. Instead, middlemen (known as *mastans*) stepped in to take over unoccupied units. They fitted padlocks to the doors to control access and let them to individuals against the payment of 'hush money'; Tk2500 (£42) in 1974. Later, would-be occupants had to make initial payments rising to Tk120,000 (£2000) in 1988 to vacating residents. This sum represents a putative value whereas the earlier payments to *mastans* were arbitrarily set.

From the early days, illegal connections to the electricity mains were made, tubewells were sunk and latrines served by soakpits were fitted. After a few years, HSD was faced with a *fait accompli*: there were too many occupants to evict so they were allowed to stay on a rental basis. The municipality then constructed the lanes

Figure 25. Bastuhara *housing in close to original condition*
Photograph: Shahidul Ameen.

Figure 26. The original provision in Mirpur
Note the latrine blocks, constructed but not serviced, and the brick window.

(known locally as by-lanes) between the house blocks in the herring-bone brick paving conventional in Dhaka. The occupants have since taken the lanes' edge to be their front boundary regardless of any easements for pipes, etc. Recently, when sewers have at last been laid, these have had to go under the brick paving and the disturbance has ruined the surface.

The HSD is currently implementing the sale of the Bastuhara housing to the occupants. A survey has been done to find out who is the occupier of each house (and each has been photographed, according to the residents) and sub-tenants have to say who the 'owner' is. The occupiers will be charged Tk134,000 (£2230), calculated from a land cost of Tk63,360 (£1056), plus a house cost of Tk103,775 (£1730)2 depreciated by 18 years at 2 per cent per year (none for the first two years so it is calculated over 16 years).

Several residents told us that Tk172,000 (£2870) was the price but this probably includes interest. The sale entitles the occupant to 99 year leasehold with limitations on their rights to sell for some years.

According to HSD, the people are rushing to buy, but residents have a slightly more sanguine impression of demand. The money must be paid in five annual instalments (which would be Tk25,800 or Tk34,500 (£430 or £575) depending on who has the correct estimate of cost) but some residents were told nine payments are due biannually.

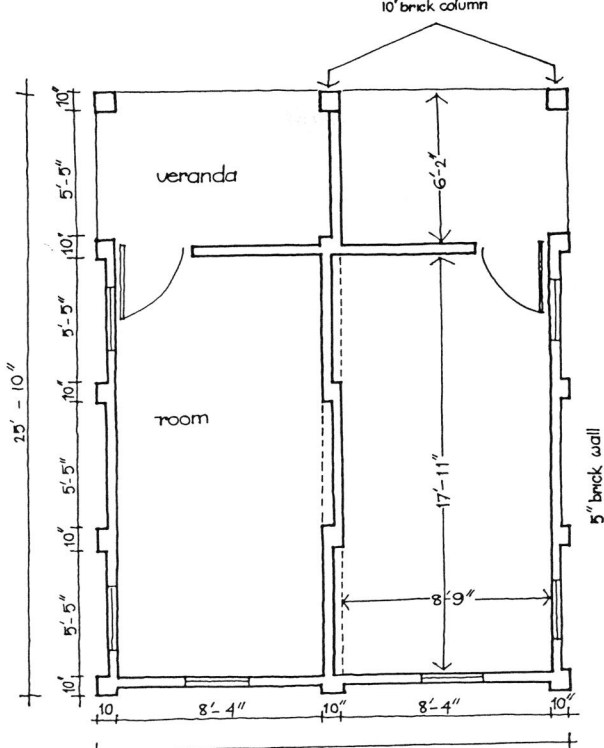

Figure 27. Original plan of a pair of dwellings, Mirpur
Source: Shahidul Ameen

We will see elsewhere that those households who have bought possession during the last five years have already paid Tk150,000 (£2500) and above for the possession of a rented house. This was, therefore, seen by them to be the value of a low-rent lease on an extended version of the house which is more than twice as large as the original.

Our Bangladesh sample is 386 houses of which only 12 are non-transformers. The 374 transformers are divided into 245 established and 129 recent.

Socioeconomic characteristics of households

The following information describes the main household (renters) of houses which have, or have not, been transformed. The occupants described as non-transformers are, with only two exceptions, living in transformed houses but have bought the lease and moved in after the work was completed so are, themselves, non-transformers. There are only 12 households in the non-transformers sample, and only two in non-transformed dwellings, so they are of little use as comparators.

As in the main part of the book, three measures are given in each table cell in these appendices: a measure of centrality and two giving spread. These are the median or fiftieth percentile (or central value) and the first and third quartile which show the range of the middle 50 per cent of the population (the interquartile range – IQR). We show these measures instead of means and standard deviations because most socio-economic and housing data are skewed.

Measures of permanence

In our preliminary work (Tipple, 1991a, 1992), we hypothesised that long residence in the past, or by intention for the future, increases the likelihood of transformation. It might be expected, *a priori*, that owners are more likely to extend if they have lived in the house a long time, simply because they are likely to have different household circumstances from those in which they first occupied the house. In addition, long residence is likely to foster commitment to an area, which is consequently likely to increase the desire to extend rather than to move.

The inertia element is thought to be very powerful in housing decisions. Social ties, the bother of moving, etc., cannot be quantified but are accounted for in the household's decisions to move or extend (Seek, 1983). Dynarski (1986) posited that, where the loss of residential attachment outweighs the benefits of moving, a household will remain in its existing dwelling.

The population in Mirpur is well established and there is almost no variability between established and recent transformers in measures of permanence in the place of residence. As we have seen above, 'allocation' of the houses was a somewhat protracted affair and many of the first occupants did not stay long. Our data are consistent with most of the occupants being in the first wave of 'allocations' in the years following 1975 (19 years ago at the time of the survey), or moving in within a few years of that occupation. At that time the household heads were in their twenties and thirties but they are now in their forties and fifties (median age for all subgroups = 45). Transformations were started when they were in their thirties and early forties, on average eight years after originally moving in. They are generally well educated. As we have seen, the dwellings were occupied by households who could afford to pay the *mastans*. They are likely to be well enough off to pay the 'hush money' and confident enough to take up the opportunity presented. Both of these point to some education. This notwithstanding, the median of 10 years in education for renters of single-roomed houses without services is impressive. Apart from being newer to the houses, non-transformers are no different from transformers in measures of establishment in the city and their households.

Income and wealth

We would expect transformers to be in the middle of the income range (table 48), both because of their long occupation of government-built housing, and because households who demand and supply additional housing space would be expected to be in that range (Woodfield, 1989). We would not expect transformers to be better off than non-transformers but would expect those with more expensive extensions to be better off than those with small ones.

Table 48. Measures of income and wealth, main households

Medians (and IQRs)	Established transformers	Recent transformers	Non-transformers
Household income (Tk thousand/annum)	63.8	58.1	52.4
	(48.5, 81.1)	(50.3, 77.9)	(44.7, 70.0)
Per capita income (Tk thousand/annum)	9.7	8.9	10.6
	(7.3, 12.9)	(6.8, 11.6)	(8.6, 14.5)
Expenditure on food (Tk thousand/annum)	36.0	36.0	36.0
	(27.4, 48.0)	(24.0, 48.0)	(24.0, 46.5)
Relative wealth index**	0.0033	0.0033	0.0017
	(0, 0.003)	(0, 0.003)	(0, 0.003)
Percentage with RWI of zero	22%	25%	42%
Percentage expecting to be better off next year	0%	2%	0%

**Relative wealth index (RWI) lies between 0 and 1: 1 implies ownership of all the consumer durables, i.e. radio or cassette player, sewing machine, refrigerator, freezer, television, motor cycle and motor vehicle.

Currently, Tk3000 per month or Tk36,000 per year (£50 per month or £600 per year) has been used as a threshold for low-income households (personal communication, M.S. Ameen). Mean annual income in 1991–2 for urban households in Bangladesh was Tk58,000 (just under £1000). In 1994, a rickshaw puller would earn about Tk36,000 (£600) while a skilled building worker would earn about Tk42,000 (£700), both of which are below the first quartile incomes of our sample. An unskilled labourer would earn about Tk18,000 (£300) annually. Median incomes for the different transformer groups in our Mirpur sample are Tk52,000 to Tk64,000 (table 48). Thus, we can see that our sample includes few who survive on an unskilled job or could be considered as low income in the Bangladesh context.

The median per capita incomes in our sample (Tk9000 to Tk10,000 – £150 to £167) correspond approximately to the median national urban per capita household income for 1991–2 (Bangladesh, 1995). The median is just above the national poverty threshold of around Tk8800 (£145) per annum and the first quartiles exceed the local hard-core poverty threshold of about Tk6200 (£100) per annum (Bangladesh, 1995). Thus, per capita incomes demonstrate that our sample is less well off than household incomes might indicate.

With Tk60 per £1.00 sterling, the incomes of our sample appear to be quite low at barely £1000 per annum for the household and £160 per annum per capita. However, if we multiply this sterling income by the Purchasing Power Parity factor of 4.1524,[3] the annual income becomes PPP£4150 per household and PPP£664 per capita, which is 2.8 times the absolute poverty threshold of US$31[4] (about £20) per month per capita

(£240 per year) determined by Ravallion *et al.* (1991). Expenditure on food (£600 per annum at the median) is remarkably stable across the groups, although it varies slightly in the percentage of total income it represents (from 56 to 62 per cent). The relative wealth index is extremely and consistently low, showing that the people have little disposable income. Only half have a radio, 36 per cent have a television and 10 per cent have a sewing machine, but only a very few have a fridge, freezer, bicycle or motor bicycle. None of our sample has a car. About a quarter of households have none of the goods.

We would expect *a priori* that renters who do not sub-let rooms to other households would tend to be more prosperous than their counterparts who do sub-let, notwithstanding the rental income they may acquire. This is the case for household incomes but per capita incomes show the opposite, no doubt owing to the larger households of the renters who do not sub-let. The RWI evidence shows that many more of those with sub-renters have none of the consumer durables included in the index (numbers in the non-transformers are so small that the paradoxical result in this variable need not be considered important).

House tenancy and ownership

We have seen that the dwellings were originally allocated through *mastans,* and were later regularised by the HSD as renters. Over 40 per cent of transformers and only one non-transformer came upon their tenancy by this means. However, half of the sample (and all the rest of the non-transformers) have bought possession. This is a process in which the occupant has paid a previous tenant for the ability to occupy the house but may not be known to HSD except as the anonymous payer of the monthly rent in place of a named tenant who is on the records.[5] This process has led to a significant number of occupants of transformed houses being non-transformers since they bought possession after the transformation had been made. It probably represents a form of 'raiding' or 'gentrification' where higher income groups displace lower as an area becomes more desirable or valuable. However, as the area was never successfully allocated to the target group (refugees),[6] it is impossible to determine whether the original occupants had lower incomes than the new.

The cost of buying possession of houses in Mirpur has been rising in real terms especially through the 1980s. This is probably a reflection of their increased size as well as the general increase in real value as the city becomes more crowded and the supply of housing falls further behind demand. Over the last few years, prices of Tk150,000 (£2500) and above have been commonplace but it must be remembered that all that is being purchased is the right to live in a house paying rent to the HSD; no ownership is involved.

It is very rare for renters in our sample to own a house in any urban area. The minority who possess a house tend to have it in the rural home area. There is no significant difference between transformers and non-transformers. We know, however, that 45 per cent of households in Mirpur own agricultural land (Bangladesh, 1993).

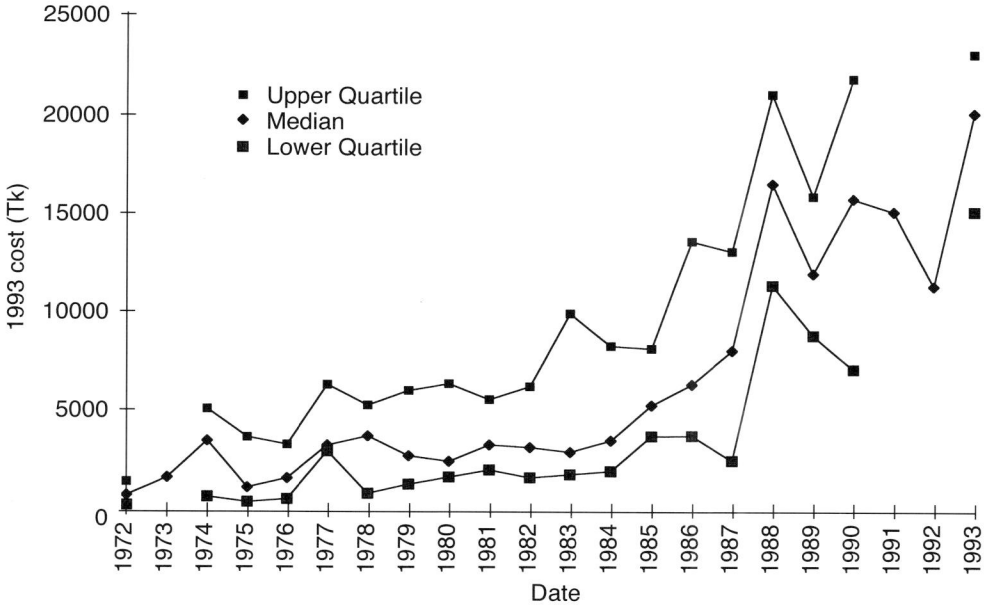

Figure 28. Cost of buying possession in Mirpur, 1972 to 1992

This is very important for our study as many will have already sold rural land to build extensions and many more will probably have sold from 1995 onwards to buy the leasehold of the house.

Household characteristics

Mean household size for Mirpur is 5.2 people. However, as table 49 shows, our sampled households tend to be slightly larger than average for Mirpur, with over 75 per cent in each group with five or more people. There are marginally more adults than children but the median of three children shows that many households are still liable to several years of stresses, triggers and shocks which may require them to find more space if at all possible. Many have alternative options for this: they can evict a tenant and use the vacated room or they can extend again. Whether the former or the latter will predominate we cannot tell at present. Non-transformers have smaller households and lower dependency ratios than transformers; they also expect to have smaller households in the future than transformers.

Guests are quite a feature of life in these crowded houses, with one per month at the median for recent transformers, and third quartiles for all transformers of 20 per annum. There is little difference in this between transformers and non-transformers.

Table 49. Household size and composition, owners

Medians (and IQRs)	Established transformers	Recent transformers	Non-transformers
Number of people in the household	6	7	5
	(5, 8)	(5, 9)	(5, 6)
Number of adults in the household	4	4	3
	(2, 5)	3, 5)	(2, 5)
Number of children in the household	3	3	2
	(2, 4)	(2, 4)	(1, 3)
Dependency ratio (no. of children per adult)	0.73	0.78	0.5
	(0.3, 1.3)	(0.4, 1.3)	(0.1, 2.0)
Expected household size in three years	7	7	5.5
	(5, 8)	(5, 9)	(5, 8)
Number of guests per annum	5	12	7
	(1, 20)	(4, 20)	3, 23)

Housing characteristics and house values for transformers and non-transformers

Introduction

In this section, we examine the physical characteristics of the original dwellings, characteristics of the housing after transformation, and the effects of the original design on extension activity. In addition, we describe the physical characteristics of the transformed house in some detail not only with respect to spatial organisation but also with regard to standards of space enjoyed by the occupants. We would expect the houses to be changing towards the conditions maintained in neighbouring areas and the city as a whole.

Increases in house size through transformations

In this discussion, we divide construction into phases to reflect the intermittent nature of the operation. When there was a pause of months or years between extensions, we regard them as being in different phases.

It can be seen in table 50 that transformation has added about 100 per cent of the original area to the house, recent transformers building more with 46 m² in total at the median. Phases tend to be small, numerous and of reasonably consistent scale, each comprising about the area of a single room at the median. There is considerable variation in the area added within a phase; in phase one, for example, the IQRs are 9.5 m² for established transformers and almost 14 m² for recent transformers. In addition, overall additions are surprisingly varied for what appears to be a very constricted standard 'plot' where only the houses next to the latrines and a few at the irregular edges of the sites appear to have extra space. In the event, our current houses vary from 34 and 36 m² at the first quartiles to 54 and 65 m² at the third for established and recent transformers respectively. The IQR for house areas is, therefore, similar to the original dwelling area. The suggestion in earlier work (Tipple, 1991a) that transformations create a variety of accommodation out of a relatively uniform stock is confirmed with respect to size of house in Bangladesh.

Table 50. Area of each phase of extension (m²)

	Established transformers	Recent transformers	The houses occupied by non-transformers
Original total built area*	22.2	22.2	22.2
	(22.2, 22.2)	(22.2, 22.2)	(22.2, 22.2)
Area added in Phase 1	9.9	8.8	16.4†
	(5.9, 15.5)	(4.9, 18.6)	(3.7, 26.2)
	(*n* = 218)	(*n* = 107)	(*n* = 11)
Area added in Phase 2	9.4	11.2	-
	(5.8, 17.6)	(7.9, 234.0)	
	(*n* = 137)	(*n* = 82)	
Area added in Phase 3	12.8	11.5	-
	(6.0, 25.6)	(8.3, 16.0)	
	(*n* = 38)	(*n* = 33)	
Area added in Phase 4	9.7	16.6	-
	(6.3, 15.1)	(7.8, 22.6)	
	(*n* = 7)	(*n* = 9)	
Area added in Phase 5	5.6	-	-
	(-, -)		
	(*n* = 1)		
Total built area	39.4	46.3	36.1
	(34.4, 53.9)	(35.8, 64.9)	(31.9, 55.3)

* Although some of the original dwellings are double sized (*c.* 45 m²), there are too few in the sample to register at the third quartile.
† This is the amalgamation of all phases because the current residents cannot differentiate as they were built by former tenants.

Habitable space is added in two distinct ways. First, the original space (14.1 m²), which consists of a habitable room and a transitional area (veranda), is rearranged to contain mainly habitable area. Second, habitable area is constructed within the extensions to add 11 and 18 m² at the medians for established and recent transformers respectively. Non-transformers live in houses which have been extended by similar amounts before their arrival. Total habitable space of more than double the original house has been achieved by transformation. Recent transformers have larger amounts of habitable space than established transformers, by 4.4 m² at the median and 7.6 at the third quartile. This suggests that, in Mirpur, by separating recent transformers as those who have extended in the last three years, we have captured those who are furthest advanced in a continuous process of extension.

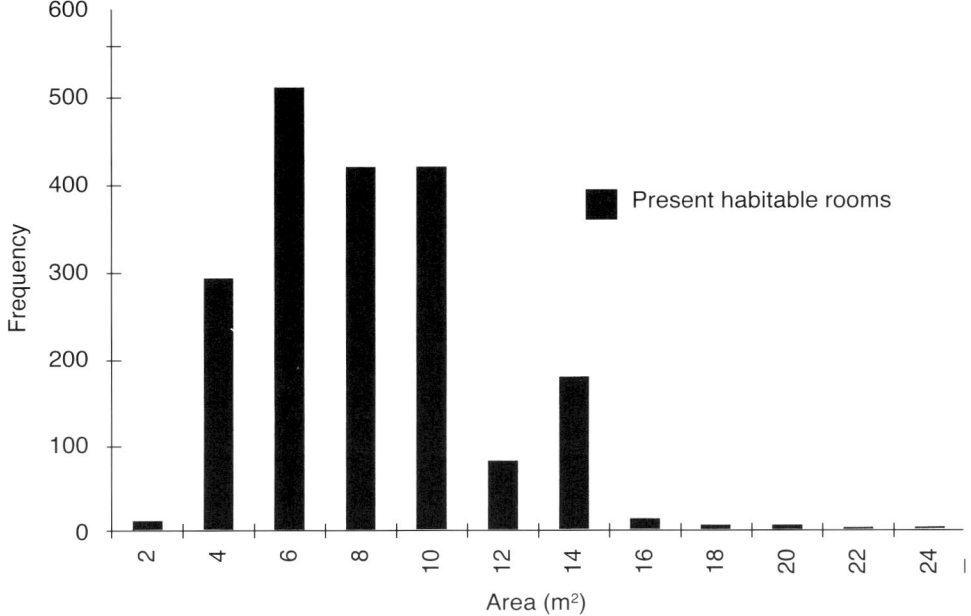

Figure 29. Frequency of habitable rooms by area, Mirpur

All the original rooms are 14 m² in area. It can be seen that the new rooms, including those which have been carved out of the existing one in phase 0, are smaller and much more varied. They are chiefly grouped in the 6–10 m² range and we shall see below how this leads to quite respectable occupancy rates (people per room) but very little habitable area per person.

The original houses were not particularly efficient in providing habitable space as the verandas were quite large (8 m²). There has been a large increase in the proportion of the enclosed space which is habitable, from only 62 per cent to about 90 per cent. Indeed the main purpose of the transformation process appears to have been to increase living area. The residents have almost universally removed the verandas and they have not replaced them elsewhere (as they have in Egypt, for example).

Few houses have rooms in them specifically devoted to commercial uses (11 per cent of the sample). Where they exist, they tend to be at least the area of a single room and a large minority are as large as the original dwelling.

In a study of informal sector activities in houses elsewhere in the sub-continent, Lall (1994) found a considerably higher percentage of the house (38 per cent) taken up by the workplace. However, there are likely to be many more commercial, manu-facturing and service industry uses which are not registered in our study because they do not take place in separate areas and we were not concerned with picking up space used partly for commercial use and partly for living (usually at different times of day). There are 298 people reported as working in the houses in our sample. Spaces dedicated for commercial use tend to be rooms facing a street at the side of an end house. Shops tend to be small (2–3 m wide and roughly the same deep) and typically sell a range of food and household goods, or specialised goods such as clothing or electrical appli-ances. There are also barber's shops, tailor's shops and stationers/photocopiers. Three houses have specialised space for manufacturing, two of them for making shoes.

Some transformers may prefer to use rooms for non-residential purposes because, apart from the higher rent which may be chargeable, they would reduce the pressure on bathrooms, toilets and kitchen spaces in the house. It is likely that increasing levels of commercial activity both follow from and generate demand for transformations.

Transformers have increased the habitable space through reorganising the original structure. There are now three rooms at the median for established transformers and two for recent transformers in the original structure. After this, the phases of extension tended to add a single room for each phase, and a total of two additional rooms at the medians. The median rooms per house is now four for established and five for recent transformers, an increase of over fourfold. Services are added by most transformers in phases one or two as most of the original dwellings had none.

Increases in space per person

We have no data on who lived in the houses before transformation. However, as discussed in chapter 2, we have used three proxies for original space occupied per person in the houses. The first, in which we adopt the non-transformers as represen-tatives of households before transformation, cannot be used in Bangladesh owing to the lack of non-transformed houses (recall that non-transformers almost all live in transformed houses). Thus, we must rely on the others. The second (HoOo) assumes that the original house (Ho), is occupied only by the current main household as the nearest approximation to the original occupants of the house (Oo). This assumes that extra people are attracted to the house only in proportion to its increasing size. A third proxy (HoOc) assumes that the original house (Ho), whose size we know, is occupied by all the current occupants (Oc). This measure has the advantage that it shows how much improvement has been made through the extensions. However, it has the disad-vantage that it assumes that all the current occupants are likely to have come to the house regardless of space available. The latter is not much of a problem where a single household occupies the transformed house but it is unrealistic in houses with additional rented rooms. However, it does give some impression of the crowding which might have been dispersed throughout the rest of the housing stock had not extra space been generated through transformation. These two measures are compared with the current housing space enjoyed or endured by the current occupants (HcOc). Table 51 demonstrates the effects of transformation on total space occupied according to these measures.

Table 51. Changes in space per person

	Established transformers	Recent transformers	Non-transformers
Current housing space per person (m²) (HcOc)	3.9 (3.0, 5.4)	3.7 (3.0, 4.9)	5.1 (3.5, 7.2)
Original housing space per person (m²) (HoOo)	3.7 (2.8, 4.5)	3.2 (2.5, 4.5)	4.5 (4.3, 7.4)
Original housing space per person (m²) (HoOc)	2.2 (1.6, 3.2)	1.9 (1.4, 2.5)	3.7 (2.0, 4.5)
Current rooms per person	0.57 (0.46, 0.80)	0.55 (0.43, 0.72)	0.63 (0.56, 0.91)
Original rooms per person (HoOo)	0.17 (0.13, 0.20)	0.14 (0.11, 0.20)	0.20 (0.19, 0.33)
Original rooms per person (HoOc)	0.10 (0.07, 0.14)	0.08 (0.06, 0.11)	0.17 (0.09, 0.20)

Originals (HoOo) are generated assuming that the original occupants (Oo) can be represented by the current main household.
Originals (HoOc) are generated assuming that all the occupants of the current house (Oc) would have occupied the original house (Ho).

The increase in space per person achieved from the main household's representing the original occupants (HoOo) is only marginal (5 and 16 per cent) but more significant in terms of rooms per person (235 and 293 per cent). This shows the importance of the division of the original structure into smaller rooms. The increase evident when using current occupants as a proxy (HoOc) for the original occupants is more marked at 74 and 98 per cent in space terms and 470 and 587 per cent in terms of rooms per person.

Reflecting what we have seen earlier, habitable space per person has been improved more efficiently than total space. HcOc has improved habitable space per person over HoOo by 38 and 60 per cent and habitable rooms per person by 141 and 186 per cent, both considerable improvements. HoOc, however, shows even greater improvements: 130 and 174 per cent in space per person and 310 and 400 per cent in rooms per person. Thus, transformation has improved habitable space provision per person by at least 38 per cent and habitable rooms per person provision by at least 141 per cent.

Increases in space occupied by main households[7]

Although the house has increased in size by over 100 per cent at the median, the main household does not occupy all the area. The area occupied by the main household has increased only by 25 and 34 per cent respectively for established and recent transformers. However, the habitable area available to them has increased by 44 and 73 per cent respectively. They tend to occupy most or all of the original dwelling and only a small proportion of extensions. Recent transformers are, however, more likely to occupy extensions, with a median of 5.5 m² used there. These data show that the extensions are frequently not for the main household's exclusive occupation but for renting out to others. In addition, they show how a variety of space occupied is being produced out of uniformity: from all households having 22 m² (14 m² habitable) there are now IQRs of over 20 m² for all space and for habitable space occupied by the main households.

In urban Bangladesh, the mean floor space per person is 5 m² but this drops to between 1.4 and 1.9 m² in some of the more densely populated areas, such as Islambag (the old part of Dhaka), where 6000 people per hectare are reported (UNDP and Bangladesh, 1994). Our main households have around 4 m² per person at the median but habitable area of only 3 m² for established transformers and 3.5 m² for recent transformers. Thus, they are midway between the urban mean and the most densely populated areas. When we consider that a western single bed is about 1.6 m² in area, each person in the median household has a habitable area at their disposal equivalent to two single beds.

The data in table 52 illuminate the issue of density and occupancy raised in the preliminary work on transformations (Tipple, 1991a, 1992) in which we posited that 'transformations increase the local population and generate higher population densities but tend to reduce occupancy rates' (Tipple, 1991a: 77). The future occupancy rate picks up whether a household is likely to be larger or smaller in three years' time. Housing adjustment theory (based mainly in industrialised countries) holds that extensions or alterations are likely to be triggered by 'shocks' such as increases in household size through births or elderly people moving in with their children (Seek, 1983). The future occupancy rate indicates whether households expect such 'shocks' in the near future. Table 52 shows that the households of both transformers and non-transformers in our Bangladesh sample tend to be on a very level trajectory in terms of size.

We have seen in table 49, however, that, with three children at the median, transformers could still require more space in the future. The data on rooms and space occupied show that main households occupy two to three habitable rooms and a little over 20 m² habitable space at the medians. Occupancy rates are high, as would be expected in a low-income area in a city with a gross housing shortage. Third quartiles of more than three, combined with the small size of rooms, demonstrate severe crowding for at least some households. The higher occupancy rates for recent transformers contrast with their greater habitable space per person and may demonstrate their having slightly larger rooms than established transformers.

In table 53, the changes in space are brought together for comparison. There is now about twice as much housing space as was originally built. It is evident that the transformers have gained considerable space in a very constricted area but their gains have

Table 52. Measures of occupancy, main households

Medians (and IQRs)	Established transformers	Recent transformers	Non-transformers
Rooms occupied by the household	3.5	3	4
	(2, 6)	(2, 6)	(2, 9)
Habitable rooms occupied by the household	2.5	3	2
	(1, 4)	(2, 4)	(1, 4)
Space occupied (m²)	27.8	30.0	35.6
	(14, 39)	(16, 38)	(21, 48)
Habitable space occupied (m²)	20.3	24.4	24.5
	(5, 30)	(14, 33)	(7, 33)
Occupancy rate (persons per habitable room)	2.3 (1.6, 3.6)	2.5 (1.7, 3.5)	2.3 (1.6, 4.4)
Future occupancy rate (persons per habitable room)	2.3 (1.6, 4.0)	2.5 (1.7, 3.8)	2.3 (1.6, 4.5)
House occupancy rate (persons per habitable room)	2.4 (1.9, 3.0)	2.5 (2.0, 3.2)	2.3 (2.0, 3.7)

Table 53. Comparison of increases in rooms, space, etc. (original median equals 100)

	Established transformers	Recent transformers	Non-transformers
Total space per house	177	208	162
Habitable space	241	272	200
Number of habitable rooms	400	500	400
Area occupied by the main household	125	134	160
Habitable area occupied by the main household	144	173	174
Habitable rooms occupied by the main household	250	300	200

been even more significant in terms of habitable space, particularly through converting the verandas. The increase in habitable rooms is particularly spectacular but must be seen in context: rooms in transformed houses are considerably smaller than the original ones. However, the improved privacy which is possible with several small rooms rather than one large one must be an important factor for transformers in this Islamic country, especially if rooms are to be rented out. The inner courtyard, narrow though it is, provides the separate access to rooms required for privacy. This supports our preliminary impression that, among the urban poor, several small rooms are preferable to one or two large ones; transformation provides more rooms as well as more room.

The pattern between variables is similar for the house and for main households except that the latter's gains are more modest than those in the house as a whole. There is, however, sure evidence of improved housing conditions for the main household. While it might have been thought that they had merely subdivided the original structure to gain more habitable rooms but left the new space for renting, in fact they have more space and more habitable space as well as space for renting out.

Space occupied by subsequent households

Few main households admitted to having rent-paying tenants, most claiming that the extra households were relatives. Tenant and other subsequent households undoubtedly occupy smaller areas than the main households; almost all of them have only one room and a mere 9 m² habitable area per household at the median. Even at the third quartile, only 13 to 15 m² is available per household.

Sub-tenants do not appear to suffer much worse occupancy rates than main households, however, as they have means of three persons per room. This is probably just as well as we have already seen that main households are very crowded because rooms are small.

Space per person for all households

The main household occupies the lion's share of the house with a median of two-thirds and third quartile of 100 per cent. Sub-tenant households[8] therefore occupy one-third of the house at the medians. The amount of space each sub-tenant household occupies is inversely related to the number of households in the house reducing from about 25 per cent (at the median) when there is only one sub-tenant household to only 13 per cent in the few where there are four sub-tenant households. It follows, therefore, that the percentage of space occupied by the main household reduces as more sub-tenants are housed – down to 44 per cent with four. These data demonstrate that there are disadvantages for sub-tenants in living in a *bastuhara* house with several households.

Increases in people accommodated

We have no data on original population so can only discuss probabilities – what is likely to be the effect of transformation on increases in population in the sampled houses.

We can only estimate the planned population for the *bastuhara* housing through comparison with the mean household size in Dhaka of 5.2 (Bangladesh, 1993). Certainly it is unlikely to have been intended for more than six persons per dwelling in the absence of transformation. In this work we have seen that there are means of 11.5 people per house for established transformers and 13.8 for recent transformers. Thus, there has been an increase of about 100 per cent in population, more or less matching the increase in space and habitable space in table 53.

Occupancy rates are likely to have reduced. Habitable rooms have increased four- to sevenfold, while the single household planned per house has been increased to two or three at the medians, and around three at the mean, by the addition of a mean of about two tenant households.

Improved service levels

There is a tendency for services to be quite high priorities in transformations in our sample, most houses having them added in the first two phases. Subsequent phases may also add further services. We cannot separate toilets and washrooms at this stage but it is clear that the tendency to replace use of public toilet and bathing facilities with private ones early in the process of transformation, found elsewhere in the sub- continent (Benjamin, 1985; Dasgupta, 1990), is repeated here.

According to official statistics, only 5 per cent of households in Mirpur have no toilet facilities (Bangladesh, 1993). From a virtual absence of toilets in the *bastuhara* houses, we now have almost 90 per cent of houses having at least one. Although sewer lines have recently been laid down the lanes between house blocks, often with cata- strophic effects on the brick paving, many households continue to use pour-flush latrines soaking into pits which, in such small plots and with a high water table, may not be a sustainable solution in the long term. Again, according to official statistics, water supply in Mirpur generally is better than in Dhaka with 72 per cent of house- holds having taps to the dwelling and 21 per cent using tubewells (Bangladesh, 1993). Most of our sample now have a tap in the house.

House physical condition

The original buildings are what is called in Bangladesh '*semi-pucca*' construction, not qualifying for the *pucca* category because the roof is not a concrete slab. All are built in burnt bricks with corrugated metal sheet roofs. Most of the extensions are in materials similar to the original houses and most conform to *semi-pucca* construction although some brick walls are only 7.5 cm thick (with the bricks laid on their sides). Bricks are available for Tk2000 (£33) per thousand and are universal in Dhaka.

Bamboo matting is used as walling material in 18 per cent of transformed houses, usually in combination with other materials. The bamboo mats are available from local weavers at a price of Tk50 (£0.8) per square metre. The original intention of separating off the transformers who had used only bamboo matting was abandoned because only 6 per cent of transformers do not combine bamboo with other materials. The use of organic materials would lead local officials to label these extensions *kutcha* or temporary.

Roofing follows the originals in using corrugated metal sheets almost universally, although many will be secondhand. The originals are prone to leaking as they are oxidising. Indeed, in the photographs of the area, one crude way of identifying the original room is through the pinkish roofing in contrast with the silver-grey on the new work. The original unglazed windows are not emulated by most transformers. Instead, they tend to fit glazed windows.

The original structures are in only indifferent condition after their 20 years of life with a large minority having cracks in the walls (41 per cent) or leaking roofs (47 per cent). These conditions also affect the extensions but to a slightly lesser extent. These data provide only the most marginal support to the notion that transformation is a means of upgrading the physical conditions of the houses in an area. This is in contrast with the massive increase in services available to residents, mainly through their own efforts.

There are many very small rooms in the Bangladesh sample; about 70 per cent of houses appear to have at least one habitable room of less than 6 m² area and about 40 per cent have two, but rooms less than 4 m² are much less common; only about 14 per cent of houses have one.

Plan forms

As we have described in chapter 5, there seems to be a tendency to create the 'plot' into a walled area to which access is gained by a door. This leads into an open corridor running from front to rear which leads to the original building, and any new rooms which usually open directly off it. Washing and cooking areas may be part of this corridor/courtyard or may be inside rooms. There is, thus, a distinct enclosure of space behind high boundary walls or within the buildings, the focus of which appears to be the corridor/courtyard space. The door to the road forms a distinct threshold where public space is succeeded by semi-private space. As we will see below, the open corridor/courtyard tends to take up about one-third of the 'plot' area. Some of this corridor may be covered with a clear corrugated sheet roofing to keep out the rain but allow some light in. This undoubtedly causes a deterioration in ventilation.

It is now almost universal for all rooms to open off the open space or narrow corridor. Where rooms lead off each other, the inner one usually has some alternative access to the corridor in addition. Only in a few cases has the access to the original room been left through the veranda space. The latter is almost always subsumed in a larger new room.

Cost of transformation phases

Established transformers tend to have built more expensive phases than recent ones (both phases one and two are more expensive than the latter's phase one), probably because life is generally becoming more expensive for low income households. In general, the phases tend to diminish in cost after phase one (table 54) but even phase five extensions have a median cost of Tk12,000 (£200), about 10 per cent of median house cost.

Table 54. Cost of phases in the extension process in thousands of taka

Medians (and IQRs)	Established transformers	Recent transformers	All transformers
Phase 1 (*n* = 369)	39.3	25.0	33.3
	(20.8, 69.1)	(12.9, 44.8)	(17.3, 59.5)
Phase 2 (*n* = 244)	26.0	18.0	22.4
	(15.6, 46.0)	(10.0, 36.1)	(12.8, 42.0)
Phase 3 (*n* = 85)	19.0	11.9	15.8
	(9.4, 43.5)	(6.9, 22.4)	(7.5, 28.7)
Phase 4 (*n* = 18)	17.8	9.5	12.3
	(10.0, 35.8)	(2.7, 23.1)	(7.4, 27.6)
Phase 5 (*n* = 6)	11.6	12.3	12.3
	(4.8, 31.7)	(-, -)	7.4, 20.2)
Total cost of transformations	62.8	46.1	56.1
	(37.5, 106.4)	(25.0, 80.0)	(31.6, 98.4)

All costs are adjusted to 1993 values.

The total spending on transformations is higher for the established transformers, with a median of Tk63,000 (£1050), than for recent transformers, whose median is Tk46,000 (£767). The overall median of Tk56,000 (£933) is a substantial amount – about one year's income, but the third quartile of Tk98,400 (£1640) shows that some have spent even more prodigiously, especially the established transformers.

The mean spending on transformations per house is Tk75,040 (£1250). If we assume that our sample is representative of the whole *bastuhara* housing (which it should be), the 4304 houses have probably had a total of Tk323 million invested in their transformation. This converts to £5.4 million or PPP£22.35 million.

Increases in house value and cost

We asked the main household in the house what their perception was of its value and rebuilding cost (table 55). In addition, they were asked to estimate what they would be willing to pay to rent similar accommodation if they lost their current house.

We have no ability to compare perceived values of transformed houses with those which are not transformed because there are only two of the latter in our sample, despite efforts to find more. There is a general consensus among occupants as to the value of Mirpur transformed houses at Tk150,000 (£2500) at the median and Tk30,000 (£500) per habitable room. Values per square metre are slightly higher for established transformers (Tk3500, £58) than recent transformers (Tk3200, £53). All the values

Table 55. Value of the house

Medians (and IQRs)	Established transformers	Recent transformers	Non-transformers
Value of the house	150	150	150
(Tk thousand)	(100, 200)	(100, 200)	80, 200)
Value of the house per room	22.2	21.5	20.0
(Tk thousand)	(16.7, 30.0)	(16.7, 29.2)	(17.1, 31.3)
Value of the house per habitable room	30	30	40
(Tk thousand)	(24.0, 44.7)	(23.2, 40.0)	(33.3, 50.0)
Value of the house per square metre	3.46	3.18	3.43
(Tk thousand)	(2.4, 4.6)	(2.5, 4.2)	(2.4, 4.8)
Percentage higher than average	55	58	83

are quite varied (IQRs are more than half median values) even though the medians are similar across transformer sub-samples. The non-transformers perceive themselves to have bought possession of higher-than-average value properties, again adding to the impression that there might be some 'gentrification' occurring as households buy into the area.

Table 56. Rebuilding cost of the house

Medians (and IQRs)	Established transformers	Recent transformers	Non-transformers
Rebuilding cost (Tk thousands)	120	100	100
	(100, 200)	(100, 200)	(80, 200)
Rebuilding cost per room (Tk thousands)	20	16.7	20
	(13.5, 28.5)	(12.5, 25.0)	(14.0, 25.0)
Rebuilding cost per habitable room	30	24	33.3
(Tk thousands)	(20, 40)	(17, 33)	(19, 50)
Rebuilding cost per square metre	3.01	2.47	2.77
(Tk thousands)	(2.17, 4.14)	(1.89, 3.56)	(2.24, 3.16)

Rebuilding costs quoted (table 56) are generally slightly lower than values, indicating either that some attention is being paid to the price of the land or that housing is worth more than it costs to build. If land cost is an issue, house occupants are slightly underestimating its value at Tk40–50,000 (£670–830) as HSD assesses average plots of 12.5 m by 4.9 m (about 60 m^2) at Tk63,360 (£1056). Established transformers have consistently higher estimates of costs, not only for the whole house but also by unit area.

It is surprising that the recent transformers have lower cost estimates as they would be expected to be up to date on costs and newer building appears to be as good quality as, or better than, older transformations. Theirs, however, are probably the more accurate estimates at Tk2500 (£42) per square metre. Thus, building cost per square metre is roughly 75 per cent of value at the median.

Ameen (1995) gives two costs per square metre for new building in Dhaka using Public Works Department data for 1993. The first, for standard low-cost (*pucca*) construction suitable for several storey buildings, is Tk8420 (£140). This represents construction with a 25 mm brick wall, reinforced concrete slab roof, plaster and paint finishing, plumbing and electrics. Our sample undercuts this first estimate by over Tk5000 per square metre at the median, so 3 m^2 are supplied for the 'official' cost of one. A second standard, *semi-pucca*, with thinner walls, without concrete slab roof, finishings or the strength of foundation required for several storeys, is estimated by the PWD at only Tk4100 (£680) per square metre but our sample undercuts this also. Recent transformers (who should know the cost of construction) reckon on Tk1600 per square metre less.

The much reduced costs quoted by our sample are most likely to be a reflection of the savings available by using the informal sector in construction work. We see below that most householders use single tradesmen rather than contractors. These are likely to be operating outside the formal system of registration and control, and to have smaller overheads and narrower profit margins than the formal sector represented by PWD.

The coincidence of our survey with the decision to sell the leases of the houses gives us another measure of value against which to judge our transformers' efforts, the price of the land and original 22 m^2 structure. As we saw above, the structure is valued at Tk103,000 less 32 per cent depreciation (Tk70,567 – £1170) or Tk3167 per square metre. As we can see, most of our sample value their house more highly than that, after all most are much larger, but the value per square metre is similar. Replacement costs estimate approximately the equivalent to rebuild the whole of the transformed structure, not just the original dwelling.

The PWD prices could be said to show us the cost of alternative housing for this group, if it existed. For Tk150,000 (£2500), a Mirpur resident who had the need to sell up and move could obtain a similar plot (for, say, Tk63,000) and less than 20 m^2 of *semi-pucca* house with some services; in other words a core house. In the Chittagong sites and services scheme, where land is much cheaper than in Dhaka, a 60 m^2 serviced plot is priced at Tk47,000[9] (Rahman, 1995). For the balance of the Tk150,000, the householder could erect only 25 m^2 of *semi-pucca* rooms. Thus, even if we assume that smaller scale formal sector contractors can make efficiency gains over a government department, the transformed *bastuhara* houses represent excellent value both as housing and as investments for their occupants in comparison with newly built alternatives.

There is a degree of agreement about rent values of transformed houses with medians of Tk1500 (£25) per household, Tk500 (£83) per room, and about Tk55 (almost £1) per square metre per month. The spreads of rents per room and rents per square metre for established transformers are very large (IQRs equal Tk750 per room and Tk69/per m²), both being greater than the median value.

The value of a habitable room in terms of monthly rents gives an indication of how long it would take a developer to pay off the investment and, thus, assess whether it is attractive. At the medians, these rooms in Mirpur would take less than six years to pay off, not counting interest. This makes them a very good investment and we can be confident that transformations will continue as long as land is available. Such buoyant rent values *vis-à-vis* house cost also suggest that people buying into the area might see it as a good investment. This again suggests that there may be some 'gentri-fication' occurring, or at least there is some potential for it.

The value and rebuilding cost of the portion of the house occupied by each household show even more clearly how inexpensive the transformed accommodation is. They assume that only the portion of the extended house which is actually occupied by a household acts as a cost to its exchequer. Main households occupy about Tk90,000 (£1500) worth of housing at the median while their tenants make do with a third of that. Rebuilding costs are marginally lower at only about Tk80,000 (£1333). It is evident, therefore, that transformers can provide accommodation for a tenant household for between Tk20,000 and Tk30,000 (£333–500). The variety of value and rebuilding cost of areas occupied by main households is very great considering how constricted the plots are: IQRs are Tk82,000 and Tk63,300 (£1367 and £1055) respectively for established transformers.

It is useful to compare what a household could achieve in the Chittagong sites and services scheme with Tk90,000. Here, the cheapest alternative providing the most accommodation would be a 30 m² plot at Tk14,000 (Rahman, 1995) which could be developed with 18.5 m² of built floor space for Tk76,000 at the project prices. This would represent a cut of at least 10 m² in floor space at the median and a plot only half as large as the current one.

The Mirpur area was not originally divided into plots but, in our analysis, we have assigned plot boundaries to the houses. In most cases, householders have built a wall along boundaries which appear to be defined as follows. At the sides, boundaries follow the centre of the party wall on one side and the centre line between the two houses on the other. Where the common latrines were installed, a line dividing the area between the two neighbouring houses into equal parts defines the plot boundary. At the rear, the boundary follows the mid point between the houses or the edge of the storm-water drain if there is one. At the front, the boundary is the edge of the brick carriageway installed by the local authority. Where the plot abuts empty land, the boundary is wherever transformation development has stopped.

In a seemingly uniform area, quite marked variations can be found. Nevertheless, median plot sizes of almost 60 m² in a narrow rectangle represent quite constricted conditions for extensions.

The initial plot ratio of 0.4 at the median has been increased to 0.7 which is close to the requirements in *pucca* areas in Dhaka for one-third of the plot to be left free of buildings. Plot ratio and floor-space index are identical because there were no second storeys in our sample and only the occasional one in the *bastuhara* houses as a whole. This is likely to change when the current sales exercise is carried out as households are likely to feel it worth their while to demolish the original structure and build two or three storeys on the plot.

The space use within the house is much more varied after transformation than before. Almost all houses now have either a toilet or a washroom or both, and about 11 per cent have commercial activities. Most houses also now have a kitchen area, usually a part of the courtyard reserved for that and partly enclosed. Almost no one has preserved or built a veranda.

The data in this and the previous section support the notion that transformation creates variety out of uniformity. From uniform single-roomed dwellings, each with a veranda, have been produced:

- a varied range of house sizes (IQRs of 20 to 30 m²);
- a variety of spaces occupied by the main households (which equate to dwellings – IQRs of about 20 m²);
- additional space of varied amounts for tenants;
- a range of house values and costs (IQRs in excess of £1000);
- floor-space indexes and plot ratios of widely differing values (IQRs of about 0.4);
- a variety of room uses including commercial activities accommodating 298 jobs and offering such services as retailing (typical small shops sell dry goods such as rice by weight, soap, biscuits, cigarettes, tinned foods, eggs and small household goods), hairdressing, laundries and tailoring, and repairing electrical goods, cycles and rickshaws, motor cycles and baby-taxis (auto-rickshaws).

That this all takes place in an area where the standard 'plot' allows under 2 m extra width alongside the original buildings, is a measure of the ingenuity of the house-holders and their builders, the desperate need for new housing for low-income groups in Dhaka, and the willingness of the occupants to occupy small and narrow spaces.

The process of transformation

Motivation for extension

The most important reason for extension in Bangladesh is to increase the habitable area available to the household as it increases both through children growing older ('stress' or 'triggers') and more people joining ('shocks'). In all, 74 per cent of established transformers and 60 per cent of recent transformers selected these as the most important factors.

Economic factors are only considered important in respect of renting out rooms; this is more important for recent transformers as more than one-third cited it as the main factor in extending. From Ameen's previous work (Ameen, 1988), we know that rents charged for rooms are three to eight times higher than the rent for the house paid to HSD. In addition, UNCHS (1989) demonstrates that owning and renting out rooms are symbiotic, each enabling the other. Thus, we would expect renting to be an important function for extensions. Although the percentage who admitted to its being paramount (32 per cent overall) is not particularly high, in a context in which admitting to having tenants might cause problems, it is likely to be very conservative, hiding a much larger true figure.

In considering why house owners decide to improve rather than move, it is useful to divide them by those who might not have even considered a move and those who did consider moving but could not. The former are about 40 per cent. There is a strong recognition that their housing is a bargain and so rent-seeking behaviour would keep them from moving elsewhere, especially into the non-subsidised market. The remaining 60 per cent could not find a suitable or affordable alternative, showing that the occupants are aware of the advantages of their current housing in comparison with others available.

Problems encountered in the extension process

Respondents were asked to rank the problems encountered in their extension activity by selecting first, second and third in order of difficulty from finance, building materials, labour, services, permissions, and an 'other, specify' option. Finance is obviously by far the most intransigent problem, and increasingly so, so that it now dominates as the first choice. Would-be transformers must raise the money for a whole phase as a lump sum at the beginning of the building operation and pay for the whole job probably within only a week or two. Thus, capital is the *sine qua non* of the construction process. However, the work often over-runs the estimate and then borrowing from friends takes place, probably in something of a hurry.

Second place in these problems goes to building materials, especially for recent transformers. This is surprising in one sense in that there is a large brickworks on the boundary of Mirpur, but it makes high-quality ceramic bricks which most transformers would not require. As the house occupier is involved in obtaining the materials with the builder (see below), the complications involved will be brought starkly into focus for the respondent which may account for the high score of building materials in the difficulties list.

The construction process

The informal sector construction process in Dhaka occurs either through self-help or by using tradesmen in the way outlined in chapter 6. This is a very labour-intensive method of construction involving very little sophisticated construction technology. An example of this is in the foundations which are achieved without concrete work. Simple brick foundations are assembled beginning four bricks thick (20 inches, 500 mm) for one course, three bricks (15 inches, 375 mm) for the next, and then the 10 inch wall is begun at ground level. Where the superstructure is only one-brick-thick walling, the foundations will start with the three-brick layer.

The five inch (125 mm) brick walls will preferably only be built to 1.5 m height at a time to allow the mortar to harden and stabilise before continuing to add more weight. In order to add stability, the mortar will be mixed 1:4 cement to sand rather than the more usual 1:6. In our study area, bricks, sand and aggregates are not usually brought down the by-lanes but are stored close to the nearest road and head-loaded to site. There is remarkably little theft from piles of building materials.

A total of five phases of extension construction have been found in the Mirpur sample: 66 per cent have implemented two phases while 23 per cent have added three. The extension activity began in earnest in the early 1980s. Since that time, a significant body of extension work has been maintained. Many houses have been subjected to second and subsequent phases in relatively quick succession, despite the very confined nature of the original development.

The median date for the first transformation is 1986 for established and 1990 for recent transformers. The nature of the sample, selecting recent transformers as those active in the last three years, ensures a later date for the most recent phase than would be evident in the established transformers. However, for each group there is obviously a fairly rapid succession of extensions with six in our sample having completed five phases. More than half the sample had extended twice.

Although there are considerable annual fluctuations in the delivery of extensions, there is a generally growing and relatively high level of activity stretching from the mid-1970s to date with second and third phases starting as far back as the early 1980s. The recent transformers have been involved in extending for as long as established transformers and most are not on their first phase.

There is no room in the current transformation process in Mirpur for contractors. The majority of households use separate tradesmen and 30 per cent build for themselves. This relatively high incidence of self-help construction is, perhaps, not surprising as the complexity of building in this case study is very low. This is especially so for bamboo matting extensions which are quite common though few houses have been extended only with bamboo matting.

Almost all households have used their own funds to finance the extensions; only 11 per cent have borrowed the majority of the money for an extension and most of these did so from savings schemes. Occupants' own funds in the Bangladesh case may mean formal savings in the banking system but are also likely to include the sale of jewellery and land in the rural area.[10] There is also probably a significant component of remittances under the Workers' Earnings Scheme whereby expatriate Bangladeshis in the Gulf States and elsewhere can repatriate their foreign exchange through the private sector at higher than the official rates.

No one had asked for planning permission to extend the houses. This does not, however, render the transformations illegal under planning and building regulations. The *bastuhara* houses are defined as '*semi-pucca* tin sheds' in the certificate of lease

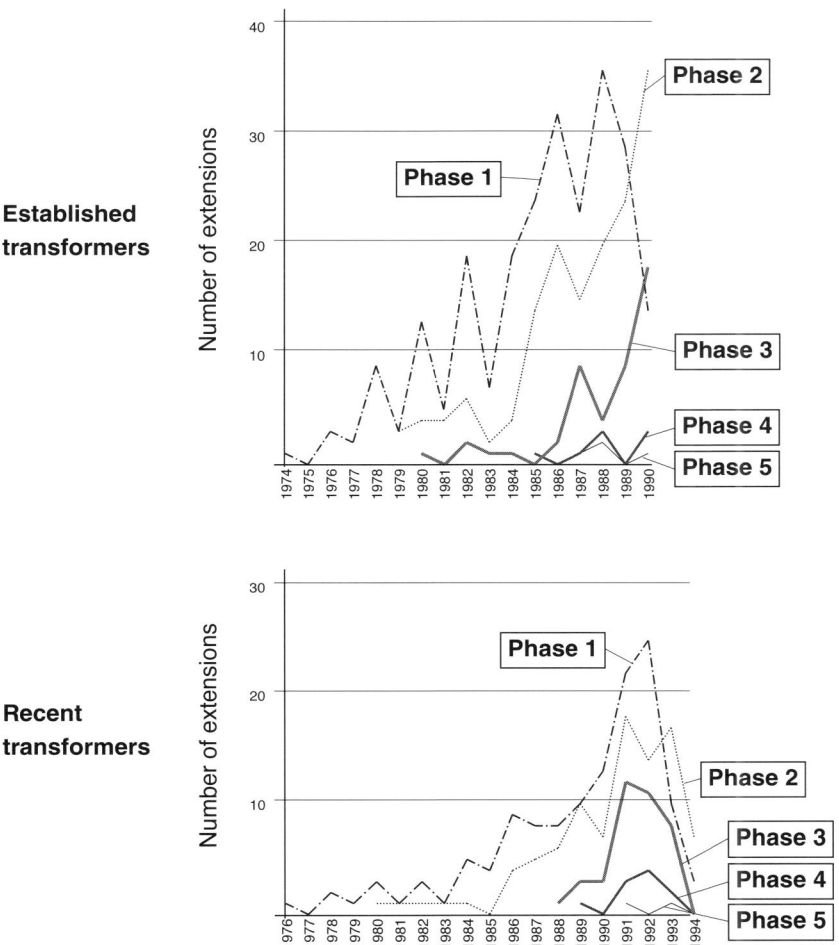

Figure 30. Number of extensions recorded in the Mirpur sample, by year

being issued by the HSD. Only *pucca* construction is governed by building and planning law. Thus, residents of Mirpur can alter and extend their houses as much as they like within the plot without contravening the law. However, this notwithstanding, 13 per cent of established transformers and 9 per cent of recent transformers had received threats from people in authority about their extensions although only one had had to make a change to the plan in response.

If, after purchasing the lease, occupants wish to demolish the original '*semi-pucca* tin shed', they must construct any new development to *pucca* standards (i.e. masonry with a concrete slab roof), fulfil building regulations and honour set-backs, etc. This will radically reduce the amount of the plot that can be covered.

Intention for disposing of the house

Currently, there is almost no one with the intention to sell the houses; almost all main households intend to remain and pass the house on to their relatives. Long residence in the past and anticipation of remaining in the future encourages transformation as a way of increasing use value, regardless of market value.

The sale of the leaseholds to these properties is likely to alter occupants' intentions for them when they no longer want to occupy them. It is more than likely that a lively market will develop in plots especially as current occupants try to consolidate their holdings by buying adjacent properties so that they have a squarer, more usable space. At this point, following the Umoja I, Nairobi, experience, we would expect to see demolition of existing structures and the construction of multi-storeyed flats and flatted factories even though this will be contrary to the planning laws governing *pucca* construction. There are such buildings on the periphery of the area and it is likely that such development would become more normal within the *bastuhara* areas. In this case, the likelihood is that the current population will gradually be displaced by higher income households as such developments lead to higher prices. Currently, however, our preliminary suggestion that 'transformations provide a means of increasing the capital investment which can be realised through the sale of the improved dwelling' (Tipple, 1991a: 77) appears to be partly true and partly false. Households that have bought possession of transformed houses demonstrate some support for this suggestion. However, the long time already spent in the area by current tenants and their intention to stay offers evidence of stability and a resistance to 'gentrification'.

Summary

The occupants of Mirpur *bastuhara* housing are generally well established in the city and their homes but remained renters until after our survey when sale by the HSD was agreed. Even in the very small and narrow plots of the *bastuhara* housing in Mirpur, transformers have been able to add 144 per cent more habitable space at the median. The extensions have been built quite cheaply and to a very high plot ratio. Transformers have undoubtedly benefited from the *laissez-faire* attitude of the authorities to their '*semi-pucca* tin-sheds' in being able to extend cheaply and to very high plot ratios.

Although the population of the area has increased as a response to the extra housing available, the original residents have improved their own housing conditions, especially through reduced occupancy rates and improved services. At the same time, sub-rented accommodation for about two more households per house has been provided.

The new additions are in relatively good condition and are perceived to have greater value (a 200 per cent increase) than their building cost. If generalised up to the entire *bastuhara* project, the occupants could be regarded as having added PPP£22.35 million worth of new housing. The survey has highlighted the remarkable achievements of the transformers in Mirpur, who are just above the national poverty line in terms of per capita income, in providing housing goods.

Income measures had a positive effect on whether a household extended the house in Bangladesh and the extent to which resources were spent on the transformation. Thus, policies that improve households' overall financial position are likely to be influential in encouraging good quality extensions. In addition, the influence of the smallness of the house on extension activity indicates that, where small houses are occupied elsewhere in the city, extension activity is likely. As a corollary, the provision of core housing of one or two rooms is likely to generate extension activity in Bangladesh. This would be more productive if plots were larger and wider than the 66 m^2 area and 5 m width of the *bastuhara* housing in Mirpur.

Notes

1   In 1994 there were about 60 taka to a pound sterling.
2   Tk94,341 for the structure and an additional 5 per cent each for electricity and sanitation.
3   The factor relating the actual GNP per capita of $210 to the adjusted real GDP per capita of PPP$872 (UNDP, 1993: table 1).
4   The US dollar has a PPP of 1.0, of course, as it is the base for the calculation.
5   This must be one of the weakest forms of tenure for which a relatively large sum of money is paid.
6   Only the 662 allocated to low-paid government workers can be said to have 'hit the target'.
7   Where there are non-habitable spaces (toilets, kitchens) in shared use, these are not allocated to the main household in this analysis.
8   That is, those admitted to by our sample.
9   For non-commercial locations.
10   As we have seen earlier, 45 per cent of occupants of Mirpur *Thana* claim to own land in the rural homeland.

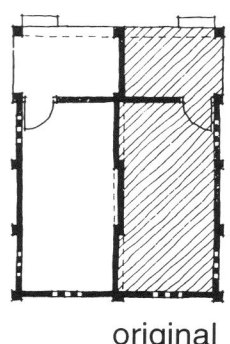

original

One of the few houses to use bamboo mats for walling, the extensions were very cheap and the whole house is only valued at Tk100,000, twice the household's annual income. The five-person main household (a couple and their three children) occupies one room. There are 12 people in the house in three households. The kitchen space and toilet are at the extreme rear of the plot. The original house has only been altered by the addition of a side door to the main room.

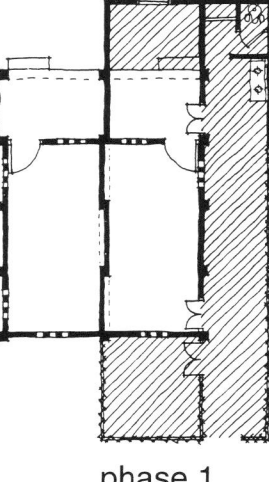

phase 1

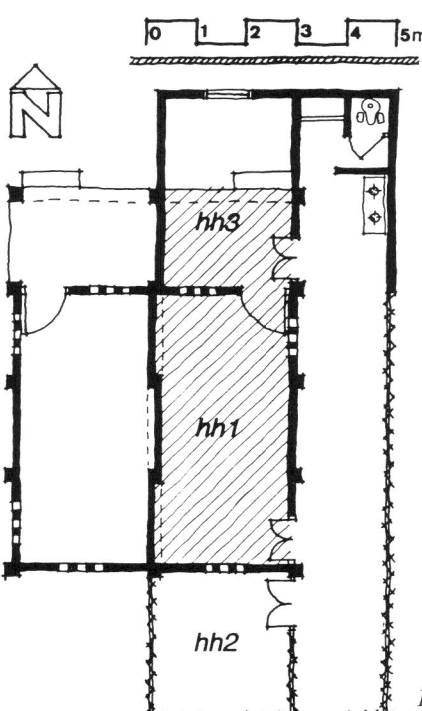

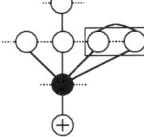

Figure 31. Extension using bamboo matting, Mirpur

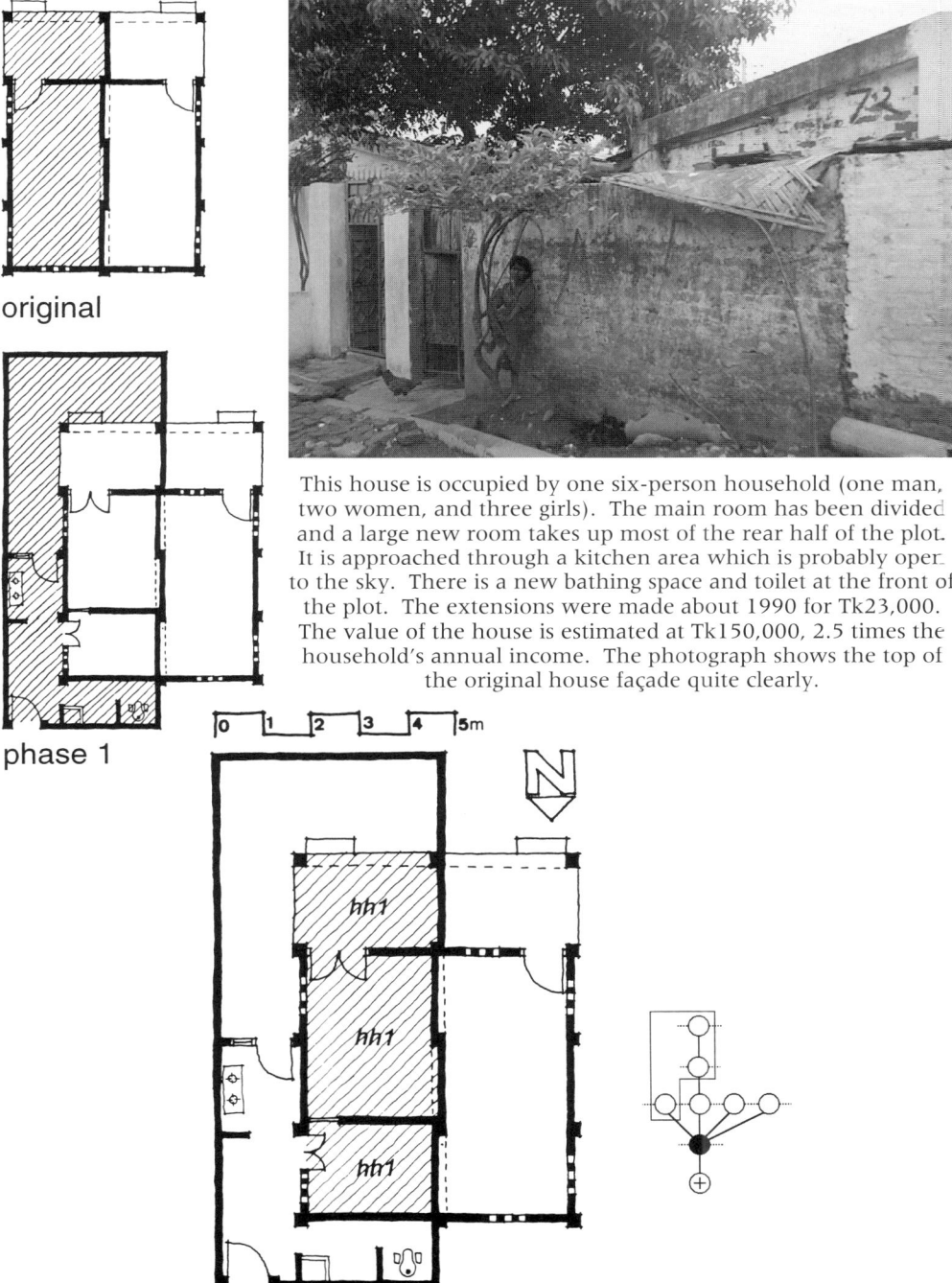

original

phase 1

This house is occupied by one six-person household (one man, two women, and three girls). The main room has been divided and a large new room takes up most of the rear half of the plot. It is approached through a kitchen area which is probably open to the sky. There is a new bathing space and toilet at the front of the plot. The extensions were made about 1990 for Tk23,000. The value of the house is estimated at Tk150,000, 2.5 times the household's annual income. The photograph shows the top of the original house façade quite clearly.

Figure 32. A hardly-extended house with only boundary wall and internal changes, Mirpur

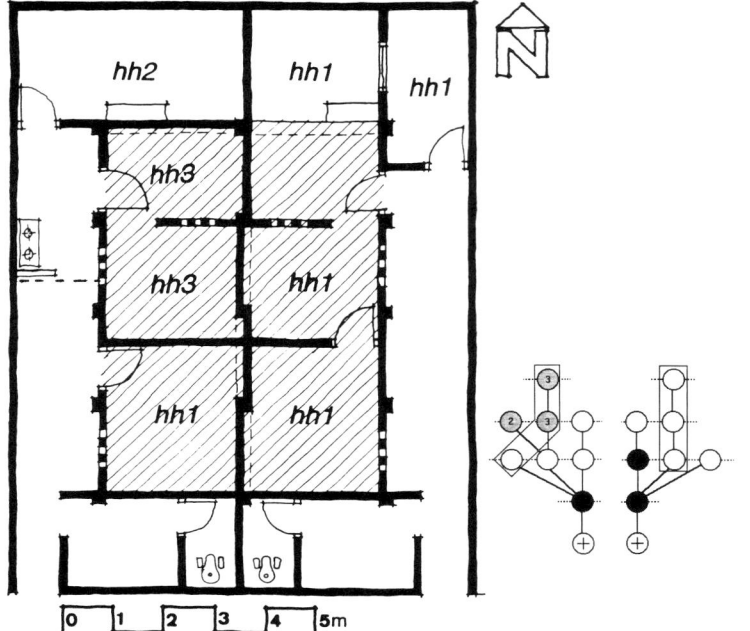

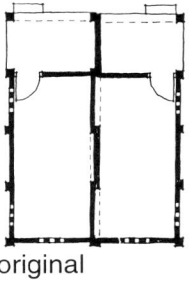

The possession was bought in 1974 and 1983 for a total of Tk7000. Similar extensions were made to each: phase 1 in 1987 costing Tk20,000 and phase 2 in 1989 for Tk30,000, but they provide differing accommodation. Both have toilet and bathroom suites on the south side. One has two rooms to the north, the other has a large room taking the whole of the north end with a covered kitchen space acting also as an access way to two rooms. Both original dwellings have been subdivided and one has a side door giving shallower access to the southern room. Seven people occupy the easterly house. Three single-person households live in the westerly house.

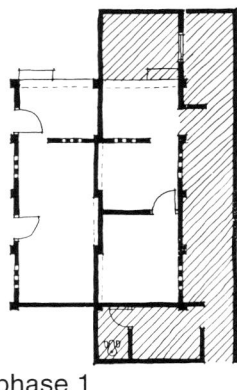

original

phase 1

phase 2

Figure 33. Neighbouring dwellings now with a single main renter, Mirpur

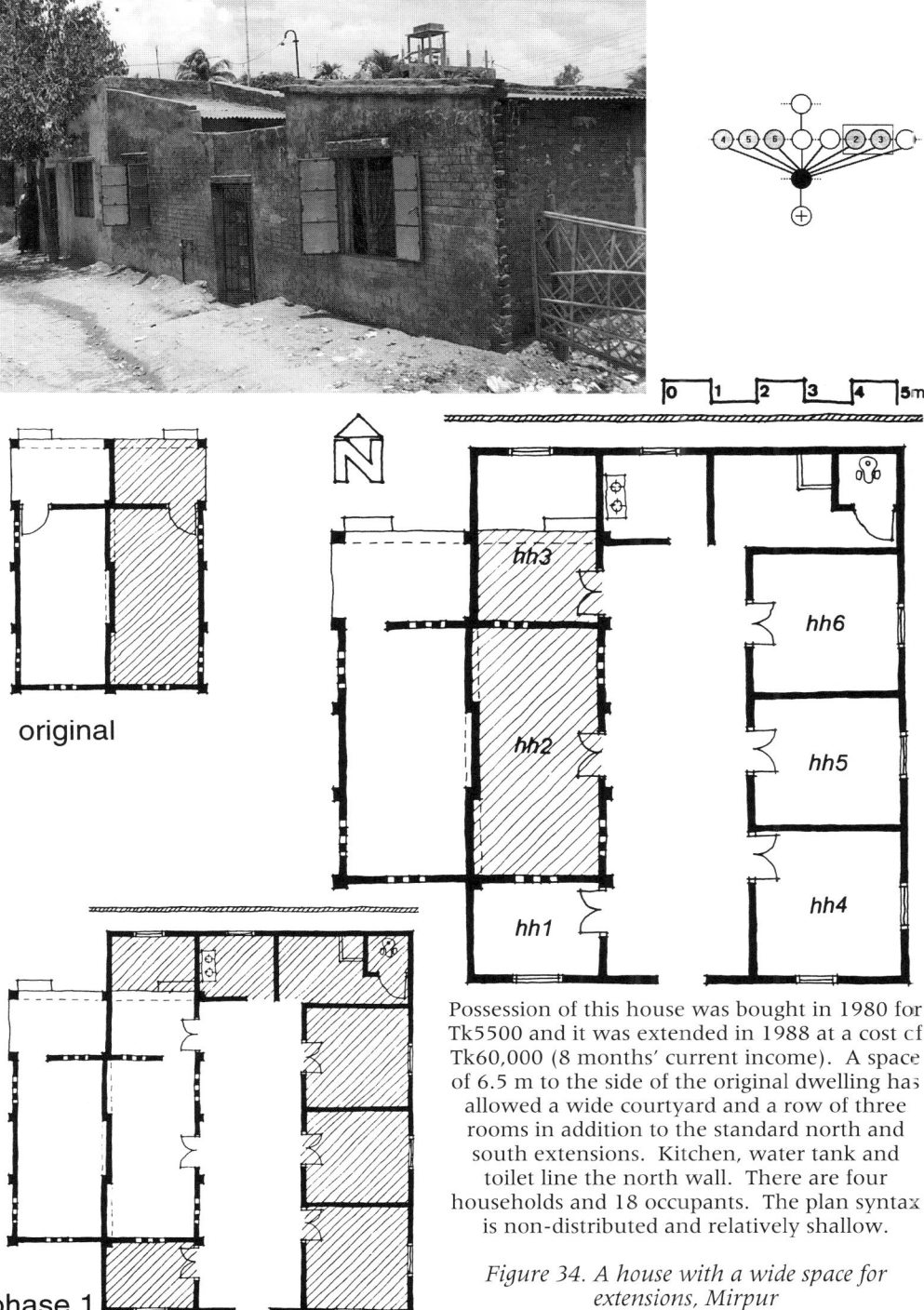

original

phase 1

Possession of this house was bought in 1980 for Tk5500 and it was extended in 1988 at a cost of Tk60,000 (8 months' current income). A space of 6.5 m to the side of the original dwelling has allowed a wide courtyard and a row of three rooms in addition to the standard north and south extensions. Kitchen, water tank and toilet line the north wall. There are four households and 18 occupants. The plan syntax is non-distributed and relatively shallow.

Figure 34. A house with a wide space for extensions, Mirpur

Figure 35. A typical street scene in the bastuhara *housing, Mirpur*
Extensions fill the spaces between original dwellings and the street.

Figure 36. Extensions in bamboo matting
Such extensions were much less common than we had expected from earlier visits.

Figure 37. Front façade and entrance showing low door, Mirpur

Figure 38. A brick extension with the original structure clearly visible behind, Mirpur

Figure 39. A corner site with two lock-up shops and residential accommodation, Mirpur

Figure 40. High-quality built environment but with poor surfacing following fitting a sewer line, Mirpur

Figure 41. A large corrugated iron and bamboo matting extension on a wide plot, Mirpur

Appendix 2. Transformations in Egypt

Introduction to Medinet Nasr, Cairo, and Workers' City, Helwan

The Egyptian case study is particularly interesting because the dwellings involved are multi-storey walk-up flats. The visit to Workers' City, Helwan, with its extensions crowding onto the façades, was one which began our interest in transformations and in the reasons why some people transform and others do not.

Cairo is the capital of Egypt and a regional centre for North Africa and the Middle East. Greater Cairo is by far the largest city in Egypt with a population of 12 million in 1991, and the largest city in which our study has been undertaken. Greater Cairo consists of three governerates: Giza, Kalubia and Cairo, the last of which contains both our study areas, Medinet Nasr and the Economic Housing of the Workers' City, Helwan.

In the Cairo Governerate in 1991, there were an estimated 1.46 million households with an average of 4.9 people; a population exceeding seven million. The annual population increase is estimated at 125,000, there are 50,000 marriages every year and the number of new households is estimated to grow at 2.6 per cent per annum (Kardash, 1994). Helwan is an industrial town south of central Cairo but within the Cairo Governerate.

Cairo is a city of great inequalities in housing provision. While households at the top of the income range hold three and more flats empty against the day when their children reach maturity, others crowd into very rudimentary accommodation in high-density areas in conditions graphically described by Wikan (1980). Thus, while the number of dwellings (1.73 million in 1986) exceeds the number of households, many households are severely crowded and find alternative accommodation impossible to locate. According to the 1986 census, the average occupancy rate in Cairo was 1.5 people per room and there were 15 m² of floor area per person; 22 per cent of dwellings are owner-occupied and 56 per cent are rented; there was a vacancy rate of about 15 per cent.

About 70 per cent of Cairo's population live in poor quality housing generically described as '*Ahiaa Shabbiaa*', literally meaning 'popular quarters'. This categorisation would include the majority of public housing projects (including our case-study neighbourhoods), the informal settlements, and the Fatmid core of Cairo. The remaining 30 per cent live in middle- and upper-income areas such as Heliopolis, Zamalek and Maadi, where public services and utilities are to a relatively high standard.

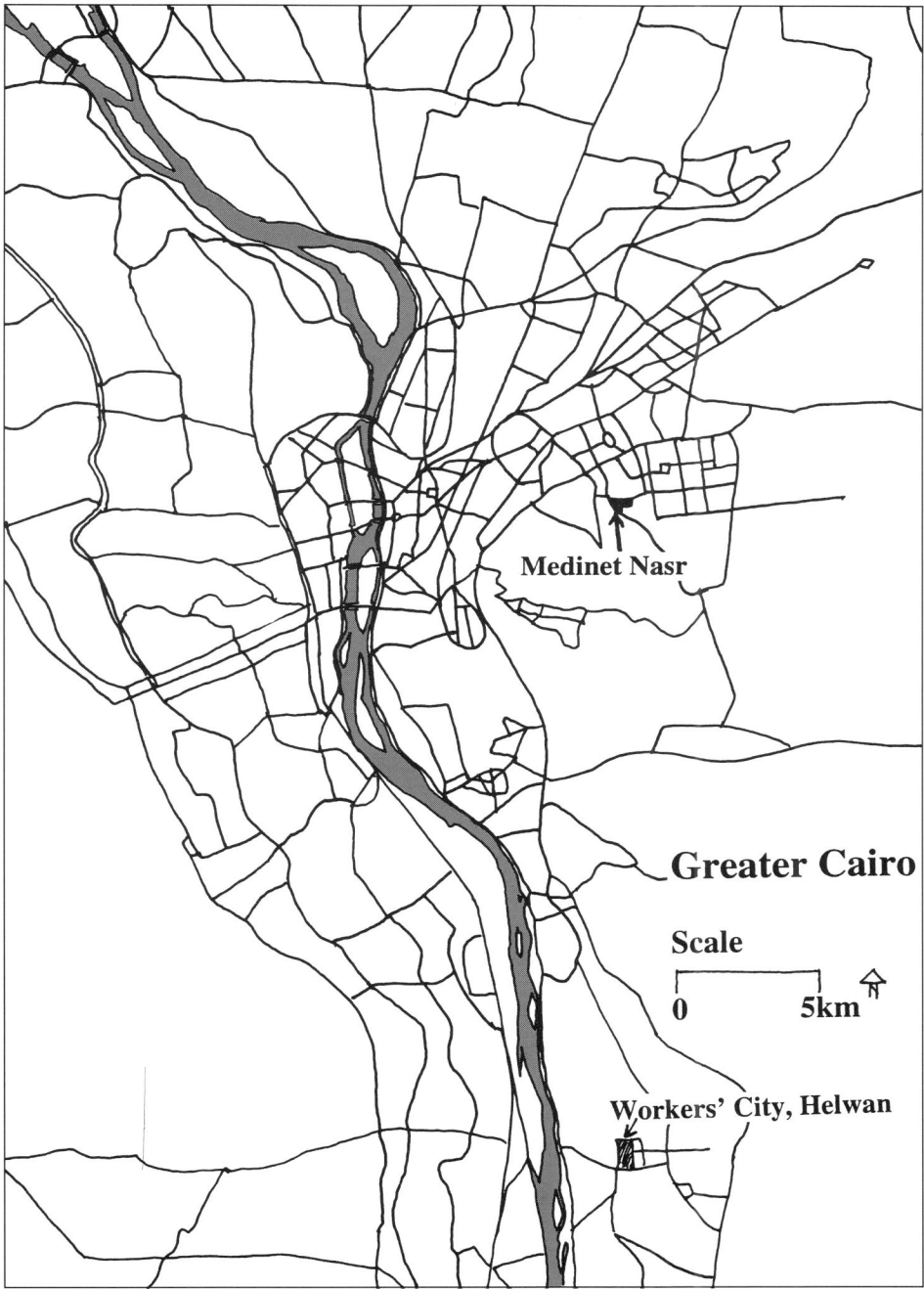

Figure 42. A map of Cairo
Source: Arnand, J-L., 1989, *Cartographie de l'Egypte, Observatoire Urbain du Caire Contemporain*, CEDEJ, Cairo.

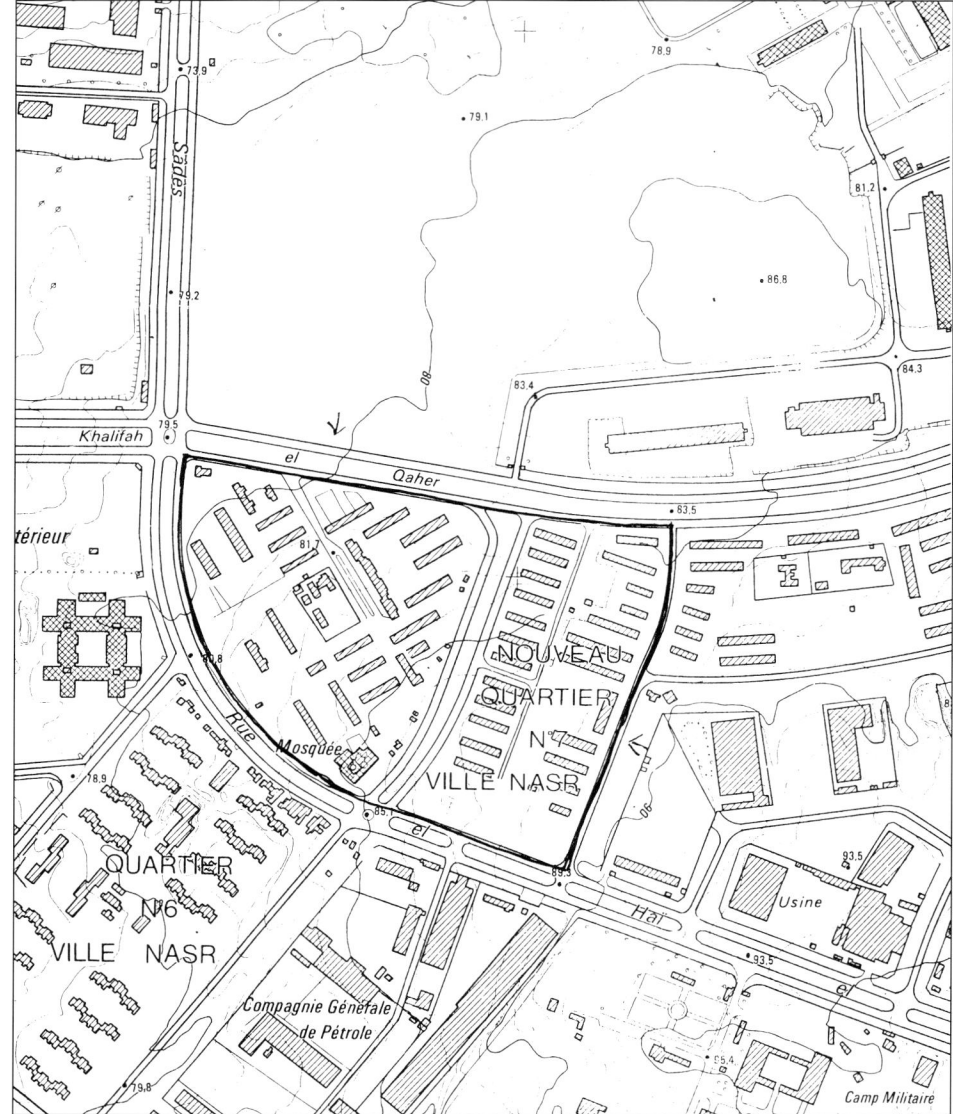

Figure 43. Plan of Medinet Nasr estate, Cairo

Most Cairians live in blocks of flats commonly referred to as '*Aimara*' of three to seven storeys. The flat would have two or three habitable rooms, a kitchen and a bathroom/toilet. Each room would have a window opening onto the street or a light-well whose width is stipulated as not less than 3 m or one-third of its height (whichever is greater). The building height should not exceed one and a half times the width of the street. In informal areas, which are built to similar physical standards to public housing, there are poorer services and the streets tend to be narrower than stipulated in the law – sometimes only 3 m in areas with five to seven floors.

While the occupants of the popular quarters might be expected to be homogeneously poor, this is not (now) the case. Two trends have served to increase heterogeneity in the poorer housing areas. The first is the influx of remittances from Egyptians working in the oil-producing Middle Eastern states. The uncertainty about whether this money will continue (not misplaced in the light of recent events in Iraq and Kuwait) prevents long-term movement out of the popular quarters into middle-class neighbourhoods which the current annual income may suggest to be appropriate. The second is a shortage of rental housing for newly formed middle-income households who can only find rental units in the popular quarters even though they have incomes above the norm there.[1] The classification of households by income, education or the neighbourhood occupied is no longer suitable in the complex situation of Egypt in the 1990s. Lifestyle and behaviour patterns are now truer indicators of class and status.

Since the early 1960s, the Egyptian Government has been embarked on a programme of building low-cost housing in large numbers and mainly in four- and five-storey walk-up blocks of flats. During the 1980s, for example, the annual production of such housing exceeded 20,000 dwellings. At the same time, the private sector provided up to five times as many dwellings, also mostly in flats. Annual housing construction rates have been high historically, in 1983 the figure reached eight dwellings per 1000 people, in 1991 it was seven per 1000. The Cairo Governerate provides about half of the annual housing production, followed by the Building Co-operatives Authority (22 per cent) and the New Communities (18 per cent).

Medinet Nasr Estate

The Gamal Abdel Nasser public housing project in Medinet Nasr, Cairo, is located adjacent to the student accommodation for Elazhar University (reputedly the oldest university in the world) east of the centre of Cairo. There are 1200 flats in the project designed for low-income earners. Some units were kept aside for emergency use, typically for newly married couples or for households suffering eviction. Construction began in 1965 and allocations began in 1967. Only one month's advance rent was required on allocation. The construction involved two large contracting companies: El Gomhoria Public Company and Atlas.

While the land remains the property of the state, the flats are on a hire-purchase arrangement. When the 180th monthly instalment is paid, the flat passes into owner occupation but the land remains the property of the Governerate. Thus, most of the sales will have been completed about 10 years ago. The selling prices for the flats were £E1080 for three rooms, £E540 for two rooms, and £E360 for one room. The real cost of provision is not known but it is obvious that these prices are highly subsidised.

Workers' City, Helwan

The Economic Housing at Workers' City, Helwan was built in the early 1960s west of the town of Helwan and close to heavy industries. The nearly 2460 five-storey walk-up flats were built in monotonous rows with occasional open spaces. The external spaces are all public, from the road verges, through to the access staircases which serve 10 or 20 flats each. The spaces between the buildings appear to be undifferentiated as

Figure 44. Plan of the Economic Housing of Workers' City, Helwan

to use: they are access tracks, parking, play spaces, dumping grounds, and grazing land for goats and other livestock. The only vegetation is in areas captured by individual households as gardens or the occasional mature tree.

The structures are *in-situ* reinforced concrete post and slab with brick infill. The staircases provide added stiffness to the structures. Within a block, all floors are identical. There is no access to the flat roofs. Flats appear to have been let to workers according to their status in the company, the three-roomed flats being reserved for supervisory staff. Extensions appear to have started in earnest in 1979 (Kardash, 1990) and to have passed through at least two stages. In the beginning, ground-floor occupants seem to have built load-bearing brick extensions. Their neighbours above may have taken advantage of these to add a small extension but they could not support many storeys. The concrete framed, cooperative extensions now constructed up the side of the buildings appear to have evolved out of the earlier form. The scale and pace of development in the mid-1980s can be judged from three of the photographs of the same building in January 1984, January 1985 and 1993.

Figure 45. Views of a block taken in 1984, 1985 and 1993, Helwan.
Note the scale and pace of extension activity.

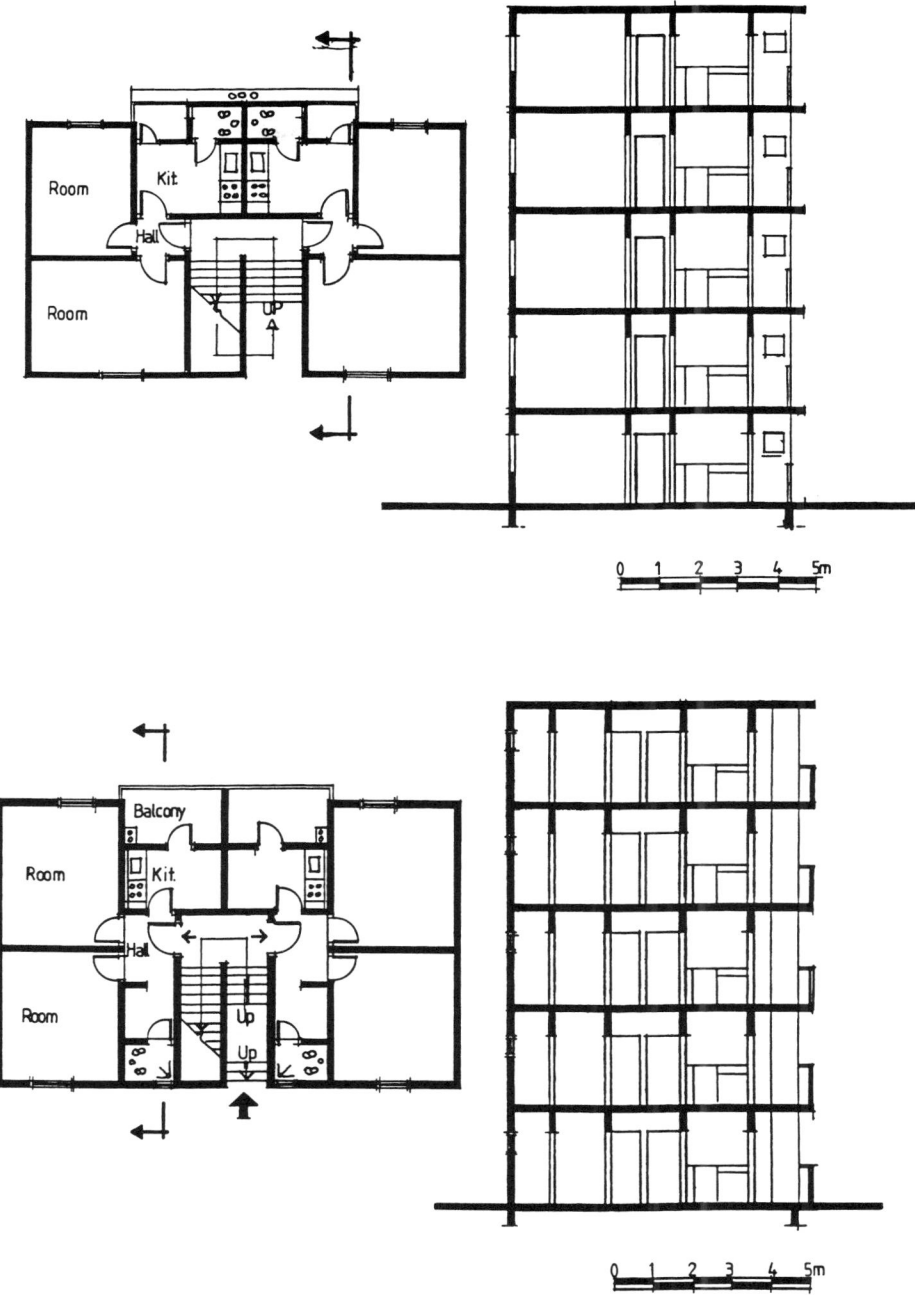

Figure 46. Plans and sections of pairs of two-roomed flats in Helwan

The sample of 329 flats includes 76 non-transformers. There are 169 established and 84 non-transformers.

Socioeconomic characteristics of households

Measures of permanence

If extension is a common phenomenon, which it is in the estates studied, it might be expected that householders would be more likely to be extenders as time passes and the head ages. In other words, non-transformers would be a vestigial group. We would expect, therefore, that transformers would be older, would have lived in the flats longer, and would be more stable in their employment than non-transformers.

As the households were allocated their flats in the 1960s (1963 in Helwan and 1967 in Medinet Nasr) as young couples (heads aged mainly between 25 and 35), they are now grouped in their middle to late working lives (medians of 53 to 60 years with non-transformers the oldest). In 75 per cent of cases, occupants did not start transformation until the head was over 40; the median age was 49 for established transformers and 52 for recent transformers. At least 25 per cent were in their upper fifties before work began.

This seems very late considering the needs of a growing family in Islamic culture (particularly separation of the sexes among teenagers) and the energy with which the process has been implemented, but it must be heavily influenced by the need to pay

Figure 47. Flats in untransformed condition, 1984, Helwan

15 years' monthly instalments before transformations could be made. Before the last payment was made, the flat belonged to the authorities who could evict an occupant who made changes. After, it was owner-occupied and only subject to planning and building control.

Established transformers and non-transformers have been staying in the flat since first allocation; their median date of arrival is 1963. No change has taken place for them as it is so difficult to move from one flat to another and the rule that allows ownership after 15 years of occupation encourages long stays in flats. The recent transformers, however, appear to have a majority of newer arrivals, with a median arrival date of 1971 and a third quartile after the median of the others. In our original review, we suggested that transformation is likely in housing markets where moving is difficult, and it is undoubtedly difficult in Egypt. As extending represents 'moving while staying still', it could be expected to occur as soon as (and in so far as) it is tolerated by authority.

As the housing was originally tied to employment, length of time in employment is close to the stay in the house with medians close to 30 years. There are a few household heads who have retired but also some who were established in their company before being housed and are still to retire.

Most of the household heads are uneducated; the median years in education is zero for all sub-samples. Only a minority have primary education but recent transformers have secondary education at the third quartile. The ability of uneducated people in Egypt to be involved in urban housing supply to the extent that they are through transformations is, therefore, a tribute to their ingenuity and their desire for improvements in housing conditions.

Income and wealth

Incomes in our sample vary between £E4200 and £E5500 (£700–917) at the medians per household and between £E852 and £E1097 (£142–183) at the medians per capita (table 57). To convert these to international spending power (Purchasing Power Parity – PPP), we multiply by 3.26.[2] This gives median household incomes for established and non-transformers of PPP£2280 and for recent transformers of PPP£3000 per year. Annual per capita incomes vary from PPP£463 to PPP£600 at the medians.

As non-transformers would be expected to be in higher positions at work (owing to their occupancy of three-roomed flats), it is, perhaps, surprising that their median income is lower than that of recent transformers and similar to that of established transformers. However, it is likely that there are sufficient widows and retired heads of household to reduce incomes to this unexpectedly low level. Recent transformers are undoubtedly better off than their peers, with 30 per cent more household income at the median. Most of the sample appear to fit into a very broad band of what the Egyptian government regards as stable low-income earners (£E3600 to 18,000 per annum). However, 38 and 20 per cent of the established and recent transformers sub-samples respectively have household incomes below £E3600 and have still managed to extend their flats. Established transformers and non-transformers have similar

Table 57. Measures of income and wealth, owners

Medians (and IQRs)	Established transformers	Recent transformers	Non-transformers
Household income* (£E thousand/year)	4.2	5.5	4.2
	(2.9, 5.6)	(3.8, 7.9)	(2.8, 5.9)
Per capita income* (£E /year)	904	1097	852
	(557, 1357)	(758, 1615)	(617, 1619)
Expenditure on food* (£E thousand/year)	2.9	3.6	3.0
	(1.8, 3.6)	(2.4, 4.3)	(0.6, 4.2)
Relative wealth index**	0.178	0.038	0.178
	(0.038, 0.218)	(0.038, 0.208)	(0.038, 0.218)
Percentage with RWI of zero	0	0	1
Percentage expecting to be better off next year†	43	25	32

* Expenditure as a proxy.
** Relative wealth index (RWI) lies between 0 and 1: 1 implies ownership of all the consumer durables, i.e. radio or cassette player, sewing machine, refrigerator, freezer, television, motor cycle.
† Those who expect a lower cost of living next year.

expenditures on food, about 70 per cent of income at the median for established transformers and non-transformers, but recent transformers spend 65 per cent at the median. These are quite high proportions of expenditure to devote to food and demonstrate how little ready cash and spending power the people in the flats have.

A large majority of the sample own the same items (radio, refrigerator and TV) so have very similar but low RWIs; only recent transformers are shown to be considerably better off than non-transformers.

House ownership

All our sampled main households own their flat. Though three-quarters of the households have bought their flat direct from the public authority who provided it originally, there has been a little market activity, shown by the 15 per cent of established transformers and 19 per cent of recent transformers who have bought from an individual. Only 12 per cent of non-transformers have acquired their flat this way. Inheritance is still relatively unimportant as a means of acquisition (less than 10 per cent) but is likely to increase as original owners, now in their fifties, die.

As might be expected, about 90 per cent of households do not own a house elsewhere, though some have their rural home. Eight per cent of recent transformers own a house elsewhere in the city; it would be worth keeping watch on trends in this as there might be an increasingly commercial motive in the extensions which is not evident as yet.

Household characteristics

As table 58 shows, household sizes are broadly similar across the three sub-samples both at the medians and in IQRs, although non-transformers have marginally the smallest households with a median of 4.5 people. There are few children in the flats, most occupants being over 16. There is thus a low dependency ratio of around 0.2 but recent transformers are pulled up to 0.29 by the larger numbers of households with three or more children. Few households expect much change in size in the next three years and guests do not appear to impose many constraints.

Table 58. Household size and composition, owners

Medians (and IQRs)	Established transformers	Recent transformers	Non-transformers
Number of people in the household	5	5	4.5
	(4, 7)	(4, 7)	(3, 6)
Number of adults in the household	4	4	3.5
	(2, 5)	2, 5)	(2, 5)
Number of children in the household	1	1	1
	(0, 2)	(0, 3)	(0, 1)
Dependency ratio (no. of children per adult)	0.20	0.29	0.18
	(0, 0.6)	(0, 1)	(0, 0.5)
Expected household size in 3 years	5	5	4
	(3, 6)	(4, 6)	(3, 6)
Number of guests per annum	2	1	0
	(0, 4)	(0, 4)	(0, 4)

Thus, the data in table 58 indicate that households are in a relatively late stage of development with few 'shocks' likely in the form of extra children or stress from children starting school, etc. (Seek, 1983). However, the four adults per household is an important stress factor in a society where privacy is required. With a married couple and two over-16 children around, three rooms become virtually mandatory.

The nature of the flats and the allocation procedure has ensured that, at the medians, there is no relationship between household size and rooms occupied. Indeed, the median household occupying two rooms is larger than that in three rooms. All sizes have a median of three rooms. Transformers, on the other hand, do have limited flexibility within the tightly constrained sites and limitations of building five-storey structures cooperatively. They have achieved a median of four rooms in the larger household sizes.

Housing characteristics and flat values for transformers and non-transformers

Introduction

It is important to note how the extensions are built in the Egypt sample. Dwellers of flats above and below each other cooperate in having a stack built alongside and attached to their flats' façades. The external dimensions of the stack are common for its full height except where balconies are cantilevered out beyond the columns.

Although it has few awkward internal corners and few especially restricted sites, the Helwan estate and parts of Medinet Nasr are fairly cramped. The flats are in rectangular blocks which are set parallel with, and/or at a distance from, the next block. The space between blocks is limited, though not too narrow for 3 or 4 m deep extensions. In addition, the flats are restricted in their width and the façades available for extension, especially the single-roomed flats with only one façade. In such circumstances, some locations are more favourable than others. They include ends of blocks, where not only might there be extra open space to capture but also there are additional façades open to extension. In top-floor flats, the ability to exploit the roof is an additional resource. Ground-floor dwellers also have an advantage in that they can extend beyond the cooperative stack if they wish to without resorting to complex technology, or they can simply capture open space as a garden. Thus, with these caveats, we could expect there to be relatively little variability in the extended flats.

In order to account for the opportunity to extend presented by the flats' position in the block vertically and horizontally, four types of orientation are recognised horizontally and these are divided into three vertically.

As we can see from table 59, the 'orientation' of a flat can significantly affect whether a household will extend or not. In the unusual blocks of back-to-back two-roomed flats, almost all have been transformed (mostly before 1991). Both of the flat types which are 'straight through' (1 and 3) appear to have very similar distributions of transformers. In both cases, approximately one-quarter of flats in our sample remain untransformed.

Within each flat type, the ground-floor occupants are consistently the most likely to have extended, and to have done so early. Consequently, ground-floor non-transformers are relatively rare. However, there is no significant correlation between storey and propensity to extend. Orientation of the flat appears to be more influential than the storey.

The most puzzling point from table 60 is that those living on the top floor in an end flat (orientation type 1) seem to have only recently begun to extend. From table 60, it is evident that ground floor transformations are generally larger than middle-floor transformations, and the latter are larger than those on the top floor; i.e. there is a slight pyramidal tendency. We would, perhaps, have expected top-floor flats to be larger at the mean than middle-floor flats as they could use the roof for extensions. Only in the middle units is this at all evident but here the mean is lifted considerably by this ability, even above ground-floor flats.

Table 59. Orientation and storey of flats and percentage transformed

	Established transformers	Recent transformers	Non-transformers
1. End unit, straight through with			
3 extendible sides (*n* = 116):	**46**	**27**	**27**
Ground floor	59	16	25
Middle floors	47	27	26
Top floor	14	50	36
2. Corner unit, back to back with			
2 extendible sides (*n* = 27):	**82**	**7**	**11**
Ground floor	100	0	0
Middle floors	74	13	13
Top floor	83	0	17
3. Middle unit, straight through with			
2 extendible sides (*n* = 179):	**47**	**28**	**25**
Ground floor	52	29	19
Middle floors	49	25	26
Top floor	38	38	24
4. Middle unit, back to back with			
1 extendible side (*n* = 11):	**91**	**9**	**0**
Ground floor	n/a	n/a	n/a
Middle floors	91	9	0
Top floor	n/a	n/a	n/a
All types:	**52**	**25**	**23**
Ground floor	60	20	20
Middle floors	52	24	24
Top floor	37	37	26

Table 60. Mean area of extensions by orientation and storey (m²)

	Ground floor	Middle floors	Top floor
1. End unit, straight through with 3 extendible sides (*n* = 116)	17.0 (*n* = 31)	14.9 (*n* = 70)	10.3 (*n* = 14)
2. Corner unit, back to back with 2 extendible sides (*n* = 27)	30.8 (*n* = 5)	24.5 (*n* = 16)	16.7 (*n* = 5)
3. Middle unit, straight through with 2 extendible sides (*n* = 179)	12.1 (*n* = 31)	11.1 (*n* = 119)	14.2 (*n* = 27)
4. Middle unit, back to back with 1 extendible side (*n* = 11)	-	21.9 (*n* = 11)	-

Increases in house size through transformations

Total built area has been extended by transformers by over 20 m² at the medians from around 40 m² to 64 and 62 m² for established and recent transformers respectively (55 and 58 per cent increases). Most have added all the space in one phase equivalent to about half the original flat or two rooms. Where there is a second phase (only 17 out of 254), it tends to be of about the same area with a median of just over 20 m².[3] Non-transformers have about 10 m² more space originally (a median of 51 m²). This reflects the finding by Wilkinson and Tipple (1991) that occupants of three-roomed flats were less likely to extend than those in two or fewer rooms.

Given the restrictions imposed by location of the flat and the limited number of façades available for extension, the scale of transformation activity is very impressive. IQRs in the original built areas are small (only 5–7 m² or 10–15 per cent of the median). The current dwelling size is remarkably consistent among transformers (medians only differing by 2 m²) with IQRs of only 14 and 13 m² (established and recent transformers respectively). Increases in habitable space are slightly more marked than increases in space overall. The original dwellings appear to have been very effective in providing habitable area with over 73 per cent for all sub-samples at the medians. Surprisingly substantial improvements have been made by the established transformers, who now have 81 per cent habitable space at the median, but the recent transformers have accepted a slightly lower percentage of habitable space than their original 76 per cent. These minor gains in habitable space have been possible through rearranging the original dwelling, mainly from absorbing the balcony. Throughout urban Egypt, the modification of balconies is evident at all income levels. Wealthy occupants of Heliopolis and Maadi enclose their balconies in glazing set in aluminium frames. At the other end of the spectrum, wooden shutters are common and some households fill the openings with masonry except for a small window. Only 22 per cent of original balconies are still extant.

The extensions themselves (phases 1 to 3) have added 15–16 m² of habitable space (at the medians) with IQRs of about 6 m². At the median, established transformers have 43 m² habitable space while recent transformers have rather less with 40 m². Non-habitable space has almost doubled in the case of the recent transformers as they have extended kitchens, washrooms, passageways and storage rooms. As extended flats become more complex, it would be expected that passageways would become longer. This has not happened very often. Instead, access to new rooms is gained through living rooms.

Although balconies originally provided have largely been subsumed in other spaces, some new balconies have been added that tend to be larger than the old ones, at about 4 m² at the median. This comes as a surprise as we would expect that the privacy issue would lead householders away from large balconies, especially as the extended flats are closer to their opposite neighbours' windows than before they were extended. It infers that the blocking in of balconies here and elsewhere may be less of a privacy strategy than one to gain more living space. Indeed, some new balconies are now blocked in partly or as a whole.

Non-transformers have 90 per cent habitable space. This reflects the plan of the three-roomed flat which has a large room that residents use as a living area with almost an alcove for a kitchen and a tiny bathroom/toilet (see figure 48).

Increases in rooms

The original flats had two or three rooms intended as living rooms but transformers' flats now have three at the median. The original three-roomed flats have almost all had their kitchens altered to serve as a living room without changes to internal walls. Thus, many of the non-transformers (who are more common in the three-roomed units than elsewhere) have four habitable rooms.

While the median area of each phase was found to be equivalent to two rooms (above), the number of rooms added appears to vary more than might be expected from those data. This illustrates the ability of extenders to subdivide their (generally fairly standard) new spaces in many different ways. The range of sizes of new rooms seems to be similar to the originals.

Other than these variations in internal division, relatively little extra variety has been added to the slightly variable original housing stock. The initial suggestion that transformations create a variety of accommodation out of a relatively uniform housing stock is hardly confirmed as far as overall size of transformed flats is concerned, but is confirmed by other measures. For example, if non-transformers are (rightly) included in the range, there is a greater variety of flats available. In addition, variety occurs within the originally homogeneous flat-size groups as differently sized extensions are made and divided up into different room sizes. Thus, households occupying two-roomed flats can now boast from a minimum of two to a maximum of six rooms.

An important measure of the effectiveness of transformation as housing supply is the amount of habitable space transformers have per person compared with what they would have had if they had not transformed. In our Egypt sample, we have data on the number of occupants of the flats before the transformation was done. Table 61 demonstrates the effects of transformation according to this measure.

Table 61 shows that, although there has been an increase in habitable space per person over non-transformers, improvements over the households in occupation on the eve of transformation are very marked. Thus, transformers have more habitable space and more habitable rooms per person than they would have had if they had not extended. In both these measures, improvements are greater than is evident by using non-transformers as the control group.

Established transformers' flats might be expected to be saturated with relatives. However, they have more space and more habitable space per person than recent transformers. The number of habitable rooms available per person has changed by 100 per cent for established transformers but only 20 per cent for recent transformers.

There are only 15 households who have another household in their flat with them.

This three-roomed flat has been extended only by capturing the balcony space into a new larger central room. The original kitchen function has been confined into the tiny alcove at the bathroom/toilet door. Six people (a man, two women, a boy and two girls) occupy the flat. The plan syntax is shallow and non-distributed with only the bathroom/toilet not opening directly off the central living room.

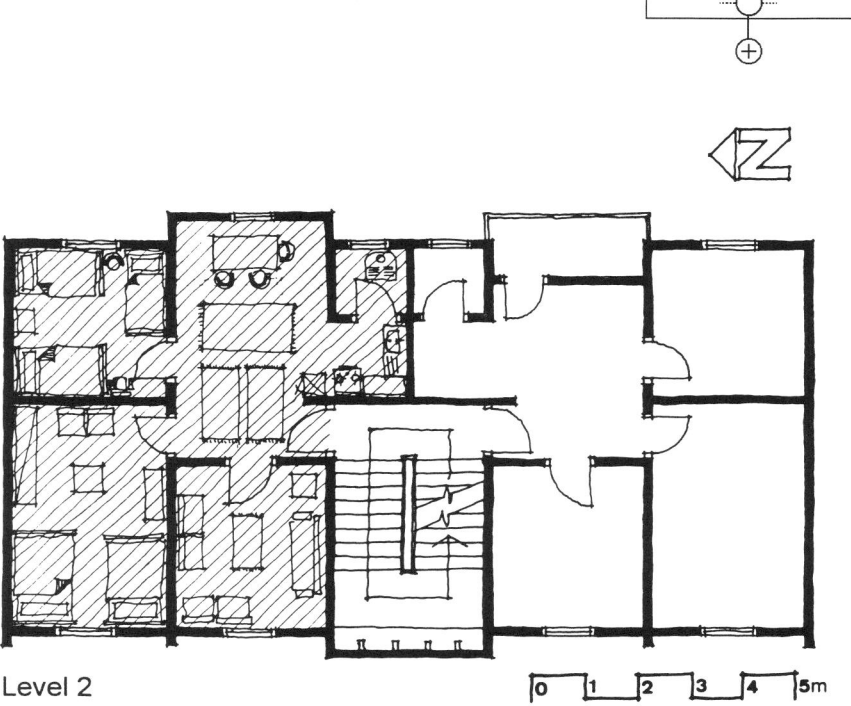

Level 2

0 1 2 3 4 5m

Figure 48. A three-roomed flat in almost original condition, Helwan

Table 61. Increases in habitable space per person for the whole house

Medians (and IQRs)	Established transformers	Recent transformers	Non-transformers
Current habitable space per person (m²)	8.5 (6.7,12.1)	7.8 (5.4, 10.3)	6.6 (4.8, 13.1)
Original habitable space per person (m²)	4.0 (3.3, 5.7)	4.4 (3.7, 6.4)	-
Current habitable rooms per person	0.67 (0.5, 1.0)	0.60 (0.3, 1.0)	.063 (0.4 1.0)
Original habitable rooms per person	0.33 (0.3, 0.6)	0.50 (0.3, 0.8)	-

The data for main households are sufficiently similar to those for all households that a separate section is not required in this case study.

We can see from table 62 that transformations have added about 50 to 60 per cent more space at the medians and 65–80 per cent more space at the third quartile. It is gratifying that habitable space has increased slightly more than total space. There is little difference in the gains made between space and rooms as new rooms are of similar size to the original ones.

Table 62. Comparison of increases in rooms, space, etc.

Original median equals 100	Established transformers	Recent transformers	Non-transformers
Total space per flat	149 (141, 168)	155 (142, 165)	100
Habitable space	159 (147, 178)	158 (128, 170)	100
Number of habitable rooms	150 (125, 150)	140 (120, 150)	100

Increases in people accommodated

Transformations increase the local population and generate higher population densities but tend to reduce occupancy rates. Thus demand for services and utilities will be increased while problems of crowding will be reduced. (Tipple, 1991a: 77)

The above can be demonstrated if there appear to be more people in the area as a result of transformations. This is different from the premise that transformers act to accommodate an inevitable increase in population. The Egyptian case is a unique example to study this because we have a variable which does not appear in the others: number of people in the flat at the time of the extension.

Contrary to the above expectation, however, there are generally fewer people in the flats now than when they were extended, even for recent transformers. In general, established transformers had slightly more people in the flat at the time they decided to extend (seven at the median) than recent transformers had (six at the median). But both now have five at the median. This finding contradicts the impression that transformations increase the population of a neighbourhood. In the Egypt case, therefore, the extensions are undoubtedly a reaction to increased need for space for the existing population not a contributing factor to population increase in a neighbourhood.

There has been very little increase in households per flat (or tenant households) in our sample as a result of the transformation activity. The layout of the flats makes it difficult for any additional households to live independent lives in extended flats. Whether this changes as internal alterations become more complex in the future, only time will tell.

As yet, only 22 out of 256 transformed flats have two households. However, if it remains difficult to find alternative accommodation, it is likely that more flat owners will modify the flat to accommodate at least one grown-up son and his wife and children. Thus, unless the efficiency of the rental housing market increases, the number of household in transforming estates is likely to grow.

The improvement in occupancy rate through transformation has been very marked, especially for established transformers whose median has reduced from 3.0 before transformation to only 1.5 currently. As expected from the above, recent transformers have improved less but from a lower starting point (from 2.0 to 1.7 at the medians). Non-transformers have a median occupancy rate of 1.5 persons per room so exhibit no more housing stress from this feature than established transformers.

Improved service levels

All the original and present houses have at least one toilet. There appear to be very few additional toilets through transformation although two roof-top extensions each have a full set of new services.

House physical condition

If transformation is a mechanism whereby areas are upgraded by their residents, we would expect to find improvements in the physical condition of the houses and their environment and/or improved services: more toilets, water points, etc.

All the original flats are built with reinforced concrete frame and brick infill, with reinforced concrete slab roof and glazed windows. Generally, transformations utilise

Figure 49. The first stack to be built, seen in 1984, 1985 and 1993 (anti-clockwise from top left)

the same materials as the originals and as residential development in the city. How far this reflects a wish to fit into the general urbanisation process of continual improvement and upgrading (Gosling *et al.*, 1993) and how far it is simply a function of what is available is difficult to tell (but one expects the latter).

Data on physical problems show that only 5 per cent of original structures and only 1 per cent of extensions show any cracks. This confirms our impressions of the areas and the photographs we have that the construction is sound in both original[4] and new structures and that the extensions are of good quality construction in sound condition.

Transformations in Egypt are carried out in defiance of planning and building codes so we would expect to find a relatively large number of breaches of regulations. This expectation is part of the instinctive objection of development controllers against unauthorised development. They tend to see every breach as the thin end of the 'building slums' wedge. One indicator of this which we use in each case study is the occurrence of small habitable rooms, especially where rooms planned as kitchens or other non-habitable spaces are modified for habitable uses, or where extensions are built on relatively constricted sites. In Egypt, the building regulations stipulate a minimum area of 10 m^2 for habitable rooms. However, for comparative purposes, we use 6 m^2 and 4 m^2 as our room size values to test for very small rooms.

Habitable rooms of less than 4 m^2 or 6 m^2 area are not very common. The conversion of balconies and kitchens to living rooms without incorporating them into other rooms, and the spatial constraints imposed by the cooperation with extenders on other floors, are likely to be responsible for the few rooms smaller than 6 m^2.

Plan forms

As we have seen in chapter 5, the balcony tends to provide the means by which the plan breaks through the original built envelope. In the back-to-back flats, where two rooms are present at the façades, the extension can have two rooms each opening off the room inside. In others, the kitchen and toilet are so arranged that ventilation is required for at least half the façade.

All extensions tend to add greater depth to the circulation pattern. Whereas only balconies were more than one room deep from the hallway, now some living rooms may be reached through two others. In almost all transformations, the original balcony is subsumed into other rooms or simply acts as circulation space. The kitchen is also commonly used for access into the new rooms so that, with almost all the transformed flats, a very small area is left with fittings to act as the kitchen for what become very large flats with a median of seven residents. End flats have major advantages in the ability to ventilate inner rooms through new windows punched through the end wall as well as having the potential to extend beyond the end wall of the blocks.

Cost of transformation phases

Phase 1 extensions cost about one year's income at the median and vary only slightly between established and recent transformations; the former build more expensive first phases (table 63). Although similarly sized, second phases are much less expensive than phase 1. This is probably heavily affected by the frequency of ground-floor extensions (five out of 16) which are cheaper as no major structural work need be undertaken. The similar third quartiles for phases 1 and 2 show that the larger extensions continue in similar cost ranges. As there are so few second and third extensions, total extension costs in our sample resemble those of phase 1 at about a year's income. There has been a reduction in the cost of extension over the years from a median of about £E10,000 between 1977 and 1981 (in 1993 prices) to less than half that in 1992–3.

Table 63. Cost of phases in the extension process (thousand £E)

Medians (and IQRs)	Established transformers	Recent transformers	All transformers
Phase 1	5.06	4.44	4.56
	(3.2, 7.6)	(3.2, 6.7)	(3.2, 7.4)
	($n = 166$)	($n = 83$)	
Phase 2	2.50	2.55	2.50
	(0.7, 6.0)	(0.5, 6.8)	(0.6, 6.0)
	($n = 12$)	($n = 4$)	
Phase 3	0.89	-	0.89
	(-, -)		(-,-)
	($n = 2$)		
Total cost of transformations	5.20	4.44	4.60
	(3.2, 7.8)	(3.3, 6.7)	(3.3, 7.4)
	($n = 166$)	($n = 83$)	

All costs are adjusted to 1993 values.

It is possible to predict the total money spent on transformations in the two estates by using the mean spending on transformations per flat (£E6089) and multiplying by the number of flats in the estates (3660). Thus, £E22.3 million (PPP£12.1 million) has probably been invested in extra housing goods by the occupants of Workers' City, Helwan and Medinet Nasr, Cairo.

Increases in flat value and cost
Non-transformers were not asked the value, the cost of rebuilding the property or the maximum rent they were willing to pay. Consequently the figures in this section have been produced by using the average value per square metre, rebuilding cost per square metre, and rent per square metre from the transformers information. Only the rebuilding cost of the transformation was given; to find the cost of rebuilding the whole flat, we assumed that this cost per square metre would also apply to the original building.

Table 64 shows that non-transformers' flats are perceived to be almost as valuable as established transformers'. An important component of this is the frequency of larger flats (with three rooms) among the non-transformed flats. These large flats are more valuable per original unit than the others and so inflate the non-transformed value. In addition, the potential to transform may have a perceived value.

Table 64. Value of the flats

Medians (and IQRs)	Established transformers	Recent transformers	Non-transformers
Value of the flat (£E thousand)	12.0	17.5	11.8
	(10, 15)	(14, 20)	(10, 12)
Value of the flat per room (£E thousand)	1.71	2.29	2.00
	(1.5, 2.0)	(1.8, 3.0)	(2.0, 2.0)
Value of the flat per habitable room (£E thousand)	3.38	5.50	2.97
	(2.83, 4.33)	(3.75, 9.88)	(2.96, 4.53)
Value of the flat per square metre (£E)	224.5	320.7	268.0
	(189, 267)	(268, 423)	(268, 268)
Higher or lower than average?*	1	1	1
	(0, 2)	(0, 2)	(1, 1)
Percentage higher than average	27	32	0

* 0 = lower, 1 = average, 2 = higher.

Given the relatively high value of non-transformed flats discussed above, table 64 shows that the transformed flats are perceived to be more valuable than they were before. This is especially true of recent transformers who are mainly concentrated in Medinet Nasr. Not only are the flats of the recent transformers perceived to be more valuable than both established transformers' and non-transformers' by a factor of almost 50 per cent, but they are also more valuable per square metre and per habitable room. The values per habitable room are particularly important as they are a good measure of residential quality. Established transformers have improved slightly on non-transformers but recent transformers have added considerable value, virtually doubling that of non-transformers. While established transformers are not perceived to maintain value per square metre to the level of the original block, recent transformers are improving on it.

The variety of values in transformed flats is also notable. The range from the lowest quartile of established transformers to the highest quartile of the recent transformers is £E10,000 for the whole flat, and £E7000 per habitable room.

Estimates of rebuilding costs (table 65) are significantly lower than estimates of value for recent transformers but higher for established transformers. Non-transformers estimate costs to be slightly higher than value. Recent transformers are likely to have an acute understanding of the cost of building based on the informal sector contractors who specialise in extension stacks. Our local surveys suggest a building cost of approximately £E220–300 per square metre, very close to the estimate made by our householders. Where value is estimated to be higher than cost, we could expect that transformers regard their extensions as well worth the investment not only for its use value but also for the increased market value which accrues.

Table 65. Rebuilding cost of the flats

Medians (and IQRs)	Established transformers	Recent transformers	Non-transformers
Rebuilding cost (£E thousand)	15.25	12.74	12.36
	(9.57, 23.1)	(10.5, 19.1)	(10.5, 12.4)
Rebuilding cost per room (£E thousand)	2.34	2.03	2.07
	(1.59, 3.34)	(1.58, 2.64)	(2.06, 2.07)
Rebuilding cost per habitable room (£E thousand)	4.55	4.99	3.10
	(2.87, 6.44)	(2.92, 10.4)	(3.09, 5.06)
Rebuilding cost per square metre (£E)	280	280	280
	(185, 400)	(225, 354)	(280, 280)

A further estimate of value was found by asking how much was the maximum rent occupants would be willing to pay for the same amount of space they currently occupied. Rents for similar property in Cairo Governerate are between £E60 and £E100 per month. Malpezzi (1986) found that casual observation suggested that Cairo rental levels were about half what the market rents would be. However, if account is taken of side payments including key money, utilities, maintenance and repairs by tenants, the discount for the typical (median) tenant reduced to about 29 per cent (i.e., the median tenant paid 29 per cent less rent plus side payments than market rent would be). There were, however, large variations leading to some paying over market rents and others benefiting from much larger discounts.

Respondents, both established and recent transformers, offered similar rental levels to those elsewhere in the Governerate. Established transformers would pay off the value of a room in approximately 18 years while recent transformers would take almost 23 years (assuming zero interest rate). Thus, rents quoted in our survey could pay back the cost of building only after a generation or more if any reasonable interest rate is included.

As almost all our sample occupy the whole of the flat, the value of the portion of the house occupied by the main household is the same as the whole flat in the Egypt sample.

Differences between types of original flat

When built, most of the flats were in plain rectangular blocks set like dominoes on the site. The space between them was designed as public open space in the manner customary for this type of development. There were, therefore, sufficient opportunities presented by the availability of open space around the blocks to make transformation likely, at least in one direction for each block (as suggested in Tipple, 1991a). Furthermore, as the spaces between the flats are considerably wider than traditional urban streets in Egypt, the reduction in space between the buildings is likely to be acceptable to the residents. In such a hot climate, narrow streets have advantages as they remain cool owing to the shade being cast across the whole space for most of the day.[5] As the balconies provide the opportunity to break out of the building envelope, there is less easily used space for extension where blocks are sited face to face rather than back to face.

The density of the estates appears to be lower than privately built estates of flats in Cairo so it could be argued that they would present the occupants with opportunities for extension to a density similar to those estates (Gosling *et al.*, 1993). Transformations have increased the built area by about 60 per cent at the median. Thus, where the Helwan flats covered 24 per cent of the ground area, it is likely that they now cover 40 per cent, and their estimated estate floor-space index (for five floors) of 1.2 is now probably 2.0.

In order to assess the differences in the scale and value of transformations among different flat types, an analysis of variance (ANOVA) technique was used to develop adjusted values. The factors adjusted for were the estate (on the grounds that different estates presented different physical environments in which the extensions could be made); the storey in which the flat is located, the plan type, the orientation of the flat, and the household income.

Table 66. Value of the flats (£E thousand) according to their orientation

Medians (and IQRs) Adjusted means in bold	Established transformers	Recent transformers	Non- transformers
1. End unit, straight through with 3 extendible sides (*n* = 116)	12.0 (10, 16) **15.5**	17.5 (14.7, 20) **17.9**	11.8 (10, 11.9) **11.5**
2. Corner unit, back to back with 2 extendible sides (*n* = 27)	10.0 (9.3, 12.0) **9.9**	14.5 (-, -) **12.3**	7.1 (3.6, 7.1) **5.8**
3. Middle unit, straight through with 2 extendible sides (*n* = 179)	12.0 (10, 15) **14.8**	18.0 (12, 20) **16.9**	11.8 (10, 11.9) **11.3**
4. Middle unit, back to back with 1 extendible side (*n* = 11)	9.0 (8, 12) **8.4**	10.1 (-, -) **9.2**	-

As can be seen in table 66, transformation appears to increase the value of flats by between 31 and 112 per cent at the means depending on type. There seems to be a premium on having a flat which passes all the way through the building (types 1 and 3) and, therefore, benefits from the ventilation and lighting advantages of this orientation. These middle units (type 3) appear to be almost as valued as the end ones (type 1); only £E1000 premium appears to attach to the end location. By contrast, back-to-back flats are valued at only about 60 per cent of the straight-through flats. There is, thus, a trace here of the value presented by the potential extendibility (see Gosling *et al.*, 1993) for the same in the UK).

From a relatively narrow distribution of flat types, the transformers have created variety within each flat type. Overall, however, variety is not a consistently demonstrable result of the transformation process. On the one hand, in contrast with the other studies, there is little more variety than before:

- a similar range of flats but more with three and four habitable rooms than before;
- little difference in the range of habitable space in the flats (IQR of 24 m²);
- no tendency as yet to provide space for tenants.

On the other hand, there is some variety appearing:

- values of flats have increased in variety with an increase in IQR from PPP£1000 to £4000;
- great variety in appearance and façade surface;
- a growing tendency to use ground-floor and road-frontage units for commercial purposes.

The impression formed is one of structures being consistently added to by relatively similar extensions and a few much larger developments on particularly favourable sites.

The process of transformation

The decision to extend

The most important reason for extending in the Egyptian sample (58 per cent) is the need for more space to house additional members of the household. From assumptions made in earlier work (Tipple *et al.*, 1985, 1986), it is surprising how few identified the children's getting older as their main reason. We had previously assumed that the requirements of separating growing children under the privacy tenets of Islam had driven householders to add an extra room. Indeed, Kardash (1990) indicates that the contractor she interviewed (see below) felt that it was his calling to help his clients separate the sexes in the home.

As we expected, renting is a minor motive (14 per cent), though more common with established than recent transformers. The particular logistics of extending five-storey walk-up flats generated a factor unique to the Egyptian case study: being persuaded to join in with neighbours. This was chosen as the main motive by 22 per cent of recent transformers but only 8 per cent of established ones. It is evident that the prospect of having light cut off by a slab at floor and ceiling level outside the window, gossip about not being able to manage money well enough to afford the same extension as neighbours, and neighbourly approbation through not joining in to bear the cost, are sufficient in combination to persuade households to become reluctant transformers (22 per cent is one per stack of five).

Motivations for extending rather than moving could be expected to centre on loyalty to the area and difficulty of finding an affordable alternative. The problem of finding suitable accommodation in urban Egypt is well known. Parents of grown-up children are particularly concerned about the difficulty of their married offspring's having a place to live not too far away so that inter-generational support can continue. It is not surprising, therefore, that, while loyalty to the neighbourhood is very low as a motive to stay and extend (4 per cent), the unavailability of alternative accommodation at the right price or in suitable condition score highly (69 per cent together).

The higher percentage of established (25 per cent) than recent transformers (10 per cent) who did not consider a move is counter-intuitive. As transformation becomes the norm, it would be expected that more households would automatically decide that extending was the best way to improve their housing. That this does not seem to be supported by this evidence is interesting. The reason may lie in the 30 per cent higher incomes of recent transformers and the lumpiness of housing supply. As aspirations rise, households may decide to move to a more salubrious neighbourhood but, on searching, find that the step up to an evidently better flat requires a major increase in expenditure which is beyond their resources. Thus, only reluctantly, perhaps, they decide that 'stay and extend' is the best way to improve their housing.

Problems encountered in the extension process

Respondents were asked which problems they encountered in their extension activity by selecting from finance, building materials, labour, services, more than one of these problems, and an 'other, specify' option. Finance dominates with about 60 per cent singling it out. This would be expected in a process where other inputs are collected together by a single contractor (see below). A few households identified other problems as follows:

- lack of technical advice and experience;
- some problems with the local authorities arising from the illegality of the extensions (see below);
- delays in the supply of materials.

The construction process

The construction process for transformations in Egypt involves contractors who tackle the whole construction task and deal directly with the client. The extensions are made cooperatively by householders and implemented by small-scale contractors. In both estates studied, contractors who were interviewed were well known in the community. They employ skilled workers on a permanent basis, paying medical insurance, social security and bonuses, and unskilled workers on temporary terms, paid by the day, hour or job for each kind of work. No women are employed. Skilled workers, who are used for concrete mixing and casting, block laying, finishings, etc., constitute at least half of the workforce.

The engineering design of these five-storey structures is done by the contractors based on experience rather than any formal training. They tend to be over-designed but have some problems with exposed reinforcement bars owing to poor concrete pouring. In addition, the concrete will not be cured for long, if at all, but this is common in informal sector contracts and in hot, dry countries.

Some contractors insist on a written contract, others do not. All provide materials and all the labour; some provide mains services, others depend on the householder to negotiate them. Where permissions are applied for (e.g. in Medinet Nasr), it is the responsibility of the owner.

Kardash (1990) describes the work of a contractor who employs a carpenter, a black-smith and three helpers as permanent staff and hires labour on a daily basis. He obtains work through personal contacts in the area where he has lived all his life. Not only does he assist the extenders with the financing of their project through working on credit, with a 50 per cent down payment and 20 months to pay the rest, but he also assists workers to set up on their own by buying them enough timber for shuttering to lay 5 m² of concrete, again on credit with time to pay. Even though the contractor appears to be the personification of a public-spirited entrepreneur, he has to complete his work rapidly to avoid problems with the police because the extensions encroach on public land. He has served six months' imprisonment, paid £E10,000 in fines, and has learned to keep some labourers standing by in case his workers are arrested while constructing an extension stack. Although he knows he is acting illegally (and has suffered for it), he believes that he should continue to help people to follow the tenets of Islam and separate boys' and girls' sleeping accommodation by extending the one- and two-roomed flats (while at the same time making a living, we would assume).

According to the contractors, a typical extension in Medinet Nasr (18 m²) in 1994 cost about £E3900 (£E222 per m²), which is paid for in two instalments: one of £E1500 on completion and the rest over two years. In Helwan, the typical 20 m² extension cost £E4200 (£E215 per m²)[6] which is paid for in similar instalments.

There is an obvious upsurge in transformation activity from 1982 when the residents had recently completed paying for their flats (15 years after moving in). In this case, therefore, ownership is seen as a virtual *sine qua non* of transformation in Egypt. For most households, only one transformation has been carried out, probably because the site is too constricted for many phases. Recent transformers also tend to be first-timers, very few of them having previously extended.

Most households (73 per cent) borrow in order to extend but not from the formal

Figure 50. A Medinet Nasr block in original condition

Figure 51. Construction work at Medinet Nasr
Note the labour-based technology in a multi-storey context

financial sector. Though Kardash (1990) indicates that credit from the contractor is common, only 4 per cent of our sample claim this as a major source of funding because they would not regard the arrangement with the contractor as credit. They see it not as borrowing but as paying over a short period by instalments. Only 22 per cent of households used savings as the majority source to finance the work.

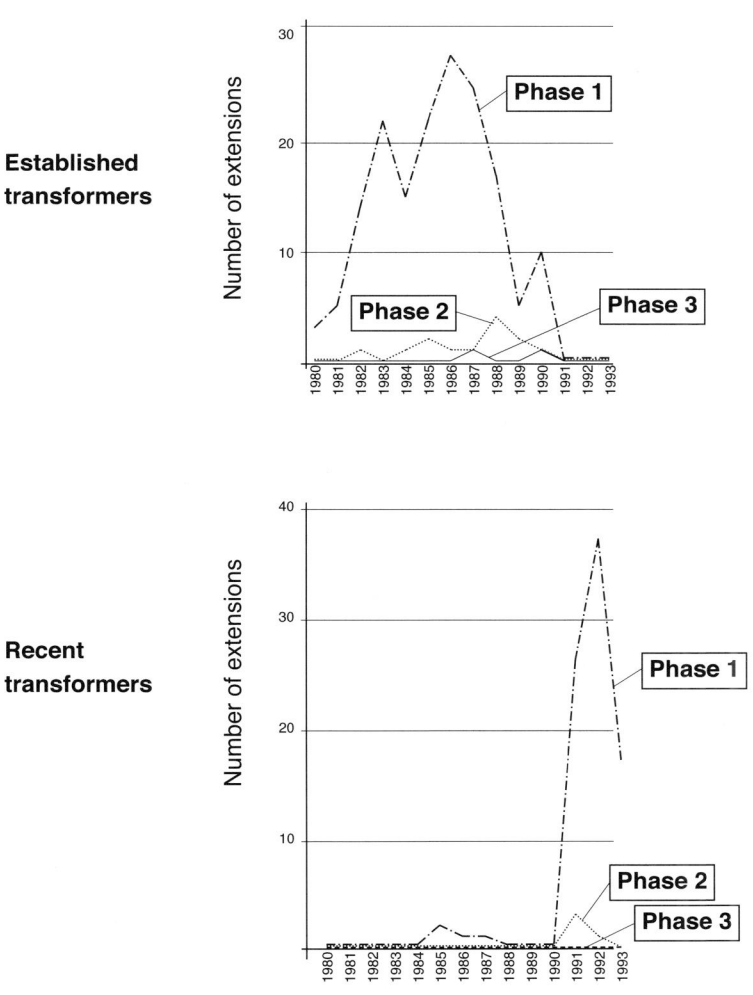

Figure 52. Number of extensions recorded in the Egypt sample, by year

The small-scale, informal sector contractors organise and carry out the work in 97 per cent of our sample. Very few households organise the work themselves through separate tradesmen and no one appears to use classical self-help methods. This is not surprising as, in almost all cases, the extensions involve a five-storey structure. It is, indeed, comforting to know that such structures are not subject to the inadequate technical knowledge of lay people, rather they are constructed by trained craftsmen well versed in post-and-slab construction in *in-situ* reinforced concrete.

Permissions

Only the recent transformers in Medinet Nasr have asked for permission but most who asked (63 per cent) were granted it. Very little action has been taken by the authorities against transformations considering their scale and their exposure to public and official view; only an unlucky few have suffered demolition.

There is an interesting historical anecdote which Kardash (1990) tells about the first stack builders in Helwan (figure 49). One day, a bulldozer arrived at the block which is, unfortunately, situated opposite the police station. A steel hauser was fastened to one of the stack uprights and the bulldozer was put into reverse. As the tension increased, two things happened: the brick infill fell out of some walls and the façade of the original building showed signs of being pulled away. At this, the demolition exercise was stopped. As a result, a third strengthening pillar was added to the damaged stack and it has remained in place, later to be further extended.[7]

Intention for disposing of the house

The complete reluctance to sell is complemented by a significant reluctance to leave the flat. Thus, only 2 per cent of our sample are likely to dispose of their flat outside the family. As it is unlikely that the respondents would have considered events beyond their death, and we could not have asked them to do so, almost all extended flats will stay in the family. This is supported by the finding (given above) that few transformers (5 per cent) are motivated by increased value.

Summary

The Egyptian case study is perhaps the most spectacular of our examples of transformation in practice. Relatively poorly paid factory workers are sculpting an entirely new five-storey high townscape around the monotonous blocks of flats in which they have lived for almost 30 years. Indeed, it was Workers' City, Helwan, which first sparked our interest in transformations.

The construction activity appears to have been accompanied by little increase in population as yet as almost all the flats are still occupied by the single household that has lived there over a long period. There is 40 per cent more habitable space than planned, even within this multi-storey environment with no planned private open space. Recent work is of particularly high standards of finish.

There is a wider variety of accommodation resulting from transformations than was originally planned, particularly in perceived value. The variety in scale is constrained, however, by the need to work in common with four other households living above and/or below as the stack is erected cooperatively and by a single contractor. It appears that one in five transformer households is reluctant, only joining in because they would lose social standing otherwise.

Though most households need more room, the decision to extend was not affected by the household size before extension nor by measures of income or wealth. Instead, the main influence was the intrinsic characteristics of the flat; smaller ones with more (smaller) rooms are most likely to be extended. Occupants of more rooms spend more on the extension when it is done.

While the Egyptian government continues to house its low-income workers in flats, it is likely that transformation will occur wherever it is tolerated. Its effects should, therefore, be accounted for in designing flats and neighbourhoods to allow enough space for extensions and circulation, and to design the flats so that ventilation and daylighting can pass into the centre of the extended flat (Wilkinson and Tipple, 1987). In addition, it is likely that the enabling policies required to improve housing supply in general, especially a supply of housing finance, would increase the occurrence and expense of transformations.

The future of transformed flats as single-household dwellings must be in doubt as they are inherited by the next generation. If they sell out or subdivide them into smaller flats, population increase and some problems of internal access and sharing of services are likely to occur. There are gains to be made by monitoring whether this takes place in the future so that suggestions can be made for divided access to parts of the flats and for fitting extra toilets, bathrooms and kitchens.

Notes

1   Such 'raiding' of low-income housing by higher income groups is common in developing countries.
2   The factor relating the actual GNP per capita of US$610 to the adjusted real GDP of PPP$1988 (UNDP, 1993: table 1).
3   There is only one third phase in our sample, of 4 m^2.
4   However, they are generally run-down and neglected. There are many cases of poor maintenance reflected in local damage to sills, string courses, rendering, pipework and other details.
5   This also imposes a problem of dampness as the ground floor walls may never by warmed by the sun sufficiently to expel moisture.
6   This is less than the rebuilding cost of £E280 estimated by the owners (table 65) but similar to the amount suggested by our local survey.
7   So the result so far is: Transformers United 1, Cairo City 0.

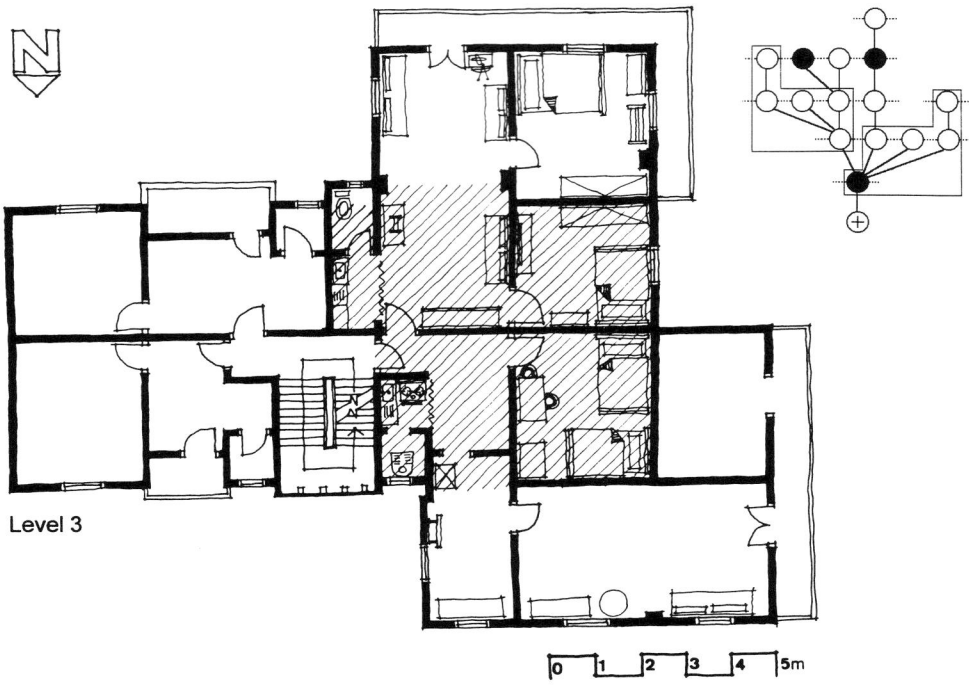

Level 3

These end flats have been bought from previous owners and made into one simply by moving one outer door 1m into the stairwell. A seven-person household with three boys and a girl under 16 occupy the flat which has been extended in three directions to eight rooms at a cost of £E14,000 (35 months' income). Both original balconies have been subsumed into new rooms but two substantial new balconies have been added. The plan syntax is non-distributed with considerable depth as new rooms are only accessible through original rooms. One room is without daylighting and ventilation.

Figure 53. A pair of transformed two-roomed, back-to-back flats, Helwan

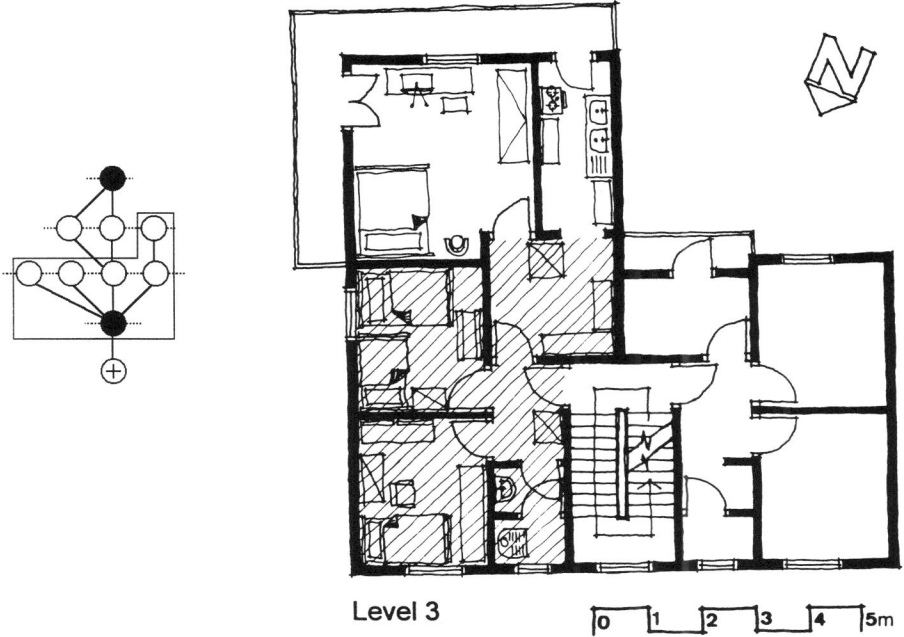

Level 3

This second floor end flat occupied by seven people (four adults and three girls) has been extended to provide a large kitchen and a third bedroom, both of which open onto a new long balcony. The extension cost £E5000 (33 months' income). The original kitchen and balcony are now joined into a living room. The new balcony gives a measure of distribution to the plan syntax at the deepest level.

Figure 54. A transformed two-roomed end flat, Medinet Nasr

This two-roomed flat has, unusually, been provided with a balcony on the entrance façade as well as room extensions and a new balcony on the balcony façade. The total cost of transformation was £E3000 (11 months' income). It is occupied by 13 people (five men, four women, two boys and two girls). All rooms are used for sleeping and two double up as living rooms. The plan syntax is non-distributed and four layers deep; one of the new rooms requires access through two others.

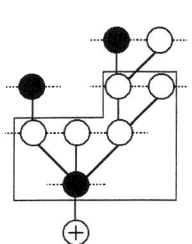

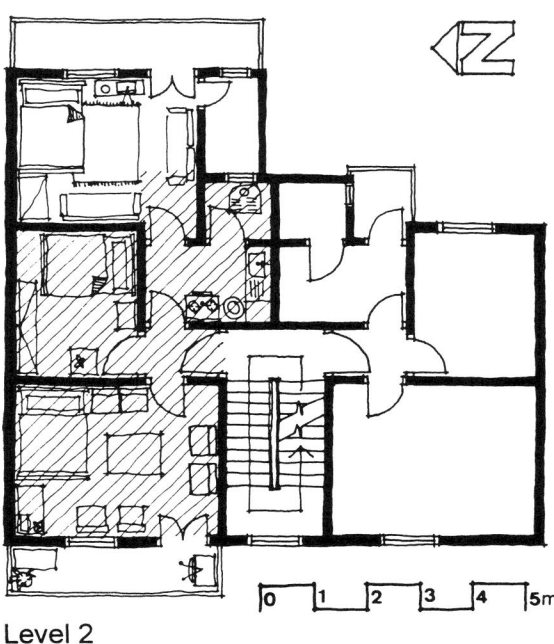

Level 2

Figure 55. A two-roomed flat extended on both façades, Helwan

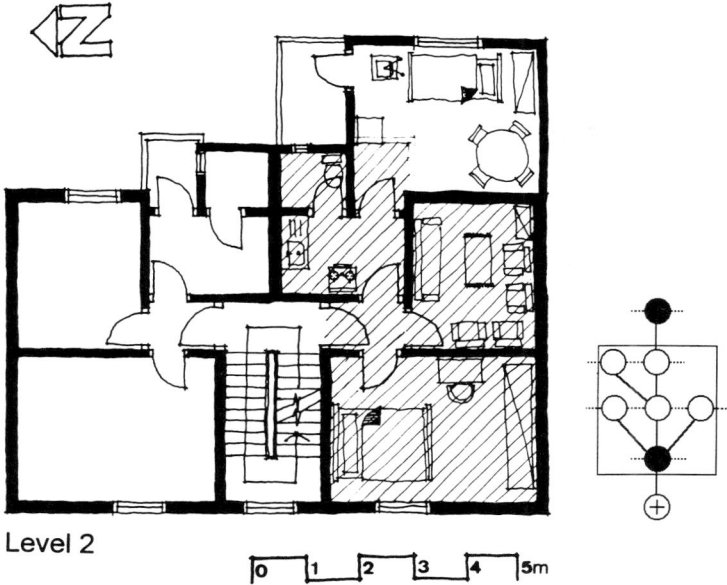

Level 2

0 1 2 3 4 5m

This first floor flat, extended to three rooms, is occupied by a 30-year-old man, his wife and another adult woman. The extension of one room and a balcony cost £E1500 in 1985 and provides a bedroom/dining area with a balcony at the side allowing light and ventilation to the toilet. The plan syntax is a common one for the sample: non-distributed and four layers deep. The new balcony requires access through a kitchen and the new room.

Figure 56. A typical extended two-roomed flat in Helwan (on extreme left of the photo)

*Figure 57. A series of extensions in the
study areas, Egypt*

The end space is used as a garden with balconies erected over it. The nearest stack was completed before 1984.

Very major extensions under construction flanking two-roomed flats.

Figure 57 (continued)

Appendix 3.
Transformations in Ghana

Introduction to Asawasi and Suntreso, Kumasi

Kumasi is the second largest city in Ghana and capital of the former Asante Empire. Founded at the beginning of the 18th century, it was devastated by the British at the turn of the 20th century only to be rebuilt on the same site. Little of the traditional culture was destroyed in the colonial period; the *Asantehene* (king of the Asante people) resides in the Manhyia Palace, close to our Asawasi study area, and the traditional system of land-holding and loyalties have survived almost unchanged.

The population statistics for the city are subject to some disagreement, largely owing to a very low figure from the 1984 census. The author estimates that in 1990 there were about 800,000 (extrapolated from Tipple's 1986 data), but the 1984 census (Ghana, 1987) shows 490,000 in 1984 and suggests that there were only about 600,000 people in the city in 1990.[1]

Compound houses dominate Kumasi (57 per cent of houses in 1986). When completed, they are roughly square on plan with seven to 12 rooms per storey opening off a central courtyard. As over 70 per cent of households occupy one room, and mean occupancy rates in the city are in excess of three persons per room, single-storey compounds tend to accommodate 20 to 30 people. Multi-storey compounds (16 per cent of houses) contain a mean of 17 rooms (Malpezzi *et al.*, 1990).

Non-compound housing tends to be in the form of bungalows or two-storey buildings set in relatively spacious plots. Though non-compound types constitute 43 per cent of houses, their small size relative to compounds reduces the number of people for whom they provide accommodation.

Although there is nothing inherent in the compound form to generate this, residents of the compound houses tend to occupy single rooms and have particularly poor access to services. In 1986, only 12 per cent of households in Kumasi (almost all of who are in non-compound housing) had a toilet that was not shared with other households and 30 per cent had no access to a toilet in the house (and most of these were in compounds). Owners have tended to have much better access to services than other tenure groups, 46 per cent having exclusive use of a toilet and only 14 per cent having none (Malpezzi *et al.*, 1990).

The city has benefited from recent renovation of the roads and water supply system. Further details on housing conditions in Kumasi can be found in Hellen *et al.* (1991), Malpezzi *et al.* (1990), Tipple and Willis (1991a, 1991b) and Willis *et al.* (1990).

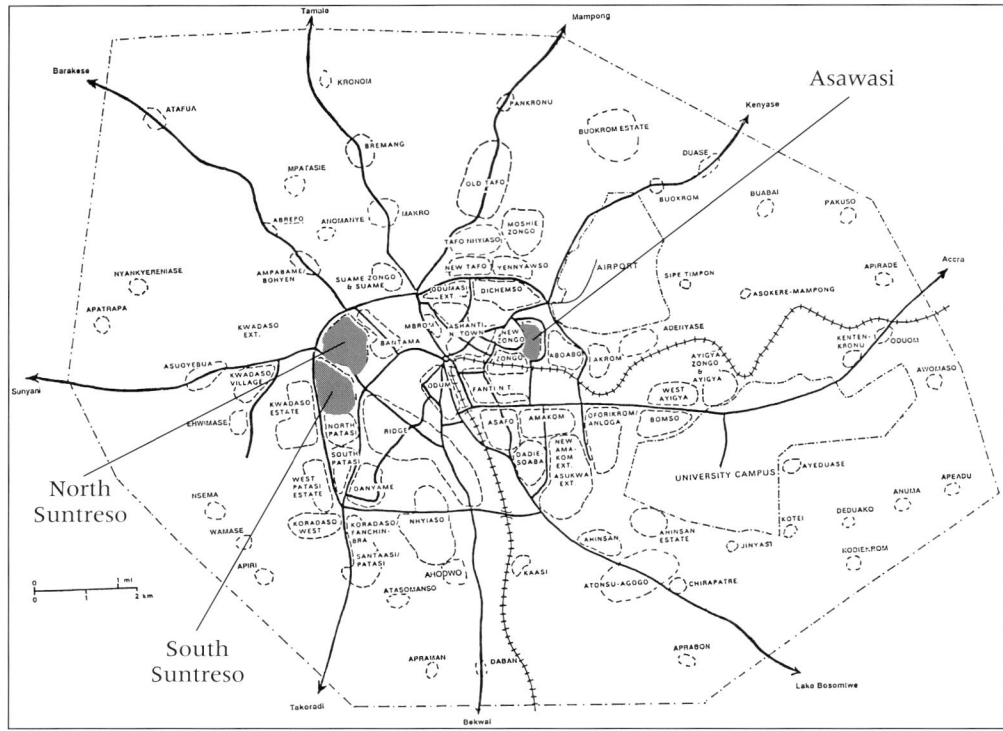

Figure 58. Map of Kumasi showing major residential areas and other land areas
Source: Original map by the author but often reproduced in the press.

The government-built housing sector is relatively small in Ghana, representing only about 5 per cent of urban housing. In Kumasi, government agencies had built approximately 4400 dwellings by 1988 (survey by S. N. Boapeah). Thus, the government's direct building effort represented only about 6 per cent of the 220,000 rooms extant in 1988 (according to Boapeah's survey). Government agencies have completed only a few hundred since then, giving a total of about 5000. In all, the originally planned dwellings probably constitute between 10,000 and 15,000 rooms.

The Ghana sample was chosen from two older government-built estates in Kumasi, Asawasi and Suntreso (which itself is divided into an earlier North estate and a later South). Both areas were built in a continuous and overlapping programme between 1945 and 1956 (Tipple, 1987) as part of the post-Second World War investment in low-cost housing that was implemented across the British Empire at that time (see Tipple, 1979, for similar developments in Zambia). The land on which Asawasi stands was leased by the government direct from Asantehene and will revert back to his control at the end of the lease (Gold Coast, 1948). North and South Suntreso are on State Land. Both Asawasi and Suntreso are wholly or mainly within the area established as Kumasi Town Lands in 1901.

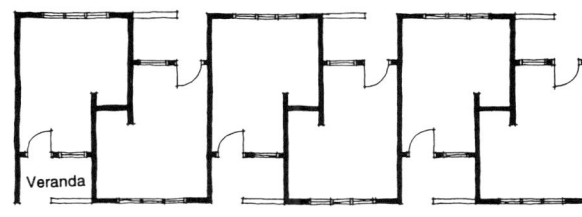

1. A terrace of single rooms.

2. A semi-detached dwelling.

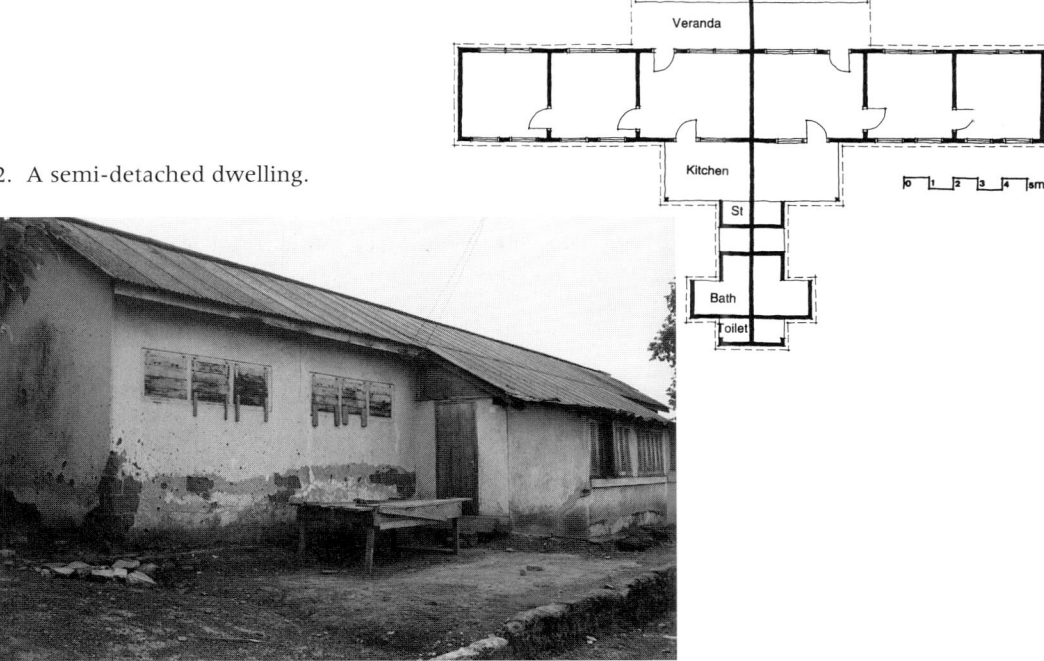

Figure 59. Original dwellings in Asawasi

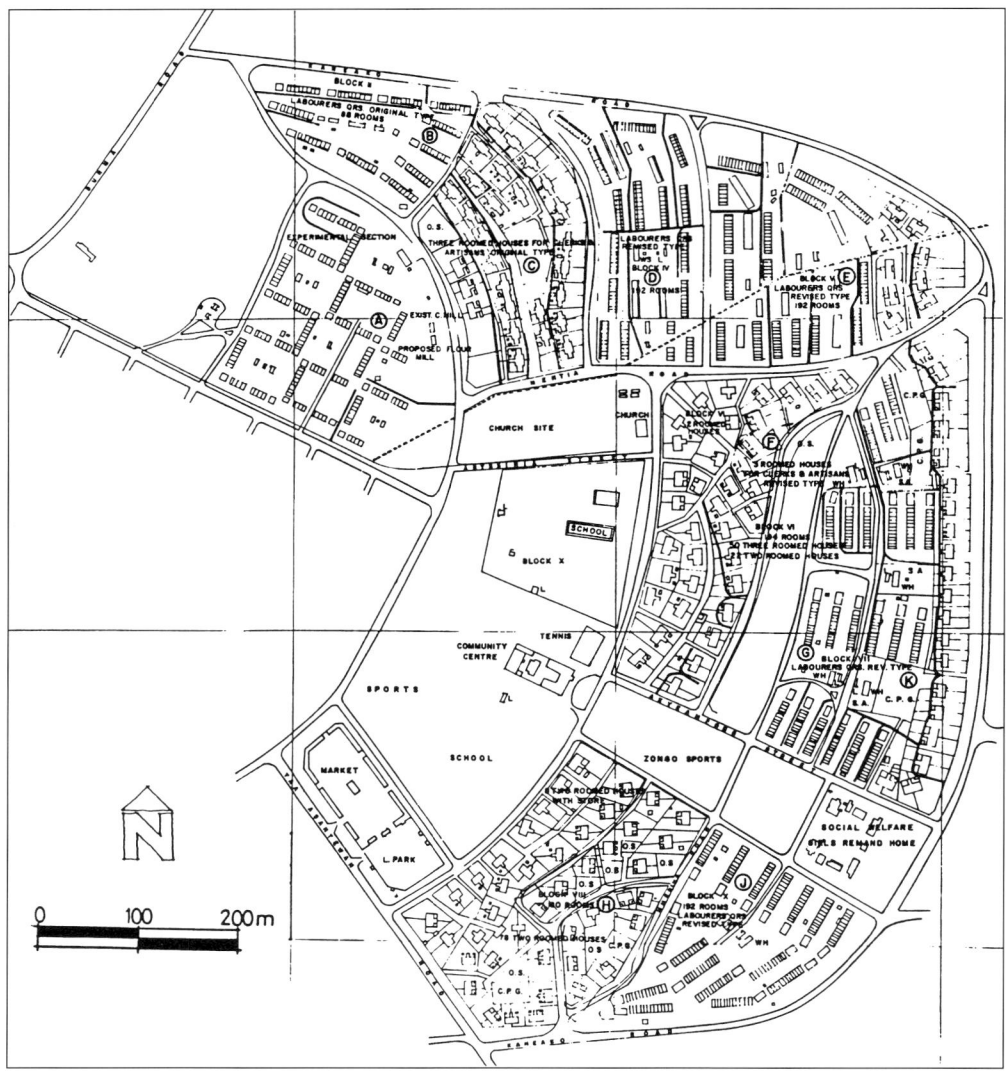

Figure 60. Plan of Asawasi

Asawasi

Asawasi estate is situated about 1 km from the centre of Kumasi, surrounded by residential development; its market is an important one being, *inter alia*, the main source of wrapping leaves[2] in the city. The estate was built in the late 1940s to the design and under the supervision of Maxwell Fry and Jane Drew. The design of the houses and the estate followed an experimental phase ('A line') designed by A. E. S. (Bunny) Alcock who was Town Engineer at the time. Earth blocks stabilised with a small quantity of cement were used and small-scale mass production was set up for roof

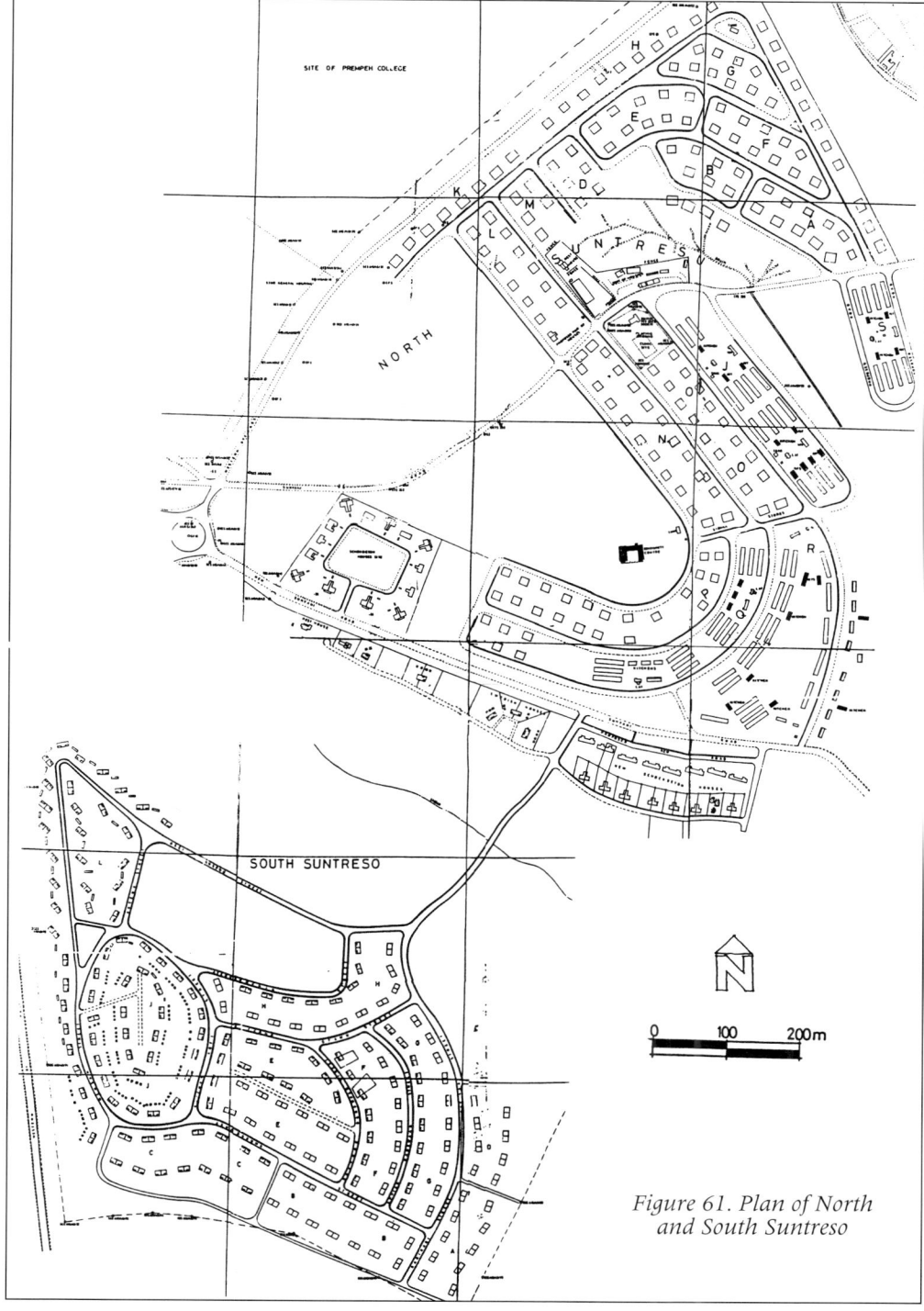

Figure 61. Plan of North and South Suntreso

trusses and other woodwork (Gold Coast, 1946; Alcock, 1952). The main project continued in this vein and its use of stabilised blocks and lean cement roofing tiles attracted comment from around the colonial world. As we shall see, the materials have stood the test of time very well. Although the main houses were re-roofed in 1960–1 in corrugated asbestos-cement sheets (BRRI, 1970), many of the kitchens are still tiled and the implication that the re-roofing was unnecessary is hard to dispel.

Asawasi originally had 1313 dwellings of which 1041 were single rooms and 272 had two or three rooms (a mean of 1.3 rooms per dwelling). The single-roomed dwellings were provided with separate 9 feet by 5.5 feet (2745 by 1650 mm) kitchens arranged in blocks back to back and side to side (in fours, sixes, or even twelves), those in 'A Line' being larger and shared one between two dwellings. Toilets were in public latrine blocks; washing and bathing places were communal.

Although the houses were intended for returning war veterans and established civil servants, only some of those eligible took up their options. Local Akans were put off by the distance from the city centre and the proximity of Aboabo, a large northerner-migrant area. Consequently the remaining houses were allocated to northerners, some of whom had been displaced by the building of Zongo police station. Because of this, and its closeness to the main mosque, Asawasi is an important area for muslim migrants from the north of Ghana and other West African countries.

Suntreso

Situated to the west of Kumasi city centre, the estate is divided into North and South by a wide undeveloped area to the south of the Sunyani Road. North Suntreso was started in 1949 and completed in 1952. South Suntreso followed, being completed in 1956. North Suntreso is mainly one- and two-roomed terraced dwellings with detached kitchens. There are 1200 dwellings in all. The two-roomed dwellings are simply two single rooms side by side with the verandas joined into one. Toilets and bath-houses were in most cases communal facilities. The South Suntreso Estate has 463 two-room and three-room dwellings, each with a bucket latrine and bathroom. In the late 1970s, the State Housing Corporation (SHC) built a few single- and two-storey detached houses along the northern boundary of South Suntreso.

Several experimental houses were included, notably the 21 'Schokbeton' prefabricated dwellings built in North Suntreso. The prefabricated housing experiment, recommended to the Gold Coast Government by N.V. Schokbeton of Kampen, Holland, entailed first the importation and then the local manufacture of large brittle concrete panels which were assembled on site by slotting them between precisely positioned uprights. The 168 houses built in Ghana by 1956 cost a then huge $7000 each and were discontinued following advice from the UN Mission in 1956 (Abrams *et al.*, 1956). Twelve timber dwellings (four detached and eight semi-detached) of Swedish manufacture were also constructed.

A report published in 1946 explaining the policy behind the new housing (Gold Coast, 1946) noted that rents were to be subsidised at 33.3 per cent for the one-roomed,

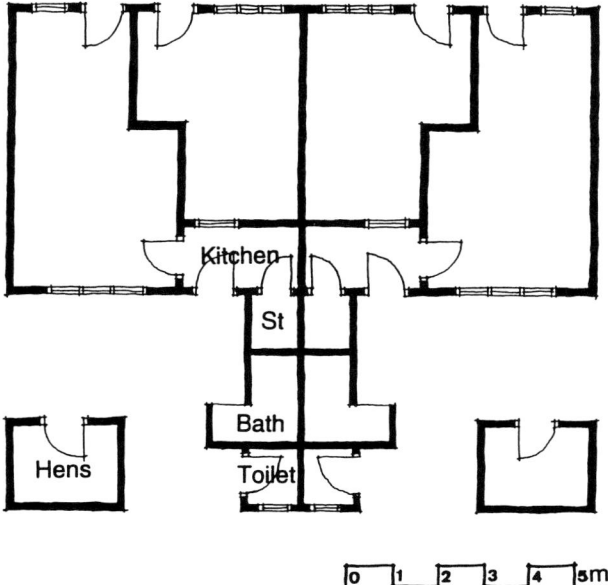

Kitchen

St

Bath

Hens

Toilet

At Asawasi, the houses were built with landcrete blocks, with battened doors and windows. The single-roomed units were originally roofed with tiles, but in about 1960–1 the tiles were replaced with corrugated asbestos sheets. The houses at Suntreso were built with cement blocks and were roofed with asbestos sheets. They had ceilings and were wired for electricity supply. All the houses were initially rented at highly subsidised rents and the Gold Coast (later State) Housing Corporation was responsible for allocation, maintenance and the collection of rents. From about 1960 government started selling the units on hire purchase to the occupants and very few remain rented from SHC.

Figure 62. Original semi-detached dwellings in Suntreso

25 per cent for the two-roomed, and 15 per cent for the three-roomed types, an attempt at income redistribution. All were for tenancy, monthly for the majority but with optional 10-, 20- or 30-year leases for the three-roomed types. Electrical connections were available in all house types except the 'standard' single rooms, for £1 after one year's 'good behaviour'. Live fences (i.e. hedges), shrubs and trees were to be planted and maintained without additional charge, but the rents did not cover private conservancy[3] for the two- and three-roomed types, which had their own toilets, or internal water and electricity charges.

The standard and superior one-roomed dwellings were rented at 6/3 (£0.32) and 9/- (£0.45) per month at a time when labourers were paid £3/11/6 or £3/18/- (£3.6–£3.9) per month (depending on service). Thus the rents constituted 12.5 per cent or less of a labourer's income (Gold Coast, 1946).

By 1981, 55 per cent of Asawasi tenants had become owners; in Suntreso, 72 per cent of occupants had bought their dwellings(Kwakye-Safo, 1981: 59) but there were serious arrears. According to the Effah Commission Report (Ghana, 1968), about 5800 people[4] were in arrears on hire-purchase payments to the State Housing Corporation in Ashanti, Upper and Northern Regions, owing a total of C6 million (about £1.2 million).

Our Ghana sample of 398 includes 88 non-transformers. The transformers are divided among 132 established and 178 recent transformers.

Socioeconomic characteristics of households

Measures of permanence

It might be expected that transformers would be relatively well settled in the urban milieu as they have not only qualified for ownership of a government-built house but have also taken time and trouble to extend it using personal savings. As would be expected from previous research on Ghana (Tipple and Willis, 1991b), owners of government-built houses tend to be in the latter half of their working lives or retired. In our sample, transformers' household heads are generally over 50 years old; only the youngest 25 per cent are under 49. Non-transformers are slightly younger than transformers, but transformers and non-transformers were of remarkably similar ages when they moved in, 29 at the medians and with the middle 50 per cent between 20 and 40.

As might be expected, established transformers started to transform when younger than recent transformers but they were still in their forties at the median. It is interesting that the third quartile of recent transformers started to extend when they were 62; the beginning of transformation is not confined to householders in their working career or when children are young. The relatively advanced age when transformation begins demonstrates that the house is not thought of as only a single-generation home. Instead, it is built up to accommodate the next generation in line with Ghanaian culture, which emphasises inter-generational obligations.

The inertia element seems to be powerful in Kumasi housing decisions. As moving house is relatively difficult in Kumasi, our sample showed very long periods of stay in their current house with a median of 30 years (a full parenting career). As it happens, there is relatively little difference among the sub-samples, all having medians of 30 years in the house. Thus, our sampled households are generally very settled in (and, therefore, committed to) their house, reflecting both the permanence of city life and the reluctance of Ghanaians to sell a house. In addition, most will have been tenants of the site before becoming owners. There is, thus, little sign of 'gentrification' following transformation.

Most owners are in retail or commercial business and have been in the same line for many years. Those who are employed rather than self-employed are also very settled. Medians of time in current employment are in excess of eight years for all groups. Although many are past retirement age for formal employment, it is customary to continue in business for as long as health permits.

We have two measures of education in Ghana: number of years spent and level attained. Both are used because students at the higher levels may have had a very circuitous journey through vocational colleges and private institutions before reaching higher education. The heads of household across the sub-samples are reasonably well educated, with a median of 10 years of schooling.

Non-transformers are marginally better educated than transformers. This may encourage them to stay in the original dwelling because it allows them to remain alone in their nuclear household without sharing with tenants or making space for extended family members. Alternatively, higher education levels may increase the cost of extending by leading the householders to require higher standards of construction either to satisfy themselves or to reflect their status. On the other hand, there is far from a positive correlation between education and income in Kumasi. As Asiama (1985) points out, the civil servants and other formal sector clerical, administrative and professional workers of Ghana have seen their incomes eroded while traders have been able, relatively, to prosper.[5]

Income and wealth

With a round thousand cedis to the Pound Sterling at the time of our survey, incomes can be seen to be relatively low using international comparators. If we accept a Purchasing Power Parity of 2.605 times the official exchange rate,[6] annual household incomes shown in table 67 become PPP£3220 for established transformers, PPP£3840 for recent transformers, and PPP£3157 for non-transformers at the medians. According to Ravallion et al. (1991), 'absolute poverty' is represented by per capita incomes of $31 per month ($372 or £248 per annum) or below and 'extreme absolute poverty' by incomes of $23 per month ($276 or £184 per annum) and below. Per capita incomes in Ghana of £184 become PPP£480 per annum, about twice 'absolute poverty' levels.

The minimum wage in Ghana at the time of the survey was C416 (US$0.63, £0.42) per day (about C125,000 a year working 25 days per month). It is acknowledged (at least unofficially) to be insufficient for even bare subsistence for a household of four people. Thus, it is not a measure of subsistence or a threshold for absolute poverty. Shared among a household of four, it gives only about US$4 per month per capita. Even multiplied by 2.605 to achieve PPP$10.42, this is only half of even the extreme absolute poverty threshold. As an aid to mental arithmetic, C1 million represents about eight minimum wages.

Table 67. Measures of income and wealth of owners

Medians (and IQR)	Established transformers	Recent transformers	Non-transformers
Household income* (C thousand/annum)	1240	1470	1210
	(880, 1,800)	(1,170, 1,840)	(940, 1,520)
Per capita income* (C thousand/annum)	183	197	239
	(140, 260)	(140, 300)	(160, 390)
Expenditure on food (C thousand/annum)	730	910	730
	(550, 1,100)	(730, 1,100)	(570, 910)
Relative wealth index**	0.23	0.23	0.058
	(0.1, 0.3)	(0.1, 0.3)	(0.02, 0.2)
Percentage with RWI of zero	11	7	17
Percentage expecting to be better off next year	10	10	3

* Expenditure as a proxy.
**Relative wealth index (RWI) lies between 0 and 1: 1 implies ownership of all the consumer durables, i.e., radio or cassette player, sewing machine, refrigerator, freezer, television, motor cycle and motor vehicle.

As we see in table 67, household incomes are very similar for established transformers and non-transformers at a median of about C1.25 million, 10 minimum wages. Recent transformers have slightly higher incomes. There are slightly greater differences among the two groups with respect to per capita incomes with non-transformers having more money per person (about C240,000 per annum) owing to their smaller households (see table 68). The proportions of income spent on food (at 55 and around 60 per cent respectively for transformers and non-transformers) are close to the 54 per cent national urban average.[7]

Both sets of transformers are noticeably better off than non-transformers in terms of consumer durables. Their RWI is higher than that of the non-transformers (table 67) but the difference arises primarily from the percentage of households who have RWI scores of zero (i.e., with none of the consumer durables). Expectation of increasing income is similar for non-transformers and transformers.

House tenancy and ownership

Over 90 per cent of transformed houses are owner-occupied but about a quarter of non-transformed houses are occupied by renters. The tiny proportion of transformers' houses that are rented have only one transformation which was built before the renters arrived. Inheritors own 40 per cent of the transformed and 26 per cent of the non-transformed houses.

The almost 40 per cent of owners who bought from the State Housing Corporation (SHC) will have benefited from the discounted rates offered and the ability to pay through hire-purchase. Asawasi originally cost about £60 per room to build (Fry, 1946a). Those who bought from individuals may have paid something approximating to a 'market' price but in the absence of a market in housing, it is likely that the price paid would be modest.

Ownership of a house other than the one occupied is a potent measure both of wealth and of commitment to the house in question and the city. Those who have no other house can, however, be expected to treat the house in the sample as their only home, the place with which they must exercise their functions of hospitality and sponsorship (Hill, 1966), the edifice which gives them their status as an owner of property, the place to provide them with security in their old age, and the property which they will bequeath to their heirs. Those who have another house may not have to rely so heavily on the one in the study areas and can, therefore, more easily leave it as a small, low-status affair. Thus, it might be expected that ownership of another house would reduce the likelihood of transformation in Ghana. On the other hand, a house in a peripheral village in Kumasi may be regarded as lower status than one in our study areas so we could expect the opposite effect on transformation.

Only a few owners owned another house but non-transformers had a slightly higher tendency to do so (16 per cent). The most common location of the other house was in Kumasi and surprisingly few followed what has been an expected pattern in past literature (for example, Brokensha, 1966) of building in their village. Owners in our sample so rarely have other houses that they cannot be considered to be professional landlords.

Household characteristics

Compared with a mean of 4.5 persons per household city-wide and 6.3 for owners in 1986 (Malpezzi et al., 1990), owner households in the two estates tend to be quite large, especially transformers who have a mean of 7.5[8] and over 75 per cent with five people or more (table 68).[9] However, this is not due to large numbers of young children; most households have more adults (16 years and over) than children. This is commensurate with the age pattern of owners who tend to be over 40.[10] Thus, the dependency ratio is not high: less than 1.0 in 75 per cent of households.[11] Non-transformers expected their households to be larger in the near future while transformers did not. This suggests that transformers have already coped with the growth of their households, perhaps accompanied by the extension activity, while the non-transformers may extend in the future to cope with their continuing growth.

Table 68. Household size and composition, owners

Medians (and IQR)	Established transformers	Recent transformers	Non-transformers
Number of people in the household	7	8	5
	(4, 10)	(5, 10)	(3, 8)
Number of adults in the household	4	5	3
	(2, 5)	(3, 7)	(2, 5)
Number of children in the household	3	3	2
	(2, 4)	(1, 5)	(0, 4)
Dependency ratio (no. of children per adult)	0.8	0.6	0.5
	(0.4, 1)	(0.3, 1)	(0, 1)
Expected household size in 3 years	7	7	6
	(4, 10)	(5, 12)	(4, 8)
Number of guests per annum	2	3	2
	(0, 6)	(2, 6)	(0, 5)

Transformers who have plans to extend, i.e., in the next three years, do not have larger households than those without such plans. However, non-transformers who plan to extend have larger households. This may show that they are reacting to housing stress felt within their own household by planning an extension. The number of guests entertained each year appears to be relatively small given the gregariousness of Ghanaian families and the frequent travelling done to funerals and other festivities[12] but the accuracy of these data may be relatively poor.

Housing characteristics and house values

Increases in house size through transformations

We know from earlier work that extensions to houses in Kumasi have provided a significant proportion, probably half, of new accommodation in the city through the 1980s (Garrod *et al.*, 1994). Thus, the transformation activity in government-built estates is part of an important unsolicited and usually unsupported housing strategy operated by owner householders themselves.

As can be seen in table 69, total built area has been extended by over 40 m² (over 100 per cent) at the median and by 150 per cent at the third quartile for both sets of transformers. In each phase of transformation, owners concentrate on adding more living space (habitable rooms) to the house. The first phase tends to extend the house by about 75 per cent at the median overall. Even at the first quartile, we can see substantial extensions: 17 m² and 19 m² for the first phase, well in excess of the average size of a single room. Additional phases tend to be smaller than the preceding phase either as demand for additional space declines or as there is less room for additions in the relatively cramped sites in parts of the estates.

Table 69. Area of each phase of extension (m²)

	Established transformers	Recent transformers	Non-transformers
Original total built area	39.7	40.2	39.7
	(25, 55)	(25, 53)	(33, 55)
Area added in Phase 1	36.3	28.3	-
	(19, 86)	(17, 60)	
Area added in Phase 2	29.6	28.7	-
	(6, 45)	(15, 60)	
Area added in Phase 3	6.4	31.5	-
	(2, 14)	(22, 52)	
Area added in Phase 4	10.5	12.1	-
	(-, -)	(6, 22)	
Total built area	82.5	87.5	39.7
	(49, 139)	(51, 130)	(37, 55)

There is also considerable variety in the scale of extensions which leads to greater variety in the current housing stock than in the original. IQRs in the original built areas are not small (30 m²), but they are smaller than the median house size. For the current house size, IQRs of 90 and 79 m² are similar to the current medians and much larger than the median original built areas.

A further demonstration of the increased variety of housing which arises from transformation is traceable by concentrating on only a single original house type, in this case the Asawasi terraces.

Table 70 shows that the variability in the sample represented by the IQR increases from virtually zero to 19 m² for established transformers and 30 m² for recent transformers, the latter of which is greater than the median original size. Indeed, in the first phase, variability is 16 m² for established transformers and 23 m² for recent transformers. Thus, the initial suggestion that transformations create a variety of accommodation out of a relatively uniform housing stock (Tipple, 1991a) is confirmed for the house as a whole.

With respect to habitable space only and in the whole Ghana sample, the median of 25 m² of original habitable space increases through transformation by about 100 per cent to over 50 m², and by about 140 per cent at the third quartile to about 85 m². Established and recent transformers have similar ranges of extension. The transformation process adds habitable space in at least two stages. In the first stage, the original dwelling is rearranged to increase the proportion of habitable space, partly through the use of the kitchen as a living room and partly by capturing the veranda as living space either by incorporating it into an existing room or by extending it into a new room. By this, established and recent transformers have gained 8 m² and 3 m² more habitable area respectively at the median.

Table 70. Area of each phase of extension (m²) for Asawasi mid- and end terraces only

Medians (and IQRs)	Established transformers	Recent transformers
Original total built area	25.0	25.0
	(25, 27)	(25, 27)
Area added in Phase 1	23.3	24.6
	(13, 30)	(15, 38)
Area added in Phase 2	6.04	9.74
	(4.5, 45)	(4.5, 30)
Area added in Phase 3	6.41	11.69
	(-, -)	(-, -)
Area added in Phase 4	-	5.01
		(-, -)
Total built area	44.1	48.3
	(32, 51)	(38, 68)

As extensions are made (the second stage), additional habitable space is added in one or more phases of construction adding about 20 m² at the median. The variety of habitable space reflects that found for total area in table 69 with IQRs almost as large as the median and about twice the median original area.

Median habitable room sizes are 13.9 m² in the original houses and 10.6 m² for the current houses. Thus, new habitable rooms tend to be smaller than original ones contrary to the Israel findings by Oxman and Carmon (1986) whose sample produced new rooms averaging 45 per cent larger than the originals. Our sample in Ghana has a great increase in occurrence of rooms of less than 8 m² as owners attempt to fit rooms into tight spaces.

Even though the original houses are reasonably well designed to provide two-thirds habitable space, the transformed houses are even more efficient with about 80 per cent habitable area at the median. This achievement is impressive, demonstrating that enclosed space is more highly prized for its potential to accommodate people, especially for sleeping, than for any other activity. Most of the gains in habitable over non-habitable space have been from incorporating verandas and kitchens into the

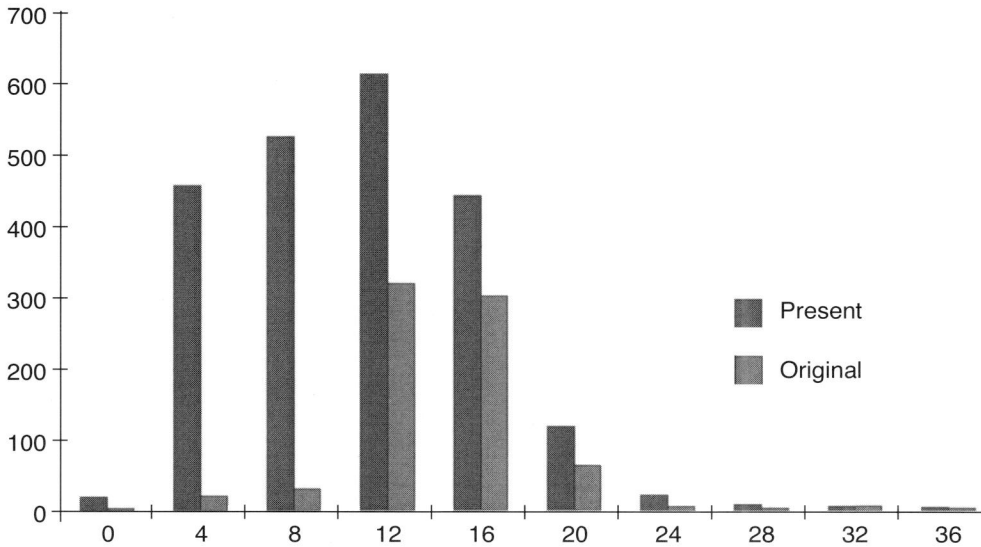

Figure 63. Frequency of habitable rooms by area, Kumasi sample

habitable space. This calls into question the long-term usefulness of verandas, except as medium-term sources of extra habitable area and 'cues' for transformation activity (Carmon and Oxman, 1981), and kitchens in a culture where cooking is mainly done outdoors. Little of the new space is taken up with non-habitable rooms or devoted to commercial activity. Early phases tend to be not only larger than later ones (table 69) but are also more likely to add a toilet or tap.

The incorporation of commercial uses into the house occurs in almost 30 per cent of houses, using 5 per cent of the area. A great variety of uses can be found including shops and kiosks selling everyday provisions, lottery kiosks, and activities such as sewing and clothes repairs, bread baking, liquor brewing and sales, tyre repairs and sales, electrical goods repair and sales, carpenters and builder's merchants, photographers, hairdressers, hotels and nightclubs. There are also mosques and churches built on house plots.

We would expect transformations to provide increases in the number of habitable rooms as well as in space. The small dwellings have had the use of their original rooms altered by modifications to the building so that there are now three habitable rooms in the original structure at the median. Thus the original veranda and kitchen (even where it is detached) are likely to be used as living rooms and some re-partitioning of spaces has been carried out.

In addition, established transformers built three, and recent transformers built two new habitable rooms at the medians. In contrast with the IQR of only two in the original houses (only one for the non-transformers), the current IQR of four or five rooms for transformers shows, once again, the impressive variety which they have built into the areas.

There is a pattern to the scale of transformations which appears to be imposed by the house types. Extension of the semi-detached types, which are larger and have plots, has been limited at the mean to just under 50 per cent of the original size at present. Mid-terraced types have means of 70 to 82 per cent, while the end terraces have a much higher 120 per cent increase. The low mean for the semi-detached types may relate more to the sample having several houses on unusually small plots (e.g. C line at Asawasi) than to the potential for expansion that those on larger plots have exploited. The largest house in our survey in Ghana now has 31 rooms.

Increases in space per person through transformation

As in the comparative analysis (chapter 2), we use three measures to assess the improvements in space available per person: non-transformers' space use, the main household as a proxy for the original household (HoOo), and the current occupants as the occupants of the original house (HoOc). The last is not very reasonable in the Ghana sample as multi-habitation is quite common and many more people live in the extended houses than would attempt to occupy the original dwelling. Table 71 demonstrates the effects of transformation according to these measures.

Table 71. Changes in space per person

	Established transformers	Recent transformers	Non-transformers
Current housing space per person (m²)	7.35	7.03	6.35
(HcOc)	(4.6, 10.9)	(4.7, 10)	4.5, 12)
Original housing space per person (m²)	5.49	5.01	7.76
(HoOo)	(3.3, 9.0)	(3.2, 8.2)	(5.0, 12.1)
Original housing space per person (m²)	3.54	3.27	6.35
(HoOc)	(2.3, 6)	(2.3, 5)	(4.5, 12)
Current rooms per person (HcOc)	1.00	0.91	0.87
	(0.6, 1.5)	(0.6, 1.3)	(0.6, 1.2)
Original rooms per person (HoOo)	0.65	0.60	1.00
	(0.4, 1.2)	(0.4, 1.0)	(0.6, 1.3)
Original rooms per person (HoOc)	0.45	0.40	0.87
	(0.3, 0.8)	(0.3, 0.6)	(0.6, 1.2)

There has been quite an increase in space per person judged by any of the three measures. The improvement over current non-transformers is the smallest, but still 1.0 or 0.7 m² and up to 0.3 rooms per person at the medians. Using just the main household to model the original occupants (HoOo), the increase is approximately 2 m² and about 0.3 rooms per person at the medians. If all the current occupants were crammed into the original house (HoOc), the improvement exhibited by current space represents a doubling of space and rooms per person. Thus, there is no question that occupants have more space than they would have had without the transformation; all that is affected by the method of measurement is the extent of the improvement.

Improvements in habitable space are larger than those in total space and constitute a large proportional increase. From non-transformers, established and recent transformers have gained 32 and 20 per cent respectively; from HoOo they have gained 45 and 52 per cent respectively and, from HoOc, their gain is 130 and 132 per cent respectively. Gains in habitable rooms per person are even greater with 85 and 67 per cent gains over non-transformers; 144 and 120 per cent over HoOo; and 239 and 224 per cent over HoOc. These are all very considerable gains in habitable space and rooms per person, representing both considerably improved conditions of occupancy and little loss to commercial and other activity. Thus we can see that extensions to space have not been fully matched by increases in the number of occupants; the 'original' occupants have, therefore, benefited from the additional space.

Increases in space occupied by main households[13]

The main households have benefited substantially from the transformation activity, occupying 40 m² at the medians which is 15–20 per cent (6–7 m²) more space than if they had continued to occupy the original dwelling unaltered (table 72). In addition, they have a greater variety of space with IQRs of 34 to 72 m² for established and 33 to 61 m² for recent transformers. In terms of habitable space, however, even greater improvements have been made; of 63 per cent (established transformers) and 49 per cent (recent transformers) at the medians.

It is clear also that transformers have better housing, in terms of habitable space enjoyed per person, than they had before and than non-transformers. This is, perhaps, counter to the popular conception that the transformed areas are overcrowded and the extensions are filled with tenants. Although there are similar numbers of rooms per person, transformers fare better than non-transformers in habitable space and habitable rooms. Established transformers now have a median of 6.2 m² habitable space, recent transformers have 5.7 m² , while non-transformers crowd in with only 4.9 m² per person. In spite of their larger households than before, main households enjoy relatively low occupancy rates (similar to those expected for owners of compound houses (Tipple and Willis, 1991b). With two persons per room or less at the medians, they are considerably better off than average for Kumasi which had means of 3.3 persons per room both in 1980 (Tipple, 1987) and in 1986 (Malpezzi et al., 1990). Non-transformers, on the other hand, have occupancy rates like those of renters of single rooms (Tipple and Willis, 1991b) even though they have several rooms.

Table 72. Measures of occupancy, main households

Medians (and IQRs)	Established transformers	Recent transformers	Non-transformers
Area per person (m²)	7.52	6.71	7.76
	(4.6, 11.7)	(4.4, 10.1)	(4.6, 12.1)
Rooms per person	0.85	0.71	0.83
	(0.5, 1.4)	(0.5, 1.0)	(0.5, 1.3)
Habitable space per person (m²)	6.20	5.69	4.87
	(3.6, 9.3)	(3.7, 8.8)	(3.2, 8.0)
Habitable rooms per person	0.60	0.50	0.33
	(0.4, 0.9)	(0.4, 0.8)	(0.2, 0.5)
Occupancy rate	1.63	2.00	3.00
	(1.0, 2.5)	(1.3, 2.7)	(2.0, 4.5)
Future occupancy rate	1.60	2.00	3.00
	(1.0, 2.5)	(1.3, 2.9)	(2.3, 5.3)

These data illuminate the issues of density and occupancy raised in our preliminary work that 'transformations increase the local population and generate higher population densities but tend to reduce occupancy rates' (Tipple, 1991a: 77).

The future occupancy rate picks up whether a household is likely to be larger or smaller in three years' time: whether they are likely to have experienced the 'shocks' of increases in household size through births or elderly relatives moving in (Seek, 1983). Recent transformers seem to expect slight growth in household size indicating continued effort to keep up with stresses by extension while established transformers show that they have stabilised or begun to experience household shrinkage and are not in need of more space. These data reinforce our finding (above) that recent transformers are in the throes of responding to housing stress (notwithstanding that they are also renting out rooms) rather than being in a comfortable and consolidated position with respect to housing space for all their own needs.

Most main households occupy all the habitable rooms within the original dwellings and also occupy at least some room in the extension, but recent transformers are less likely to occupy extended space than established transformers. They occupy medians of about 10 m², or at least one habitable room, in the extension.

The theme of greater variety through transformation is continued in terms of space occupied by the main household (table 73). We can examine only those main households who occupy the almost uniform, single-roomed accommodation in Asawasi to demonstrate that considerable variety has been produced. The number of habitable rooms available to the main household has increased to three or four and they can now occupy a median of over 30 m² with IQRs spanning 16 or 20 m². Thus, variety has indeed been created out of uniformity in Asawasi terraces.

Table 73. Comparison of increases in rooms, space, etc.

Original median equals 100	Established transformers	Recent transformers	Non-transformers
Total space per house	207	218	100
Habitable space	215	205	100
Number of habitable rooms	300	250	100
Area occupied by the main household	120	115	92
Habitable area occupied by the main household	163	149	100
Habitable rooms occupied by the main household	200	200	100

To summarise, increases in housing space are different according to which measure is used. The most dramatic effect of transformation has been in the increased space in the house overall. The median number of habitable rooms available in the houses has shown a threefold increase. Habitable space has doubled, as has total space.

Main households have increased their area occupied but not by as much as the general increase, demonstrating that other households merit some priority in allocating additional space. Once again, however, main household habitable space has increased more markedly than total space, and the number of habitable rooms available by more than habitable space. This is because the new rooms tend to be smaller than the originals. In this context, main households have improved their occupancy rates over their non-transformer peers from 3.0 to 1.6 and 1.8, established and recent transformers respectively.

The original houses, unchanged (as occupied by non-transformers) are evidently inadequate for the realities of modern urban Ghana where their relatively central locations attract relatives and hold onto nuclear family members after they could be expected to have formed their own households elsewhere. With more than 25 per cent of these households having eight members, some of these small self-contained dwellings have more than four persons per room.

Space occupied by subsequent households

Space has been generated which is now occupied by other households. We have socioeconomic data for up to two per house: one renter household and one family household living rent free which we use as representative of all subsequent households. In addition, we have data on rooms occupied by each household in the house.

Subsequent households occupy much less room than the main household in the house (only one room and about 13 m² at the median) and their accommodation is mainly in the extensions. It seems strange, however, that main households with recent transformations have half a square metre per person less habitable space while they do not claim as much of the new extended space for themselves as established transformers.

Subsequent households tend to occupy roughly similar amounts of space regardless of how many households there are in the house. This demonstrates that there is a specific range of spaces which are deemed appropriate for occupation by a household. However, with the first quartiles hovering around the 6–10 m² range, the space regarded as appropriate is quite small at the lower limit, and may indeed represent the detached kitchen connected with many of the single-roomed dwellings. Subsequent households, however, have per-person occupancy rates only marginally below those of main households because their households are much smaller.[14] In line with the findings of Tipple and Willis (1991b), rent-free (family) tenants have very slightly worse housing conditions than tenants but both have a median occupancy rate of two persons per room.

As we would expect, there is a major reduction in the proportion of space occupied by subsequent households as their number rises, especially after the first. There is also a commensurate variation in the percentage of the house occupied by the main household who have a smaller percentage share as more households are accommodated.

Increases in people accommodated

While established and recent transformers have households of 10 and 11 people at the medians, non-transformers have much smaller households (median of 6). In addition, the IQRs of transformers are greater than the median of non-transformers, demonstrating the variety of accommodation provided. Hearsay evidence would suggest large numbers of tenant and rent-free (family) households in the Kumasi estates. In addition, our pilot study undertaken in Suntreso, where the sample was selected to represent the range of transformations, showed a mean of 5.2 households per house (Tipple and Owusu, 1994). However, our random sample shows us that the mean number of households per house is only 2.14, and the median for transformers is only 2.00 households per house. At the median, households have no tenants and no rent-free (family) households. About one-third of households have tenants and the same percentage have rent-free (family) households (with much overlap). These data suggest that the sampled houses are less in multi-habitation than expected.

Improved service levels

Only the semi-detached and detached houses in the sample were originally provided with their own water tap and toilet. Thus, 35 per cent of the sample originally had a toilet; the remainder were served by public latrines situated at strategic sites in the residential area. As a result of extension activity, 56 per cent of established transformers and 61 per cent of recent transformers now have a toilet. They are mainly added in the first phase of extensions.

House physical condition

There appears to be no correspondence between the original materials in which the houses were constructed and those used in the extensions. As we saw above, the original estate houses (at least in Asawasi) were built in a spirit of experimentation using innovative materials and techniques which have stood the test of time. Thus, 38 per cent of our sample are built of stabilised soil (landcrete) blocks and the remainder have cement block (known in Ghana as sandcrete) walls. However, the acceptance of soil-based materials into general use has never been achieved either through government example or through the establishment of small-scale industries to produce and promote them. Thus, the stabilised soil blocks have been eschewed by extenders who have simply used the easily available cement (sandcrete) blocks (125 × 300 × 450mm) and corrugated aluminium sheets. The houses were originally roofed in stabilised soil tiles but have had corrugated asbestos sheets since 1960–1. All new sloping roofs are covered in corrugated metal (iron or more recently aluminium) and flat ones are reinforced concrete slabs. Almost all the original windows were unglazed, using wooden shutters in various forms instead of glass. Locally manufactured wooden louvred windows (jalousies) are still used in a majority of cases (63 per cent) but a significant minority (29 per cent) have borne the additional expense of using glass, normally in the form of louvres set in aluminium carriers screwed to wooden frames.[15]

These materials used in transformations are the same as in most residential development in the city. How far this reflects a wish to fit into the general urbanisation process of continual improvement and upgrading (Gosling et al., 1993) and how far it is simply a function of what is available is difficult to tell, but one expects the latter.

There are obviously some signs of age and neglect in these estates where the original structures have passed their fortieth year. A large minority (47 per cent) have at least minor cracks in the wall (though major cracks are quite rare – in only 6 per cent of original structures). Leaking roofs are relatively common (30 per cent in the original structures) but not the norm, while rotten or broken windows are present in most houses (84 per cent). The extensions display much better physical conditions except in respect of the windows, where 89 per cent are broken or rotten, though this may reflect an increase in the use of glazing which breaks much more easily than the formerly common wooden jalousie (or top-hinged wooden panel shutter provided originally on some windows in Asawasi). The evidence suggests that transformation activity here is indeed a form of physical upgrading, giving new life to old housing which otherwise may deteriorate beyond rescue.

As far as the State Housing Corporation (SHC)[16] officers are concerned, most transformations have planning and building regulations approval. The residents must apply through SHC who pass the applications to the Ashanti Regional Town and Country Planning Department. While it is likely that some permissions have related more to monetary exchanges than to the fulfilment of all regulations, as a result of at least a semblance of planning control we could expect there to be less blatant flouting of the regulations than would occur in an entirely uncontrolled situation.

Where rooms planned as kitchens or other non-habitable spaces are modified for habitable uses, and in extensions on relatively constricted sites, it might be expected that there would be many rooms which were smaller than regulations demand. About two out of three houses have at least one room of less than 6 m² but those of less than 4 m² are much less common (only present in 35 per cent of houses). The majority of the rooms smaller than 6 m² are the original detached kitchens or verandas which have simply been absorbed into habitable space without demolishing any walls. Because of the arrangement of the kitchens in terraces, back to back and side by side with only the narrow frontage exposed in most cases, they are particularly difficult to extend. However, most of them have been in habitable use since before 1960 (BRRI, 1970). There is also a tendency to build small rooms as additions to the narrow terraced dwellings where space is tight. Although there are new rooms which have been built too small to comply with current norms, the occurrence of small rooms owes more to short-sightedness in the original provision of these kitchens than to the additions' being made in inappropriate ways.[17]

One-fifth of the 2214 habitable rooms in the sample are less than 6 m² in area. Only 7 per cent of rooms are less than 4 m². Of these, 52 per cent are in the original building and the remainder are in the extensions.

Plan forms

We have discussed plan forms briefly in chapter 5. The most notable feature of the changes in plan form from transformation must be the prevalence of compound houses. This can be demonstrated by dividing the house forms resulting from transformation into three as follows:

- Type 1: houses without courtyards including those with fenced yards;
- Type 2: houses with rooms opening directly onto a corridor-shaped external space, sometimes via a veranda;[18]
- Type 3: houses with rooms opening onto a rectangular courtyard wider than a mere corridor.

These are enumerated in table 74.

Table 74. Transformed house types built in Kumasi study areas (percentages)

Percentages	Asawasi	North Suntreso	South Suntreso	All areas
Type 1, no courtyard	22	42	50	31.4
Type 2, corridor	34	14	0	23.9
Type 3, courtyard	44	44	50	44.7

In only 31 per cent of transformed houses has the self-contained villa form been retained. In 45 per cent of the sampled houses, the compound form with a courtyard as an internal space and the focus of circulation has been achieved, despite many dwellings being very constricted before extension. At the median, about 16 per cent of plot area is used for the courtyard.

The increasing use of the compound form and rooms opening off a corridor or open space rather than off another room increases ventilation and the flexibility of room use. Such rooms can be occupied by household members or rented out to individuals or households who live independently. If the new rooms opened off or were accessible through an internal living room there would be a reduction in flexibility and this is evidently not favoured by transformers.

Cost of transformation phases

Established transformers have spent considerably more (67 per cent more at the median) on transformation than recent transformers (table 75). Their median expenditure of C2 million constitutes 1.6 times their median annual income whereas that for recent transformers (C1.2 million) is only 80 per cent of their higher median annual income. However, the third quartile of over C8 million (£8000) represents massive expenditure for low-income households. The lower figures for recent transformers gives some support to the idea that they are merely part of the way through a larger transformation programme which may reach comparable figures to those of their established counterparts.

Table 75. Cost of phases in the extension process in millions of cedis

Medians (and IQRs)	Established transformers	Recent transformers	All transformers
Phase 1	1.88	0.64	1.25
	(0.3, 7.8)	(0.4, 2.4)	(0.4, 7.0)
	($n = 174$)	($n = 63$)	($n = 237$)
Phase 2	0.76	0.65	0.69
	(0.3, 2.5)	(0.1, 2.0)	(0.2, 2.0)
	($n = 31$)	($n = 37$)	($n = 68$)
Phase 3	11.4	0.58	0.91
	(-, -)	(0.1, 3.3)	(0.1, 6.3)
	($n = 2$)	($n = 12$)	($n = 14$)
Phase 4	-	0.35	0.35
		(0.1, 0.6)	(0.14, 0.6)
		($n = 4$)	($n = 4$)
Total cost of transformations	2.00	1.21	1.84
	(0.5, 8.3)	(0.5, 3.2)	(0.5, 7.2)

All costs are normalized to 1993 values.

There appears to be a tendency for established transformers to have built one very large phase (costing more than one year's household income – C1.9 million, £1900 – at the median) followed by a more moderately sized phase. Recent transformers have been more steady with three similarly sized phases, each at about C600,000 (£600).

The mean spending on transformations in our sample is a gigantic C34.9 million but this includes four extremely large and expensive projects (e.g. a church). If we remove these from our calculations, the mean is still an impressive C15.2 million. If we extend this to total of 5000 government-built houses in Kumasi, the contribution of transformations to the city's housing stock is likely to be about C76 thousand million (£76 million or PPP£200 million).

Increases in house value and cost

The issue of values brings into focus the analytical problems arising from the absence of a market in houses in Kumasi: for cultural reasons, houses are hardly ever sold out of the owning lineage (Tipple, 1984). Thus, our discussions also centre on the price of building replacements. As many residents have relatively accurate perceptions about the price of obtaining land and constructing (table 76), an owner may realise that the house could be improved more cheaply by extending than by seeking out a plot and building from new (table 77). However, we must be careful not to assume that the move-rather-than-improve option is available to owners in Kumasi. Although they may move by building elsewhere, they would not normally sell their current house. In that case they must build from other capital than that which would be available if they could liquidate the equity in their original house.

Table 76. Value of the whole house

Medians (and IQRs)	Established transformers	Recent transformers	Non-transformers
Value of the house (C million)	4.35	4.50	2.50
	(2.3, 7.6)	(2.5, 8.0)	(1.5, 5.0)
Value of the house per room (C thousand)	462	455	556
	(290, 670)	(280, 720)	(400, 750)
Value of the house per habitable room (C thousand)	739	785	1500
	(470, 1140)	(500, 1250)	(1000, 2500)
Value of the house per square metre (C thousand)	66.4	56.7	62.9
	(39, 87)	(36, 93)	(44, 110)
Higher or lower than average? *	1	1	1
	(1, 3)	(1, 3)	(1, 1)
Percentage higher than average	35	42	14

* 1 = less than average, 2 = average, 3 = more than average.
C1000 = £1.

Table 77. Rebuilding cost of the house

Medians (and IQRs)	Established transformers	Recent transformers	Non-transformers
Rebuilding cost (C million)	6.00	6.00	6.00
	(2.6, 10.0)	(3.0, 10.0)	(2.0, 5.0)
Rebuilding cost per room (C thousand)	600	600	733
	(330, 930)	(380, 970)	(500, 890)
Rebuilding cost per habitable room (C thousand)	1000	1000	2000
	(500, 1460)	(630, 1670)	(1500, 2500)
Rebuilding cost per square metre (C thousand)	87.2	79.2	82.4
	(44, 121)	(48, 118)	(58, 119)

C1000 = £1.

Uncertainty about house value could be expected in a place where there is almost no market in housing[19] and where market rents are unknown. In previous work attempting to value market rents (which are strongly related to values), Malpezzi *et al.* (1990) found that landlords had very low opinions of the value of their property in rental terms despite being aware of the cost of construction. It was as if years of rent controls had blunted the value predictions.

In our sample, the estimates of value are 25 per cent lower than those of replacement cost and most households appear to regard their houses as less valuable than average for their area. The latter assertion is probably inaccurate for many transformers who make it because the non-transformed houses represent a pool of least valuable houses against which at least a bare majority of transformed houses must be more valuable.[20]

Rebuilding costs estimated by the occupants appear to be a remarkably accurate reflection of formal sector costs. Building technologists at the Faculty of Environmental and Development Studies (FEDS) at the University of Science and Technology (UST), Kumasi quoted C77,000 for construction cost per square metre for housing in Suntreso in 1991 (about C800,000 per room). Median estimates from our sample are lower than this figure but not by a large margin and may well reflect savings available by using the informal sector.

Housing available through formal sector suppliers in Kumasi, notionally targeted at the low-income population but too expensive for most, is priced between C5 million and C13 million with a cost per room of C4–5 million (table 78). Our sample's estimates are lower per habitable room at the median by a factor of between four and five. Even the subsidised SSNIT (Social Security and National Insurance Trust) houses cost 2.8 times as much per habitable room as the median estimate of the transformers.

A further estimate of value was found by asking occupiers how much was the maximum rent they would be willing to pay for the same amount of space they currently occupied. Previous questions on willingness to pay for rooms asked in the World Bank study on rent control in 1986 (Malpezzi *et al.*, 1990) showed very close correlation between rent valuations and the current rental levels, and relatively little spread. Since the beginning of rent control in 1943, rental levels have never reflected the cost of providing accommodation. Instead they have been based on rather uncertain norms relating to incomes (classed as formal-sector salary levels) which in turn do not reflect consumption. At the median, they have been about 2 per cent of consumption for at least a decade (Tipple, 1984; Malpezzi *et al.*, 1990; Korboe, 1993b).

Table 78. Prices of house types available through formal-sector suppliers on the outskirts of Accra, July 1993 (millions of cedis)

House type	SSNIT	Parakuo Estates	Regimanuel-Gray
1 bedroom (two rooms)	5.4*	7.8	8.1
2 bedrooms (three rooms)	8.5*	11.2	9.65
3 bedrooms (four rooms)		12–13	

* These prices are subsidised for political and public relations reasons.
All prices include off-site cost of main services.

The maximum rental levels per room quoted by our sample, at the medians, are C667 to C833 (£0.67–0.83) per month, or two to three times the most recent controlled rent. Thus, they reflect the going rates for similar property rather than the cost of building the accommodation; nor are they a significant proportion of household consumption. The rents quoted would pay back the principal cost of building in 600 to 800 months (up to 69 years) at the medians. Therefore, they could not pay back the cost of building even after three generations if any reasonable interest rate is included.

We would expect to find a close relationship between the value of that part of the property occupied by the main household and the ability of the main household to invest in housing. This assumes, of course, that the rest of the house is financially self-sustaining which, we know for Ghana, it is not.

Although transformers occupy houses which they estimate to be worth about 80 per cent more than non-transformers, the portion which they occupy is valued at only about 20 per cent more at about C3 million (£3000) at the median. Rebuilding costs are rather higher at about C4 million (£4000) at the median for the main household and just over C1 million (£1000) for the subsequent households. Thus, the main household's portion is four times as valuable as that occupied by subsequent households in the house.

It is likely that rebuilding costs are more accurate measures of worth in Ghana and we can therefore posit a cost of accommodating owner households at about C4 million each and tenant households at a little over C1 million each. These costs show what good value transformed houses are in comparison with the formal sector's alternatives. These start at C5.4 million for SHC's subsidised two-roomed bungalow and proceed to Ghana Real Estate Developers Association (GREDA) members' offerings at C8 million for two rooms to C12–13 million for four rooms.

As indicated earlier, UNCHS (1993) found a worldwide median house-cost-to-income ratio of five but a Sub-Saharan African median of only 1.04. This probably represents under-consumption of housing goods as much as a healthy supply of inexpensive housing. Our previous work in Kumasi which showed that 73 per cent of households occupied only one room reinforces this (Malpezzi *et al.*, 1990; Tipple and Willis, 1991b). In our preliminary work on transformers in Kumasi, we found very high house-cost-to-income ratios among transformers in Suntreso, demonstrating that house owners were prepared to spend large amounts on housing improvements. There, our non-random sample generated median ratios against household income of 4.5 for the original house, 6.5 for the additions, and a total of 10.7 (Tipple and Owusu, 1994).

Our random sample, however, has picked up many more of the modest transformations added to very small dwellings. Thus, our cost-to-income ratios are more realistic. Non-transformers occupy housing costing about 2.5 times their income at the median. Transformers occupy houses with replacement costs of about four times their incomes. However, the portion of the house occupied by the main household costs 2.6 (for recent transformers) to 3.0 (for established transformers) times income (about the same as for non-transformers' houses). Thus, although Ghanaians perceive houses as large investments in relation to their income, within them they occupy only accommodation of middling value in the house-cost-to-income ratio range for developing countries.

Intensity of development

We can see from table 79 that the original very modest floor-space indexes and plot ratios have been increased considerably. As there is relatively little two-storey development,[21] the two statistics are almost the same.

While the original development could be said to be over-generous in open area so that floor-space indexes and plot ratios were unnecessarily low (at 0.25 at the median), the current situation could be cause for concern, especially if, as we argue elsewhere, transformations as they exist are only an intermediate stage of development. A third quartile of 0.73 for recent transformers represents quite high proportions of ground space covered by built area. There is probably a need for some control over the extent to which additional floor space is constructed in areas where the local plot ratio is 0.7 and above. As most of the extensions have permissions (see below), this control could be exercised but it should be seen to be even handed between current non-transformers who wish to extend and those who have benefited from the case-by-case decision-making which seems to have obtained in the past.

Table 79. Plot ratios and floor-space indexes

Medians (and IQRs)	Established transformers	Recent transformers	Non-transformers
Plot area (m²)	138.4	156.5	39.7
	(76, 320)	(88, 306)	(33, 55)
Original built area (m²)	39.7	40.2	39.7
	(25, 55)	(25, 53)	(33, 55)
Total built area (m²)	82.5	87.5	39.7
	(49, 139)	(51, 130)	(33, 55)
Ground floor built area (m²)	82.1	86.6	39.7
	(49, 137)	(51, 124)	(33, 55)
Original floor-space index	0.26	0.25	0.24*
	(0.18, 0.37)	(0.17, 0.37)	(0.2, 0.3)
Floor-space index	0.58	0.59	0.24*
	(0.42, 0.73)	(0.39, 0.74)	(0.2, 0.3)
Plot ratio	0.57	0.59	0.24*
	(0.42, 0.71)	(0.39, 0.73)	(0.2, 0.3)

* Since the majority of non-transformed houses do not have official plots, we have used the mean plot size for each transformed house type as a proxy for the plot of non-transformers in those house types.

The process of transformation

Motivation for extension

The examination of motivations for extension addresses the issue of what causes a household to make a significant change to its housing consumption rather than continuing to tolerate the *status quo*.

The transformation activity in Asawasi and Suntreso appears to be essentially intended as an increase in the supply of living space, especially space for the household and for relatives of household members. The three housing stress reasons (more people joining the household, children getting older, housing the family[22]) account for 81 per cent of the motives for needing more room. The commercial reasons (renting, business, for increased value) account for only 15 per cent of the extensions.

The low score of renting (only 7 per cent) as a motive does not contradict the frequent use of rooms for renting out. The reason for this is outlined by Korboe (1993a) who explains that renting may be practised as an interim use of rooms intended ultimately for the use of *abusua* members or spouse and children of the original owner. Rent incomes from the houses, admitted to by owners, represent a very small part of their income, less than 2 per cent at the median, and do not repay the cost of the room in any reasonable period (see above).

When asked about their motivation for extending rather than moving, householders reflected the fact that, in the Ghana context, housing is almost never sold and thus there is virtually no market.[23] In the case of the houses in our sample, which were built by an outside agency and only bought by the owners, we might expect there to be some market but little seems to be emerging. It is unsurprising, therefore, that 34 per cent of householders declared that there was no alternative at a price they could pay and 6 per cent could find no suitable alternative.

The lack of a housing market in Kumasi does not prevent mobility, it simply means that their values cannot be liquidated when houses are left. Thus, 25 per cent of transformers did not consider moving and 29 per cent expressed loyalty to the area as the main reason for not leaving.

In discussing availability of alternatives to buy, respondents would probably only be thinking of formal-sector low-cost houses built for purchase. State Housing Corporation and the few real estate developers (who together form GREDA) build a few single-household houses per annum. As we saw in table 78, these are much more expensive per room than the stay-and-improve strategy for our transformers. In so far as alternatives are available (and there are very few), it is evident that transformers perceive their small houses extended to be better value than new, larger houses.

Problems encountered in the extension process
Respondents were asked to rank the problems encountered in their extension activity by selecting first, second and third in order of difficulty from finance, building materials, labour, services, permissions and an 'other, specify' option. There is little substantive difference between established and recent transformers in their perception of problems so we do not have a significantly different housing supply context from the 1980s.[24] Finance is number one for over 85 per cent. We must remember here that there is no formal system from which transformers can borrow and informal systems are not set up for long-term borrowing. Thus, the extender builds from cash balances.

Materials are less of a problem now than in the 1970s and 1980s but still 54 per cent of recent transformers found them the second most intractable problem. Labour (which probably included relationships with main artisans or foreman) is the third most difficult problem (21 per cent placed it second, 54 per cent third). Services are seen as little problem even though many houses have none. Permissions are not a problem, either because SHC took care of the matter or because officials could be bought off easily.

The construction process
A total of five phases of construction have been found in the Kumasi sample. Most have only implemented one or two phases (97 per cent of transformers) but many of the recent transformers are now on phase three or four. Activity began in earnest back in the 1960s and progressed to such an extent that almost 40 per cent of our sample had at least one extension completed by 1980. The pattern is one of boom and hiatus

**Established
transformers**

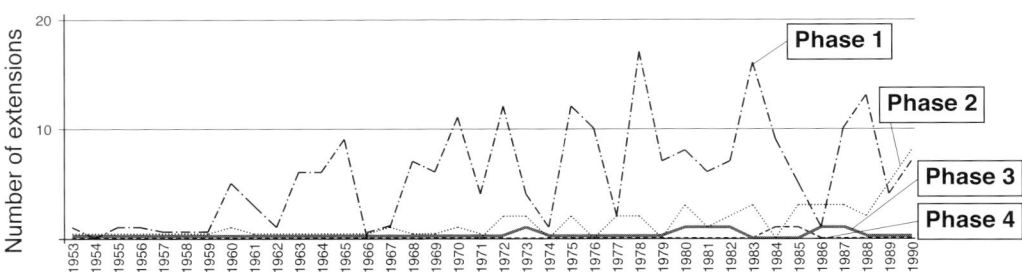

**Recent
transformers**

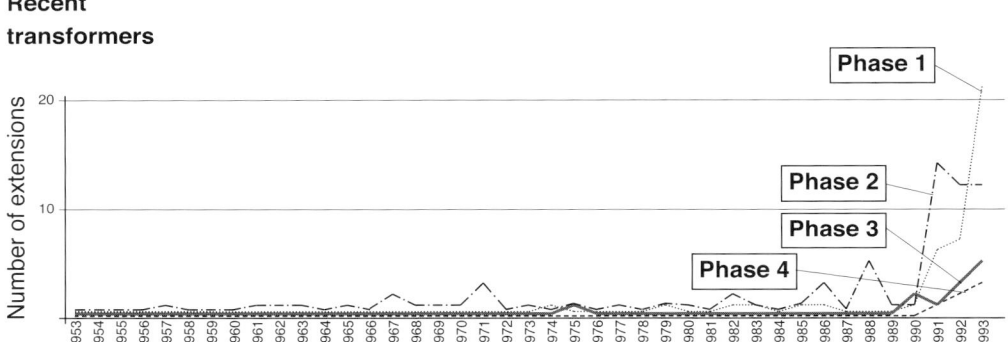

Figure 64. Number of extensions recorded in the Kumasi sample, by year

at three- to five-year intervals.

In building their extensions, most householders do not hire a contractor, in the sense of someone who handles all the trades within one organisation, they use single artisans beginning with a mason. He tends to become a leader in the building process and may influence the choice of carpenter, plumber, electrician, etc. Some masons have staff who can be building while the leader helps the client with purchases of materials and components, etc. Thus, the line between artisans and contractors can be very fuzzy.

Very large jobs (building two-storey extensions) may require a contractor, especially where speed is of the essence. In this case, the contractor will negotiate prices separately with the owner and the artisans and take his profit. While we might have expected that extenders would be less likely than new builders to use contractors, there is little evidence of this. In Lagos, Aina (1988) found that about 30 per cent of owners used contractors to build houses. In our sample, 29 per cent of transformers used contractors for extending. While contractors tended to do the larger jobs (median of five rooms but with a third quartile of 10 rooms), separate tradesmen carried out extensions with a median of four rooms in phase one.

The process of extending can be both long and intermittent. When money runs out, the workers are laid off and leave the site. When the work can proceed once again, it is likely that the same artisans will be engaged, except in cases of delinquency. When work can resume, the customer will call the relevant artisan. If he is busy, the customer might take on someone else or, more likely, wait for him to be free.

The engagement of single tradesmen (masons for the floors and walls, carpenters for roof and doors/windows, electricians and plumbers) appears to be increasingly popular and contractors are losing ground out of their meagre market share. Recent transformers used tradesmen for 75 per cent of extensions and single contractors for 19 per cent while established transformers used tradesmen for 62 per cent and contractors for 34 per cent. Within our sample, the costs of projects carried out by single contractors are very similar to those done through separate tradesmen.

Although extensions to existing houses are ideally suited to self-help through family labour, self-help is an insignificant component in the extensions in Kumasi. If there are teenage or older boys in the house, they may contribute some casual labour but it would be minimal, e.g., unloading materials. Household members who are artisans or builders' labourers would be used but they are unlikely to be the leading contributors to the work. In our sample, only 4 per cent of owners declared using family labour alone or as an adjunct to hired workers. These data can be compared with those of Blankson (1988) who found that, in extensions in government estates in Ghana, 81 per cent of the households used local artisans, 10 per cent of the households built the extensions themselves, and the remaining 9 per cent used registered contractors.

Clients supply materials (and in some cases tools as well) and pay for labour. Under such arrangements, the artisans are paid a daily rate. The small-scale local artisans (masons, carpenters, plumbers, electricians, welders, etc.) usually build at cheaper rates than the formal sector, most probably because their overheads are very low and many do not pay taxes on their earnings. A contractor or artisan can be paid in three different ways:

1. He may be paid the full amount at the end of the contracted work. In this case the contractor pre-finances the whole development.
2. Portions of the work may be estimated and paid for when the client is satisfied with the work done. This payment arrangement continues until the whole house is built.
3. A proportion (usually one-third) of the agreed total may be paid at the start of work, another one-third about halfway through, and the remaining one-third on completion.

Unlike formal-construction-sector practice, the majority of informal-sector contractors and artisans involved in transformation activities do not enter into written agreement with the house owners. However, the conditions under which jobs are awarded to them – the fees and payment schedules, and the supply of materials – are usually discussed in the presence of witnesses. Within local culture, decisions taken in these discussions constitute a valid agreement.

Informal interviews with contractors and artisans engaged in transformations in Asawasi and Suntreso found masonry work on a room where the site is fairly level costs C30,000 (£30) from foundation level to roofing level, excluding plastering, for a client perceived to be poor and C80,000 (£80) for one assessed to be rich. The fee for plastering one standard room (10 ft by 10 ft or 3 m²) is C18,000 for inside and screeding the floor, and C15,000 for rendering the outside. The fee for building a roof ranges from C8000 to C10,000 (£8–10) per room with an additional C10,000 (£10) for a ceiling. One of the contractors interviewed had charged C300,000 (£300) in February, 1994, for roofing a 13-roomed two-storey house. In addition, he charged C3000 for fixing each door and C1000 for fixing each window. Thus, labour costs for a room are between C80,000 and C130,000 (£80–130).

The contractors and artisans have their own financial issues to confront. Temporary workers demand payment immediately the work is completed because they feel that the contractor would not be able to pay large sums of money in arrears. However, a problem may arise if the client has not paid the contractor in advance for the building work and the latter has no cash in hand. Problems also arise owing to the constant increase in the price of materials. Contractors tend, however, to shift this onto the client through an initial agreement that he/she must purchase and supply the materials for the work. This removes a major source of conflict between client and contractor or artisan but increases delays which may lead to laying off the contractor. Some clients do not pay regularly, others complain that contractors make frequent demands for payment.

The relationship between implementer and cost of the job is, perhaps, what we would expect. The single contractors are called in for the more expensive extensions (median C1.2 million – £1200) and self-help labour by household members is only used for small jobs (median less than C200,000). Single tradesmen carry out jobs with a median value of more than half of those for which a contractor is engaged. This probably tells us more about the small scale of the contractors than the ambitiousness of the tradesmen.

Like housing generally in Ghana, extensions are financed out of the owner's 'own funds' (57 per cent of our sample) and 'family funds' from *abusua* relatives or their children (34 per cent of recent transformers, 24 per cent overall). Building with 'own funds' here means using whatever money can be wrested from the household's meagre budget without seriously affecting food and other essentials. It is unlikely that this would go as far as the ambitions towards home-ownership of some of the poor house-holds in Cairo that have led to reductions in basic food consumption (Wikan, 1990). In line with Aina's (1988) findings for Lagos, very few householders borrowed money from the formal sector (2 per cent) or, indeed, in any formal way even from relatives and friends. Most owners, therefore, end the construction with little outstanding debt; when the building is finished it is fully paid for.

For those in business, earnings are used to buy the materials as money becomes available. Building and road contractors, whose profits tend to be large, own houses in the estates. For employees in the formal sector, lump-sum end-of-service benefits may have been used.[25] For some there might be windfall gains (e.g. lottery winnings) and rent advances to contribute towards paying for subsequent extensions.[26] More often recently, however, remittances from abroad are used (9 per cent of recent transformers). As Aina (1988) found in Lagos, any substantial sum of money which a householder comes across is likely to be devoted to furthering his or her housing goals.

It is obvious that, in the absence of large savings or loans and with the need to pay builders in cash, payment will be a problem. In Kumasi this is allowed for through the following mechanisms:

1. Lengthening of the spending period by collecting materials in advance of building. Although there is wastage through storing, it is obviously perceived to be a smaller loss than leaving the cash in a bank through years of inflation.
2. Relatively long building period. In our housing supply study in Ghana (referred to above), the mean length of building period for a house in Kumasi was 59 months or 9.4 months per habitable room.

A small majority of the extenders have made and been successful in at least nominal efforts to gain permission. Even for the remainder, little trouble from the planning authority seems to have resulted. Only 11 per cent of established transformers and 18 per cent of recent transformers had been harassed in any way by the authorities. Of these, almost all found no action taken against them, about 8 per cent had changes forced on them, half as many had to pay a monetary penalty (a bribe), and only a minute proportion had actually to stop work.

Intention for disposing of the house

As we described above, the selling of a house is very unusual indeed and only 1 per cent of households declared their intention to sell if ever they left the house. The remainder's intention to pass it on to the family or not to leave indicates that, whatever investment is made in transformations, the family will benefit from long-term use value.

Summary

In the Ghana sample, owners are changing small terraced and semi-detached villas into substantial compound houses. Through up to four phases of transformations, households have doubled floor space within the houses. There are about 75 per cent more people and twice as many households accommodated in the area than before extensions. However, conditions are not more crowded within the houses. Main households have about 20 per cent more housing even though many tenants, both rent paying and rent free, have been accommodated. In parallel, there has been a great increase in the services provided as households have eschewed using public facilities when they can provide private ones. There is a also a much greater variety of accommodation than existed originally.

While there is undoubtedly an improvement in the value of houses, there is a tendency to add rooms at the lower end of the market for tenant households. Thus, while the housing in general is filtering up in an upgrading process, there is an opportunity for new households to begin their upward filtering at the bottom of the housing ladder.

Transformation appears to be a very good bargain in relation to the cost of alternative housing but rental incomes will never pay off the cost of rented rooms if any reasonable interest rate is accounted for. Some parts of the study areas are now very heavily developed, perhaps over-developed. But these are mainly areas where only very narrow open spaces are available.

The decision to extend is influenced mainly by characteristics of the house itself; small size, the design of the estate, etc., but there are some socioeconomic characteristics of the households which have significant effects. Low income and short stay in the house seem to be inhibiting to transformation. Once the decision to extend has been taken, the cost of the extension is strongly influenced by the house type and household size.

Finance is the major problem for extenders and could usefully be addressed by policy. Availability of loans to finance extensions is likely to increase greatly the efficiency of the supply process through transformation. Even without finance from formal lending sources, a total of PPP£200 million worth of extensions have probably been added to the 5000 government-built dwellings in Kumasi.

Notes

1   There is a general consensus that the 1984 census figures are low for urban areas.
2   Many goods bought in the market are wrapped in a particular type of leaf.
3   The semi-detached and detached types had 'pan' latrines from which excreta was emptied daily by 'conservancy' labourers employed by the local council.
4   Which must have been just about everyone with a house!
5   Our past experience of working in Kumasi has led us to use expenditure as a proxy for income. This tends to overcome the problem of low formal-sector salaries as it reflects the real benefits accruing to formal-sector workers (except perquisites in kind such as access to housing) and other incomes in the household.
6   Calculated on the basis of the GDP per capita of $400 and the UN International Comparisons Programme (ICP) 'international dollar' (which equalises prices internationally to give purchasing power parity) estimate of GDP per capita of $1042 (UNDP, 1993: table 1).
7   The national urban average is implied by the weightings attached to the 'food, beverages and tobacco' index numbers in the Consumer Price Index.
8   The mean household size of non-transformers is 5.8.
9   Recent transformers have slightly larger households than established transformers; both have larger households than non-transformers.

10   In Ghana a man is likely to father children for a longer period of his life than is common in industrialised countries. Multi-generational households are also common.

11   The number of income earners may well be lower than the number of adults because many remain at school well beyond their sixteenth birthday. On the other hand, many teenagers have some income-generating potential as an extra pair of hands at their mother's trading stall, pushing a cart, or in one of a myriad of informal-sector jobs in which they can be seen participating around the city.

12   Many visitors for funerals and festivals may go to family houses in the traditional areas of Kumasi.

13   Where there are non-habitable spaces (toilets, kitchens) in shared use, these are not allocated to the main household in this analysis.

14   But the median room size for first subsequent households is only 8 m² so they will feel more crowded than main households.

15   A 1.3 m wide, 1 m high window with 8 glass louvre blades cost C10,000 (£10) in 1992 (C13,000 with anti-burglar bars).

16   SHC became a private company after the research was completed.

17   It is possible that at least some of these habitable rooms which used to be verandas (122 in the sample) are no longer separate rooms. Our GIS analysis sometimes could not distinguish between the original wall and the current one, thus giving two rooms where there is in fact only one. Thus, the data on small rooms may be an over-estimate.

18   This is similar to the 'face me, face you' style of housing common in other parts of West Africa (Aina, 1988).

19   For discussion on the cultural importance of houses and the lack of a market in housing. see Tipple (1987).

20   The reason why valuations are lower than estimated costs of rebuilding may include the following: (1) value calculations may be based on known cost when built by the informal-sector tradesmen whose low overheads allow remarkably cheap construction; (2) it may be that the familiarity which people have with the cost of building is suspended when thinking of value; (3) the lack of maintenance usual among house-owners may give housing the price characteristics of the consumption good as which it seems to be regarded, i.e., that it becomes less valuable with age.

21   Though what there is tends to be impressive in its scale of investment and probably represents the way forward for many more transformers.

22   This means providing accommodation for members of the extended family as separate households.

23   The sacral nature of houses in Ghana is dealt with in Tipple (1984).

24   This is, perhaps, surprising as the availability of building materials has improved very greatly.

25   Although now cancelled, end-of-service benefits were a substantial portion of career earnings. For example, at the university, for workers with over 10 years' service they were one third of the final year's salary times years of service.

26   Since 1986, rent advances of two to five years' payments have become a normal way of increasing the net present value of the very low rents charged in Kumasi (Malpezzi et al., 1990). In our housing supply study (sponsored by the Leverhulme Trust), the mean rent advance paid in Kumasi was C158,000 (£158) or 51 months' rent. Hearsay suggests that it is not uncommon now for a landlord to collect such advances for two rooms and finance the building of a third therefrom. However, our data give no support to this being a common occurrence. A very recent subterfuge to arise is for a houseowner to allow a prospective tenant to add a room to the house in exchange for a number of years' rent-free tenancy.

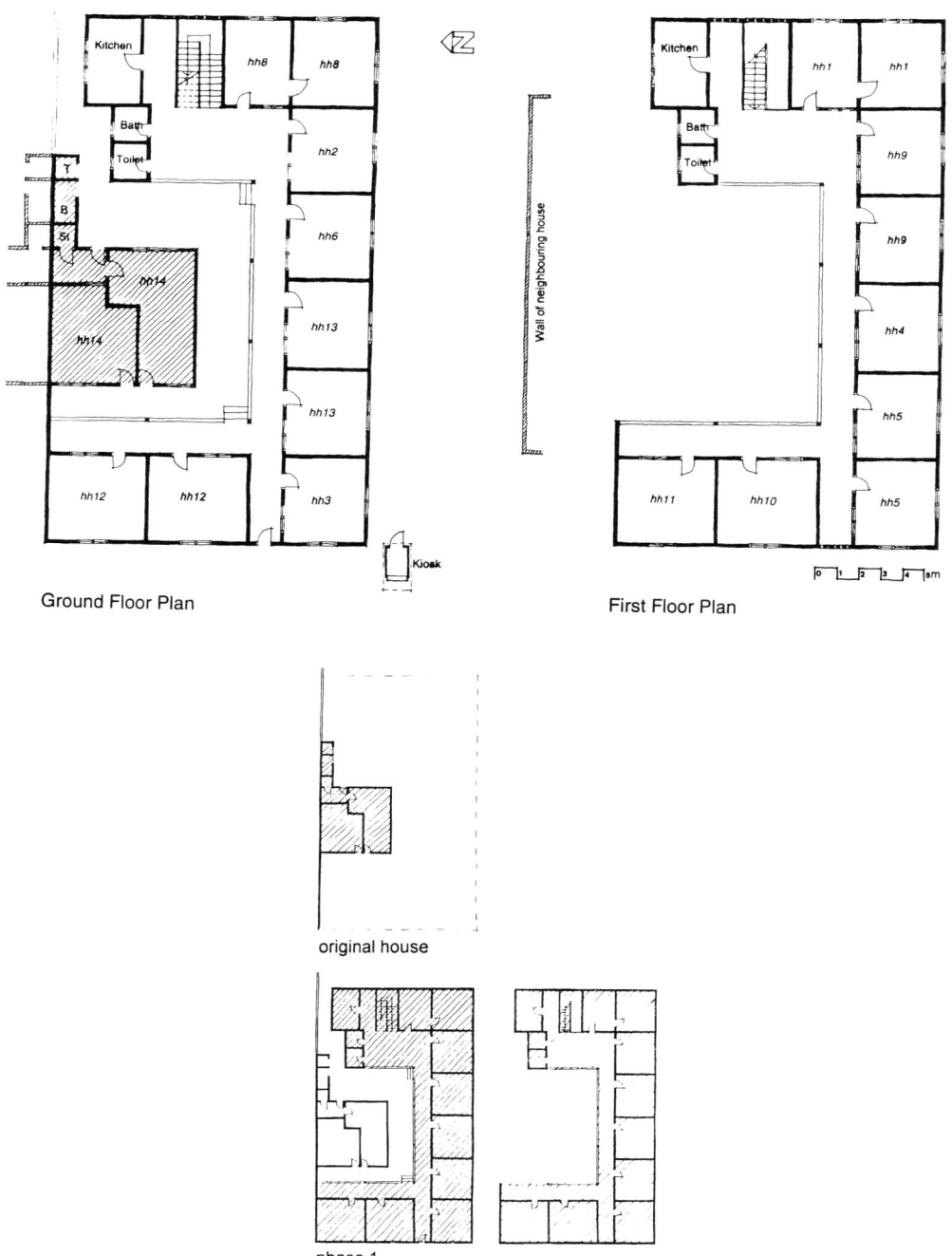

Ground Floor Plan   First Floor Plan

original house

phase 1

Figure 65. A major transformation in Kumasi

This is a single phase extension converting a semi-detached two-roomed villa into a two storey compound house containing 21 habitable rooms currently accommodating 14 households.

Figure 66. A three roomed semi-detached dwelling transformed into a modest six-roomed compound, Kumasi

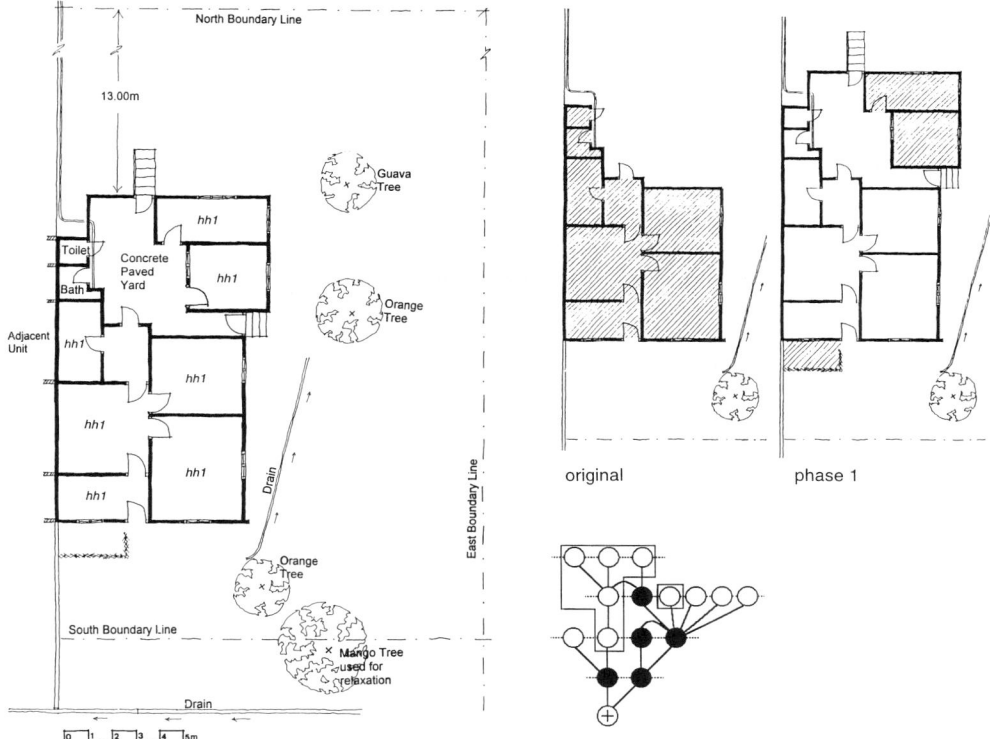

This three-roomed semi-detached house in Asawasi has been extended by the addition of a rear yard with rooms opening into it. The 13-person household (3 men, 4 women, 3 boys and 3 girls), headed by a 78-year-old woman, occupies all seven rooms. The extensions were made in 1978 but no record has been kept of their cost. No attempt has been made to occupy the whole plot with a courtyard dwelling; it is used as a garden with fruit trees. The plan syntax is fairly distributed through the many entrances from the garden and the new courtyard. There is a cluster of new rooms at level 3 while the original dwelling occupies the deepest spaces.

Figure 67. A three-roomed semi-detached villa extended, Kumasi

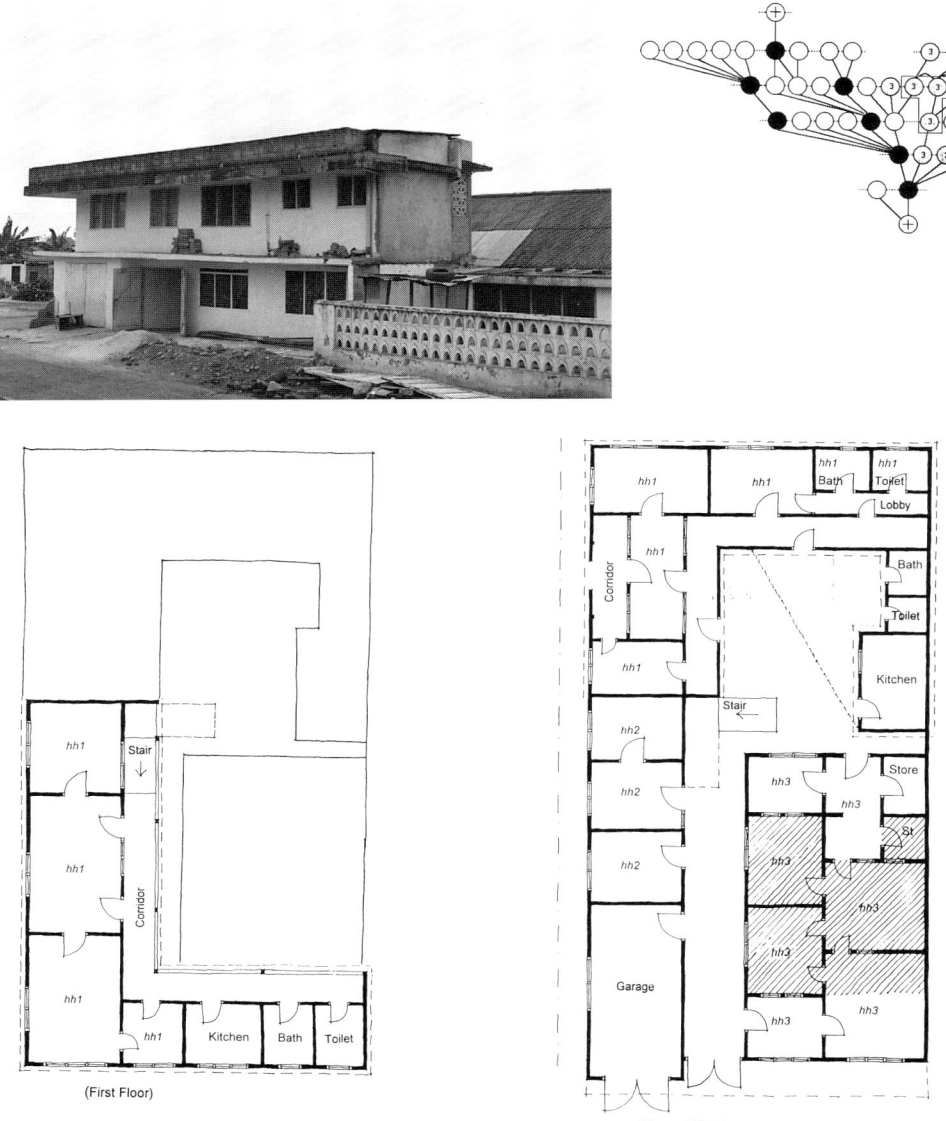

Figures 68 and 69. Two neighbouring impressive transformations, Kumasi

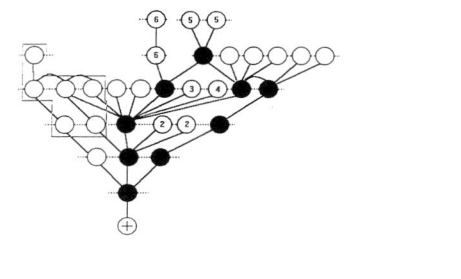

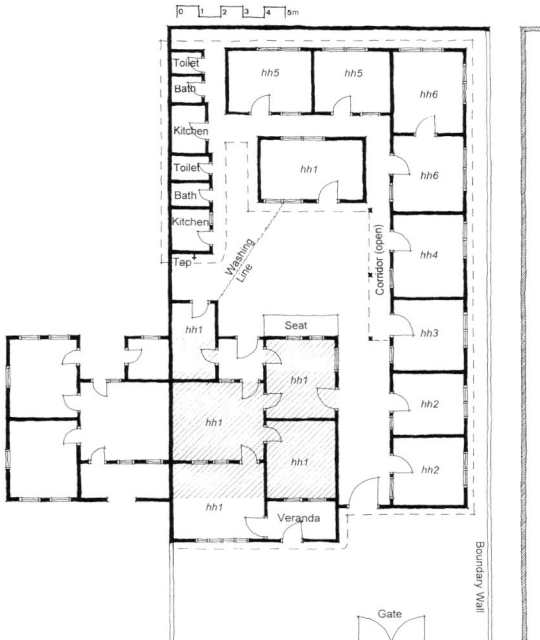

This pair of 59 sq.m., three-roomed, semi-detached cottages has been extensively converted into compound houses. The one on the opposite page has an area of 219 m² and 27 rooms which currently accommodate only 15 people. The upper storey (at the front) is not yet occupied. The house is owned by an elderly woman who has lived there since the early 1960s. Her household of two women and two children occupies rooms at the rear of the ground floor. There are two other households, one in the extended original dwelling and one in the front of the new wing. One is paying rent, the other lives rent free as family of the owner. The extension was made in 1985 at a cost of C3 million.

The house on this page has 180 m² of accommodation, with 22 rooms occupied by 26 people. There are 5 tenant households. The owner, whose household of three adults and four children, occupies the extended original dwelling and a further room, has lived there since 1955. The extension was built in one phase in 1978 at a cost of C12,000 (about £2400 at the time).

The space syntax of both houses demonstrates the contrasting designs of the original and the new. The extended original dwellings (in rectangles) are relatively distributed with several routes to some rooms. The new areas, apart from some distribution around the side entrance of one, are distributed with series of rooms opening off circulation spaces at different depths. This demonstrates the tendency to build rooms that open off open space or corridors and are, therefore, easy to use for tenants or family members living independently. They are very well designed for traditional inheritance (in common by a large number of relatives).

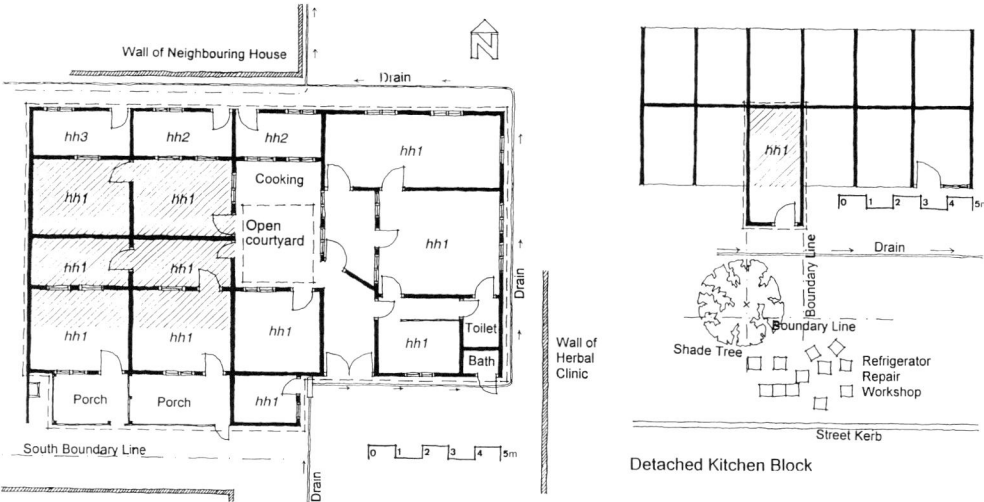

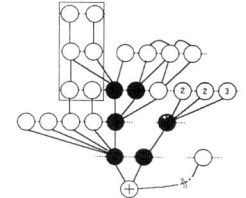

This end-terrace, two-roomed dwelling has been extended into a 14-roomed house with 16 occupants. The main household is 11 people (3 men, 3 women, 3 boys and 2 girls). The main household occupies 11 rooms while two tenant households have three rooms between them opening outwards onto a lane only 1.3 m wide. Unusually for our sample, the rooms tend to be arranged in suites of two (known locally as a chamber and hall). The extensions are wrapped immediately around the original structure. To the side is a complex series of access spaces with a corridor opening into an open courtyard and an enclosed hallway. The plan syntax diagram shows a relatively bifurcated pattern, one side being non-distributed and clustered around access spaces. The other side, wholly occupied by one household, is relatively distributed, especially at levels 3 and 4. The house would cost C7 million to rebuild, 2.8 times the annual household income.

Figure 70. A major transformation on a two-roomed dwelling, Kumasi

*Figure 71. A heap of sandcrete blocks awaiting use in a building project, Kumasi.
Block-saving like this is a common feature of Ghanaian urban areas*

Figure 72. Manufacture of sandcrete blocks on site, Kumasi

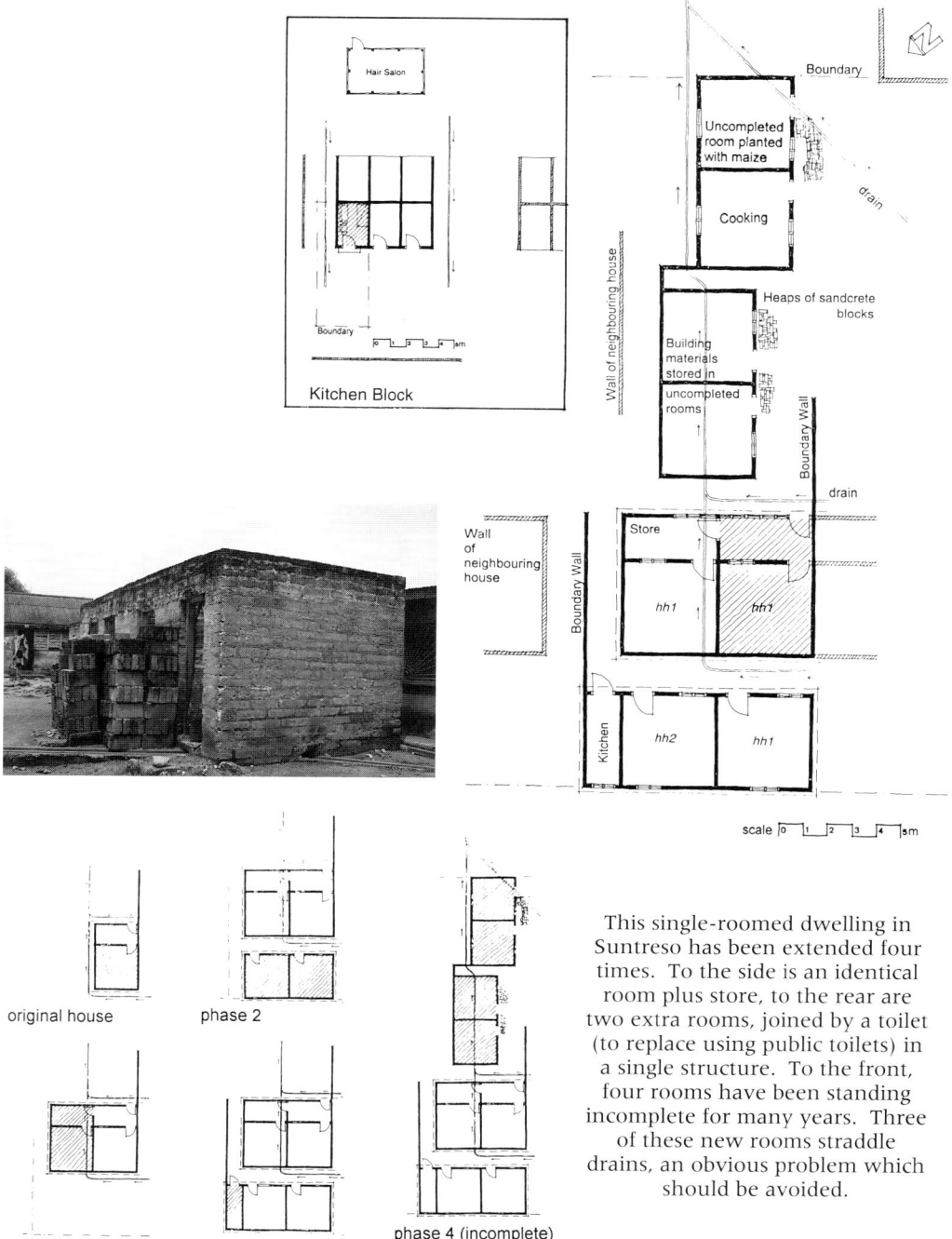

This single-roomed dwelling in Suntreso has been extended four times. To the side is an identical room plus store, to the rear are two extra rooms, joined by a toilet (to replace using public toilets) in a single structure. To the front, four rooms have been standing incomplete for many years. Three of these new rooms straddle drains, an obvious problem which should be avoided.

Figure 73. A multi-phase transformation, Kumasi

Figure 74. Several extensions to single-roomed terraced dwellings in Asawasi

Appendix 4. Transformations in Zimbabwe

Introduction to Mbare and Highfield, Harare

Harare, formerly called Salisbury, is the capital of the Republic of Zimbabwe (formerly Rhodesia) in Southern Africa and has a population of just over one million. Situated about 1400 metres above sea level, the city was founded as Fort Salisbury on 13 September 1890, and developed by the British South Africa Company, as the culmination of a military expedition to occupy the area between the Zambezi and Limpopo rivers on behalf of Britain.

All urban settlements in Zimbabwe have an early and long history of racial segregation. In Harare racial segregation in terms of housing for the African population began as a early as March 1892 when the Sanitary Board promulgated regulations to establish a 'Native Location' at a site about 1 km south of the main town centre (and farthest away from the White suburbs north of the town centre). The location was under the supervision of a European superintendent who supervised construction of buildings and administered a curfew that ensured that 'African workers were not outside the location or their masters' premises after 9 pm' (Jackson, 1986: 8–9). By the turn of the century 26 huts had been built and the municipality gradually replaced African-owned huts with its own housing. In 1907 a new location (the basis of the present day Mbare) of some 25 ha was established about 4 km from the town centre and further south. It provided accommodation mainly for male workers whose families were expected to remain in the rural native reserves.

The policy of racial segregation gained momentum in 1923 when Southern Rhodesia was given responsible self-government by Britain. New housing estates or 'townships' were developed where houses were leased and tied to employment. However, by the 1950s it became evident that some African workers could not return to the rural areas and were destined to remain even after retirement in urban areas. To allow for this, home-ownership schemes (based on long leases rather than on freehold title) were developed. Under the Land Apportionment Act of 1963 Africans were allowed freehold to land but only in designated rural and urban areas.

Following the Unilateral Declaration of Independence in 1965 and the strengthening of ties (as well as policy objectives) with apartheid South Africa, moves were initiated to remove Africans from urban areas altogether. Using the example of Soweto in Johannesburg (in South Africa) the government set about establishing dormitory settlements for Africans. These were to enable Africans to work in and service the

White towns and cities and at the same time live separately. The first houses in the dormitory new town of Chitungwiza, situated about 20 km south of Harare city centre, were built in 1974.

The struggle for independence escalated into civil war in the 1970s when neighbouring countries such as Zambia and Malawi (former partners with Rhodesia in the Federation of Rhodesia and Nyasaland) had ruled themselves for a decade but it was

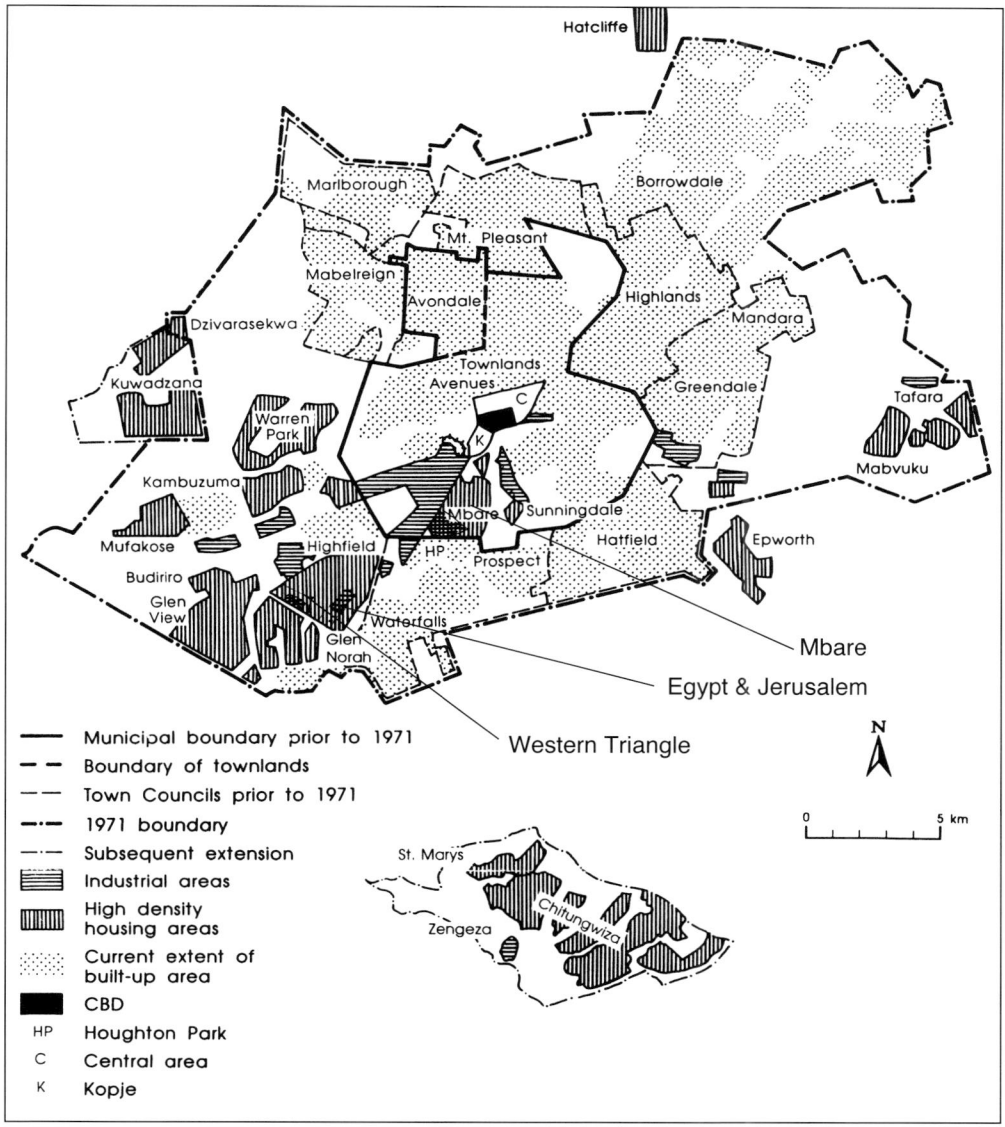

Figure 75. Map of Harare showing study areas
Source: Rakodi and Withers (1995: 188).

not until 1978 that the process of repealing and replacing of racial laws was started.

Squatter settlements developed around bus termini and on open spaces in African townships. Government and local authorities set up 'temporary' squatter rehousing areas in Chitungwiza and the other townships. There were waves of refugees flocking into Salisbury and being housed in official emergency shelter schemes or joining the squatters, especially in Epworth on land owned by the Methodist Church.[1]

The city of Harare in independent Zimbabwe inherits, therefore, a dual administration system, one for African townships and the other for the remainder of the city. In addition, residential areas were planned and located as, *inter alia*, means of racial control. In colonial times, Africans were not allowed to own land in urban areas, their movements in and out of the urban areas were controlled, and they were regarded as temporary urbanites. All housing for Africans was rented, strictly segregated from the Whites' city, and operated by a different administration, the Department of African Administration. The movement towards the 'stabilisation' of the African population, which had been influential in neighbouring Northern Rhodesia/ Zambia since the Eccles Commission of 1944 (Tipple, 1981) was only joined in Southern Rhodesia (as Zimbabwe was then) in 1963 when the Land Apportionment Act was amended to allow Blacks to acquire freehold tenure of urban land.

In an attempt to unify the administration of urban areas and remove racial connotations from the past, African townships were renamed 'high density areas' and the White suburbs renamed 'medium and low density areas'. By 1988 the Harare City Council administered 17 high density residential areas. The more recent of these have adopted site and service approaches, with or without core houses or wet cores usually on 300 m² plot sizes. New regulations were passed in 1992 allowing for greater flexibility in plot size as well as in materials used in construction. Even these recent modifications to the regulations have not changed the general way in which high-density areas developed in the past and are expected to develop in the future.

It can be seen from table 80 that government-built so-called 'high-density' estates have contributed a considerable part of the housing stock of Harare. Although single dwellings on such substantial plots are hardly high density in international terms,

Table 80. Housing stock in high-density residential areas, Harare, 1988

Area	Freehold family	Rented family	Institutional	Single person	Hostel	Total
Mbare	3316	2395	236	218		6165
Highfield	5428	1940	320	2395		10,083
Other estates*	51,837	7635	313	11,563	11,866	83,214
Total	60,581	11,970	869	14,176	11,866	99,462**

Source: Rakodi and Mutizwa-Mangiza (1989).
*Including Epworth which is not officially part of Harare.
**Total in the original table (91,682) is not consistent with table contents.

these low-income housing areas accommodated over three-quarters of Harare's 1978 population on 8 per cent of the residential area of the city (Rakodi and Mutizwa-Mangiza, 1989). According to Musandu-Nyamayaro (1992), there was a deficit of 70,000 dwellings in Harare in 1991.

Mbare

The oldest township in Harare, Mbare, is situated to the south of central Harare, east of the arterial Simon Mazorodze Road. It was developed from about 1907 onwards as a township for Black workers (housed as single males) with jobs in the city. Employers paid the rent for the council-built structures and later bought them for renting to their workers. There were no formal plot surveys. By the 1960s, three-storey barrack-style hostels, with rooms shared by three to five people, were constructed to house single males either working in Harare or in transit to the South African mines. During the 1960s and 1970s, core housing (two- to four-roomed semi-detached and terraced dwellings) dominated the new provision for married couples.

By 1975, as the fighting between government forces and guerillas intensified, many people flocked into Salisbury and Mbare township. The government built precast post and panel dwellings with asbestos-cement roofs as temporary accommodation. Needless to say, temporary has become permanent as housing supply falls behind demand. Figures from Harare City Council Housing and Community Services

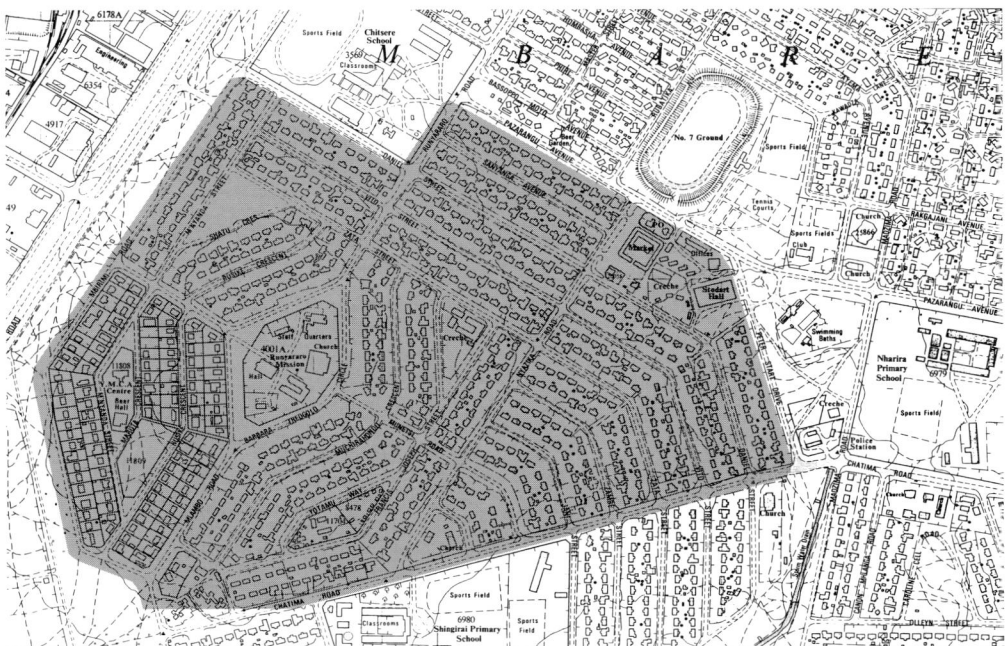

Figure 76. Plan of the study area, Mbare, Harare

Department show 29,266 dwellings constructed city-wide in the 1971–91 period (about 1500 per annum) while the housing waiting list grew to over 70,000 (Pritchard, 1993).

The area chosen for study in Mbare is located in the south-west of the estate, an area commonly known as 'National'. It is on the south-west of the township, close to the large Southern and Ardbennie industrial estates. It consists of 1450 semi-detached dwellings in various stages of transformation. The study area is served by a shopping and community centre complex where there is a market-place, wood vendors, arrays of shops, a crèche, a community hall and a beer garden. Chitsere School and Shingirai Primary School adjoin the area to the north and south respectively. A sports ground stands immediately to the north.

The houses in the study area were constructed as so-called four-roomed core units, comprising two bedrooms, a living room and a kitchen. The tiny toilet/bathrooms are entered from outside. Typical dwellings in our study area are 52 m² in area set on plots measuring 27 to 29 m in depth and about 9 or 10 m wide. Each has electricity, piped water and sewerage reticulation on the plot. They are built of bricks set in cement/sand mortar and rendered in places, floors are concrete, roofs are asbestos-cement sheeting on timber rafters. There are no ceilings.

Highfield

Highfield was begun in 1935 by central government as a township for Africans employed in the public sector and as a response to overcrowding in Mbare. Originally outside city limits, its administration passed to Salisbury City Council in August 1972, following the extension of the city boundaries. It is situated to the south-west of Mbare on land originally known as Baxter's Farm. Between 1935 and 1953, two-, three- and four-roomed dwellings were built for married couples. The tenants paid no rent but had to stay with their wives and to keep the house and garden clean as required by the township ranger (Pritchard, 1993).

In 1955, as part of the government's acceptance that some Africans would retain their urban identity after retirement, home-ownership housing was introduced (for the first time) in Highfield. In fact the 'Old Highfield' part of the estate (where home ownership and long-term leases were possible) is seen as the home of the 'armed struggle for independence' as it is here that leading politicians such as Robert Mugabe, Joshua Nkomo and others had houses.

It was also during this period that four new areas were opened up for housing, including our study areas of Jerusalem and Egypt, which consist of 1058 two- and four-roomed dwellings in rigid grid-iron blocks (113th to 133rd Streets) on the south-east of Highfield, just to the east of a site containing Highfield Secondary School and three primary schools. To the south-west is a shopping centre and bus terminus. The houses are mainly detached and vary from 47 m² to 56 m² in area containing four rooms and (usually) a veranda. Plots of about 12 m × 21 m are shorter and wider than those in Mbare.

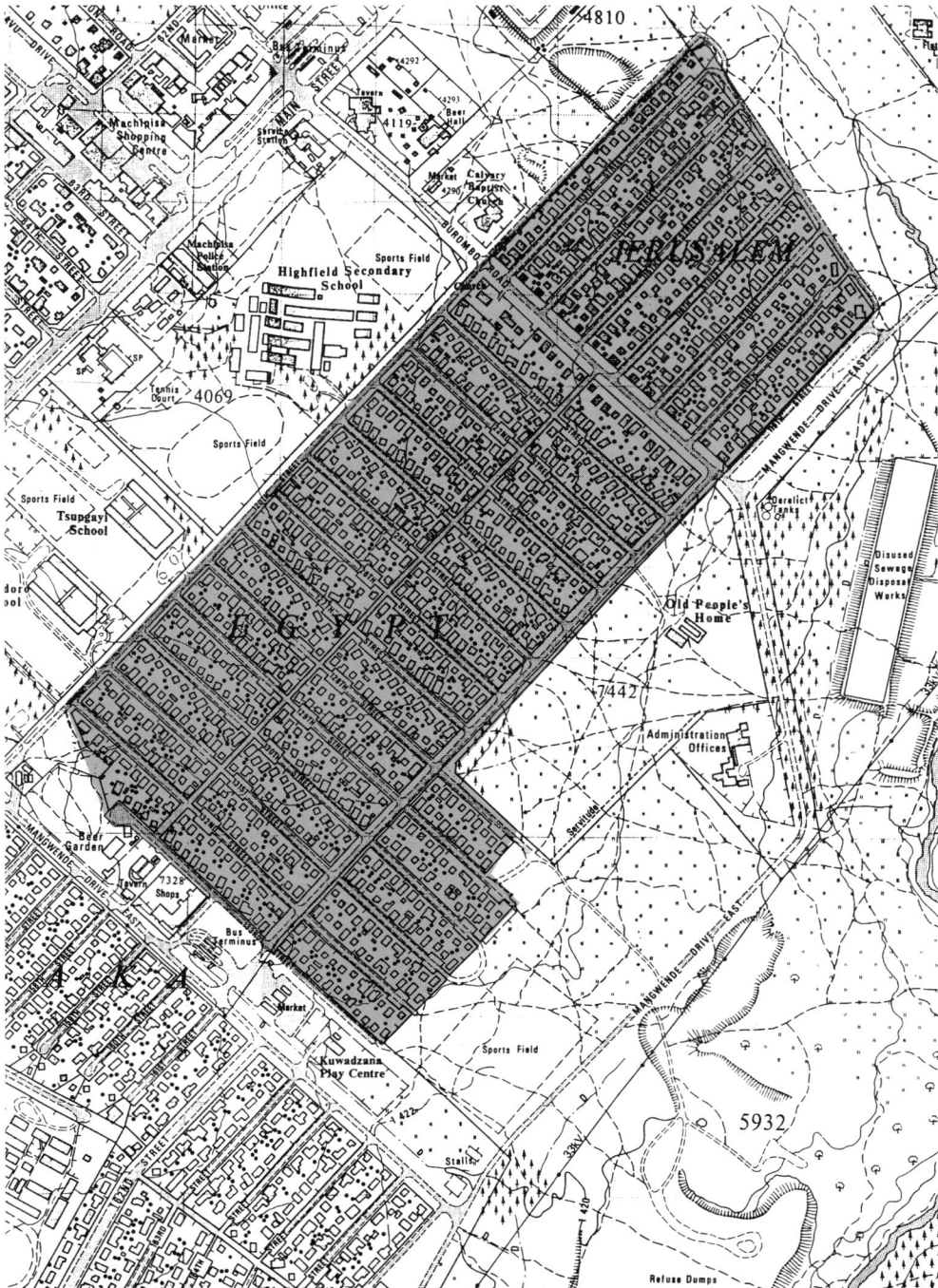

Figure 77. Plan of the Egypt and Jerusalem study areas, Highfield, Harare

Figure 78. Plan of the Western Triangle study area, Highfield, Harare

Figure 79. A non-transformed dwelling in Mbare

The New Canaan area was constructed at the westerly corner of Highfield in 1961 as a mix of 2- and 4-roomed detached, semi-detached and terraced dwellings for renting to non-government workers through their employers. The part of the study area known as Western Triangle is a mixture of detached and semi-detached dwellings built after 1965 initially to cater for domestic workers from white suburbs. Houses were constructed of cement blocks or precast panels. Stand sizes are small, being 250 m² for semi-detached and 300 m² for detached units.

The New Canaan/Western Triangle study area is a grid-iron plan (mainly 238th Street to 242nd Street) with modification for the triangular site. It contains a YMCA and adjoins Kwayedza Secondary School to the north, Zororu Social Youth Centre to the east, and a bus terminus serving Glen Norah to the south.

Many of the houses in this area are laid out using a wooden stencil (3.3 m × 3.3 m) for each room to produce a 6.6 m × 6.6 m, 44 m² house with four identical rooms. Toilets, with overhead showers, and kitchens were often added on to the basic square

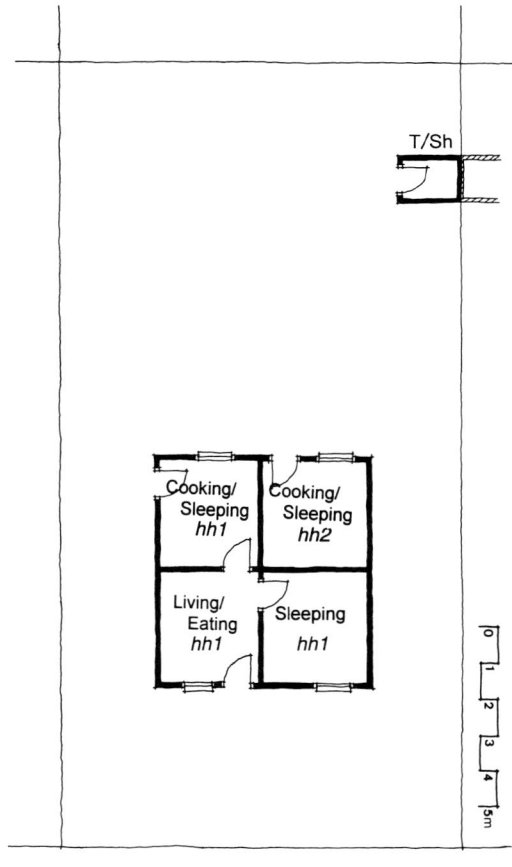

242nd Street

Figure 80. Plan of a non-transformed dwelling in Highfield

shape. Others are slightly smaller (42 m²) and semi-detached. All the plots in the two areas of Highfield are approximately 390 m² (13 m × 30 m). They are of similar construction and servicing standards to those in Mbare.

Our Zimbabwe sample is more complex than those in the other three countries. The 335 houses include 45 non-transformers but the transformers are divided into three roughly equal parts. There are 97 established transformers, 91 recent transformers and 102 shacks-only transformers. The last, those who have only added wooden rooms, are probably over-represented with respect to their frequency in order to have a usefully sized sample.

Socioeconomic characteristics of households

The Zimbabwe case study contains a sub-sample not found elsewhere, the shacks-only transformers. These are householders who have made no other extension to the house than building one or more wooden sectional sheds which are normally rented out to separate households. While they do not represent the scale of investment of an extension in permanent materials, they do add housing to the stock and households to the population. Thus, we regarded them as transformers.

Measures of permanence

House owners in the Zimbabwe sample are, as expected, a very settled group. Their household heads tend to be over 50 years of age; both recent and established transformers have median ages of 54 or over; shacks-only transformers are 50 at the median. However, even non-transformers have a median age of 48. Owners, whether transformers or not, moved in to their houses aged 30 at the median while 75 per cent of each sub-sample were under 38.

There is general similarity between the sub-samples in the age at which they first transformed the house: all have median ages of starting the extensions close to 40, and IQRs of only about 17 years. Thus, it is likely that the decision to extend was made while children were still young and growing, and new children were being born.

All owner groups display long periods of stay in the house. All have been there over 20 years at the median with only non-transformers having more than 25 per cent who have lived in their current house for less than a decade. Unexpectedly, shacks-only transformers are more settled (at least five years more at the median) than those making transformations in conventional building materials.

Length of time in current employment is shorter than expected (less than 10 years at the median for each sub-sample), and much shorter than in our other case studies. This arises from the pattern of employment before Independence and the uncertainty following it. Prior to the 1980s, very few residents of our estates were eligible for senior technical posts. The post-Independence indigenisation efforts and the shortage of white labour led to a more mobile workforce as people jockeyed for new opportunities in employment. Only those unsuited to the changed working environment are

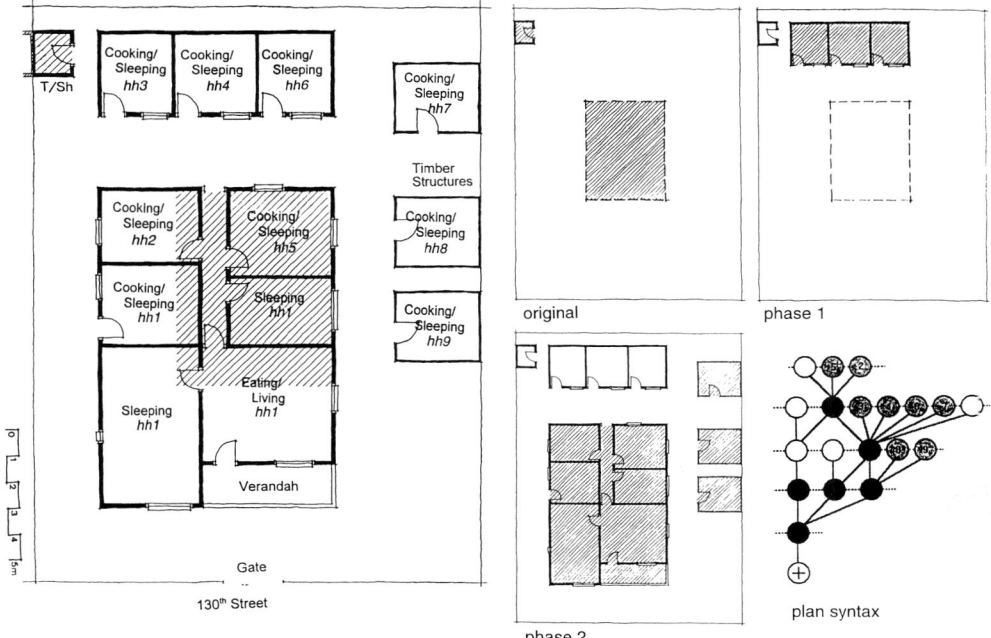

This completely altered house is owned by a five-person household whose head is 40 and has lived here for 22 years. There are eight tenants (all single-person households), a total of 13 people in the house. The transformations cost Z$30,000 in the 1980s; the house is worth Z$90,000. The plan is a short version of the corridor villa with additional external rooms facing inward like a local *kraal*. The plan syntax shows a distributed layout with three different routes to the deepest parts of the house. All rooms are accessible directly from circulation spaces. The three timber rooms are outside the building lines.

Figure 81. A completely transformed house in Highfield

likely to have remained in the same employment.

In the Zimbabwe sample, we asked about retirement and unemployment. Considerable numbers of transformers are retired or unemployed (as high as 45 per cent among established transformers). Surprisingly, transformers are more likely to be retired than non-transformers and just as likely to be unemployed. Retirement benefits are not adequate to form lump sums suitable for extension activities. However, retired people are likely to have educated adult children who are likely to assist financially in improving the parental home.

Most owners have only primary or junior secondary education, each group having a median of eight years at school. Non-transformers tend to be just as well educated as transformers.

Income and wealth

Non-transformers and shacks-only transformers have similar incomes but they are lower than other transformers (table 81). Shacks-only transformers also include a proportion of particularly low-paid people as the first quartile of Z$7200 (£720) demonstrates.

Table 81. Measures of income and wealth, owners

Medians (and IQRs)	Established transformers	Recent transformers	Shacks-only transformers	Non-transformers
Household income	15.6	20.4	13.2	13.8
(Z$ thousand/annum)	(9.9, 24.0)	(11.9, 26.4)	(7.2, 19.8)	(10.8, 18.0)
Per capita income	2.66	2.96	2.52	3.17
(Z$ thousand/annum)	(1.4, 4.6)	(2.0, 4.1)	(1.6, 4.0)	(1.9, 4.0)
Expenditure on food	5.88	6.00	4.80	4.80
(Z$ thousand/annum)	(4.8, 7.7)	(4.8, 7.2)	(2.5, 6.7)	(3.6, 6.0)
Relative wealth index*	0.109	0.159	0.050	0.077
	(0.06, 0.16)	(0.06, 0.69)	(0.02, 0.11)	(0.02, 0.16)
Percentage with RWI of zero	11	2	20	4
Percentage expecting to be better off next year	22	18	15	16

*Relative wealth index (RWI) lies between 0 and 1: 1 implies ownership of all the consumer durables, i.e., radio or cassette player, sewing machine, refrigerator, freezer, television, motor cycle and motor vehicle.
Z$10 = £1.00 in 1993.

We would expect transformers to be in the middle of the income range both because of their long occupation of council housing and because households who demand extra housing space in developing countries tend to be in the middle-income ranges (Woodfield, 1989). In Harare, labourers earn about Z$3000 (£300) per year, skilled artisans earn between Z$12,000 (£1200) and Z$60,000 (£6000), and managers begin at around Z$36,000 (£3600). Thus, the median households in our sample with incomes of Z$13,200 to Z$20,400 (£1320–2040) have more than three times the wage of a labourer and less than that of managers. Even third quartiles do not reach management wage levels.

At Z$10 to £1 at the time of the survey in 1993, annual household incomes in our sample were from £1320 to £2040 at the medians. However, the value is higher than the sterling equivalent would indicate. With a GDP per capita of US$650 per annum, the real GDP is calculated at a Purchasing Power Parity of PPP$1484 (UNDP, 1993: table 1). Thus the factor to convert local currency to PPP is 2.28. It could be said, therefore, that the £1320 to £2040 above is equivalent to £3010 and £4630 at PPP.

With per capita incomes of between PPP£570 and £750 at the medians, transformers have an income of 2.4 to 3 times the 'absolute poverty' level determined by Ravallion *et al.* (1991). Per capita incomes are very similar across the transformer sub-samples but the non-transformers' are higher owing to their smaller households. The same reason accounts for a disappearance of the low first quartile among the shacks-only transformers. Expenditure on food once again demonstrates the similarity between shacks-only transformers and non-transformers (medians of 36 and 35 per cent respectively) and their poorer circumstances than the transformers who build permanently (29 per cent for recent transformers).

The relative wealth index shows that recent transformers possess far more durable goods than any other sub-sample while shacks-only transformers and non-transformers again demonstrate their relative poverty. There is little to separate the sub-samples with regard to expecting to be better off in the near future.

If we exclude the 84 houses containing only single households, the owners who transform and have other households in the house have lower incomes than the whole sample but roughly similar per capita incomes, expenditure on food and RWIs. The difference is especially marked in the recent transformers who display almost 20 per cent less income (Z\$16,800 – £1680) and a lower per capita income (Z\$2730 – £273) than the whole sample. This shows either that housing with tenants can so supplement income that house ownership (or in this case house extension) can move down the income range, or that renting out some of the rooms helps the household to transform. In both cases, there is evidence of the symbiotic relationship between owner-occupation and renting (UNCHS, 1989).

House ownership

The houses were sold to sitting tenants by the City Council; about 75 per cent of these purchasers still own them and few have resold although there is a market in houses in the area. Only in the recent transformers (14 per cent) have more than 10 per cent bought from individuals. Inheritance is likely to increase with the passing years. It is interesting that inherited houses are more likely to be occupied by shacks-only transformers or non-transformers (14 and 19 per cent respectively). It may be that inheritance passes the houses down the income range to people for whom permanent extensions are beyond the scope of their incomes. More likely, though, is the 'prisoners' dilemma' issue attached to property which is inherited in common. Inheritance in Zimbabwe tends to vest property in the family as a group, not in a senior individual. Individuals are unlikely, therefore, to invest in the improvement of an asset which does not belong exclusively to their household. Where parents are still alive and living in a family home, however, it is likely that extensions would be financed by their children. Almost consistently, half the respondents have a house in their rural home area and only the odd one or two have other houses in the city.

Household characteristics

As might be expected, non-transformers have smaller households than the others and shacks-only transformers have smaller households than recent or established trans-formers (table 82). This seems to be in line with expectations as both groups are making little effort to increase the size of their own housing; the shacks-only transformers tend mainly to provide rooms to rent out (only 24 per cent occupy any space in the extensions compared with 81 per cent for established transformers and 75 per cent for recent transformers). Transformers all have similar numbers of adults at the medians (and more than non-transformers), only varying in the number of children in the household. Recent transformers may be responding to the pressure of three children at the median (and a median dependency ratio of 0.73) in deciding to extend. Only shacks-only transformers expect a change in household size, in this case downwards, probably reinforcing their decision to extend with only cheap perishable materials. There is little difference in expectation of guests and their presence is unlikely to motivate transformation.

Table 82. Household size and composition, owners

Medians (and IQRs)	Established transformers	Recent transformers	Shacks-only transformers	Non-transformers
Number of people in the household	7 (4, 9)	7 (5, 8)	6 (3, 8)	5 (3, 7)
Number of adults in the household	4 (2, 6)	4 (2, 5)	4 (2, 6)	2 (2, 5)
Number of children in the household	2 (1, 4)	3 (1, 4)	1 (0, 4)	2 (1, 3)
Dependency ratio (no. of children per adult)	0.60 (0.2, 1.0)	0.73 (0.2, 1.3)	0.43 (0.0, 1.0)	0.67 (0.3, 1.5)
Expected household size in three years	7 (4, 9)	7 (5, 8)	5 (3, 8)	5 (4, 7)
Number of guests per annum	5 (3, 11)	4 (2, 7)	4 (2, 7)	4 (2, 10)

Housing characteristics and house values

We would expect the former African township houses which form our study area to be in the process of renewal and improvement in a manner observed in South Africa by Andrew and Japha (1978) and Beinart (1971) and both to be moving towards conditions in the houses in neighbouring areas and the city as a whole.

Increases in house size through transformations[2]
Total built area has been extended by up to 33 m² at the medians by both established

and recent transformers, to around 80 m² at the median, but only by 14 m² by shacks-only transformers. The area added at the medians in the first phase is substantial, over 30 m² and 60 per cent of the original house, but tends to tail off in later phases (table 83). It is unlikely that this is due to cramping on the site because there is still a substantial area of garden on the plots, but it may be evidence of trying to keep within the building lines. Recent transformers appear to be working in more equal phases with about 27 m² at the median even in phase three. The shacks-only transformers work in smaller phases of 12 to 14 m² at the medians and increasing between phases one and two. This might be as they gain greater confidence in erecting and letting out shacks, and they are unfettered by the building lines as shacks tend to be built regardless of building and planning control.

There is greater variety in the scale of extensions than in the original houses. IQRs in the original built areas are small (as shown by the shack-only IQR of only 3 m² and the non-transformer IQR of 9 m²). For the current house size, IQRs are half the medians (at 30 to 40 m²). The initial hypothesis that transformations create a variety of accommodation out of a relatively uniform housing stock is confirmed for Zimbabwe.

Table 83. Habitable area added by transformation (m²)

	Established transformers	Recent transformers	Shacks-only transformers	Non-transformers
Habitable space in the original dwelling*	27.7 (24, 30)	26.0 23, 30)	34.4 (33, 38)	30.3 (27, 40)
Habitable space currently in Phase 0**	25.6 (18, 30)	23.4 (0, 28)	34.4 (33, 39)	32.1 (27, 40)
Habitable space currently in Phases 1–5	30.9 (22, 45)	37.7 (20, 63)	13.0 (8, 23)	- -
Total habitable space in the house	55.1 (46, 67)	55.5 (43, 67)	45.2 (38, 59)	32.1 (27, 40)

* This represents the area of the original house which is still standing; in a few cases, some demolition has taken place.
**Phase 0 represents the original house whether or not the rooms are as built or have been subdivided or joined together.

Unlike in the other samples, there appear to be no gains made in habitable space through rearranging the original dwelling. Only a few house types in the sample have verandas to capture as living space either by incorporating them into existing rooms or by extending them into new rooms. At the medians, about 100 per cent more habitable space is added by the extensions. In total, at the median, the current house has about 55 m² of habitable space.[3]

As we would perhaps expect, little non-habitable space has been added (only 5 m² per house at the medians of established and recent transformers), demonstrating that

enclosed space is more highly prized for its potential to accommodate people, especially for sleeping, than for any other activity. Verandas have increased in size and
frequency, contrary to expectation.

Phases of extension are quite substantial, each adding a median of two or three
rooms and only slowly fading through the successive phases. Transformation increases
the number of habitable rooms in a house from three to six or seven at the medians
(four for shacks-only transformers). In contrast with the nil IQR in the original houses,
the current IQR of two rooms for established transformers and three for recent transformers shows that variety in the number of rooms available has been built into the
otherwise fairly uniform housing stock.

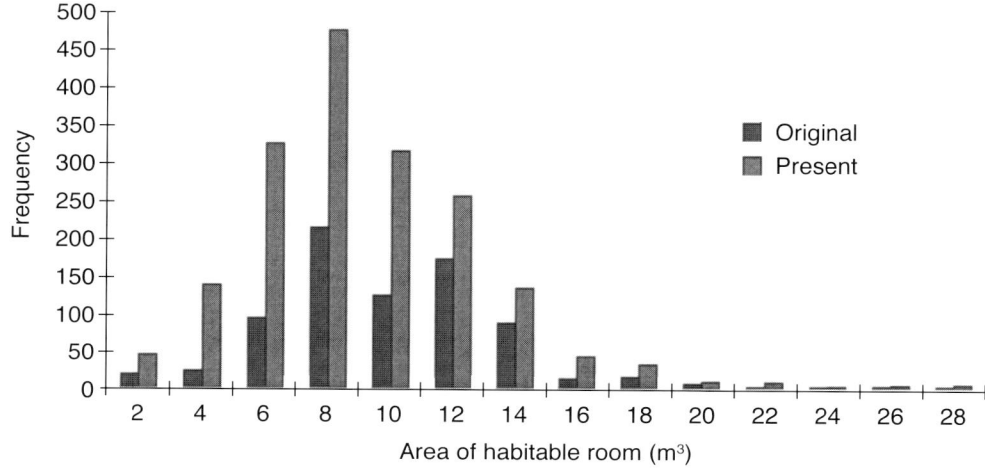

Figure 82. Frequency of habitable rooms by area, Harare sample

Our Zimbabwe sample seems largely to maintain the size distribution of the original
rooms. The greater concentration in the 8 m² class is owing to the large numbers of
shacks erected as both the only transformations and also mixed with permanent
construction. Our sample focused on the shacks-only transformers more than their
actual distribution merited in order to have a large enough sample for analysis.
Thus, it is likely that the actual distribution would feature a smaller hump in the
graph at 8 m².

Increases in space per person through transformations

Using the three different proxies for original space occupied per person in the houses,
there is general consistency in the fact that most transformers have more space than
they would have had if they had not transformed. First, using non-transformers as a
proxy, each transforming sub-sample has more space at the median, but established
transformers only marginally so. Broadly similar results occur when number of rooms

are examined but here the shacks-only transformers show lower values than non-transformers.

When original space use per person (HoOo) is generated by assuming that the original occupants (Oo) can be represented by the current main household, non-transformers show a reduction in space used per person. On the other hand, improvements of 46 and 65 per cent are recorded for established and recent transformers at the medians,[4] but only 16 per cent by shacks-only transformers. The last group show a reduction in rooms occupied per person, as do non-transformers, both indicating the propensity of households to rent out space even when it is tight in the main dwelling.

When original space use per person (HoOc) is generated assuming that all the occupants of the current house (Oc) would have occupied the original house (Ho). space use has doubled except for shacks-only transformers who have made only marginal improvements. The same is true for rooms used.

Table 84. Changes in space per person

Medians (and IQRs)	Established transformers	Recent transformers	Shacks-only transformers	Non-transformers
Current habitable space	4.59	4.84	5.63	4.50
per person (m²) (HcOc)	(3.7, 6.4)	(3.6, 6.7)	(4.0, 7.1)	(2.3, 10.0)
Original habitable space	4.10	3.91	5.89	5.67
per person (m²) (HoOo)	(3.0, 6.2)	(2.9, 5.2)	(4.2, 8.5)	(4.5, 9.3)
Original habitable space	2.47	2.58	3.96	4.50
per person (m²) (HoOc)	(1.9, 3.7)	(1.8, 3.5)	(3.0, 5.8)	(2.3, 10.0)
Current habitable rooms	0.50	0.60	0.50	0.43
per person (HcOc)	(0.4, 0.7)	(0.5, 0.8)	(0.4, 0.7)	(0.3, 0.5)
Original habitable rooms	0.44	0.46	0.50	0.50
per person (HoOo)	(0.4, 0.7)	(0.3, 0.8)	0.4, 0.8)	(0.4, 0.9)
Original habitable rooms	0.29	0.30	0.33	0.43
per person (HoOc)	(0.2, 0.4)	(0.2, 0.4)	(0.3, 0.5)	(0.3, 0.5)

Table 84 shows the habitable space currently occupied per person by the main household and allows comparison with the three proxies for the original conditions. Again, there is a general increase through transforming. Compared with non-transformers, established and recent transformers have only slight increases in habitable space per person, but shacks-only transformers have an increase of over 1 m² at the median.

With respect to the number of habitable rooms, however, recent transformers score the greatest increase and the established and shacks-only transformers share similar smaller gains. Measure HoOo shows small gains for established transformers and recent transformers but only marginal and negative gains for the shacks-only transformers and non-transformers. HoOc shows an approximate doubling in space available for established and recent transformers compared with the space per person if all the current occupants had to crowd into the original dwelling. Similarly, increases are valid for rooms occupied per person. Shacks-only transformers have made smaller, but still significant gains.

Increases in space occupied by main households

Transformers' main households tend to occupy about the same space as was available in the original dwelling while non-transformers have lost 13 m² at the median as tenants ('lodgers') are now accommodated even though there are no extra rooms (table 85). Only recent transformers have a median area appreciably greater than the original dwelling.

Table 85. Measures of occupancy, main households

Medians (and IQRs)	Established transformers	Recent transformers	Shacks-only transformers	Non-transformers
Area originally occupied*	38.9	35.7	48.3	50.0
(total original built area)	(28, 43)	(3, 40)	(48, 57)	(39, 60)
Space occupied by the main	42.5	50.6	42.9	36.5
household (m²)	(31, 60)	(32, 68)	(37, 52)	(29, 48)
Habitable space occupied by	32.6	39.0	34.1	27.5
the main household (m²)	(23, 46)	(23, 52)	(29, 41)	(22, 36)
Habitable rooms occupied	4	4	3	2.5
by the main household	(2, 5)	(3, 6)	(3, 3)	(2, 3)
Occupancy rate (persons per	1.8	1.6	2.0	2.2
habitable room)	(1.3, 3.0)	(1.0, 2.3)	(1.5, 2.7)	(1.5, 2.9)
Future occupancy rate (persons	2.0	1.6	2.0	2.0
per habitable room)	(1.4, 3.0)	(1.0, 2.3)	(1.3, 2.7)	(1.4, 3.0)

* The portion of the original building which is still standing.

Except for the shacks-only transformers who seem loath to move out of the main house into the shacks, most transformers occupy as much space in the extensions as in the original dwelling. In line with our photographic evidence, this probably demonstrates that the new rooms are of at least as high quality as the old.[5] The medians of 19 m² and 21 m² extension space occupied (established and recent transformers respectively) indicate at least one large habitable room or two small ones being devoted to the main household.

While the shacks-only transformers tend to have similar numbers of rooms and occupancy rates to non-transformers, those whose extensions are more permanent have four rooms at the median and less than two persons per room. That recent transformers have more habitable space and rooms (both in all and per person, see table 86) than established transformers may demonstrate that they are still enjoying the extra space in the extensions rather than filling it with extra households. This is reinforced by the lower occupancy rates than any other group but not by their prediction of no increase over the next three years (table 85).

The theme of greater variety through transformation is partly continued in terms of space occupied by the main household: established transformers occupy a wider range of total space than their original dwellings presented (IQRs of 29 and 36, established and recent). The size range of original houses was very small (IQR of only about 10).

As we can see in table 86, established transformers' main households have lost out slightly on area and rooms per person, while the other transformers have gained a little. The picture changes slightly for habitable space, however, as all transformers have more habitable space and rooms at the medians than non-transformers. Shacks-only transformers fare particularly well for habitable space per person but less well than others with respect to habitable rooms, in which they are similar to non-transformers. This probably demonstrates the similarity of the main dwelling to that which has not been transformed. However, less of the original dwelling has to be used for lodgers as shacks are available for them.

Table 86. Housing space per person for main household

Medians (and IQRs)	Established transformers	Recent transformers	Shacks-only transformers	Non-transformers
Area per person (m²)	6.20	7.00	7.19	6.46
	(4.8, 9.8)	(5.0, 10.6)	(5.4, 10.6)	(5.1, 12.3)
Rooms per person	0.80	1.00	0.68	0.83
	(0.5, 1.2)	(0.7, 1.3)	(0.6, 1.0)	(0.5, 1.0)
Habitable space per person (m²)	4.72	5.33	5.55	4.51
	(3.3, 7.2)	(3.9, 8.0)	(4.2, 7.9)	(4.1, 8.8)
Habitable rooms per person	0.56	0.63	0.50	0.46
	(0.3, 0.8)	(0.4, 1.0)	(0.4, 0.7)	(0.4, 0.7)

These data illuminate the issues of density and occupancy raised in the preliminary work in which we suggested that transformations increase the local population and generate higher population densities but tend to reduce occupancy rates (Tipple, 1991a). Transformers certainly have achieved a reduction in occupancy rate and those building in permanent materials have improved more than those building only shacks. The future occupancy rate picks up whether a household is likely to be larger or smaller in three years' time: whether households expect 'shocks' or 'triggers' in the near future (Seek, 1983). Numbers in the households of both transformers and non-transformers tend to be on a very level trajectory.

Main households appear to occupy at least as many rooms as were available in the original house, some considerably more. Virtually all houses had only three habitable rooms originally but main households in transformed houses now occupy four at the median and up to six at the third quartile. On the other hand, non-transformers have only 2.5 habitable rooms at the median. Established transformers and recent transformers occupy as many rooms in the extensions (two at the medians) as in the original house.

Table 87. Comparison of increases in rooms, space, etc. (original median equals 100)

	Established transformers	Recent transformers	Shacks-only transformers	Non-transformers
Total space per house	215	222	132	100
Habitable space	198	213	131	106
Number of habitable rooms	200	230	133	100
Area occupied by the main household	109	142	89	73
Habitable area occupied by the main household	118	150	99	91
Habitable rooms occupied by the main household	133	133	100	83

The summary information in table 87 demonstrates that, though the variables differ in degree or extent, established transformers and recent transformers have consistent and considerable improvements (even taking the effect of part-demolitions into account) while shacks-only transformers have less and non-transformers have had to endure constant or poorer conditions. Habitable space has improved slightly less than total space for established and recent transformers, while non-transformers have actually gained in this through reorganisation of the original dwelling. Because room sizes are roughly similar to the originals, there is no great difference between gains in space and gains in rooms.

The main households have benefited from the extensions but only marginally in all variables for established transformers; indeed the effect of demolitions may cancel out any improvement and leave them with roughly similar space. Recent transformers have had quite significant improvements, especially in habitable area. Main households in the houses of shacks-only and non-transformers, on the other hand, have less space, especially in the total area.

Space occupied by subsequent households

The tenant households occupy about one-quarter of the space occupied by main households but there seems to be a slight reduction in space for each as more households

occupy the house. When there is only one tenant household, it tends to enjoy 9 m²
or 10 m² (16–18 per cent of the house) at the median but this falls to 6–8 m² (about
10 per cent of the house) when there are four tenant households. Counter to our
expectations, the subsequent households in shacks-only transformers do not occupy
smaller amounts of space than in houses with permanent extensions. With IQRs of
3–6 m² the variability of tenants' accommodation is relatively small, only about half
the medians. Main households retain between 62 and 74 per cent of transformed
houses for their own use; subsequent households only have between 9 and 18 per
cent at the medians.

Rent-paying tenants do not suffer much worse space standards per person than the
main households despite occupying much less of the house. Though they are confined
to single rooms mostly, their occupancy rate is kept to similar levels to main households (two persons per room) by their smaller households. On the other hand, rent-free
(family) households crowd to a much greater extent with almost three persons per
room at the median.

Increases in people accommodated

Taking non-transformers as the control, established and recent transformers have
increased the population accommodated by about 60 per cent (to about 12 people per
house at the median) while shacks-only transformers have added about 30 per cent
at the median (to nine people per house) (table 88). There are larger increases in
households, however, by the addition of a median of two per house by established
and recent transformers and a median of one by shacks-only transformers. Thus, at
the median, three households are accommodated in houses originally designed and
equipped for a single household. These data show how the new environment accommodates additional smaller households so that the very significant increase in
households has not been altogether reflected in population growth.

Table 88. People currently accommodated

Medians (and IQRs)	Established transformers	Recent transformers	Shacks-only transformers	Non-transformers
People per house	12	11	9	7
	(8, 15)	(8, 14)	(6, 11)	(5, 9)
Households per house	3	3	2	1
	(2, 5)	(1, 4)	(1, 4)	(1, 2)
Number of tenant (lodger) households	2	2	1	0
	(0, 3)	(0, 3)	(0, 2)	(0, 1)

Improved service levels

The original houses were designed and built so that all had a toilet and water supply. There are so many additional households in the houses and relatively few additional services that there has been a reduction in the service level per household.

House physical condition

Generally, transformations utilise the same materials as residential development in the city. How far this reflects a wish to fit into the general urbanisation process of continual improvement and upgrading (Gosling *et al.*, 1993) and how far it is simply a function of what is available is difficult to tell (but one expects the latter). The main non-conformity to this are, of course, the shacks. Here, sectional timber buildings are utilised because of their cheapness and ease of assembly which obviously outweigh the problems of rotting and termite attack which shorten their life. The timber sections are sold locally, often from the side of the road in front of a house in the neighbourhood.

Most of the extensions are built in burnt brick with only a small minority in cement blocks which were the main material used in the original walls (over 60 per cent). The latter, however, seem to be growing in popularity as 27 per cent of recent transformers used them in comparison with 18 per cent of established transformers. The popularity of asbestos-cement sheeting for roofs instead of corrugated metal can be seen through the 91 per cent of extension roofs using this material in the extensions. All non-transformed roofs appear to be corrugated metal sheeting. Though almost all original windows were glazed, just over 20 per cent of windows in extensions are not glazed, using shutters instead of glass.

Wall materials are becoming a problem in the original houses with 58 per cent showing structural cracks, but roofs are generally sound (only 18 per cent leak). In the new buildings, however, roofs are leaking in almost a third of cases and the newer walls have almost as much of a crack problem as older ones. However, when the shacks-only sub-sample is removed,[6] there are considerable reductions in structural problems reported especially in extensions where only 25 per cent have structural cracks and 20 per cent leaking roofs.

Thus, the transformations in permanent materials have only a small minority with obvious defects. These data appear to confirm that there is some element of neighbourhood upgrading in the transformation work.

As far as the Harare Department of Housing and Community Services officers are concerned, most transformations have planning and building regulations approval. To obtain planning and building approval, residents must submit plans (prepared to a high technical standard) together with a processing fee to the Department of Housing and Community Services. It is likely that some violations of planning and building approval procedures occur out of ignorance of the procedures and fees required rather than as deliberate efforts to avoid building in accordance with the law. As such, there is a semblance of order and adherence to planning control and ordered building, even where extensions are based on unapproved plans. This is contrary to what might be expected in a completely uncontrolled situation.

In Zimbabwe, the building regulations require habitable rooms to be 7 m² in superficial area. However, for comparison with the other country samples, we have looked at how many habitable rooms have areas less than 4 m² and 6 m². Each house was originally built with at least one room less than 6 m² in area intended for cooking in but many have now been commandeered for habitation. A small majority of transformed houses have at least one room of less than 6 m² but those of less than 4 m² are much less common (31 per cent in recent transformers). Counter-intuitively, shacks-only transformers have almost no small rooms, probably as a result of the standard-sized shack which they can purchase and erect. Unlike other areas studied, space constraints are unlikely to be responsible for the small rooms.

Small habitable rooms may be constructed as such, converted from non-habitable rooms (such as kitchens), or formed by dividing up existing habitable rooms. In all, 21 per cent of rooms in the sample are less than 6 m² in area; only 3 per cent of rooms are both less than 6 m² in area and in the original dwelling. Only 5 per cent of rooms are less than 4 m² in area; almost all of them are in the extensions. Thus, the majority of small rooms have been added in the transformation process.

Plan forms

We have commented briefly on plan forms in chapter 5. In our sample, the form of house created by the transformation process appears to follow four patterns:

1. There is a living room, kitchen, etc. as in a self-contained bungalow but a corridor which is usually accessible from the rear of the house serves all the other rooms. This allows access to rooms without passing through either the kitchen or living room and allows them to be rented out to one or more separate households.
2. The original house is extended with free-standing rooms facing towards the main house, usually at the rear but sometimes also at the side. This is a little like a compound or Zimbabwean *kraal*. This form is most suited to shacks-only transformation but is not limited to that category.
3. The original house is extended by a set of rooms, separately accessed or as a suite, which have a separate entrance usually at the side or rear of the original building and with no internal access to it. This can be rented out as a unit or as individual rented rooms.
4. The original house is simply extended into a large self-contained single-household bungalow.

These forms are also used in combination but all except the last tend to result in most rooms opening off a corridor or part of the open plot, as in the traditional *kraal*. This gives a level of flexibility in room use which is not found in the original self-contained dwelling but which is particularly useful when the house is to be used by several households. Very few transformers block the open way through to the rear by building across it. This may be in response to the building lines (although this does not stop shacks from being illegally built close to boundaries) or it may demonstrate how important maintaining independent access to the large rear plot area is for house-holders with an eye on renting out rooms there.

Cost of transformation phases

As we noted earlier, phase one is normally the major extension, those coming later being smaller. Recent transformers' phase three is exceptional in this. The low cost of shacks can be seen very sharply in table 89 and seriously biases the 'all transformers' results. It is obvious that the shacks provide very cheap additional accommodation and allow income to be obtained very cheaply, much more so than any of the other methods of transforming. The shacks are, therefore providing a source of rental income at very low cost indeed and new housing at the bottom end of the market. In contrast with shacks-only transformers, others spend considerable amounts of money on trans-formations. The third quartile shows the very major investment entered into by the top 25 per cent, especially of the established transformers.

Table 89. Cost of phases in the extension process in thousand Z$

Medians (and IQRs)	Established transformers	Recent transformers	Shacks-only transformers	All transformers
Phase 1	42.6	30.0	1.48	11.5
	(21, 102)	(9, 65)	(1.0, 2.2)	(1.8, 54)
Phase 2	28.3	7.14	1.30	4.36
	(2.3, 77)	(2.2, 15)	(0.7, 2.6)	(1.8, 19)
Phase 3	1.57	21.8	1.58	1.88
	(1.3, 2.1)	(21, 35)	(-, -)	(1.3, 17)
Total cost of transformation	53.4	31.6	2.0	16.1
(thousand Z$, 1993 prices)	(21, 106)	(16, 66)	(1.0, 2.4)	(1.9, 61)

All costs are adjusted to 1993 values.

Increases in house value and cost

The housing market in Zimbabwe has been active for many years in the low- and medium-density (high and medium cost) areas. Rakodi and Withers (1993) report property sales of at least Z$330 million in 1988. There are now several high-density (low-cost) houses advertised for sale in the daily newspapers every day, and residents of Mbare and Highfield must be well aware of price levels prevailing in their neigh-bourhoods. Thus, we can probably expect realistic estimates of value as well as of building cost. In table 90, the value of established and recent transformers' houses appears to be almost double that of their non-transformer neighbours, and their value per room holds up very well at Z$7700 and Z$8300 (£770 and £830 and 77 and 83 per cent of non-transformers' values) respectively. Recent transformers feel that they have actually achieved higher value per room than either established transformers or non-transformers. More importantly, value per square metre is estimated to be greater for established and recent transformers than for non-transformers, supporting impressionistic evidence of the relatively high quality of many of the newer transformations in Zimbabwe. This is in contrast with our Ghana sample where values appear to collapse. In addition, the IQRs of transformed houses are larger than non-transformed, supporting the notion that transformations increase variety.

Table 90. Value of the whole house

Medians (and IQRs)	Established transformers	Recent transformers	Shacks-only transformers	Non-transformers
Value of the house (Z$ thousand)	75 (55, 100)	82.5 (60, 116)	50 (40, 56)	45 (35, 60)
Value of the house per room (Z$ thousand)	7.69 (5.7, 10)	8.29 (6.1, 11.5)	6.94 (5.0, 8.6)	10.00 (7.5, 12.0)
Value of the house per habitable room (Z$ thousand)	11.7 (9.0, 17.1)	12.1 (9.3, 20.0)	11.0 (8.0, 12.7)	16.7 (15, 20)
Value of the house per square metre (Z$ thousand)	1.05 (0.8, 1.4)	1.16 (0.8, 1.7)	0.79 (0.6, 1.0)	1.00 (0.8, 1.6)
Higher or lower than average?*	1.5 (1, 2)	2 (1, 2)	1 (1, 2)	1 (1, 1)

* 1= less than average, 2=more than average.

However, the shacks-only transformers perceive their additions to have added no appreciable value. As they have more rooms, the value per room has reduced from Z$10,000 to only Z$6940 and per square metre from Z$1000 to only Z$790.

Rebuilding costs, as shown in table 91, approximate to values (table 90) minus land cost. Non-transformers are the least costly to replace but have the highest cost per room. They are not the most expensive per square metre, though, as established and recent transformers are more costly. As would be expected, shacks-only transformers have a low estimate of replacement cost at only Z$5000 above non-transformers. There is remarkable consistency among transformers who have used permanent materials, at around Z$10,000 (£1000) per habitable room and Z$900 (£90) per square metre. Only the per square metre cost shows any significant variation and, as would be expected, shacks-only transformers have lower replacement costs per unit of area.

Our rebuilding cost per room is different from prices in Mbare and Highfield in table 92. The fact that our sample give lower estimated costs than values, and that they are lower than those in the newspapers, is probably more a reflection of the low construc-

tion costs available in the informal sector and the effect of not having to pay for the
land than of inadequate estimates of value.

Table 91. Rebuilding cost of the house

Medians (and IQRs)	Established transformers	Recent transformers	Shacks-only transformers	Non-transformers
Rebuilding cost	60	70	45	40
(Z$ thousand)	(40, 100)	(45, 96)	(30, 65)	(25, 50)
Rebuilding cost per room	6.25	6.31	6.38	8.00
(Z$ thousand)	(4.5, 9.0)	(4.2, 9.1)	(4.3, 9.0)	(5.6, 11.0)
Rebuilding cost per habitable	10.0	10.0	10.0	13.3
room (Z$ thousand)	(7, 15)	(6, 15)	(6, 14)	(10, 17)
Rebuilding cost per square	0.85	0.92	0.69	0.83
metre (Z$ thousand)	(0.6, 1.3)	(0.6, 1.3)	(0.5, 1.1)	(0.6, 1.1)

Table 92. Average advertised sale price for houses in Mbare and Highfield, 1986–91
(Z$ thousand)

	1986	1987	1988	1989	1990	1991	1992	1993	1994
Mbare:									
House price					46.5	63.8	70.0	70.0	100.0
Price per room					7.8	12.9	10.0	10.0	12.0
Highfield:									
House price	24.1	19.0	30.1	40.0	66.7	175.2		65.0[a]	116[c]
								116[b]	260
Price per room	4.9	3.8	6.2	7.6	12.4	28.1		18.1	30.0

Source: 1986–90: Rakodi and Withers (1993: 266).
        1991-94; *Herald* newspaper advertised prices.
(a) Price for a four-roomed 'core' house (August 1993).
(b) Price for a six-roomed house (core + extensions) (July 1993).
(c) Price for an eight-roomed house (April 1994).

Our third means of valuation is through perceived rental values, the maximum rent
a household would be willing to pay to live in the same amount of space they currently
occupied. According to Rakodi and Withers (1993), mean monthly rents in 1991 were
Z$50 (£5) per room in high-density areas of Harare but some households paid up to
Z$100 (£10) per month per room. By 1995, monthly rents in Mbare and Highfield
had increased to about Z$150 per room. The 1993 estimates in our sample (with sub-
sample medians varying from Z$80 to Z$86 – £8 to £9 – per room) are, therefore,
realistic. The higher figure for recent transformers (Z$86) shows their better quality.

Rental levels in Zimbabwe appear to reflect the cost of providing the accommodation. The rents estimated would pay for the rooms in less than eight years (with zero interest rate), a realistic period to give a market return on investment. Rakodi and Withers (1993) found that households with incomes below Z$2400 (£240) per annum spent an average of 39 per cent of their income on rent but our sample of tenants ('lodgers') pay much less than this norm (about 10 per cent at the median and 16 at the third quartile) and our owners do not value the house to that extent of their income (they would be willing to pay about 20–25 per cent of their income to rent a replacement). These data represent the known propensity of house-cost-to-income ratio being higher for owners than renters (Malpezzi et al., 1990). According to UNCHS (1993), renters in Sub-Saharan Africa average 10 per cent of income on rent.

There is little evidence of a collapse of value per room or per square metre in Zimbabwe such as happens in Ghana, except in the shacks-only transformers when it would be expected because of the cheap and temporary nature of the extensions. Oddly enough, though shacks-only transformers show significant reductions in value and cost per room (of about 20 per cent), the same is not so true per square metre where values are more similar to other transformers. This probably arises from the consistently modest size of rooms added by shacks-only transformers.

Overall, with transformation, there is a slight reduction in value per room and per square metre but a more marked reduction in cost, especially cost per room. The 'there goes the neighbourhood' syndrome which might be expected by jaundiced observers of transformations does not appear to occur as a result of the established or recent transformers' activities but neither is there 'gentrification', filtering up out of the reach of the original occupants.

Table 93. *Value and rebuilding cost of the portion of the house occupied by the household (Z$ thousand)*

Medians (and IQRs)	Established transformers	Recent transformers	Shacks-only transformers	Non-transformers
Value of the area occupied by the main household	41.8 (20, 66)	49.5 (35, 88)	32.2 (23, 47)	42.5 (35, 50)
Value of the area occupied by the tenant household	9.8 (7, 15)	9.8 (6, 16)	7.3 (5, 10)	11.4 (9, 13)
Rebuilding cost of the area occupied by the main household	36.0 (18, 61)	40.8 (27, 69)	30.0 (20, 46)	35.4 (21, 50)
Rebuilding cost of the area occupied by the tenant household	8.8 (5, 13)	8.5 (4, 14)	7.2 (4, 9)	8.5 (5, 15)

Established and recent transformer main households occupy housing worth between Z$40,000 and Z$50,000 (£4000–5000) at the medians while their tenants occupy a quarter or less of this (only about Z$10,000 worth) (table 93). These compare favourably with prices of housing on the market (table 92) and demonstrate that the private-sector rental market can provide accommodation at the bottom of the market (£1000) for a fraction of the cost of a whole bungalow on a plot. Of course, shacks are even cheaper at only about Z$7000 (£700) per household.

Intensity of development

The first four rows of table 94 remind us of the data presented in earlier parts of this section. Even though there have been increases in built area of over 60 per cent in established and recent transformers, and 27 per cent in shacks-only transformers, plot ratios and floor-space indexes are still only 34 per cent at the highest median and only 42 per cent at the highest third quartile. These figures do not represent over-building and seem to allow for additional extensions in the future. There is only a very low correlation between plot size and scale of transformation but this could be expected because plots are not very variable in size and they are large enough not to be a seriously constricting factor.

Table 94. Plot ratios and floor-space indexes

Medians (and IQRs)	Established transformers	Recent transformers	Shacks-only transformers	Non transformers
Plot area (m²)	240.7	237.5	294.8	274.1
	(223, 255)	(203, 263)	(262, 341)	(223, 306)
Original built area (m²)*	38.9	35.7	48.3	50.0
	(28, 43)	(3, 41)	(48, 57)	(39, 60)
Current built area (m²)	83.8	79.1	63.6	50.0
	(66, 96)	(61, 102)	(57, 81)	(39, 60)
Plot ratio	0.33	0.34	0.23	0.18
	(0.3, 0.4)	(0.3, 0.4)	(0.2, 0.3)	(0.1, 0.)
Original floor-space index	0.20	0.20	0.17	0.18
	(0.2, 0.2)	(0.2, 0.3)	(0.1, 0.2)	(0.1, 0.2)
Floor-space index	0.33	0.34	0.23	0.18
	(0.3, 0.4)	(0.3, 0.4)	(0.2, 0.3)	(0.1, 0.3)

* This represents the area of the original house which is still standing; in a few cases, some demolition has taken place.

It could be argued that the original very low floor-space indexes render extension activity not only inevitable but also preferable to continuing with generous space provision. The current state may not be regarded as over-building but the past could be said to be under-building.

We can see from the above discussion that transformation in Zimbabwe has created not only more living space but also considerable variety in the seemingly rather uniform township environment. Variety has occurred in:

- a varied range of house sizes (IQRs of 30 to 40 m²);
- a variety of spaces occupied by the main households (IQRs of about 30 m²);
- additional space for a variety of tenants or 'lodgers';
- a range of house values and costs (IQRs of £5–6000);
- floor-space indexes and plot ratios varying by about 0.1 (IQR).

The process of transformation

Motivation for extension

In examining motivation for extension, we address the issue of what causes a household to make a significant change to its housing consumption rather than continue tolerating the *status quo.*

As shacks-only are over-represented in the sample, they bias the all transformers data through their radically different distribution. The most important reasons for extending in the shacks-only transformers sample are economic. Half built their shacks to rent them out and a further 7 per cent had other business reasons. They are popular as kiosks. Other transformers are less concerned with renting rooms – but still over 30 per cent have it as their main motivation. 'Housing stress' and 'shocks' (Seek, 1983) generating a need for more space for residential use account for 34 per cent in shacks-only transformers. In the others, 57 per cent of transformers are driven by need for more accommodation for the household and extended family. Within these housing stress motives, the children getting older appears to be the most powerful. No one transformed primarily to improve services, probably because they were universally provided on the plot.

Only 19 per cent of respondents reported that they did not consider a move rather than transformation. There is a reasonably active market in houses in the areas which would suggest that considering a move is an available option for most would-be housing adjusters. However, 59 per cent had probably entered the market looking for another house but either could not meet the price for which their extended house could be provided (35 per cent), or could find no suitable alternative (24 per cent).

There is little loyalty to the neighbourhood articulated as the reason for staying and extending, although it is more common among those extending in permanent materials. However, some who had looked for other houses may well have done so within their neighbourhood or close by.

Problems encountered in the extension process

Respondents were asked to rank the problems encountered in their extension activity by selecting first, second and third in order of difficulty from the housing supply inputs, and an 'other, specify' option. Shacks-only transformers differ again as their main difficulty was avoiding the local authority (46 per cent ranked it first). This is not a problem for recent transformers and only rarely for established transformers as they generally have permission.[7] Established transformers' overwhelming problem has been in the financing (65 per cent ranked it first) while recent transformers have had fewer financial problems and more problems with building materials (56 per cent ranked it first). In the lower ranks, both established and recent transformers have chosen building materials and labour as being problematic (over 20 per cent ranking both either second or third). Services are not a problem in these well-serviced areas.

Phases of construction

A total of three phases of construction have been found in the Harare sample but most transformers have only implemented one phase (79 per cent). There is a long experience of transforming in the study areas; a few started in the 1950s but momentum gathered in the 1970s and 1980s. The shacks which exist have been added only since the 1980s. Prior to the mid-1980s, the local authority constantly demolished timber shacks as they appeared but stopped in the face of social and political pressure. However, even if some escaped the demolition, they tend to be assembled from second-rate timber and so have a short lifespan.

Self-help, in the form of actually building the structure, is relatively uncommon in the Zimbabwe sample (16 per cent) except for shacks-only transformers (30 per cent)

Figure 83. The construction process in Harare

Established transformers

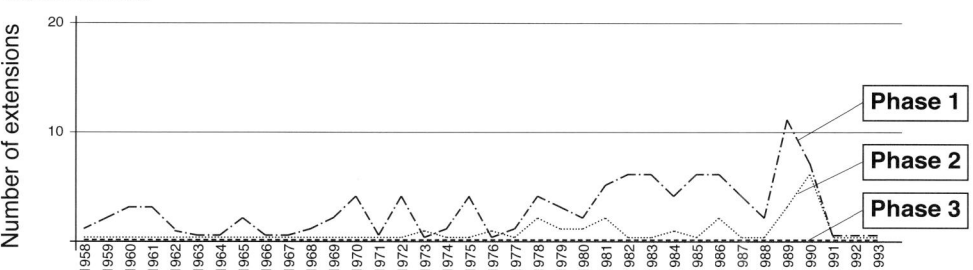

Recent transformers

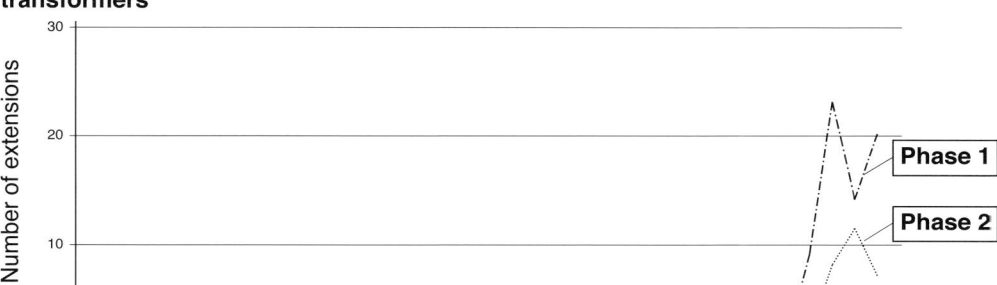

Shack transformers

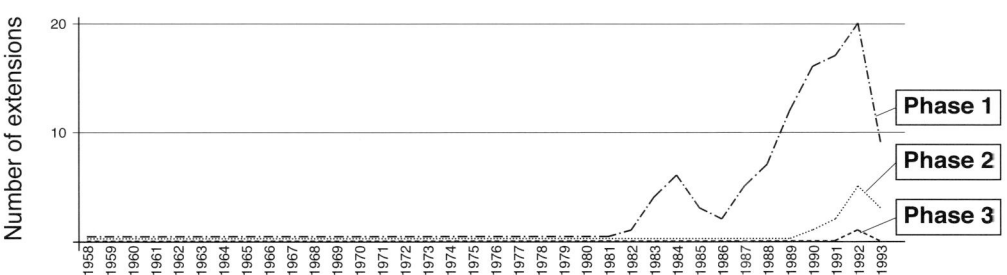

Figure 84. Number of extensions recorded in the Harare sample, by year

who can purchase the room in sections ready to be nailed together at the corners. Contractors who bring together several trades are also uncommon in the transformation process (13 per cent), whereas the single tradesmen dominate the scene (67 per cent). One of the main reasons for this is the form of payment customary in each case. If a contractor is engaged, payment tends to involve large sums as the work proceeds quickly and all processes are completed in a short time. If single tradesmen are engaged, however, the owner can have delays between them so that money can be gathered and payments strung out to suit the owner's resources.

It can be seen from table 95 that, while self-help is utilised for less costly extensions, there is little to separate the jobs done by single tradesmen and contractors by cost. Both tackle large extensions and both have a large range of job costs (IQRs are similarly extensive). In the Zimbabwe case, the extensions where self-help has been combined with tradesmen are the largest at the median and have a third quartile of Z$137,000. This suggests that, for the very large jobs, owners are reluctant to leave all the tasks to paid help and feel the need to economise by having household members help. In addition, such extensions are likely to be so large and complex that the opportunity for tasks to be accomplished over the weekend or between stages is greater than for simple one-room additions.

Table 95. The median cost of the first extension and implementer* (Z$ thousand)

Medians (and IQRs)	Number of observations	1993 cost of extension
Self-help, household members	15	5.80
		(2.8, 31.6)
Single contractor	26	36.30
		(20.1, 76.3)
Separate tradesmen	138	40.20
		(13.0, 87.2)
Self-help plus tradesmen	12	50.00
		(7.5, 137.1)

* Shacks-only transformers have been omitted.

Most transformers use savings and earnings to finance the extension operations. There is little formal-sector borrowing for the extensions as only 18 per cent of recent transformers and far fewer established transformers have borrowed from a bank. The popularity of saving with institutions such as the Central African Building Society (CABS) is undoubtedly important as a channel for funding large items of expenditure like extensions and 'own funds' will incorporate many institutional savers. Family funds are especially important for the retired heads of household, many of whom receive money from sons and daughters to assist or enable the transformation activity.

Permissions

Officers of Harare Department of Housing and Community Services are satisfied that most transformers have planning and building regulations approval for their extensions. They appear to be content with the semblance of order which is maintained in the estates, contrary to what might be expected if there were blatant flouting of the regulations. Shacks, however, appear to attract universal opprobrium from officials in informal conversations and have been subject to demolition in the past.

The overwhelming majority of (non-shack) transformers asked for and received planning permission for (at least some of) their extensions. While we have no reason to believe that all have followed the plan for which permission was granted, neither have we reason to suppose that such breaches are any more likely in transformations than in any other area of planning control.

The shacks are a different story as virtually none of them have planning approval and most breach the building lines by being too close to the plot boundary. In fact, 68 per cent of shacks-only transformers had received threats from the local authority with respect to their shacks but in only half of these had work stopped. Only one-quarter of the other transformers have received any harassment from the authorities over their extensions and most have led to nothing or only a change in the design.

Intention for disposing of the house

Despite a reasonably brisk market in houses, there is still a reluctance to sell. Thus, only a small percentage of the houses (13 per cent) are likely to transfer to owners other than family members. However, there is a higher incidence of willingness to sell among recent transformers than in the other sub-samples. Half the households intend to pass the house on to the family and one-quarter claimed that they would not leave it.

Summary

The Zimbabwe sample represents a settled population of working people and a considerable group of retired people whose children assist them to extend their houses. The shacks-only transformers are, as expected, more like non-transformers in their socio-economic characteristics but are, surprisingly, longer occupants of their houses than other transformers. Owners who rent out rooms to tenants tend to have lower incomes than those who do not, suggesting that renting out allows ownership by lower income people than if it were not possible.

Several extension phases are generally used, each of which adds substantial amounts of accommodation (two to three rooms). The transformation in total adds three to four rooms at the median and makes substantial gains in habitable space per person by any measure. However, one extra room only for shacks-only transformers leads to a loss of habitable space per person as they receive tenants onto their plots. Main households are generally better housed than before even though they have also made room for many tenant households (known as lodgers in Zimbabwe). The lodgers have only about a quarter the space of the main households, and generally only one room per household. Even with much less space, tenant households do not have very crowded conditions as their households are relatively small.

Generally the extensions are built to at least as high a standard as the original structure, except that shacks are only timber sheeting. Indeed, transformed houses appear to retain or increase their value, even at the square-metre level when other countries' transformations do not. Shacks are, as expected, a very cheap way to add housing space and allow people to gain an income from rents very easily and with a very short amortisation period. In plan, most transformations produce houses which can be occupied by more than one independent household.

Many households extend in order to make an income from rents. Most transformers face problems in raising finance but there has been a sustained level of extension activity for many years, involving large amounts of money. In fact, with a mean spending on transformations of PPP£12,708, transformers throughout Mbare and Highfield are likely to have invested PPP£166.6 million in extending and modifying the housing stock, a prodigious achievement.

Notes

1   The village of Epworth in Lincolnshire, UK, is the birthplace of John and Charles Wesley, the founders of the Methodist Church.
2   In this analysis we have come across a shortcoming of the GIS system which we used and which causes some inaccuracies in our calculations. In the house plans, the original house is registered as Phase 0. If any part of it is demolished in the transformation process, phase 0 becomes smaller by that amount. It is reasonably rare but does throw up smaller house sizes than were in fact existing. The difference seems to be about 10 m² at the median.
3   The fourth row in the table is not a simple sum of lines 2 and 3 because the median extension may not be added to the median original house.
4   This might be an over-estimate owing to the reduced original area caused by the method of recording phase 0 in the GIS package.
5   During the fieldwork it was noticed that finishes to extensions are generally of better quality than the originals but the workmanship varied greatly.
6   Several of the remaining sample have some shacks on the plot in addition to their extensions in permanent materials.
7   It should be noted that our transformer sample was largely chosen through planning records so it is likely that our established and recent transformer sample will have permission for at least some of their transformations. They may, however, have some unauthorized extensions in addition to those for which permission was granted (or may have deviated from the permitted development). In fact, 34 per cent of our sample have both extensions to the house (which probably have permission) and free-standing extensions (which probably have not).

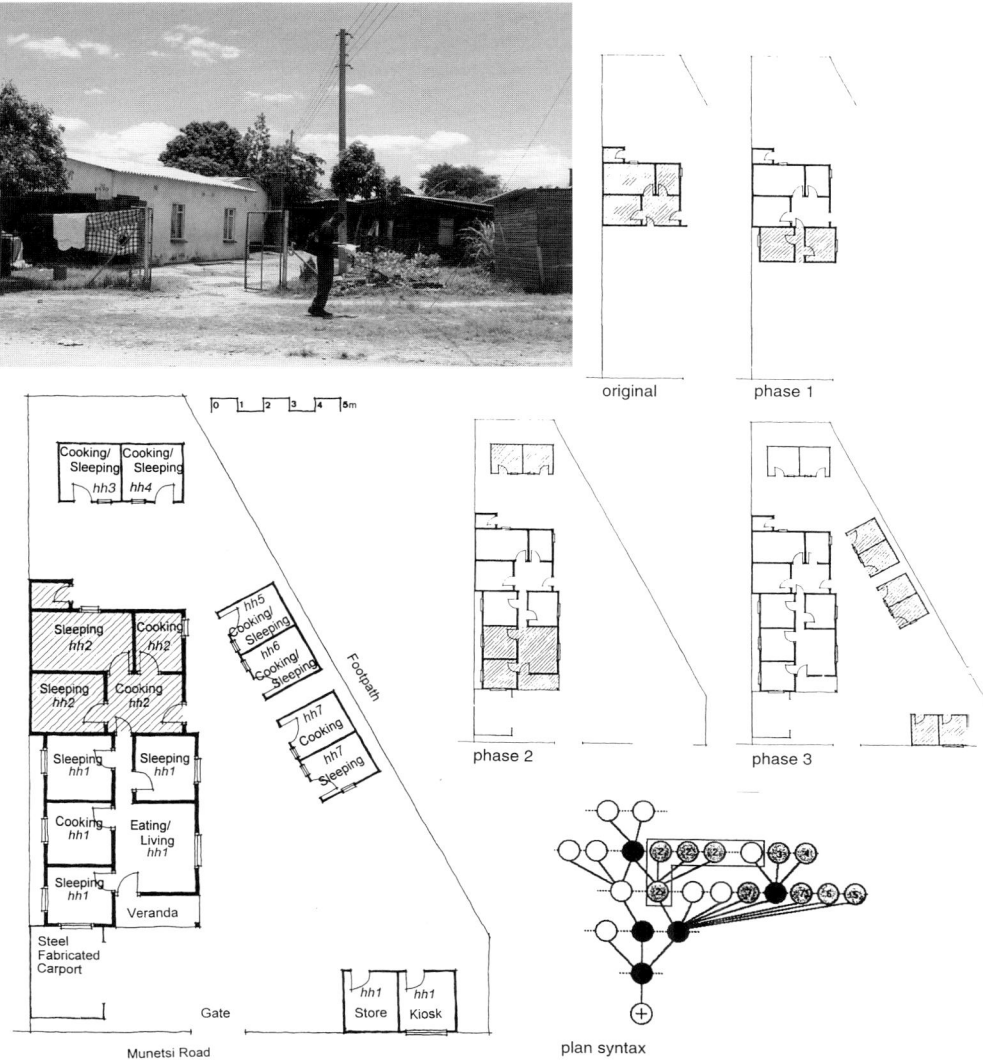

This semi-detached house has been extended into a combination of two suites of four and five rooms plus several single rooms in wooden shacks opening onto the yard. In order to light and ventilate the forward extension from a semi-detached villa, a narrow space has been left towards the boundary. The transformations were carried out in 1983 for Z$3000 and the 1990s for Z$40,000. The value of the house is about Z$150,000, eight times the owning household's income. The original seven-person household is augmented by seven tenant households giving a total of 26 people on the plot.

Figure 85. Large plots allow great complexity, Harare

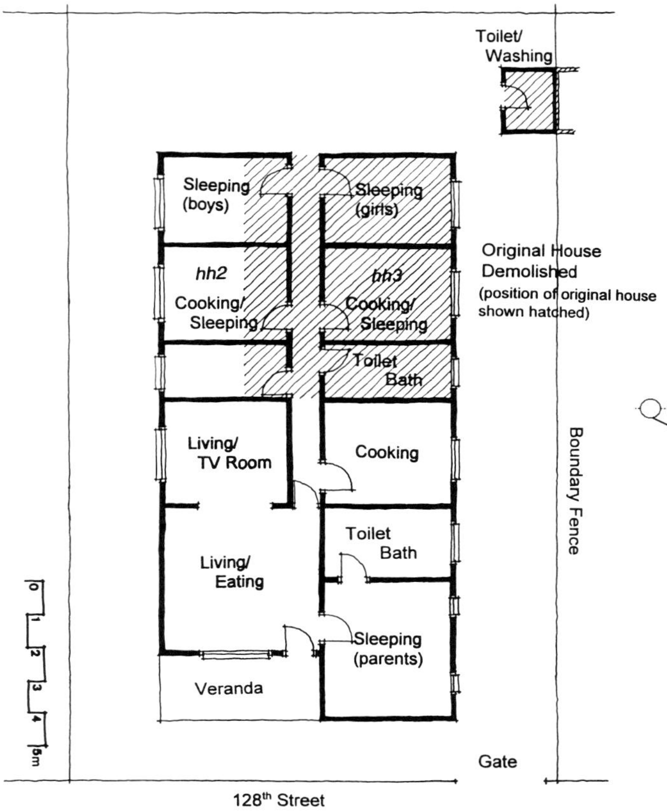

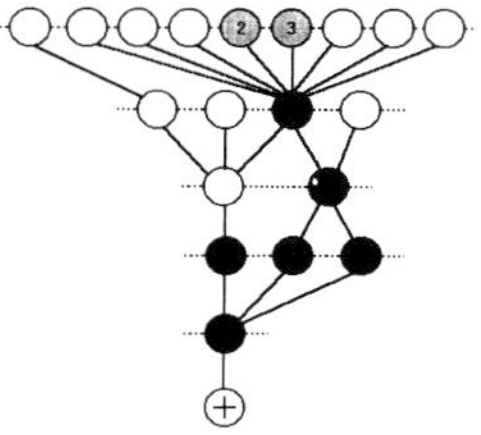

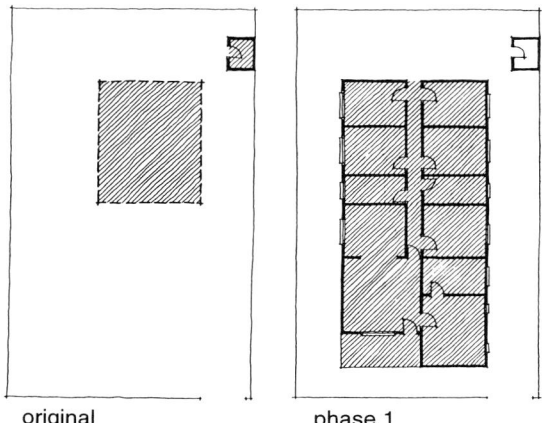

Toilet/
Washing

Sleeping
(boys)

Sleeping
(girls)

hh2

hh3

Cooking/
Sleeping

Cooking/
Sleeping

Toilet
Bath

Original House
Demolished
(position of original house
shown hatched)

Living/
TV Room

Cooking

Living/
Eating

Toilet
Bath

Boundary Fence

Sleeping
(parents)

Veranda

Gate

128th Street

0
1
2
3
4
5m

This house is an enlarged villa with a rear corridor to provide flexibility in use of many of the rooms. It is owned by a nine-person household and occupied by them and two extra households, a total of 14 people. It is worth about Z$55,000, just over two years' income for the owner household. The transformations were carried out by separate tradesmen in 1990 at a cost of Z$45,000.

original

phase 1

Figure 86. A typical transformed house with a rear corridor, Harare

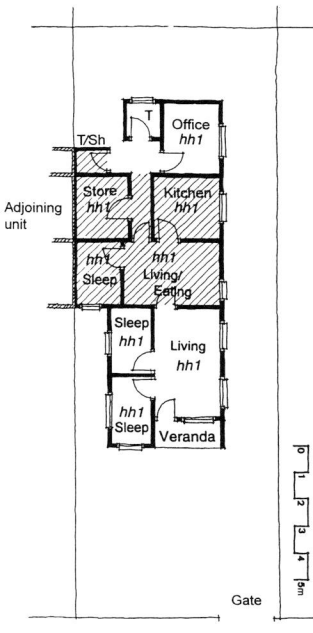

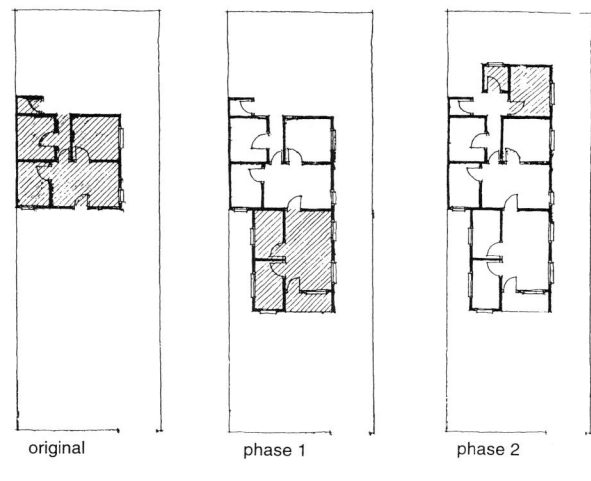

original   phase 1   phase 2

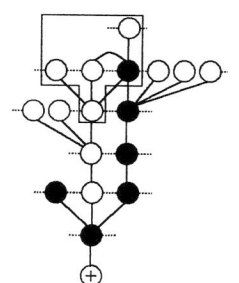

This 48 m² semi-detached villa has been extended to 84 m² and 8 rooms. There is an office at the rear. It now appears from the outside as a modern detached, higher status villa though it is still a semi-detached house at the rear. The 31-year-old male household head reports being unemployed. There are three adults and three children in the house. The owner estimates its total worth at Z$125,000. Its design results in a very deep space syntax, with some distribution provided by the internal corridor and external spaces. The original structure is now very deeply placed (levels 4–6).

Figure 87. A forward extension on a dwelling originally sited towards the rear of the plot, Harare

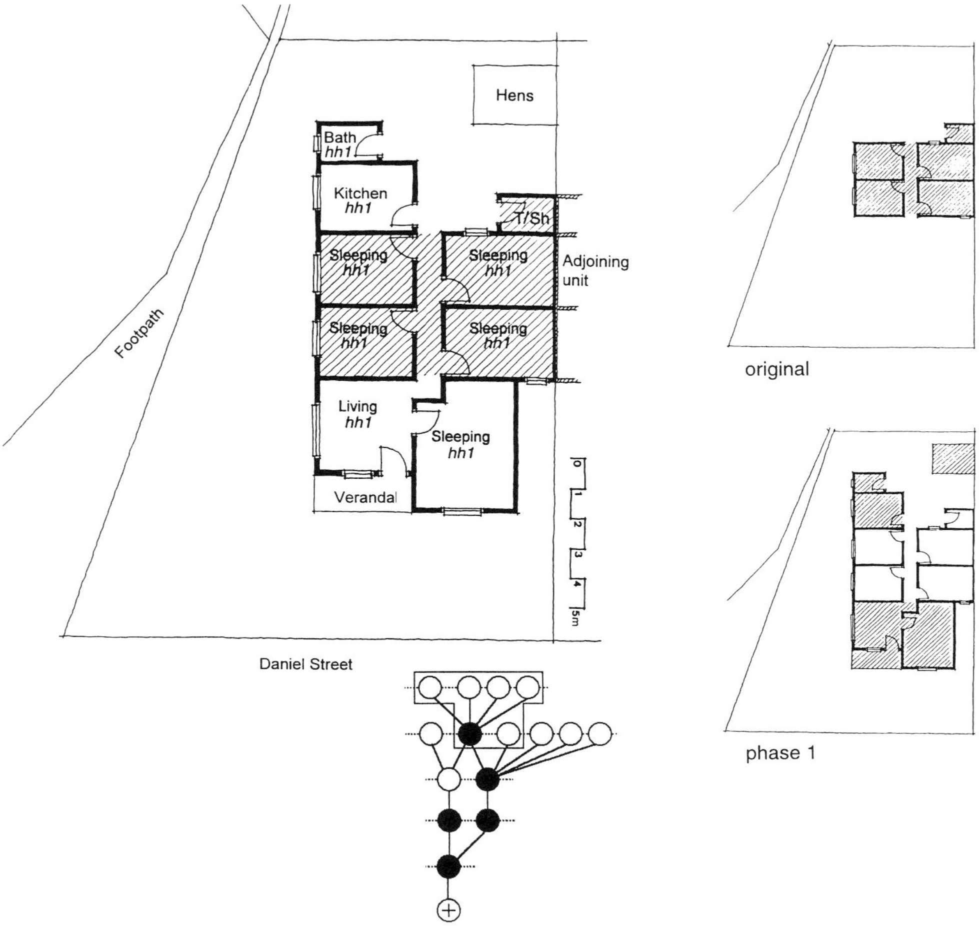

Hens

Bath
hh1

Kitchen
hh1

T/Sh

Sleeping
hh1

Sleeping
hh1

Adjoining
unit

Sleeping
hh1

Sleeping
hh1

Living
hh1

Sleeping
hh1

Verandal

Footpath

Daniel Street

0 1 2 3 4 5m

original

phase 1

The common villa with corridor access at the rear has been created here by rearranging the original dwelling into the corridor and rooms at the rear and building a new suite of front rooms. A kitchen and bathroom have been added to the rear. The single household (six adults and one child) occupy all 124 m² The head has lived in the house for 43 years. The transformation was made in 1985 for Z$5000.

Figure 88. A conversion turning the original dwelling into corridor access, Harare

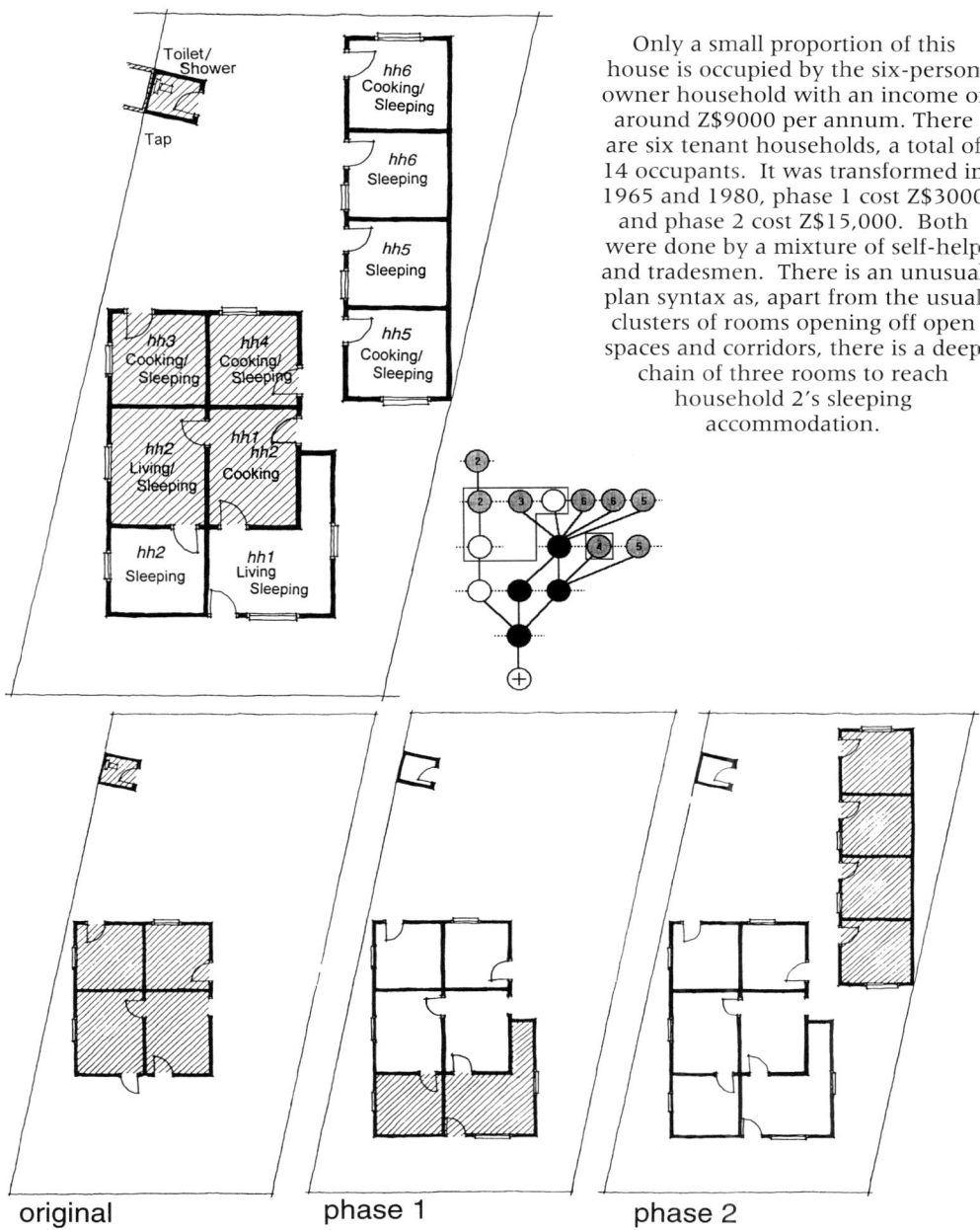

Only a small proportion of this house is occupied by the six-person owner household with an income of around Z$9000 per annum. There are six tenant households, a total of 14 occupants. It was transformed in 1965 and 1980, phase 1 cost Z$3000 and phase 2 cost Z$15,000. Both were done by a mixture of self-help and tradesmen. There is an unusual plan syntax as, apart from the usual clusters of rooms opening off open spaces and corridors, there is a deep chain of three rooms to reach household 2's sleeping accommodation.

original   phase 1   phase 2

Figure 89. Transformations used to house tenant households, Harare

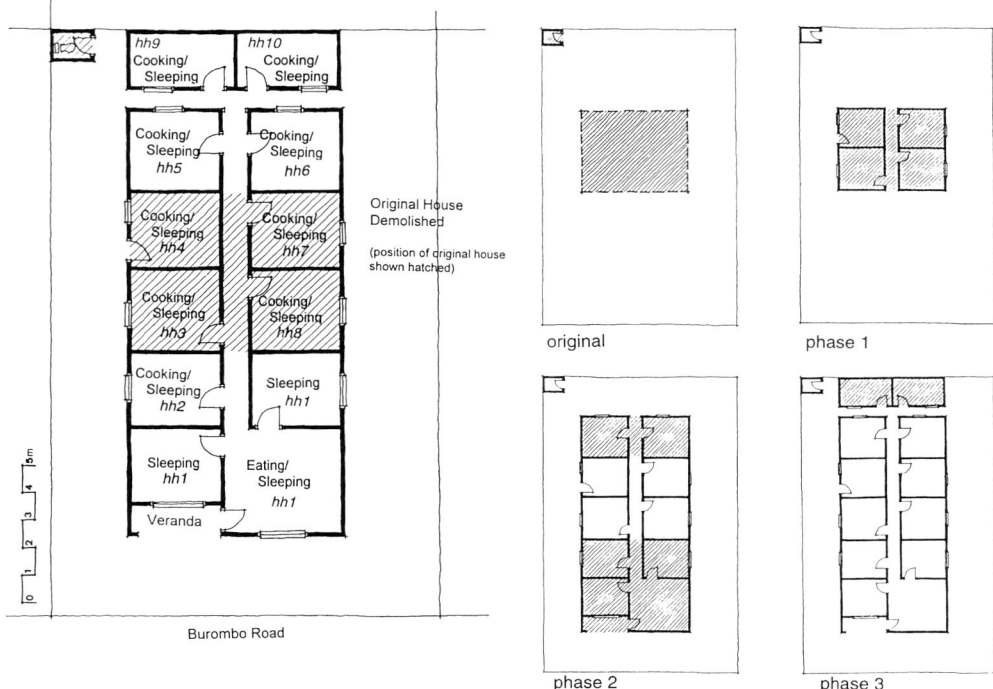

original

phase 1

phase 2

phase 3

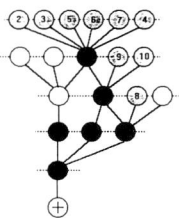

The 15-person main household in this house occupies only three rooms even though there are others available, and obviously prefers to rent the others for the income. There are 42 people in the house in 10 households. This is a perfect example of a house in which the main household has accommodation at the front and other rooms are ranged along a central corridor accessed only from the rear. It gives a high level of flexibility in who occupies the rooms. There is also the option of opening any of these rooms to the side of the house, as for household 4. The transformations cost Z$11,000 in 1981. The two rear rooms (phase 3) are shacks located outside the building lines. The house is worth about Z$120,000, five times the owning household's annual income.

Figure 90. An extreme form of the corridor-access rooming house, Harare

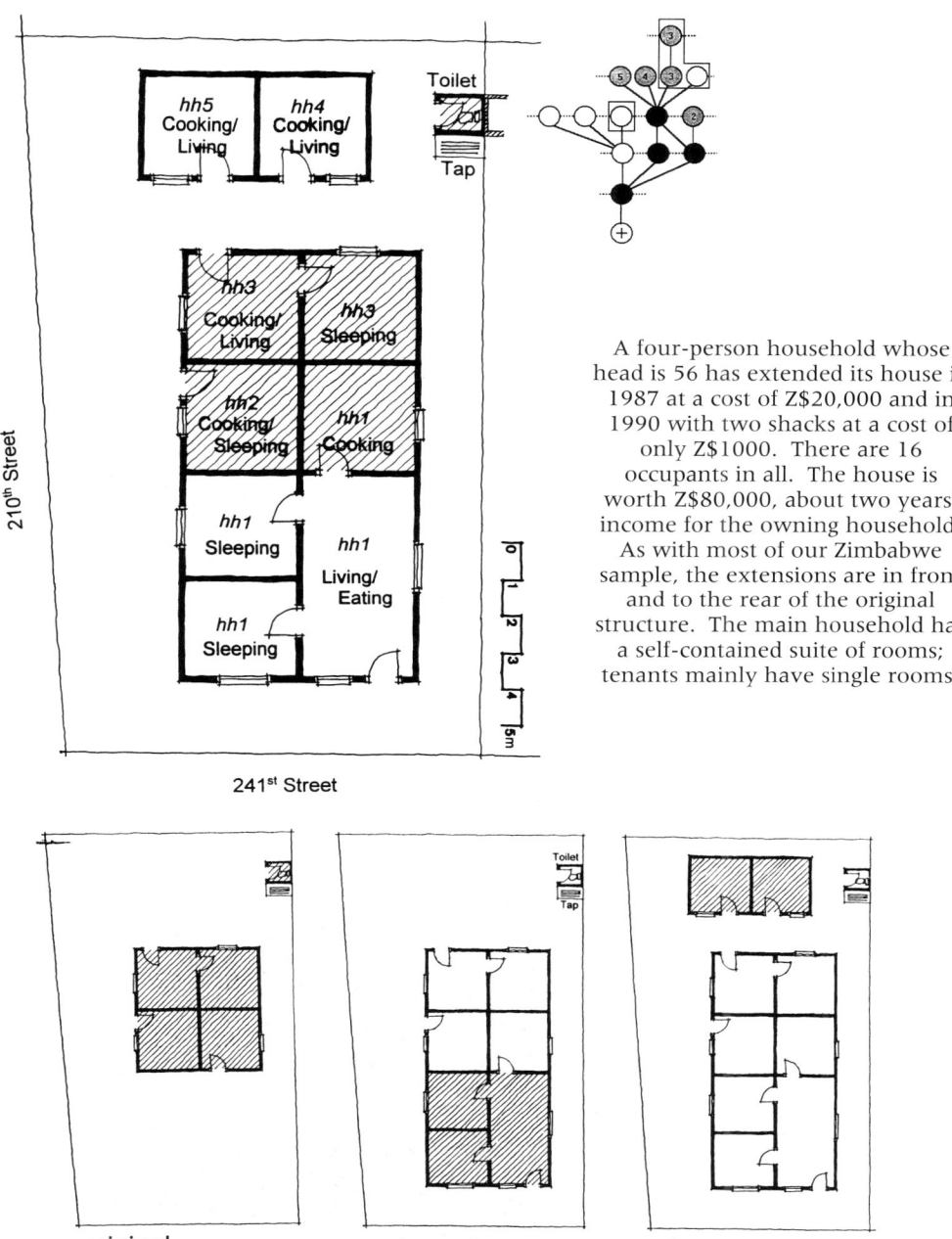

A four-person household whose head is 56 has extended its house in 1987 at a cost of Z$20,000 and in 1990 with two shacks at a cost of only Z$1000. There are 16 occupants in all. The house is worth Z$80,000, about two years' income for the owning household. As with most of our Zimbabwe sample, the extensions are in front and to the rear of the original structure. The main household has a self-contained suite of rooms; tenants mainly have single rooms.

Figure 91. An extended house in Harare

Figure 92A. A large brick forward extension under construction
The original structure is still visible through the window (centre)

Figure 92B. A simple forward extension giving one room and a large porch

Figure 92C. Many extensions require the roof line to be raised

Figure 92D. A row of rooms made from concrete fencing panels.

Appendix 5. An assessment of the decision to transform

In this appendix we examine the characteristics that distinguish transformers from non-transformers. By so doing, we can point out the issues which could be addressed by policy in order to increase the efficiency of transformations as a housing-supply mechanism.[1]

Predicting the transformation decisions

The data on transformers and non-transformers provided the basis for a two-step econometric analysis of the decision to transform. The factors that influenced the decision to transform were identified, and then the amount spent on the extension was modelled. The analysis is similar to that used by Ziegert (1988) and Garrod *et al.* (1995) and was based on the two-stage Heckman procedure (Heckman, 1976, 1979).

In a similar way to that described in Garrod *et al.* (1994), we used a probit model (in SAS) to find which variables are affecting the decision to extend. Not all the variables looked at by Garrod *et al.* were available from our study, e.g., ethnic group or whether a respondent has worked abroad. However, the following variables were used in the modelling procedure:

ExtCost	Cost of extension indexed to 1993 prices.
Age	Age of head of household.
IncPC	Income estimated by household expenditure per head: in Bangladesh, in thousands of taka; in Egypt, in £E; in Ghana, in 100,000s cedis; in Zimbabwe, in Zimbabwe dollars.
IncDiff*	Difference in annual income of household and mean annual income for other households in their estate: in Egypt, in thousands of £E; in Ghana, in 100,000s of cedis; in Zimbabwe, in Zimbabwe dollars.
Sex	0–1 variable: whether respondent is female.
HseStay	Number of years spent in the house.
EmpStay	Number of years in current employment.
RBefExt	Number of rooms in the house in 1990.
ABefExt	Area of house in 1990.
OwnElse	Other houses owned (0–1 variable).
EducYrs	Years spent in education.
Estate	The estate within the country sample: i.e. in Egypt, Helwan or Medinet Nasr; in Ghana, Asawasi, North

Suntreso or South Suntreso; in Zimbabwe, Mbare, Highfield (Egypt and Jerusalem), or Highfield (Canaan and Western Triangle).

Acquire*   Method of acquisition; bought, inherited or rented.

StayCity   0–1 variable: whether respondent intends to stay in the city.

Depend   Dependency ratio (number of children/number of adults).

SellL   0–1 variable: whether the respondent will sell on leaving.

Family   0–1 variable: whether respondent will pass house to family.

AgeArrv   Age when moving into house.

HHSize   Household size (1993).

* Not used in Bangladesh

These variables relate to the fundamental characteristics of the respondent households and their houses or flats, and the relationships specified by Mendelsohn (1977) in his model. Except in Bangladesh, the presence of non-transformers in the sample made it possible to generate a variable representing the difference between the income of the transformer's household and the mean for the area.

The first-stage analysis utilised a binary dependent variable 'Ext', which took the value one if a household extended its house during the period 1990 to 1993 and zero otherwise. Thus, all recent transformers (1990–3) in the survey took the value one, and all non-transformers zero. The probability of transforming was then modelled as a function of the households' characteristics during the period being examined. This was not used in Bangladesh as there were so few non-transformers in the sample.

In stage two of the Heckman procedure, we modelled the decision on how much to spend (in 1993 prices) on the transformations once the decision to transform has been taken. Only recent transformers were included to determine the variables for this stage though all transformers were sometimes modelled. The same variables are used as in the first stage.

Lambda, the inverse Mills ratio, was output by the first-stage probit analysis and was entered into the second-stage analysis to counter any possible sample-selection bias. This was necessary because the observed data in the second-stage model are not sampled randomly from the population, but as a result of the extension decision. If the data had been treated as having been randomly sampled from the population of house-owners, rather than from the sub-population of extenders, then potentially serious biases could have occurred (Heckman, 1979). Thus, in each sample for which we have carried out the first stage of the procedure, account has been taken of the difference between the proportion of the sample who are recent extenders and the proportion of them in the area as a whole. The latter was roughly estimated from our experience of the areas involved. This allows the calculation of weights for the observations reflecting the ratio of the observed to true mix of extenders to non-extenders in the population (see Manski and McFadden, 1981).

Goodness-of-fit statistics are generally employed to find how well a model describes the data set at hand. In essence these statistics work on the principal that, under a 'null hypothesis', a mathematical function of the residual variation of each data point from its estimated value (given by the model) will conform to a known distribution. Thus, in layman's terms, finding that the usual 'null hypothesis' that the model is a good explanation (fit) of this data set is true implies that we will find that the goodness-of-fit statistic will not differ significantly from the known distribution (i.e. we achieve a non-significant result.) The binary nature of our data (recently transformed or not) suggests we use Pearson's statistic and the log-likelihood statistic.[2]

These goodness-of-fit statistics show that our models are not particularly good fits although generally the log-likelihood statistics are not significant. It is notoriously difficult to find a perfect goodness-of-fit statistic for probit analysis because the dependent variable consists of only two values, zero and one.

Bangladesh

In Bangladesh, income was measured not by the difference from others in the neighbourhood but by its actual size through a variable:

TotEx   Total annual household expenditure (as a proxy for income) in thousands of taka.

In addition, an acquisition variable was added:

Acquire   Means of acquisition of the house: 0 = rent from public sector; 1 = buy possession.

Because there were so few non-transformers as a comparator in the Bangladesh sample, only the second stage of the model was relevant.

The probit model was estimated using LIMDEP 5.1 (Greene, 1989). The influential variables, all of which were significant at the 0.15 level, are as given in table 96. The variables are given in decreasing order of significance and this model explains 22 per cent of the variability.

Table 96. Variables which affect the amount spent on transformations, Bangladesh

Variable	Coefficient (*t*-value)
Constant	9.665 (40.95)
RBefExt	-0.131 (4.24)
Totex	0.12 (3.83)
Acquire = bought possession	0.361 (2.19)
R-squared	0.22
Adjusted *R*-squared	0.199
F-statistic	10.37

The covariate 'RBefExt' has a negative coefficient implying that the fewer rooms a house has in 1990 the more will be spent on the transformation. 'TotEx' (in thousands of taka) has a positive coefficient implying that the more affluent a householder is. the more money (s)he will spend on transformation. The effect of the 'Acquire' variable is quite marked. Adjusted mean extension cost for householders who buy possession of the house can be calculated at Tk25,514 whereas for the remainder, who rent from the public sector, it is only Tk17,800.

As we might expect, incomes have some small but significant effect on whether a house is transformed and a larger effect on how expensive the transformation is once the decision is taken to go ahead. However, the smallness of the house before the extension (expressed as area in the first stage and number of rooms in the second) is more important.

In Bangladesh it seems that householders will transform if they have smaller houses i.e., if there is still space on their plot, and they will build as many rooms as they can afford. Those who bought possession, and are thus demonstrably willing to invest in housing, are capable of building the most expensive extensions.

Egypt

The Egypt study had a number of unique variables which were included in the model These are as follows:

HHbefExt   Number of people in the household before any extension.
HseType   Flat type:
           1 = Helwan 2-roomed back to back narrow;
           2 = Helwan 2-roomed back to back wide;
           3 = Helwan 2-roomed straight through;
           4 = Helwan 3-roomed straight through;
           5 = Medinet Nasr 2-roomed straight through;
           6 = Medinet Nasr 2-roomed straight through.
Floor   Floors 1 to 5.
Estate   1 = Helwan;
           2 = Medinet Nasr.

The usable sample for the Egypt data set consisted of 69 (25 per cent) recent extenders and 208 (75 per cent) respondents who had not extended their houses since 1990. This tallied with informal estimates of a recent transformation rate of around 20 per cent for this period. The sample was adjusted slightly to take account of the small discrepancy between observed and expected numbers of extenders.

The probit model was estimated using LIMDEP 5.1 (Greene, 1989) on the weighted observations. The results are given in table 97. Again, all variables shown entered the model at the 0.15 significance level.

Table 97. Variables which appear to affect the decision to transform*

Variable	Coefficient
Constant	-2.213 (-2.50)[a]
Estate = Medinet Nasr	3.193 (7.37)
EducYrs	0.050 (1.95)
RBefExt	0.218 (1.56)
ABefExt	-0.039 (-1.57)
IncDiff	0.0001 (1.92)
Inherit	0.991 (2.42)
Unrestricted log likelihood	-41.467
Restricted log likelihood	-154.336
Likelihood ratio test[b]	225.7
Pseudo *R*-squared[c]	0.731
Correct predictions (%)	94.5 per cent

*Unweighted parameter estimates in order of significance.
(a) *T*-values are shown in parentheses.
(b) The likelihood ratio test statistic is computed as twice the difference between the initial and maximum log-likelihood values: asymptotically this statistic has a chi-squared distribution with *n* [number of restrictions, see Gujarati (1995)] degrees of freedom. At the 95 per cent confidence level the critical value of the chi-squared distribution is 12.59 with 6 df.
(c) Pseudo *R*-squared is computed as 1-(restricted log-likelihood/unrestricted log-likelihood) and is, according to McFadden (1974), an alternate measure of goodness-of-fit for probabilistic choice models.

Households in Medinet Nasr were more likely to transform than those in Helwan because by 1990 most flats in Helwan had already been transformed. There was a strong correlation between the number of rooms in the flat in 1990 and the area of the flat at that time and, as a result of this, these variables were only significant when entered into the model jointly, rather than singly. As a result, it was difficult to separate out their individual effects on the decision to transform. One reasonable interpretation may be that the impetus to transform was the combination of a relatively small floor area divided into a large number of rooms. Conversely, fewer rooms in a large area would discourage transformation, probably because it suggests that the householder had transformed prior to 1990. Thus, cramped conditions may be an important stimulus to the decision to transform, both before and after 1990. This may seem somewhat counter-intuitive, as we would expect Muslims to wish to divide up space so as to maximise privacy and therefore would expect more smaller rooms in houses that had already been transformed. However, this does not mean that they would not wish these rooms to be as large as possible.

A greater number of years in education and a higher rate of income than the average for the area both increased the probability that a householder will transform. The chances of transformation also rose if the householder acquired the house through inheritance.

The goodness-of-fit statistics suggest that our model was a good approximation of reality, in that it provides a very good fit for the data and correctly predicts over 90 per cent of all recent transformations.

The second-stage empirical analysis estimated a linear model of the cost of the extension (ExtCost) using the 69 extenders, mostly from the Medinet Nasr estate. The inverse Mills ratio, Lambda, linked the two stages of the empirical analysis by controlling for sample-selection bias. Aside from the Mills ratio, variables which were not significant at the 0.15 level were discarded from the model. The results of the second-stage analysis are given in table 98. The explanation of just over 30 per cent of the variation in the dependent variable was satisfactory.

Table 98. Variables which affect the amount spent on transformation, Egypt

Variable	Coefficient (*t*-value)
Constant	3093.3 (2.18)
RBefExt	558.78 (3.34)
EducYrs	-101.15 (-2.75)
Sex of head	-868.19 (-1.47)
Floor	-271.80 (-1.69)
Helwan: 3-room straight through	-3851.3 (2.73)
Helwan: 2-room back to back wide	-6154.9 (-3.03)
Lambda	350.61 (0.63)
R-squared	0.302
Adjusted *R*-squared	0.222
F-statistic	3.77

Physical structure seemed to be an important determinant of spending on transformations. The flats on higher floors had less spent on extensions (presumably a logistical issue, as larger extensions are less practical on higher floors), and certain original layouts of flats in Helwan also seemed to attract lower expenditures. The 1990 flat layout was correlated with the number of rooms in the flat before 1990. However, the variable RBefExt was a highly significant and positive determinant of spending in the model specified, either with or without layout variables. This again tallies with the notion that respondents living in the most cramped conditions are most eager to extend and, here, suggests that this will lead to a high spend. However, in this case, there is less evidence to support this notion as the area of the flat before extending is not a significant factor in explaining spend. Surprisingly, the more educated Egyptians are spending less on transformations. This may suggest that they have spent money on extensions previously or, if they are younger, may be dividing their resources between work on their flats and on bringing up their children.

The Egyptian government seems intent on continuing to build walk-up flats. The most obvious response to the first-stage analysis is to suggest that new housing is built with future transformations in mind. Flats should have at least three rooms, with the smallest being those rooms most easily continued into the extension.[3]

Ghana

The Ghana data set included a useful variable specifying house type:

Hsetype   1 = Semi-detached 2-roomed;
           2 = Semi-detached 3 or 4 rooms;
           3 = End terrace 1 room;
           4 = End terrace 2 rooms;
           5 = Mid terrace 1 room;
           6 = Mid terrace 2 rooms.

Our sample is essentially a random one with the exception that non-transformers are over-represented. Although it is estimated that approximately 90 per cent of houses have been transformed and 10 per cent remain non-transformed, our sample had a ratio of 78:22. This is mainly because there are very few non-transformers left in Kumasi and we needed as many examples as possible. Hence weights were used to reduce this bias and reflect a more representative view of the population.

There were 392 usable observations in the Ghanaian data set, 72 (18 per cent) recent extenders and 320 (82 per cent) respondents who had not extended their houses since 1990. The relative proportion of recent extenders was probably slightly higher than this, with perhaps around a quarter of households extending between 1990 and 1993 (see Garrod *et al.*, 1995, for a discussion of this issue).

As before, we are primarily interested in the dependent variable 'Ext' which takes the value 1 if the house has been extended between 1991 and 1993 and the value 0 otherwise. The probability of extending (that Ext = 1) is then estimated using LIMDEP 5.1 on the weighted observations. The results are given in table 99. All variables shown entered the model at the 0.15 significance level.

Owners of semi-detached houses were more likely to extend than those who owned terraced houses. Houses occupied by the owner who acquired them from the State Housing Corporation, or his/her representative (caretaker), were more likely to be transformed than those which had been inherited. Respondents with higher incomes than their neighbours were more likely to extend, as were those with larger households and, therefore, more pressure on space. The number of rooms in the house before 1991 was also influential: the more rooms there were in the house at that time, the less likely it was to be extended. This is probably because previous extensions had already been built and it would then tally with the analysis of extension decisions in non-government built housing in Ghana carried out by Garrod *et al.*, (1995).

Table 99. Variables which appear to affect the decision to transform, Ghana*

Variable	Coefficient (*t*-value)
Constant	-1.086 (-3.73)[a]
Acquire = bought from SHC	0.509 (1.94)
Acquire = owner's representative	0.613 (2.27)
Semi-detached, two rooms	0.989 (4.68)
Semi-detached, three or four rooms	0.798 (3.97)
RBefExt	-0.102 (-5.42)
HHSize	0.047 (2.28)
IncDiff	0.263×10^{-6} (2.24)
Unrestricted log likelihood	-190.24
Restricted log likelihood	-227.95
Likelihood ratio test statistic[b]	75.42
Pseudo *R*-squared	0.165
Correct predictions (%)	79.33

*Parameter estimates in order of significance.
(a) *T*-values are shown in parentheses.
(b) At the 95 per cent confidence level the critical value of the chi-squared distribution is 14.06 with 7 df.

The goodness-of-fit statistics suggested that the model was reasonable and that it provided an adequate fit for the data, correctly predicting nearly 80 per cent of all recent transformations.

The second-stage empirical analysis estimated a log-linear model of the cost of the extension (ExtCost) based on the 72 extenders from the first-stage model. Apart from the Mills ratio, variables which were not significant at the 0.15 level were discarded

Table 100. Variables which affect the amount spent on transformation, Ghana

Variable	Coefficient (*t*-value)
Constant	12.113 (15.75)
ABefExt	0.018 (3.63)
End terrace, two rooms	-1.409 (-1.77)
Mid terrace, two rooms	-0.898 (-1.75)
Acquire = bought from SHC	0.645 (1.57)
LAMBDA	0.867 (1.37)
R-squared	0.290
Adjusted *R*-squared	0.236
F-statistic	5.39

from the model. The results of the second-stage analysis are given in table 100. The explanation of around 30 per cent of the variation in the dependent variable was reasonable given the data available.

The area of the house before transformation was a significant factor in this case, with householders in larger houses spending more on their extensions. Again, this may have been an effect of the greater affluence of respondents already living in larger (extended) houses. These respondents may have had more disposable income to spend on transforming their houses and the space necessary to achieve their objectives. Living in two-room terraces reduces spending on their extensions. Those respondents who acquired their house directly from SHC spent more on their extensions than those who left the house in the hands of a representative or who had inherited. Owners are under pressure to provide accommodation for extended family members, either in the form of space in their own household or as rent-free rooms separate from their own households' rooms.

The analysis seems to suggest that space to extend is an important factor in the decision to extend and on how much is spent. House-owners do not want only two or three rooms in a country where traditional houses are much larger and accommodate more people. Thus, they will build more if they have the space. This suggests that future housing policies should avoid small two- and three-roomed dwellings unless they are built as core housing with enough space around them to permit future transformation when and if the householder desires.

Zimbabwe

The usable sample of 282 observations consisted of 138 (49 per cent) recent extenders and 144 (51 per cent) respondents who had not extended their houses since 1990. The relative proportions of these two groups in the population were probably less even than this, with approximately 30 per cent of households estimated to have extended their houses since 1990. The probit model was again estimated using an appropriately weighted sample. The results are given in table 101. All variables shown entered the model at the 0.15 significance level.

The area of the house in 1990 was found to be an important factor in the decision to extend, although the number of rooms in 1990 was not. Unsurprisingly, the larger the house, the less likely was it that the householder would transform between 1991 and 1993. It would seem that the area of the dwelling, rather than the number of units it is divided into, is the crucial factor in the extension decision.

Differences between estates also proved to be important. Houses in Highfield (Egypt and Jerusalem) were the most likely to be transformed in the period of interest, while householders in Mbare were the least likely to transform because most of them had already done so prior to 1991. The positive sign on the plot area coefficient suggests that the larger the plot, the more likely the householder is to extend. This makes intuitive sense given that sufficient area within which to extend is a prerequisite of such activity.

Table 101. Variables which appear to affect the decision to transform, Zimbabwe*

Variable	Coefficient (*t*-value)
Constant	0.920 (1.94)[a]
ABefExt	-0.049 (-7.56)
Estate = Mbare	-0.385 (-1.64)
Estate = Highfield (Egypt and Jerusalem)	0.665 (2.21)
Plot area	0.0050 (3.08)
Unrestricted log likelihood	-125.6
Restricted log likelihood	-195.4
Likelihood-ratio test statistic[b]	139.6
Pseudo *R*-squared	0.357
Correct predictions (%)	69.9

*Parameter estimates in order of significance.
(a) *T*-values are shown in parentheses.
(b) At the 95 per cent confidence level the critical value of the chi-squared distribution is 9.49 with 4 df.

The goodness-of-fit statistics suggest that our model is a reasonable approximation of reality, in that it provides an adequate fit for the data and correctly predicts nearly 70 per cent of all recent transformations.

The second-stage analysis used the same variables as in the first stage but added:

Shack   0–1 variable reflecting whether a house has only a shack transformation or not

The second-stage empirical analysis estimated a log-linear model of the cost of the extension (ExtCost) using the 138 extenders from the first-stage model as the source

Table 102. Variables which affect the decision on cost of transformation, Zimbabwe

Variable	Coefficient (*t*-value)
Constant	9.60 (30.20)
Sex	0.589 (2.64)
Shack	-2.819 (-14.01)
HseStay	-0.018 (-2.21)
RBefExt	0.126 (2.19)
Lambda	0.060 (0.19)
R-squared	0.659
Adjusted *R*-squared	0.646
F-statistic	50.96

data. Apart from the Mills ratio, Lambda, variables which were not significant at the 0.15 level were discarded from the model.

The results of the second-stage analysis are given in table 102. Considering the data available to model the cost of the extension, the explanation of around 65 per cent of the variation in the dependent variable was highly satisfactory. This was not necessarily evidence of the theoretical validity of the model: there may have been much stochastic variation in the data overshadowing the systematic influence of variables. Nonetheless it did provide important evidence of reliability.

As expected, householders transforming shacks spent considerably less on transformation than other respondents. The length of stay in the house was also a significant explanatory variable, though surprisingly its effect was negative, with those who had spent longest in their houses spending the least. This may be because these respondents had already completed most of the transformations they desired in the past. The fact that the head of household had retired was not a factor for determining spending. There was no significant difference in spending on recent extensions between households where the head was retired and those where the head was still employed. More surprisingly, those respondents who already had most rooms spent the most on their transformations. Number of rooms may be an indicator of affluence, and respondents who already have more prestigious houses may have spent more than those whose houses are more modest. The area before extending was not a significant factor, nor is any conventional indicator of affluence such as per capita income.

This analysis seems to point to the inevitability of extensions. If a house has not been extended, it will be, and if there remains sufficient room on the plot this process may be repeated. Those wishing to build prestigious dwellings will lavish the most money on them as householders invest in accommodation for this and the next generation. Those who build humble shacks can extend cheaply and the ability to provide some extra housing space can be achieved on low budgets.

Conclusions

The main conclusion from this exercise is that, in the decision to extend, the house is more influential than the household. In the cost of extension, however, the influence of the house reduces and that of the household increases. If a household has a plot, its members are very likely to extend and to spend considerable amounts of money on the extension. The physical characteristics of the house are likely to have more effect on the decision to transform than the household's income or composition. However, the degree to which the household is committed to urban life and the neighbourhood appears to be influential. The influence of income and household size on the cost of transformations is not as important as might be expected, and certainly not as important as house characteristics.

We can assert from the model that anyone who has the space to transform is likely to do so. If policy is required to encourage transformations in housing areas currently being planned, plots should be clearly demarcated and large enough to accommodate several new rooms. Though the usual assistance with finance and the other inputs would be useful as in all housing supply, if there is private space to put them on, extensions appear to be almost inevitable in the life of low-cost housing in developing countries. These issues are addressed in the policy proposals in chapter 8.

Notes

1   This material is drawn from a paper written with two colleagues Gill Masters and Guy Garrod. Their major contribution to it is acknowledged.

2   For those more mathematically inclined the definitions of the goodness-of-fit statistics are given below:

$$\text{Pearson's} = \sum i \sum j (r_{ij} - n_i p_{ij})^2 \,/\, n_i p_{ij}$$

$$\text{Log-likelihood} = 2 \sum i \sum j \ln (r_{ij} \,/\, n_i p_{ij})$$

where the sum on i is over 'grouping' (from the independent variables included in the model; for example, group 0 in the variable 'sex' defines the males and group 1 the females) and the sum on j is over levels of response (i.e. zero and one). r_{ij} is the weight of the response at the jth level for the ith group, n_i is the total weight at the ith grouping and p_{ij} is the fitted probability for the jth level at the ith grouping.

3   Indeed this would solve one of the major problems of the flats once extended, that the internal room loses daylight and ventilation. This way either the original room is continued out into the extension or the first part of the extension allows a window to be opened into the original room before a new room is created further into the extension.

References

Abrams, C., V. Bodiansky, and O, Koenigsberger. (1956). *Report on Housing in the Gold Coast*, New York: United Nations.

Aina, T. A. (1988). 'The construction of housing for the urban poor of Lagos', *Habitat International* 12(1): 31–44.

Alcock, A. E. S. (1952). *Earth Building in West Africa*, Pretoria: Comission Pour la Cooperation Technique au Sud Du Sahara (CCTA).

Ameen, M. S. (1988). *Housing for Low-income People in Third World Peri-urban Areas: A Case Study of Dhaka, Bangladesh*, Newcastle upon Tyne: School of Architecture, University of Newcastle upon Tyne.

Ameen, M. S. (1995). *Qualitative Report on Bangladesh for Transformation Research Project*, Dhaka: Bangladesh University of Engineering and Technology.

Amole, B., D. Korboe, and A. G. Tipple. (1993). 'The Family House in West Africa: a forgotten resource for policy makers?' *Third World Planning Review* 15(4): 355–72.

Andrew, P. and D. Japha (1978). *Low Income Housing Alternatives for the Western Cape*, Cape Town: Urban Problems Research Unit, University of Cape Town.

Angal, A. (1991). The conflict between the built environment created by the recent housing schemes in Algiers and the expectations of those for whom they are designed, Unpublished PhD Dissertation, University of Newcastle upon Tyne.

Arditi, C., R. Sepulveda, and A. Toro. (1990). 'Vivienda social: technologias apropiadas y cambio residencial'. Paper presented to the Third National Construction Congress (3er Congreso Nacional de la Construccion), Vina del Mar, Chile, April.

Aref, H. (1989). The Latent Potential of the low-income in housing projects, Masters Thesis, Cairo University (in Arabic).

Asiama, S. O. (1985). 'The rich slum-dweller: a problem of unequal access, *International Labour Review* 124(3): 353–362.

Bamberger, M., B. Sanyal, and N. Valverde, (1982). *Evaluation of Sites and Services Projects: The Experience from Lusaka, Zambia*, Washington, DC: World Bank.

Bangladesh, Government of, CWFP, and ICCDDR (1995). *The Urban MCH-FP Initiative: a Partnership for Urban Health and Family Planning in Bangladesh*, Dhaka: Government of Bangladesh.

Bangladesh, Government of, (1993). *Bangladesh Population Census 1991, Zila: Dhaka*, Dhaka: Bamgladesh Bureau of Statistics.

Bangladesh, Government of, (1995). *Summary Report of Household Expenditure Survey, 1991–92*, Dhaka: Bangladesh Bureau of Statistics.

Behloul, M. (1991). *Post Occupancy Evaluation of Mass Housing Estates in Algeria: The Case of Four Mass Housing Estates in Algiers*, Unpublished PhD Dissertation, University of Sheffield.

Behloul, M. (1996). 'Mass housing estates: residents' responses in Algeria, Egypt and Jordan', XXIVth IAHS World Housing Congress, Ankara, Turkey, 27–31 May.

Beinart, J. (1971). 'Government-built cities and people-made places', in *The Growth of Cities*. Ed. D. Lewis, London: Elek Books.

Benjamin, S. (1993). *Urban Productivity from the Grass Roots*. New Delhi: Human Settlements Management Institute.

Benjamin, S. J. (1985). 'India: Formal v. informal', *The Architectural Review* (1062): 32–36.

Bhatt, E. (1989). 'Towards empowerment', *World Development* 17(7): 1059–1065.

Blankson, C. C. T. (1988). 'Housing estates in Ghana: a case study of middle- and low-income residential areas in Accra and Kumasi', in *Slum and Squatter Settlements in Sub-Saharan Africa: Towards a Planning Strategy*, Eds R. A. Obudho and C. C. Mhlanga, New York: Praeger.

Boehm, T. P. and K. R. Ihlanfelt (1986). 'The improvement expenditures of urban homeowners: an empirical analysis', *AREUEA Journal*(14): 48–60.

Bouchair, Y. (1984). The problem of adaptability in low cost housing in Algeria, MPhil dissertation, Centre for Architectural Research and Development Overseas, University of Newcastle upon Tyne.

Brand, S. (1994). *How Buildings Learn: What Happens after They're Built*, New York: Viking Penguin.

Brokensha, D. (1966). *Social Change at Larteh, Ghana*, Oxford: Clarendon Press.

BRRI (Building and Road Research Institute) (1970). *Report on Asawasi Housing Estate Survey, A Survey of the Living Conditions of Asawasi Housing Estate*, Ghana: Building and Road Research Institute.

Carmon, N. (1992). 'Housing renovations in moderately deteriorated neighbourhoods: public–individual partnership in Israel and its lessons', *Housing Studies* 7(1): 56–73.

Carmon, N. and T. Gavrieli (1987). 'Improving housing by conventional versus self-help methods: evidence from Israel', *Urban Studies* 24: 324–332.

Carmon, N. and M. Hill (1988). 'Neighbourhood rehabilitation without relocation or gentrification', *Journal of the American Planning Association* 54(4): 470–481.

Carmon, N. and R. Oxman (1981). *Self-help Housing Rehabilitation in Distressed Neighbourhoods in Israel*, Haifa: Samuel Neaman Institute for Advanced Studies in Science and Technology, Technion – Israel Institute of Technology.

Carmon, N. and R. Oxman (1984a). Responsive Public Housing: An Alternative for Low Income Families, Faculty of Architecture and Town Planning, Technion – Israel Institute of Technology (mimeo).

Carmon, N. and R. Oxman (1984b). 'Small is beautiful in public housing as well', in *Cities, Communities and Planning in the 1980s*, Eds F. D. Soen, A. Lazin and Y. Neumann, Aldershot: Gower.

Chana, T. S. (1984). 'Nairobi: Dandora and other projects', in *Low-Income Housing in the Developing World*, Ed G. K. Payne, New York: Wiley: 17–36.

Danby, M. (1989). *Durability and Social Acceptability of Stabilised Soil Buildings, Ghana*, Newcastle upon Tyne: Centre for Architectural Research and Development Overseas, University of Newcastle upon Tyne.

Dasgupta, A. S. (1986). 'Producing activities and dwelling transformation: implications for innovative design', paper presented at the International Seminar on Income and Housing, HSMI/HUDCO and IHS (Rotterdam) New Delhi, Nov. 14–15.

Dasgupta, A. S. (1987). 'Spatial planning and home based economic activities: design considerations'. Unpublished paper, New Delhi.

Dasgupta, A. S. (1990). 'Negotiating for growth and change: a study of user initiated transformation of formal housing', *Open House International* 15(4): 34–40.

Davidson, F. and G. Payne (1983). *Urban Projects Manual. A Guide to Preparing Upgrading and New Development Projects Accessible to Low Income Groups*, Liverpool: Liverpool University Press in association with Fairstead Press.

Devas, N. (1992). 'Financial aspects of sustainable urban development', paper presented at the International Workshop for Sustainable Urban Development, Cardiff, 13–17 July.

Durande-Lasserve, A. and R. Pajoni (1993). 'The regularisation of irregular settlements in cities in the developing world: techniques, procedures and policies', background paper to the Seminar on Managing the Access of the Poor to Urban Land: New Approaches for Regularisation Policies in the Developing Countries, Mexico City, 24–26 February.

Dynarski, M. (1986). 'Residential attachment and housing demand', *Urban Studies* (23): 11–20.

El Fortea, S. (1989). 'The courtyard house versus progress and development in Libya: a case for compromise', *Open House International* 14(2): 13–17.

Ferchiou, R. (1982). 'The indirect effects of new housing construction in developing countries', *Urban Studies* 19: 167–176.

Fisher, R. M. and L. B. Winnick (1961). 'A reformulation of the filtering concept', *Journal of Social Issues* 7(1/2): 47–85.

Forrest, R. and A. Murie (1994). 'The dynamics of the owner-occupied housing market in Southern England in the late 1980s: a study of new building and vacancy chains', *Regional*

Studies 28(3): 275–289.

Forrest, R., A. Murie, D. Gordon, P. Burton, K. Doogan and A. Franklin (1993). *New Homes for Home Owners: A Study of New Building and Vacancy Chains in Southern England*, London: HMSO.

Fromm, D. (1985). 'Alternatives in housing, 1: Peru: Previ', *Architectural Review* (1062): 48–54.

Fry, E. M. (1946a). 'Developing in 'the most beautiful town in West Africa' – Kumasi', *West African Review* (June): 625–627.

Fry, E. M. (1946b). 'Developing the most beautiful town in West Africa', *West African Review* (June): 624–626.

Garrod, G., K. Willis and A. G. Tipple (1994). *Housing Extension Decisions in Kumasi: Ghana. A Two-stage Analysis*, Newcastle upon Tyne: Centre for Research in European Urban Environments, Department of Town and Country Planning, University of Newcastle upon Tyne.

Garrod, G. D., K. G. Willis and A.G. Tipple (1995). 'A two-stage econometric analysis of the housing extension decision in Kumasi, Ghana', *Urban Studies* 32: 949–966.

Ghana, Government of (1968). *Report of the Commission Apppointed to Enquire into the Manner of Operation of the State Housing Corporation* (Chairman, D.S. Effah), Accra: Government of Ghana.

Ghana, Government of (1987). *1984 Population Census of Ghana: Demographic and Economic Characteristics, Total Country*, Accra: Statistical Service.

Gilbert, A. (1993). *In Search of a Home*, London: UCL Press.

Gilbert, A. and A. Varley (1990). 'Renting a home in a Third World city: choice or constraint?' *International Journal of Urban and Regional Research*, 14(1): 89–108.

Gilbert, A. G. (1988). 'Home enterprises in poor urban settlements: constraints, potentials, and policy options', *Regional Development Dialogue* 9, 4(Winter): 21–37.

Gilbert, A. G. (1991). 'Comparative analysis: studying housing processes in Latin American cities', in *Housing the Poor in the Developing World: Methods of Analysis, Case Studies and Policy*. Eds A. G. Tipple and K. G. Willis, London: Routledge.

Gold Coast (1946). Pamphlet setting out certain plans and policy for government and government-sponsored housing schemes in the Gold Coast, Department of Social Welfare and Housing, Government of the Gold Coast, Accra.

Gold Coast (1948). The Asawasi Housing Scheme: Building in stabilised laterite, Department of Social Welfare, Gold Coast Government, Accra.

Gosling, J. A., G. T. Keogh and M. J. Stabler (1993). 'House extensions and housing market adjustment: a case study of Wokingham', *Urban Studies* 30(9): 1561–1576.

Greene, W. H. (1989). *LIMDEP*, New York: Econometric Software, Inc.

Greger, O. and F. Steinberg (1988). 'Transformations of formal housing: unintended evolutionary developments as inspiration for innovative design', *Open House International* 13(3): 23–35.

Grigsby, W. G. (1971). *Housing Markets and Public Policy*, Philadelphia: University of Pennsylvania.

Gujarati, D. N. (1995). *Basic Econometrics*, New York: McGraw-Hill.

Habraken, N. J. (1975). *Supports: An Alternative to Mass Housing*, London: Architectural Press.

Habraken, N. J. (1980a). *Design for Adaptability, Change and User Participation in Housing Process and Physical Form*, Singapore: Media.

Habraken, N. J. (1980b). 'Design for adaptability, change and user participation', in *Proceedings of Seminar Three, Architectural Transformations in the Islamic World*, Jakarta, March, The Aga Khan Award for Architecture: 23–29.

Harmon, O. R. (1988). 'The income elasticity of demand for single family owner occupied housing: an empirical reconciliation', *Journal of Urban Economics* 24: 173–185.

Harmon, O. R. and M. J. Potepan (1988). 'Housing adjustment costs: their impact on mobility and housing demand elasticities', *AREUEA Journal* 16: 459–478.

Hassan, M. M. (1992). 'Low-cost housing finance in developing countries: with reference to Egypt', in *Housing in the Third World: Analysis and Solutions*, Eds L. Kilmartin and H. Singh, New Delhi: Concept: 317–328.

Hays-Mitchell, M. (1993). 'The ties that bind. informal and formal sector linkages in streetvending: the case of Peru's ambulantes', *Environment and Planning A* 25: 1085–1102.

Heckman, J. J. (1976). 'The common structure of statistical models of truncation, sample selection and limited dependent variables and a simple estimator for such models', *Annals of Economic and Social Measurement* (5): 475–492.

Heckman, J. J. (1979). 'Sample selection bias as a specification error', *Econometrica* (47): 153–160.

Heisler, H. (1971). 'The creation of a stabilised urban society: a turning point in the development of Northern Rhodesia/Zambia', *African Affairs* 70(279): 125–145.

Hellen, J. A., A. G. Tipple and M. A. Prince (1991). 'Environmental risk assessment in a tropical city: an application of housing and household data from Kumasi, Ghana', in *Geomedizinische und Biogeographische Aspekte der Krankheitsverbreitung und Gesundheitsversorgung in Industrie – und Entwicklungsländern*, Ed. E. Hinz, Frankfurt: Peter Lang.

Higdon, D. (1995). *Codes of Transformation Practice: A Householder's Guide to Making Extensions to the Home*, Newcastle upon Tyne: Centre for Architectural Research and Development Overseas, University of Newcastle upon Tyne.

Hill, P. (1966). 'Landlords and brokers: a West African trading system', *Cahiers d'Etudes Africaines* 6: 349–366.

Hillier, B. and J. Hanson (1984). *The Social Logic of Space*, Cambridge: Cambridge University Press.

Holston, J. (1991). 'Autoconstruction in working class Brazil', *Cultural Anthropology* 6(4): 447–465.

Jackson, P. (1986). *Historic Buildings of Harare (1890–1940)*, Johannesburg: Quest.

Japha, D. and M. Huchzemeyer (1995). *The History of the Development of Townships in Cape Town, 1920–1992*, Newcastle upon Tyne: Centre for Architectural Research and Development Overseas, University of Newcastle upon Tyne and School of Architecture and Planning, University of Cape Town.

Kardash, H. (1994). The housing parameters in Cairo: a qualitative background, Report prepared for the CARDO Transformations Research Project, mimeo.

Kardash, H. S. (1990). *The Transformation Process of Government Housing in Cairo: The Case of Helwan, El Tebbeen and Imbaba*, Unpublished PhD Dissertation, University of Newcastle upon Tyne.

Kardash, H. S. and N. Wilkinson (1991). 'Development within development: user extensions of 4-storey walk-up housing in Cairo – the case of Helwan', *Open House International* 16(1): 9–18.

Kellett, P. (1995). *Constructing Home: Production and Consumption of Popular Housing in Northern Colombia*, Unpublished PhD Dissertation, University of Newcastle upon Tyne.

Kellett, P. and A. Toro (1990). 'User initiated transformations of social housing: an overview of the Chilean experience', Instituto de la Vivienda (INVI), Santiago, and Centre for Architectural Research and Development Overseas (CARDO), Newcastle upon Tyne, unpublished.

Kendig, H. L. (1981). Buying and Renting: Household Moves in Adelaide, Canberra: Australian Institute of Urban Studies.

Kirwan, R. M. and D. B. Martin (1972). *The Economics of Urban Residential Renewal and Improvement*, London, Centre for Environmental Studies.

Korboe, D. (1992). 'Family houses in Ghanaian cities: to be or not to be?', *Urban Studies* 29(7): 1159–1172.

Korboe, D. T. (1993a). *The Low-income Housing System in Kumasi: An Empirical Examination of Two Neighbourhoods*, Newcastle upon Tyne: University of Newcastle upon Tyne.

Korboe, D. T. (1993b). *Qualitative Report for the Ghana Housing Supply Research Project*, Kumasi: Department of Housing and Planning Research, University of Science and Technology.

Kraria, H. (1989). *Bel-Air: Rehabilitation of an Old Quarter of Setif, Algeria*, Unpublished PhD Dissertation, Centre for Architectural Research and Development Overseas, University of Newcastle upon Tyne.

Kwakye-Safo, S. (1981). The Contribution of State Housing Corporation to Housing Development in Ghana, Kumasi: Department of Planning, University of Science and Technology.

Lall, V. D. (1994). *Informal Sector in Alwar: Status, Development and Action Plan*, New Delhi: Society for Development Studies.

Landeau, J.-F. (1991). 'Ratio analysis: a study of mortgage borrowers in Tunisia', in *Housing the Poor in the Developing World. Methods of Analysis, Case Studies and Policy*, Ed. A. G. Tiple and K. G. Willis, London: Routledge: 113–125.

Lansing, J. B. and L. Kish (1957). 'Family life cycle as an independent variable', *American Sociological Review* 22: 512–519.

Laquian, A. A. (1983). 'Sites, services and shelter – an evaluation', *Habitat International* 7(5/6).

Lerman, R., E. Borukhov and D. Evron(1985). *Project Renewal Housing Initiatives: Their Impact on Housing Conditions and Housing Values*, Jerusalem: Brookdale Institute.

Lerman, R. I. (1988). 'Project Renewal's programme for enlarging dwellings: its rationale, utilization, costs and benefits', *Megamot (Behavioural Sciences Quarterly, Israel)* 31: 3–4.

Lipton, M. (1980). 'Family, fungibility, and formality: rural advantages of informal non-farm enterprise versus the urban-formal state', in *Human Resources, Employment, and Development, Vol. 5, Developing Countries*, Ed. S. Amin: London, Macmillan.

Littlewood, A. J. and M. Munro (1996). 'Poverty and poor housing in Scotland: the relationship between income and housing deprivation', ENHR Housing Research Conference on Housing and European Integration, Helsingør, Denmark.

Littlewood, A. and M. Munro (1997). 'Moving and improving: strategies for attaining housing equilibrium', *Urban Studies* 34(11): 1771–1787.

Lowry, I. S. (1960). 'Filtering and housing standards', *Land Economics* 36(November): 362–370.

McFadden, D. (1974). 'A conditional logit model of qualitative choice behavior', in *Frontiers of Econometrics*, Ed. P. Zarembka, New York: Academic Press.

McLeod, P. B. and J. R. Ellis (1982). 'Housing consumption over the family life cycle: an empirical analysis', *Urban Studies* 19: 177–185.

Malpezzi, S. J. (1986). *Rent Control and Housing Market Equilibrium: Theory and Evidence from Cairo, Egypt*, Washington, DC: George Washington University.

Malpezzi, S. (1990). 'Urban housing and financial markets: some international comparisons', *Urban Studies* 27(6).

Malpezzi, S. J., A. G. Tipple and K. G. Willis (1990). *Costs and Benefits of Rent Control: A Case Study in Kumasi, Ghana*, Washington, DC: World Bank.

Manski, C. and D. McFadden (Eds) (1981). *Structural Analysis of Discrete Data with Econometric Applications*, Cambridge, MA: MIT Press.

Mayer, N. S. (1981). 'Rehabilitation decisions in rental housing and empirical analysis', *Journal of Urban Economics*(10): 76–94.

Mayer, R. W. and R. Enis (1981). *Development of Open Spaces in Givat Olga, Haifa*, Israel: Samuel Neaman Institute for Advanced Studies in Science and Technology, Technion-Israel Institute of Technology.

Mehta, M. and D. Mehta (1990). 'Home upgradation and income generation from housing', in *Housing and Income in Third World Urban Development*, Eds M. Raj and P. Nientied, London: Aspect Publishing.

Mendelsohn, R. (1977). 'Empirical evidence on home improvements', *Journal of Urban Economics* 4(4): 459–468.

Michelson, W. (1977). *Environmental Choice, Human Behaviour and Residential Satisfaction*, Oxford: Oxford University Press.

Mills, G. (1989). 'The shape of housing in South Africa', *Open House International* 14(3): 6–15.

Moudon, A. V. (1986). *Build for Change*, Cambridge, MA: MIT Press.

Muller, A. (1995). *Shared Knowledge and the Formal Housing Process in Namibia*, Unpublished PhD Dissertation, University of Newcastle upon Tyne.

Musandu-Nyamayaro, O. (1992). *Land, Housing and Urban Development in Zimbabwe: A Review of Planning and Housing Standards for Low Income People in Harare*, Harare: Department of Rural and Urban Planning, University of Zimbabwe.

Nientied, P., N. Bhattacharjee and M. B. Bharati (1987). 'Housing for income, practice and policy relevance', Paper presented at the International Seminar on Income and Housing in Third World Development, New Delhi, India, 30 November to 4 December.

Northern Rhodesia, Government of (1944). *Report of the Commission on Administration and Finances of Native Locations in Urban Areas (The Eccles Commission)*, Lusaka: Government Printer.

Owens, D. (1991). *The Walls Around Us*, New York: Random House.

Owusu, S. E. and A. G. Tipple (1995). *The Process of Extension in Kumasi, Ghana*, Newcastle upon Tyne: Centre for Architectural Research and Development Overseas, University of Newcastle upon Tyne.

Oxman, R. and N. Carmon (1986). 'Responsive public housing: an alternative for low-income families'. *Environment and Behaviour*, 18: 258–284.

Oxman, R. and N. Carmon (1989). 'The open form', *Open House International*. 14: 15–20.

Peattie, L. R. (1981). 'What is to be done with the informal sector? a case study of shoe manufacturing in Colombia', in *Towards a Political Economy of Urbanisation*, Ed. I. Safa, New Delhi: Oxford University Press.

Peinado, J. (1980). Case study, Cuidad Bachue, Bogotá, unpublished MPhil course work, School of Architecture, University of Newcastle upon Tyne.

Price, R. M. (1974). 'Politics and culture in contemporary Ghana: the big-man, small-boy syndrome', *Journal of African Studies* 1(2): 173–204.

Pritchard, C. B. (1993). *The Zimbabwe Case Study Qualitative Report for the Transformations Study*, Harare: University of Zimbabwe.

Ragin, C. (1989). 'New directions in comparative research', in *Cross-national Research in Sociology*, Ed. M. L. Kohn, New York: Sage Publications: 57–76.

Rahman, M. (1995). *Integrated Urban Infrastructure Development: Bangladesh Experience in Low Cost Housing Projects*, Dhaka: Housing and Settlement Directorate.

Raj, M. and B. Mitra (1990). 'Households, housing and home based economic activities in low income settlements', in *Housing and Income in Third World Urban Development*, Eds M. Raj and P. Nientied, London: Aspect Publishing.

Rakodi, C. (1995). 'Rental tenure in the cities of developing countries', *Urban Studies* 32(4-5): 791–811.

Rakodi, C. and N. D. Mutizwa-Mangiza (1989). Housing policy, production and consumption in Harare (Zimbabwe), Department of Rural and Urban Planning, University of Zimbabwe, Harare (mimeo).

Rakodi, C. and P. Withers (1993). *Land, Housing and Urban Development in Zimbabwe: Markets and Policy in Harare and Gweru*, Cardiff: Department of City and Regional Planning, University of Wales College of Cardiff.

Rapoport, A. (1969). *House Form and Culture*, Englewood Cliffs, NJ: Prentice Hall.

Ratcliff, R. U. (1949). *Urban Land Economics*, New York: McGraw-Hill.

Ravallion, M., G. Datt and D. van de Walle (1991). 'Quantifying absolute poverty in the developing world', *Review of Income and Wealth* 37(4): 345–362.

Sakr, S. (1983). In-use modification of existing public housing in Cairo, Masters Thesis, Massachusetts Institute of Technology.

Salama, R. (1997). 'Understanding user transformation of public housing', in *Tradition, Location and Community: Place-making and Development*, Eds A. Awotona and N. Teymur, Aldershot: Avebury: 205–224.

Salim, A. (1998). *Owner-occupier's Transformation of Public Low Cost Housing in Peninsular Malaysia*, Unpublished PhD Dissertation, University of Newcastle upon Tyne.

Sarkar, N. (1988). *Case Study of Dwelling Transformation*, Delhi: Rohini.

Seek, N. H. (1983). 'Adjusting housing consumption: improve or move', *Urban Studies*(20): 455–469.

Sepulveda, O. and G. Carrasco (1990). El rol del usuario, identidad y entorno socio-ambiental en la transformacion de la vivienda social en Puerto Montt, Presentacion Fondecyt, Santiago.

SKAT (1991). *Building Materials in Bangladesh*, Report for the Swiss Development Co-operation, Geneva.

Steinberg, F. (1984). 'Ain El Sira In Cairo: the 'architecture of poverty'', *Open House International* 9(2): 35–42.

Stewart, D. J. (1996). 'Cities in the desert: the Egyptian new-town program', *Annals of the Association of American Geographers* 86(3): 459–480.

Strassmann, W. P. (1986). 'Types of neighbourhood and home-based enterprises: evidence from

Lima, Peru', *Urban Studies* 23: 485–500.

Strassmann, W. P. (1987). 'Home-based enterprises in cities of developing countries', *Economic Development and Cultural Change* 36(1): 121–144.

Strassmann, W. P. (1994). 'Over-simplification in housing analysis, old and new, with specific reference to land markets and mobility', ENHR 2nd Symposium Housing for the Urban Poor, Birmingham, 11–14 April.

Summers, R. and A. Heston (1988). 'A new set of international comparisons of real product and price levels estimates for 130 countries, 1950–1985', *Review of Income and Wealth* 34: 1–26.

Tipple, A. G. (1979). 'Low cost housing policies in the copper towns of northern Rhodesia/Zambia: an historical perspective', in *Collected Papers 4*, Eds A. V. Akeroyd and C. R. Hill, York: Centre for Southern African Studies, University of York.

Tipple, A. G. (1981). 'Colonial housing policy and the 'African towns' of the Copperbelt: beginnings of self help', *African Urban Studies* 11(Fall): 65–85.

Tipple, A. G. (1984). Towards a culturally acceptable housing strategy, the case of Kumasi, Ghana, Unpublished PhD Dissertation, University of Newcastle upon Tyne.

Tipple, A. G. (1987). The development of housing policy in Kumasi, Ghana, 1901 to 1981: with an analysis of the current housing stock, Newcastle upon Tyne: Centre for Architectural Research and Development Overseas, University of Newcastle upon Tyne.

Tipple, A. G. (1991a). *Self Help Transformations of Low Cost Housing: An Introductory Study*, Newcastle upon Tyne: Urban International Press for the Overseas Development Administration, London.

Tipple, A. G. (1991b). 'Self-help transformations: infrastructure issues', 17th WEDC Conference: Infrastructure, Environment, Water and People, Nairobi, 19–23 August, WEDC, University of Loughborough.

Tipple, A. G. (1992). 'Self help transformations to low-cost housing: initial impressions of cause, context and value', *Third World Planning Review* 14(2).

Tipple, A. G. (1993). 'Shelter as workplace: a review of home-based enterprises in developing countries', *International Labour Review* 132(4): 521–539.

Tipple, A. G. (1994a). 'A matter of interface: the need for a shift in targeting housing interventions', *Habitat International* 18(4): 1–15.

Tipple, A. G. (1994b). 'The need for new urban housing in Sub-Saharan Africa: problem or opportunity', *African Affairs*(93): 587–608.

Tipple, A. G., B. Amole, D. Korboe and H. Onyeacholem (1994). 'House and dwelling, family and household', *Third World Planning Review* 16(4): 429–450.

Tipple, A. G., G. Garrod and K. Willis(1994). Housing Extension Decisions in Kumasi, Ghana: A Two-stage Analysis, Newcastle upon Tyne: Centre for Research in European Urban Environments, Department of Town and Country Planning, University of Newcastle upon Tyne.

Tipple, A. G., D. Korboe and G. Garrod (1997). 'Income and wealth in house ownership studies in urban Ghana', *Housing Studies* 12(1): 111–126.

Tipple, A. G. and S. E. Owusu (1994). Transformations in Kumasi, Ghana, as a Housing Supply Mechanism, Preliminary Study, Centre for Architectural Research and Development Overseas, University of Newcastle upon Tyne.

Tipple, A. G., N. Wilkinson and M. Nour (1985). 'The transformation of Workers' City, Helwan: multi-storey extensions observed', *Open House International*. 10(3): 25–38.

Tipple, A. G., N. Wilkinson and M. Nour (1986). 'The transformation of multi-storey dwellings by self-help: Workers' City, Helwan, Egypt'. *Planning Outlook*. 29(1): 39–46.

Tipple, A. G. and K. G. Willis (Eds) (1991a). *Housing the Poor in the Developing World: Methods of Analysis, Case Studies and Policy*. London/New York: Routledge.

Tipple, A. G. and K. G. Willis (1991b). 'Tenure choice in a West African city', *Third World Planning Review* 13(1): 27–45.

Tipple, A. G. and K. G. Willis (1992). 'Why should Ghanaians build houses in urban areas?' *Cities* February: 60–74.

Treiger, B. and E. Faerstein (1987). 'The effects of an upgrading project on income-generating activities in a Brazilian squatter settlement – the case of Pavao-Pavaozinho', paper presented at the International Seminar on Income and Housing in Third World Urban Development, New Delhi, India.

Turnbull, C. (1998). Transformations in Zimbabwe analysed using 'Space Syntax', unpublished BA dissertation, Department of Architecture, University of Newcastle upon Tyne.

Turner, J. F. C. (1972). 'Housing issues and the standards problems'. *Ekistics*. 196: 152–158.

Turner, J. F. C. (1976). *Housing by People: Towards Autonomy in Building Environments*, London: Marion Boyars.

UNCED (1992). 'Agenda 21, Chapter 7: Promoting sustainable human settlement development'. United Nations Conference on Environment and Development, Rio de Janeiro, 14 June.

UNCHS (1989). *Strategies for Low-income Shelter and Services Development: The Rental-housing Option*, Nairobi: UNCHS (Habitat).

UNCHS (1990). *The Global Strategy for Shelter to the Year 2000*, Nairobi: UNCHS (Habitat).

UNCHS (1993). *Shelter Sector Performance Indicators*, Nairobi: UNCHS (Habitat).

UNCHS (1995). *Sustainable Human Settlements in an Urbanising World, Including Issues Related to Land Policies and Mitigation of Natural Disasters*, Nairobi: UNCHS (Habitat).

UNCHS (1996a). The Habitat Agenda: Chapter III, The Habitat Agenda, http://www.undp.org/un/habitat/agenda/ch-3.html.

UNCHS (1996b). The Habitat Agenda: Chapter IV, Global plan of action: strategies for implementation, http://www.undp.org/un/habitat/agenda/ch-4.html.

UNCHS (1996c). *An Urbanising World: Global Report on Human Settlements 1996*, Oxford: Oxford University Press for UNCHS (Habitat).

UNCHS/ILO (1995). *Shelter Provision and Employment Generation*, Nairobi: United Nations Centre for Human Settlements (Habitat)/Geneva: International Labour Office.

UNDP (1993). *Human Development Report 1993*, Oxford: UNDP/Oxford University Press.

UNDP and Government of Bangladesh (1994). *Urban Sector National Programme*, Dhaka: Government of Bangladesh.

Wikan, U. (1980). *Life Among the Urban Poor in Cairo*, London: Tavistock.

Wikan, U. (1990). 'Changing housing strategies and patterns among the Cairo poor, 1950–85', in *Housing Africa's Urban Poor*, Eds P. Amis and P. Lloyd, Manchester: Manchester University Press for the International African Institute.

Wilkinson, N. and A. G. Tipple (1987). 'Are self help extensions the way forward in multi-storey walk-ups? lessons from Helwan, Egypt', *African Urban Quarterly* 2(3): 235–249.

Wilkinson, N. and A. G. Tipple (1991). 'Self-help transformation of government-built flats: the case of Helwan, Egypt', in *Beyond Self-help Housing*, Ed. K. Mathey, London: Mansell.

Willis, K. G. (1991). 'Regression analysis: discriminants of overcrowding and house conditions in Ghanaian housing markets', in *Housing the Poor in the Developing World: Methods of Analysis, Case Studies and Policies*, Eds A. G. Tipple and K. G. Willis, London: Routledge: 126–142.

Willis, K. G., S. J. Malpezzi and A. G. Tipple (1990). 'An econometric and cultural analysis of rent control in Kumasi, Ghana', *Urban Studies* 27(2): 241–258.

Wojtowicz, J. (1984). *Illegal Facades*, Hong Kong: Jerzy Wojtowicz.

Woodfield, A. (1989). *Housing and Economic Adjustment*, New York: Taylor & Francis, for and on behalf of the UN.

World Bank (1993). *Housing: Enabling Markets to Work*, Washington, DC: World Bank.

World Bank (n.d.). *The Housing Indicators Program*, Washington, DC: World Bank.

Ziegert, A. L. (1988). 'The demand for housing additions: an empirical analysis', *AREUEA Journal*(16): 479–492.

Zimbabwe, Government of (1976). *Regional Town and Country Planning Act*, Harare: Government Printers.

Index